AF607988

BAROQUE VISUAL RHETORIC

Baroque Visual Rhetoric

VERNON HYDE MINOR

UNIVERSITY OF TORONTO PRESS
Toronto Buffalo London

Toronto Buffalo London
www.utppublishing.com

ISBN 978-1-4426-4879-1

Toronto Italian Studies

Library and Archives Canada Cataloguing in Publication

Minor, Vernon Hyde, author
Baroque visual rhetoric / Vernon Hyde Minor.

Includes bibliographical references and index.
ISBN 978-1-4426-4879-1 (cloth)

1. Arts, Baroque – Italy. 2. Arts, Italian – 17th century. 3. Arts, Italian – 18th century. 4. Aesthetics, Modern – 17th century. 5. Aesthetics, Modern – 18th century. 6. Art criticism – History. I. Title.

NX552.A1M55 2015 709.03′2 C2015-905133-9

This book has been published with the assistance of the Research Board of the University of Illinois, Urbana-Champaign.

University of Toronto Press acknowledges the financial assistance to its publishing program of the Canada Council for the Arts and the Ontario Arts Council, an agency of the Government of Ontario.

Canada Council for the Arts **Conseil des Arts du Canada**

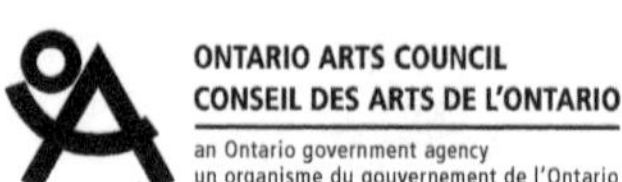

Funded by the Government of Canada | Financé par le gouvernement du Canada | Canada

For Heather

Whilst we deliberate how to begin a thing, it grows too late to begin it.

Marcus Fabius Quintilian

Contents

Illustrations

Acknowledgments

No writer stands alone. There are myriads of texts and a plenitude of sharp, critical minds forming the congregation within which writers and scholars work. Our colleagues inspire us, while the system of higher education provides us with an institutional framework for our thinking, our teaching, our discussions, and our writing. It probably is impossible to sort out where one's contributions begin and end: no single person owns an idea or an area of study, a topic or a topos. We are all in this together.

Having said that, of course, I still must (and very much wish to) acknowledge specific friends, colleagues, and institutions. First of all, my wife, Heather Hyde Minor, to whom I dedicate this book, has been by my side throughout the time I worked on these essays. As a highly productive scholar herself, she understands the discourse of critical writing and therefore has been unfailingly helpful to me. Her ways of assisting and encouraging are too many to describe. I hope my dedication conveys a true sense of obligation, love, and appreciation.

As for institutions, there are many to thank. First of all, the places where I have taught – the University of Colorado at Boulder and the University of Illinois, Urbana-Champaign – have aided my research and writing with funding and encouragement. I especially wish to thank the Illinois Campus Research Board for its support. The Ricker Library of Architecture and Art at the University of Illinois stands with the finest art libraries in the United States. Its director emerita, Professor Jane Block, shared her vast bibliographic knowledge with me and provided assistance in more ways than I can enumerate. Also unfailingly helpful is and has been Christopher Quinn, interim head and assistant architecture and art librarian.

When in Rome I have had the pleasure of reading in the Bibliotheca Hertziana, ably directed by Elisabeth Kieven and Sybille Ebert-Schifferer, both of whom I thank for their administration of an extraordinary institution. It is the best library for post-classical and pre-modern art in Italy. I also have been helped in a number of ways by Ornella Rodengo, who is in the Directors' Office at the Hertziana. For her assistance in finding an image in the Musée Grenoble (France), I thank Sylvie Portz.

The American Academy in Rome, housed in a grand McKim, Meade, and White building on Rome's Janiculum Hill, has supported me in many ways. I especially wish to thank Lester Little, Carmella Franklin, Christopher Celenza, and Pina Pasquantonio. In association with the American Academy, I also express my gratitude to the National Endowment for the Humanities for their support and funding of an NEH Summer Seminar I directed at the American Academy in 2011. In that seminar I met and worked with scholars of sparkling wit and impressive backgrounds. One and all provided me with ideas that helped in the formation of this text.

I also thank Giancarla Periti, John Senseney, and Jeffery Geller, who have read large swathes of this text and have provided very useful and encouraging comments.

When working at the Library of the Sterling and Francine Clark Art Museum and Institute, I was assisted by the very able and endlessly helpful librarian Valerie Krall and was helped in many ways by Michael Ann Holly, Keith Moxey, and Michael Conforti.

Most recently I was fortunate to be a Resident Associate at the National Humanities Center. I thank the Fellows and Residents, generous and entertaining scholars with whom I was able to share my ideas while learning much from theirs. I thank especially Geoffrey Harpham, Director and President, and Elizabeth (Cassie) C. Mansfield, Vice President for Scholarly Programs. The NHC in the Research Triangle Park, North Carolina, is a national treasure.

Finally I thank two people at the University of Toronto Press: Ron Schoeffel and Suzanne Rancourt. When I first approached Ron about my text, he responded with a long message, both cautionary (we all know the uncertain state of academic publishing) and reassuring. Although I never met him in person, just the same I experienced Ron's generosity, which shone through his frequent communications with me and his enthusiastic support of my project. Since Ron's death, I have been ably and encouragingly assisted by Suzanne Rancourt, editor at the University of Toronto Press.

All translations are mine unless otherwise noted.

BAROQUE VISUAL RHETORIC

1 Introduction

What follows are essays that in no way claim either individually or aggregately to be a systematic treatment of what I am calling "baroque visual rhetoric." On the whole my fascination lies with well-known works of European art, especially Italian, in the seventeenth and eighteenth centuries. These paintings, buildings, and sculptural ensembles have held me in thrall for decades. From the first time I walked into a museum, through my first day in an art history class, to the present day, I have felt riveted before works of art, have had that unshakeable sense not just of *vita breva, ars lunga* but that some profound tale, some essential truth lay mute within certain (but not all) paintings, buildings, and statues. I first grasped this as an intuition. I make no claims to having discovered something new or profound; I wish only to put into words what has come to me after all those moments when I have been shaken to my core or moved into other worlds.

I represent my writing as "essays," calling upon an early-modern form of discourse. Following Francis Bacon, I read mostly Italian art of the seventeenth and eighteenth centuries "not to contradict and confute; nor to believe and take for granted; nor to find talk and discourse; but to weigh and consider."[1] All of this weighing and considering comes from a unique perspective: my own. I reflect on diverse works of art, fluctuating a bit on how to approach what I sense to be determining ideas, all the while invoking critical perspectives as I see how they might fit. I hope but cannot be assured that readers will find something of value in my self-assays (as Harold Bloom translates the French *essais*).[2] By writing about his beliefs, Michel de Montaigne (1533–92) coined the word *essais* for literature; he was by turns endeavouring, testing, and attempting to know himself.

My challenge has been to write about works of art, weighing and considering, assessing and evaluating things and situations. There is nothing conclusive about an essay, nothing summed up or neatly packaged. One does not discover the essence or baroqueness of seventeenth- or eighteenth-century art. There is no process of distillation and in all likelihood no "aha!" moment. What seem to emerge from essaying ideas are inconclusiveness, somewhat messy comparisons, not altogether related occurrences, inevitable contradictions, and no very general sense of an ending. Images, objects, and monuments long precede their evaluation and tentative analysis. In the preface to his *Essays*, Bacon stressed, "To write just treatises requireth time in the writer and leisure in the reader, which is the cause which hath made me choose to write certain brief notes, set down rather significantly than curiously, which I have called Essays. The word is late, but the thing is ancient."[3]

Early-modern painting, sculpture, and architecture are happy, ludic things; Bernini's *Apollo and Daphne* has never *not* given pleasure. At Rome's Villa Borghese, spend an hour or two with this violently running pair, forever in their moment of metamorphosis, and listen to comments made in every language imaginable as visitors stroll past, marvelling, exuding pleasure. Undoubtedly there will be the occasional sourpuss, although I've never encountered one there. I once had a ten-year-old American boy, beaming with delight, explain to me the whole mythical tradition of Bernini's *Pluto and Persephone* in the next room over, his parents standing by, smiling with pride.

Although my art-historical experiences have been unfailingly eudaemonic, I remain haunted by the baroque.

2 Critical Perspectives

M. Jourdain, the hero of Molière's *Bourgeois Gentleman*, was shocked to learn that "I have been speaking prose all my life, and didn't even know it!" Art historians might also be startled to discover that we have been working all along in the rhetorical mode – and didn't even know it. At the same time, even though we are not literary critics, "poetics" as a theory of criticism, not just of literature, crops up frequently in our writing about objects and their historical circumstances. As I am using the words here, "rhetoric" and "poetics" are not topics with which we are especially familiar, despite the fact that they tend to blush unseen in the background of many art-historical practices. That is why in this text I put such master discourses in the foreground. They enrich our language and insights, and, in my estimation, they make us better art-historical critics.

Art historians know, too, that artists – painters, sculptors, and architects – wish and have wished to persuade, if often in some indefinite, non-argumentative sense. In terms of poetics, artists and architects have implicitly understood that metaphor is explicitly *figural* and therefore that painting, sculpture, and architecture in their very essences are metaphorical.

Almost from their beginnings, poetry and poetics have drawn upon the figures, schemes, tropes, and central ideas of rhetoric. Poetics and rhetoric remain distinct from one another in their generation and study of meaning in human discourse. Also as ideas or *epistemes* they have separate histories. At the same time and consistently they have become handmaidens to one another. We could say that rhetoric is to oratory what poetics is to poetry, although this is an approximate analogy. Then, as they both relate to differing practices, they together have an association with painting, sculpture, and architecture.

Theoretical poetics and *theoretical* rhetoric have to do with the art historian's craft, regardless of the historical period one studies. Theories of literary discourse, as opposed to art-historical discourse, have held centre stage in deconstructive and postmodern polemics in the second half of the twentieth century and the early decades of the twenty-first. Should art historians consider themselves above the fray? Language and images or language and "artistic" objects are not the same thing, of course, but they nonetheless remain nearly coextensive; that is, they have similar if not identical boundaries and scope. In short, those historical objects traditionally considered by art historians are and should be subject to modern critical theory.[1]

I begin with the art of criticism "as the study of how to think about language – dialectics, hermeneutics, and various modes of deconstruction and cultural critique," in Wayne C. Booth's terms.[2] Booth uses the word "language," whereas I believe that the critic can focus on how we think about images as well as texts – and that images are in many ways texts.[3] Whenever a critic attempts to write about philosophy, music, literature, or art history, he or she must come up with a metalanguage, a way of speaking that allows one to step back from a particular discourse or discipline and address it not really in its own terms but somehow differently. Michael Ann Holly reminds us that works of art come with no guarantee of translatability.[4] So, in a sense, we beat against the tides of objects and sounds, calling for arguments, interpretation, and explanation. For music, we put into words our thoughts on non-linguistic sounds arranged diachronically, while in art history we look for strong words to match compelling images arranged synchronically, *ekphrasis* by way of *enargeia*, and then fit them into what we understand about history and criticism. Mieke Bal and Norman Bryson in their pioneering essay "Semiotics and Art History" write that the word "rhetoric," as in "art-historical rhetoric," forms "the fundamental conceptual shapes of art-historical accounts."[5] In the hands of an art historian, in other words, rhetoric constitutes how one frames a narrative, forms an inquiry, and constructs a plot. The way we choose our words depends on how we conceive of the nature of the work of art, how we "read" it.

Walter Benjamin's doctor heard him say in a hashish dream "Quod in imaginibus, est in lingua" – a lapidary statement deserving Latin phrasing if ever there was one.[6] Loosely: what is in images is in language, or "Insofar as it is in images, it is in language." This could be a motto for art historians; indeed, it forms part of our very lifeblood. If something exists in an image, we believe we can talk and write about it. To return briefly to Bal, she writes in *Quoting Caravaggio*, now dealing with rhetoric in the hands of a baroque artist, that "it is a strategy of meaning-production in a performative relation between text and addressee; an effect of the real."[7] She puts her finger on the dynamic, vigorous, and protean nature of baroque visual rhetoric, how it performs – in a sense operates and unfolds – between a viewer and, say, a painting. It makes meaning.

The art of criticism has matured, even blossomed, over the past several generations. In the late 1970s, when the reign of structuralism had run its course, there sprang up a continental school of criticism that marked a "linguistic turn," using Cassirer's notion of philosophical method as *wende* – a "turn" or even a "turning point" – in literary (or philosophical) studies, one which in short order upset a fairly broad swathe of those who styled themselves as within the European and Anglo-American republic of letters.[8] I refer, of course, to deconstruction, mentioned by Booth earlier. Although it is perilous and problematic to generalize or simplify the roles and thought of Jacques Derrida, Paul de Man, Michel Foucault, and Gilles Deleuze, I would venture that the project of deconstruction sought to *interrogate*, a somewhat favoured term of their followers, the claims of the enlightenment on how the "I" and the world can (in non-religious terms) come to be seen, each in its own right, as integrated, whole, and meaningful. I think therefore I am, and therefore "I" can determine *res cogitans* and *res extensa*. Because Derrida is widely seen with some justification as deconstructing that which as well as those who – the *philosophes* – challenged the Roman Church's magisterium, its lock on telling the "greater narrative," we need to keep him in mind.

Paul de Man bears much of the credit for introducing Jacques Derrida's philosophical writings to literary critics at American universities in the early 1970s. His *Blindness and Insight: Essays in the Rhetoric of Contemporary Criticism*, first published in 1971, includes "The Rhetoric of Blindness: Jacques Derrida's Reading of Rousseau."[9] The core of de Man's critique of Derrida's critique of Rousseau is the problematic Western belief in the priority of the spoken over the written word. Prophecy is first spoken, only subsequently and therefore derivatively written. One sees speech as presence and writing as absence. Derrida shows that Rousseau's privileging of spoken language in his *Essai sur l'origine des langues* is necessarily challenged by the fact that Rousseau is *writing*, not speaking, his essay. De Man does not so much agree or disagree with Derrida as he shifts the discussion to *representation* and reviews the tradition of mimesis, another major concern of Rousseau's. That brings into view the problematics of absence and presence, mimesis and simulacrum, and finally declarative as opposed to rhetorical critiques of artistic – specifically in the present instance and for my interests, baroque – objects.

De Man bores in on "two closely related rhetorical figures discussed by Derrida": mimesis and metaphor. De Man's subtle, "argus-eyed" (as Angus Fletcher characterizes it in his review of this collection of essays[10]) readings of fairly standard tropes in the history of art criticism serve us well in our study of baroque visual rhetoric. In the world of logocentrism – "In the beginning was the Word, and the Word was with God, and the Word was God" (John 1:1) – the making of the "absent present" should not be ambiguous. That is to say, a portrait of a pope for instance, should not in any way call into question the reality of that very pope or, to put it in philosophical and de Manian terms, should not question the "ontological status of the imitated entity."[11] It nonetheless remains obvious that making the pope present underscores his absence. He does not appear; his picture does. The classical theory of the arts in the early-modern period, roughly the sixteenth through the eighteenth centuries, assumes that, once again in de Man's words, mimesis "confirms rather than undermines the plenitude of the represented entity."[12] Would that it were so!

Despite Rousseau's apparent assertion of the contrary, Derrida finds in his writings evidence for the priority of metaphorical readings over literal ones, which then leads to an undermining of the metaphysics of presence. Rousseau understands representation not so much in terms of the physical reality of something but, and here Kant would have agreed, as measured or indicated by sensations in the mind. Whether consciously or not (de Man and Derrida disagree) Rousseau sees that meaning resides in language, but not necessarily as something deposited there by the writer, who first of all (it is often supposed) had that very meaning and intention in his or her mind before putting it into words.

One of deconstruction's most useful findings is that representation is inherently rhetorical, not literal or declarative. Insofar as all painting and sculpture *represent*, all painting and sculpture is rhetorical. Baroque visual rhetoric is a subspecies of the general rhetoric of representation.

The "new science," which emerged gradually in the seventeenth century and then more rapidly in the eighteenth, interrogated and deconstructed the *Magisterium divinale et sapientiale*; "French Theory" has done much the same to Cartesianism and science. It is not, from the "baroque" point of view, exactly the case that "an enemy of my enemy is my friend." With the burgeoning of theory in the later twentieth and early twenty-first centuries, things have come nearly full circle. In all of this, as I hope to demonstrate, rhetoric, poetics, and hermeneutics have their place, especially in the North American university system, which is by no means the exclusive home of art-historical practices. But it constitutes, just the same, a significant *locus publicas* for critical discourse in the humanities.[13]

Near the middle of Louis Menand's book *The Marketplace of Ideas: Reform and Resistance in the American University*, he takes a step back to observe what he calls "the Humanities Revolution."[14] Up to this point he has tracked the development of American colleges and universities, which is the realm of tertiary education, and how beginning in the late nineteenth century and continuing until the Second World War American universities grew as professional and research-oriented institutions. Following the Allied victory, the post-war baby boom, the Cold War, the rapidly expanding American economy, the Soviet Union's launching of Sputnik and, as a consequence, the National Defense Education Act of 1958, US colleges and universities grew as they had never before. Menand terms the period from 1945 to 1970 the golden age of American higher education.

After that time higher education did not decline into a brass or iron age, but American universities and the kinds of research they support became more diversified, while faculty lost some confidence in those truths marking the golden age. In his nearly epigrammatic telling, Menand explains what happened: "The vocabulary of 'disinterestedness,' 'objectivity,' 'reason,' and 'knowledge,' and talk about things like 'the scientific method,' 'the canon,' and the 'the fact/value distinction' began to be superseded, particularly in the humanities, by attention to 'interpretations' (rather than 'facts'), 'perspective' (rather than 'objectivity'), and 'understanding' (rather than 'reason' or 'analysis')."[15] Far from bemoaning these changes, Menand sees them as inevitable developments growing from the "artificiality of Golden Age disciplinarity." He tracks the "hermeneutic turn" in his own field of study, English literature, and points out that post-structuralism grows naturally from the work of the so-called New Critics and their insistence on close readings of free-standing "verbal icons," a favoured phrase of literary criticism in the 1950s. Menand finds nothing to regret in these changes.

Art history also demonstrates an awareness of the hermeneutic turn, the move beyond the discipline's empirical underpinnings. As a relatively new mode of inquiry, art history first of all had to be empirical, had to establish its data and documents so as to determine the way things are and were – the who, what, when, and where. That kind of work is always important but is nonetheless preliminary to the hermeneutic – what and how things mean. Lurking only slightly in the background for art historians is aesthetics, a quasi-philosophical phenomenon of the eighteenth century, a concept that was almost invented for that species of "scholar" – the art historian – who barely existed several centuries ago. Now there are lots of us. Aesthesis, after all, is one's preferred mode of existence, except in those very particular situations when "anaesthesis" is called for. Art historians therefore deal with the interpretation *and* appreciation of works of art.[16]

These preliminary remarks establish in a way an apology – or, better yet, part of an apologetics – for the kinds of interpretations I am pursuing in this text. My readings could strike some as outside the traditions of art history; I maintain that they are in fact a natural outgrowth of the very nature of art history. Gotthold Lessing may have argued long ago that painting and literature have different ontologies which, he suggests, should not be confused with one another.[17] Then in the mid-twentieth century Clement Greenberg moved forcefully in the direction indicated by Lessing, insisting on "that which [is] unique and irreducible in each particular art."[18] My interest, on the other hand, lies with those theories that have had an important impact on the study of cultural artefacts, especially those productions that are acts of representation, whether verbal or visual.

As I indicate, my concerns lie with the word/image discourse within the contexts of rhetoric and poetics. Let me summarize matters as they stand to this point: Rhetoric as the art of persuasion and the tool of oratory constitutes one of the oldest traditions, somewhat pejorated by Plato as that which seeks to convince without too much concern for the truth. Then Aristotle, Cicero, and Quintilian wrote about rhetoric, their texts undergirding the rhetorical practices of the Renaissance and baroque periods. Finally we have, in the past half century or so, a newer notion of rhetoric as a tool for the literary, cultural, and art-historical critic that unpacks and examines texts and images of all sorts. Indeed,

John Summerson once gave a lecture, which he published in *The Classical Language of Architecture*, with the title "The Rhetoric of the Baroque." There he discusses, without digging very deeply into the practice and critical apparatus of rhetoric, three buildings: St Peter's, the Palais du Louvre, and Blenheim Palace.[19] These certainly are baroque buildings deserving of rhetorical critiques.

As I do with rhetoric, so I do with poetics: rather than attach either of these "forms" to something specific such as oratory or poetry, I tend to follow in the latter instance Aristotle, who saw poetics as not necessarily tied to metrical, literary forms. For him, *mimesis* ruled the roost, it being a more general and controlling idea, one not anchored in a specific artistic form.

Alberti, Renaissance Humanism, and Rhetoric

Unlike Monsieur Jourdain, Leon Battista Alberti knew precisely how and in what form he was writing. He was acquainted with Quintilian, mentioning him in *On Painting*, and wrote in the style of Cicero. John R. Spencer's study of art theory in the quattrocento finds that Alberti not only wrote like Cicero but also believed the modern painter should paint according to Cicero's rhetoric.[20]

Spencer's article, published in 1957 in the *Journal of the Warburg and Courtauld Institutes*, is foundational for anyone studying the intimate connection between early-modern painting and the traditions of rhetoric. Although the only orator mentioned by Alberti is Quintilian, Spencer nonetheless asserts that for Alberti the language of art is the language of oratory. Spencer writes that the "aims and means of the new painting envisaged by Alberti in his treatise are similar to the aims and means of the rhetoric advanced by Cicero,"[21] which in turn are similar to the aims and means in Alberti's disquisition on painting. Pope Pius II, Aeneas Sylvius Piccolomini, argued for the close association between rhetoric and painting primarily because they have narrative in common. Here, then, is one of those crucial elements – the ability to tell a story – that cemented the visual arts to rhetoric.

Consistent with Ernst Cassirer's philosophy, the visual arts constitute a coherent symbolic form; that is, baroque art – to choose a general and debatable category, yet one that serves as a subset of the arts understood by Cassirer – structures its own reality according to its own conventions, assumptions, and praxis. The protocols, manners, and rituals of the visual arts operate within society and history, which means that the shapes of symbolic forms change with time, place, and circumstance. For Cassirer, myth, language, and art each has its symbolic form, but these "interpenetrate one another in their concrete historical manifestations."[22] Both myth and language, and within language, poetics and rhetoric, "interpenetrate" the symbolic form of baroque art.

Alberti adapted many concepts used by Quintilian to painting, such as *convenevole* – appropriateness or decorum – and affective gesture. When Spencer turns to "invention," a key term in oratory and painting, he points out that for Alberti invention comes from the artist's experience. It is only later, in the sixteenth and seventeenth centuries with the advent of *maniera* and *secentismo* (mannerism and baroque) – now firmly situated in the discourses and academies of art, or what I have just referred to as art's symbolic form – that invention is found not in the common-sense world of visual experience but in history and poetry. Invention, therefore, is filtered and rarefied by these literary and historical contexts.

Spencer quotes Cicero on the make-up of oratorical invention: "acumen, then method – which we may be permitted to call art – and third diligence; for my part I am unable to refuse primacy to intellect." Spencer comments, "Alberti does not define the invention, perhaps because it is too well understood, but the recurrence of the words *ratione, arte, diligentia,* and *ingenio* throughout his treatise lead us to suspect more than a casual relationship between oratory and painting."[23]

What is the orator's aim is also the painter's, architect's, and sculptor's: each addresses an audience, often a fairly large one, and seeks to convince, move, and delight. Beginning with Petrarch and rising to a state of excitement with the discovery in the fifteenth century of original texts by Cicero and Quintilian, an intense interest in rhetoric dominated philological and visual theory. At the same time, preachers – not just humanists – were becoming ever more interested in public oratory and the great examples of ancient rhetoric, now known in original texts rather than by way of medieval commentaries.[24] A parallel development in the sixteenth century was the rediscovery and publishing in Italian by Lodovico Castelvetro of Aristotle's *Poetics,* resulting in the Horatian *ut pictura poesis,* which was a way of thinking about the connection between painting and poetry, with poetry standing for all literature. Most who write on the history of rhetoric and poetics see the two as being fairly closely associated with one another, at least until the advent of Romanticism.

Poetics, broadly conceived, thrived in early-modern Italy. Entwined with the rise of humanism, poetics as a theoretical and apologetical tool for defending ancient and modern literary texts developed theories of genres and rules of composition. The need to interpret ancient literary and philosophical texts in the light of Christianity, to appraise and assess the poetic, fictive narratives of Dante, Petrarch, and Boccaccio, contributed to the development of complex discourses on literary theory. Thanks first of all to Boccaccio's *Genealogiae decorum gentilium* (1360), the literate elite gained a rich understanding of metaphorical and figurative tropes.

There followed an ever-expanding corpus of texts on poetics in the later fifteenth century and throughout the sixteenth, a phenomenon that began in Italy and spread to Spain, England, and France. To list only two, there were Marco Girolamo Vida's *De arte poetica* (1527) and Giangiorgio Trissino's *La Poetica* (1529, expanded 1563). By the early decades of the sixteenth century, Latin versions of Aristotle's *Poetics* appeared, culminating, as I mentioned, in Lodovico Castelvetro's Italian editions of 1570 and 1576. Luis de Góngora y Argote (1561–1627) and Baltasar Gracián (1601–58) brought a different kind of sophistication to poetic theory with their tropes of *culteranismo* and *conceptismo.* Emanuele Tesauro wrote extensively in his *Il Cannocchiale Aristotelico* (*The Aristotelian Telescope*, 1654), on *figure ingeniose* and *figure metaforiche.*

Because of the close association between the literary conceit and what I am calling baroque visual rhetoric, a few further words about Tesauro and *concettismo* are in order here.

The English metaphysical poets, so named by Samuel Johnson more than a century after their appearance, translated the Italian word *concetto* into "conceit" and – following the path well trod by Giovanni Battista Marino and before him Petrarch – spun extended metaphors and disjunctive similitudes out of the thin air surrounding a witty and poetical Mt Olympus.[25] Dr Johnson wrote with some acerbity, "About the beginning of the seventeenth century appeared a race of writers that may be termed the Metaphysical poets."[26] He, a product of the neoclassical branch of the Augustan Age, did not much like those poets, their "race," or their fanciful conceptions – their conceits.

In modern English the word "conceit" more often than not refers to an exaggerated self-regard, which is related to but is not the same as the word Michelangelo or Shakespeare, Gianlorenzo Bernini or Emanuele Tesauro understood. For them conceit brought to mind a conception or an idea.

In its practical application, especially when used by artists, "conceit" (*concetto*) promoted and sanctioned vivifying, animated, and enlivened images, ones brought to very high, even startling, definition. Aristotle in his *Poetics* suggested that the metaphor – the very thing that grounds a conceit – although unteachable, is nonetheless tied to the innate human ability to see among the phenomena of this world resemblances, even unlikely ones: "It is the one thing that cannot be learnt from others; and it is also a sign of genius, since a good metaphor implies an intuitive perception of the similarity in the dissimilars."[27] The mimetic tradition, long and even deeply mysterious (think of the origin of mimesis in Dionysian mystery cults[28]) has within itself an imbedded metaphor, building perceptible similarities from paint, clay, and stone, for instance. Brain scientists may have something to say about our native ability to translate an arrangement of forms, whether two- or three-dimensional, into something they are not: marble becoming Michelangelo's *David*, for instance. We call it representation, visual intelligence, imitation, realism, or even abstraction. And of course the list can be extended. The point I want to make is that in my understanding of baroque visual rhetoric there is nearly always something metaphorical. In fact, there is always something "conceited" and disjunctively simulated about nearly *all* art. A literary conceit may extend a metaphor over an entire sonnet, as Giovanni Battista Marino does when a woman's hair becomes the sea, an ivory comb a ship, and a diamond clip the rocks upon which a lover founders.[29] A visual metaphor, even an extended one, does not sustain a comparison in quite the same way as does a literary metaphor; rather, a *concetto* in the visual arts tends to stack up layers of representation, create and exploit echelons of reality, both mimetically and diegetically, as dizzyingly existential realms, complex and sometimes mysteriously related ontologies. Furthermore, it is not that baroque visual rhetoric and visual poetics are unique in their claims on metaphor; it is, rather, that the visual metaphor in the hands of many artists of what we have come to call the "baroque period" has a higher coefficient of complexity and, one might say, metaphorical sophistication. In an eccentric sort of way, we can note that much of baroque – the category can be expanded to encompass the somewhat elastic category "early modern" – art is "conceited." An important seventeenth-century text on the conceit/*concetto* is Emmanuel Tesauro's *Il Cannocchiale Aristotelico*.

Tesauro's title, *The Aristotelian Telescope*, is paradoxical and oxymoronic first of all because Tesauro seems to argue that Aristotle can justify baroque taste and second that there is some connection between Aristotle and the telescope, a seventeenth-century invention. The reference to the *cannocchiale* (telescope), the most representative instrument of the new science, is coupled with an adjectival Aristotle, who stands as a sign of cultural conservatism, although the Jesuits, liberal and baroque by turns, also relied upon Aristotelian philosophy. Tesauro seems to assert that there is plenty of grist in Aristotle's *Rhetoric* for the baroque mill. Then there is Georg Simmel's comment on microscopic technology (a baroque phenomenon) that "coming closer to things often only shows us how far away they still are from us."[30]

Tesauro marvelled over Galileo's telescope, how it becomes an instrument of ingenious ingenuity – his way of characterizing wit – because with it one can see sunspots and measure the mountains and seas of the moon. What God has attempted to hide, a bit of glass reveals.[31]

Born in Torino in January 1592, Tesauro was the seventh son of a noble Piedmontese family. The Jesuits saw to his early education and when he was 19 brought him into the order as a novitiate. After five years studying *grammatica*, he returned to Milan and became a teacher of rhetoric at the Accademia di Brera for three years while undertaking his advanced courses in philosophy. In 1619 he was off to Cremona to assume a chair in rhetoric, tackling a number of exercises in eloquence while also studying theology. Tesauro gained from the Jesuits the right to preach in 1624.

Although he travelled about, Milan soon became his permanent residence. In the Savoyard Court he wrote satirical panegyrics and was preacher to the Duchess Cristina. He also carried out diplomatic missions between Lombardy and Piedmont. He was probably considered the most representative literary figure in the Piedmontese court. Apparently because of the complicated politics of the time and his siding with Prince Tomaso during the break with Tomaso's sister Cristina, not to mention the civil war then raging in Piedmont, Tesauro was forced to leave the Jesuit order in 1634. He remained a secular priest.

Throughout his adult life Tesauro had diplomatic duties as well as literary ones, remaining in Carignano's retinue through the separation and reconciliation between the Duchess Cristina and Prince Tomaso. Tesauro did not take up again his office as court preacher; rather, having become Cavaliere di Gran Croce dei Santi Maurizio e Lazzaro, he assumed instead the position of tutor in the Carignano family. It was at this point he began writing the *Cannocchiale Aristotelico*, with the consequence that he presented no orations for a decade. He started up again in 1653, when he climbed into the pulpit and delivered several sermons, including one for the funeral of Cristina. The municipal authorities in Torino commissioned from him a history of the city in 1666. In his later years he was tutor to the future Vittorio Amadeo II, to whom he dedicated his *Moral Philosophy*. Tesauro saw himself as old-fashioned but admitted he was "inclined toward the Copernican system."

He wrote in the *Cannocchiale* of two styles of painting ("i generi principali del favellare"), one sketched out in general terms – what we might call painterly – meant to be seen from afar, the other done finely (linear) and meant to be seen up close. The latter was for the experts, the former for the general and undiscerning population – the larger the crowd, the greater the distance from which they see. So the latter becomes the former as Tesauro goes on to characterize them; the first is the exquisite medium, the second appropriate for a concert; the first is epic, the other for scenes on a stage; one has arrows, subtle and pungent; the other is bombastic, flaming, resounding; one Attic and sour, the other Asiatic and sweet; one appropriate to Nestor, the other to Odysseus; one to Quintilian, the other to Thucydides; one to Demosthenes, the other to Cicero. These binary oppositions that Tesauro observed have become in the traditions of art history, using the language of Heinrich Wölfflin, the linear and the painterly, or more generally the Renaissance and the baroque.

Form

"Form" gives us a vocabulary for translating images into words, thereby creating one of the bulwarks of the discipline of art history. As Michel Foucault would recognize formalism, it is an *episteme*, a distinguishing idea that knocks into shape, appropriately enough, the way we view the body of art-historical knowledge.

Art history's founders – Johann Joachim Winckelmann, Alois Riegl, and Heinrich Wölfflin, among others – developed a kind of historicism that embraced style as its most telling ingredient.[32] Style for Winckelmann represented an essential element of a nation, one that informs and is informed by everything else, making it a total representation of culture.[33] He was writing at the dawn of nationalism, which in some peculiar way informed his ideas, not as a German but as a historian, one who discovered in ancient Greece a unique self-contained culture that generated and embraced a complex array of values and symbolic systems, a collective conscious and unconscious – in short, a *geist*.

By the nineteenth century in Europe, cultural and individual identity had shifted from institutions – the Roman Catholic Church and such broad if immaterial "states" as the republic of letters – to nation states. In the world of learning, the dependence on classical art and literature and the Latin language morphed into an emphasis on vernacular language and literature. From the vantage point of a later age, we can see this embracing of national identity and vernacular language sifting down to new academic disciplines, each with its own set of terms and language. Art history's demotic became style. And because of Georg Wilhelm Friedrich Hegel's positing of a ghost in the machine – the *geist* – style mutated into symbolic form.

But back to Winckelmann: the way he devised a connection between art and culture meant that after him it became difficult for an art historian to conceive of history as anything other than suffused with a culture that encodes itself in style or form. Because this way of thinking – style is art; art is culture; culture is history – persisted from the time of Winckelmann on, the emergence of art history as a discipline in an age of nationalism and vernacular culture is hardly surprising. Indeed, within this historicized system, art history was nigh on inevitable.

If Winckelmann got it right, then artistic style is a language, one that with the helpful assistance of art historians can be read. Style becomes a beam of light that shines into any and all corners of all cultures, a bolt of lightning, even, that reveals the whole, discloses a truth about culture shrouded in the imagery of art lying behind the curtain of nation, culture, and time. How could there not be a discipline of art history if its purveyors were to have control of just such a lamp? But it may also be true, as David Ferris has argued, that art history has relied precisely upon a "refusal to account for the concept of culture lying behind this history" – Winckelmann's and Hegel's history, that is. It is this very denial that "sustains art history as a discipline in its own right."[34] The concept of culture to which Ferris refers grows out of a discourse that is more aesthetic than historical, more tinged by form than by events. We turn our backs on that concept of culture to which Ferris refers, or we pretend it is not there, because Winckelmann spun his theory of art more or less out of thin air. In other words, he had no real historical, or more specifically *art*-historical, record upon which to base his assertion that the freedom of Greek sculpture of the Golden Age could appear only within the context of Greek institutions that promoted self-determination and liberty. His knowledge of Greek sculpture came through Roman sculpture. Despite the vast resources of ancient statuary available to Winckelmann in the Albani collection – he lived for a while in Rome's Villa Albani – and in the Capitoline Museum, the only piece mentioned specifically by Pliny the Elder known to Winckelmann was the *Laocöon,* then as now in the Vatican collection and not a piece of Greek sculpture of the classical age.

Heinrich Wölfflin, an epigone of Winckelmann and student of both Jacob Burckhardt and *formpsychologie,* raised the stakes on style through his brilliant formulation of archetypes. He asserted in his *Principles of Art History* that European culture of the seventeenth century could only be represented in a painterly way, in terms of patches of colour, profound spaces, oblique vectors, uncontained forces, and hypertrophic spectacle. Art of the sixteenth century assumed an oppositional visual system that is linear, planimetric, draughtsmanly, and closed.[35] The Swiss art historian wanted to sound the depths of form in more thoroughgoing ways than most nineteenth-century art historians were inclined to do. In his preface to *Classic Art,* Wölfflin wrote that people were bored with biography and "description of the circumstances of the time," which I take to mean background, something oftentimes presented to the reader more for flavour than for real explanation.[36] What he wanted to find, instead, was the "essence of a work of art." Wölfflin pointed to Adolf von Hildebrandt's complaint against those who direct their attention to the outward shape of plants without understanding the inner life of a flower, its growth, or its basic nature.

Wölfflin also was alert to the complex ways of representation and the phenomenon of a style adhering to the vernacular, to local and national cultures. His introduction to *Classic Art* is quite marvellous as a ploy to show the author's sympathy with his audience's somewhat gauche and anti-classical attitudes. He begins,

> The word "classic" has, for us, a rather chilly sound. We feel that it drags us away from the bright, living world into airless rooms inhabited not by warm, red-blooded human beings but only by shadows. "Classic Art" seems to be the eternally-dead, the eternally-old, the fruit of the Academies, the result of learning and not of life, and in us the desire for the living, the actual, the tangible, is so urgent. [There is here that baroque headlong rush of language that rhetoricians call asyndeton.] What modern man wants above all is an art with a strong smell of earth about it.[37]

It is remarkable that Wölfflin will indeed serve up classic art with at least some vapours of the earth. What is he trying to do with this apparently frank and open appeal to the reader's confidence? Wölfflin ostensibly was speaking against the "realist" tastes of late nineteenth-century German art, such as one finds demonstrated in the rural scenes made popular by Wilhelm Leibl and Hans Thoma. He concedes the pleasure of a nice picture showing, say, "a lively scene on Sunday morning in Rome's Piazza Montanara when the peasants come in to be shaved."[38] This imaginative view, which he conjures as a comparison to Raphael's *School of Athens*, is meant to stand in for quattrocento painting, a style that in Wölfflin's and supposedly our eyes is replete with ordinary detail and summons the comfort of everyday experience. The purpose of this conjoining of fifteenth-century Florentine painting with late nineteenth-century German realism is to draw in his reader, who is *bürgerlich* or – in the more pejorative sense – *spiessbürgerlich*, to the world of Florentine art, first of all of the fifteenth century, and then to lead the reader gently by the hand, as it were, to the grand and aristocratic classic style of the early *cinquecento*. Wölfflin, in other words, cajoles his German readers away from their vernacular to a different one, one still imbued with an identifiable and analysable style, hence his own excursus on the linear and painterly in *Principles of Art History*. Art history was born into a nationalist ideology but found itself soon enough in dire need of liberation from that very limitation. Or to put it in slightly different terms, style became part of the vernacular of a *discipline* rather than of a culture. Style is an inherent attribute of a new academic discipline, one that allows academic citizens – professors – to move horizontally across national and linguistic boundaries.

Style for Wölfflin has special powers. Essences and archetypes illuminate forms, just as forms betoken essences and archetypes. For art history that means form can be symptomatic of an age, with "age" taking on nearly transcendent meanings. "History" in this sense, propelled by *geist*, becomes something prior to events, and formalism as a way of critiquing art is caught up in Hegelian idealist notions of how time works.

In an important essay on formalism, German idealist philosophy, historicism, and materialist (mostly Marxist) readings of time and art, David Summers assesses the costs of formal analysis.[39] In his formalist reading of Raphael's *Holy Family*, Summers shows by way of demonstration how the grouping of figures becomes a pyramid, the horizon a horizontal, and colour an element in creating balance. Recognizable images become counters in a kind of glass bead game, one that the *magister ludi* plays in celebration of coordination and harmony. We leave out a lot of things when doing formal analysis, but it has been the belief of generations of art historians that this abstracting procedure effects distillation, the boiling away of volatile, that is to say inessential, elements so as to find the precipitate or concentrate. Form is that hard-pan, the sediment so crucial to culture.

What first strikes our eye in a painting – those pre-iconographic elements that Erwin Panofsky assigned to the (mere) first level of interpretation[40] – seem so apparent; but they really mask something deeper, something non-figurative and conceptual that has to be pried loose from that which is subliminal and apparently subconscious. As Rosalind Krauss in her palpable and pellucid language sees it, interpretation is based upon "a notion that there is a work, x, *behind which* there stands a group of meanings, a, b, or c, which the hermeneutic task of the critic unpacks, reveals, by breaking through, peeling back the literal surface of the work."[41]

It is in this substructure that, for all intents and purposes, the real work of formalism goes on. It is as if we find the deep Platonic form, the gestalt. Those who studied astronomy, at least until the time of Kepler (1571–1630), believed that the world is alive and owes its vibrancy to harmony, a harmony that may not always be obvious to the naked eye. The old number mysticism upheld the principle that by understanding the relations between numbers, which materialize in art as verticals, horizontals, ratios, and geometric forms, we understand some basic truth about the universe.

To return to Krauss: the exegete or philosopher has to penetrate a certain opacity, either in the words of the law (exegete) or in the illusory and therefore obscure aspects of our experience of nature (philosopher), so as to find the truth, the underlying form and harmony of things. In *Phaedrus* Plato wrote of the experience of the harmonious face, the face Winckelmann believed could only be Greek, a face whose proportions follow, more or less, the golden mean (or golden section), roughly equalling 1:1.618.

I give two quotations here from sources widely separated in time: they imply that visual experience has deep roots in harmony, in a beauty that has, as Luca Paccioli was later to characterize it, a godly form.

Socrates holds forth in Plato's *Phaedrus* on beauty and the effects of love. One who has been in this vale of tears for too long may have lost his ability to rise from the corruption of the world and to see genuine beauty; he will, on the contrary, merely detect in beauty something to be desired and then possessed because he has sunk to the condition of a "brutish beast." But one who still trails the clouds of glory, as it were, and remembers the perfection of the "other" world, that perfect one, has eyes that can see straight and true.

> [He] is amazed when he sees any one having a godlike face or form, which is the expression of divine beauty; and at first a shudder runs through him, and again the old awe steals over him; then looking upon the face of his beloved as of a god he reverences him, and if he were not afraid of being thought a downright madman, he would sacrifice to his beloved as to the image of a god; then while he gazes on him there is a sort of reaction, and the shudder passes into an unusual heat and perspiration; for, as he receives the effluence of beauty through the eyes, the wing moistens and he warms. And as he warms, the parts out of which the wing grew, and which had been hitherto closed and rigid, and had prevented the wing from shooting forth, are melted, and as nourishment streams upon him, the lower end of the wing begins to swell and grow from the root upwards; and the growth extends under the whole soul – for once the whole was winged. During this process the whole soul is all in a state of ebullition and effervescence.[42]

Putting aside the fairly obvious double entendres, we can see how Socrates's words can be taken as evidence of the power of a perfectly formed face, one that follows certain preordained and divine rules. Although Euclid was the first to define the golden section in approximately 300 BCE, its properties were in all likelihood known from the time of Pythagoras in the sixth century BCE. We might say, following Ernst Cassirer, that here is a symbolic form, a *morphē* instantiating an *eidos* – a form, in other words, evoking an idea – or the concept of *logos* disclosing itself through the concept of *physis*.

Thomas Mann knew the traditions of Plato and Greek sculpture, evoking them in *Death in Venice* through Aschenbach's eyes.

> Round a wicker table next him was gathered a group of young folk in charge of a governess or companion – three young girls, perhaps fifteen to seventeen years old, and a long-haired boy of about fourteen. Aschenbach noticed with astonishment the lad's perfect beauty. His face recalled the noblest moment of Greek sculpture – pale, with a sweet reserve, with clustering honey-coloured ringlets, the brow and nose descending in one line, the winning mouth, the expression pure and godlike serenity. Yet with all this chaste perfection of form it was of such unique personal

charm that the observer thought he had never seen, either in nature or art, anything so utterly happy and consummate.[43]

It is not that the boy's face brought to mind a Greek statue but that it indeed had the status of just such a statue; or better yet, it was that very face Socrates described as soliciting the clear-eyed spirit who had recently left the world of true form, one who was so moved by the vision that he began again to sprout his wings so as to fly ever closer to the True, the Good, and the Beautiful. No wonder Aschenbach was astonished.

What I believe these quotations illustrate is a long tradition of associating beauty with art and art with proportion revealed by form. Formalism leaves out many things: one is that sense of the state of *being* within or represented by the work of art. In other words, an ontological investigation of a painting, for instance, takes account of form and structure, but only as that which provides a threshold into other experiences. Also, the formalism that I have been outlining can lead to what E.H. Gombrich called the "physiognomic fallacy," which invites association with the more famous "intentional fallacy" of Wimsatt and Beardsley.[44] David Summers has already covered this ground in detail, so I will only mention here that the physiognomic fallacy asserts that form "speaks" to us across cultures and time in a universal language; all we really need do is look and listen.[45] Gombrich argued that forms by themselves do not tell us much; rather, we have to work the form back into the narrative of the original work of art and then into the original culture. We need to be, in other words, historians. And once form becomes part of history, it is not just entangled in social and political exigencies but also elicits ideas and structures of meanings from philosophy and religion and such expressive traditions as poetics and rhetoric.

Hermeneutics and Rhetoric

We as art historians may be willing to admit, while pretending we have not always been aware of it, that when we write about works of art and their circumstances – especially in Rome of the early-modern period, which is the primary if not exclusive focus of this book – we both observe and practice hermeneutics. Although the image of Hermes dashing through the sky to bring messages from gods to humans is familiar enough to art historians, hermeneutics seems to be something more in the purview of philosophers. Martin Heidegger, Hans-Georg

Gadamer, and Paul Ricouer are *not* names often bandied about by art historians, especially those studying European art from roughly 1400–1750.

Hermeneutics of the early-modern period derive from Protestant rather than Catholic sources. The Church's magisterium and the pope's infallibility in matters of meaning and interpretation of biblical text obviated to a fairly large extent the need for theories of interpretation. Protestant theologians, on the other hand, who saw sacred text as that which can sustain interpretation beyond something exclusively dependent upon episcopal authority, sought out rules and rubrics that would deal with sacred and classical texts. Those procedures were spelled out in manuals, such as J.C. Dannhauer's *Hermeneutica sacra sive methodus exponendarum sacrarum litterarum*, published in 1654. Dannhauer does not offer exegesis so much as he insists upon rules and methods for interpretation, a characteristic of hermeneutics that remains to the present day.[46]

It is worth remembering that the primary charge of the visual arts in Rome of the sixteenth and seventeenth centuries, as it had been for centuries before that, was to create a visual understanding of sacred text, to illuminate the Word. The visual arts often differ from typical – that is, written – biblical exegesis because they do for us what the world does in Genesis: they put us in the (simulated) world of God's creation.[47] And we stand in awe.

Gianni Vattimo struggles with the kind of experience I am trying to elucidate in his book *Beyond Interpretation: The Meaning of Hermeneutics for Philosophy*.[48] He begins with a story of entering Borromini's Sant'Ivo alla Sapienza in Rome for the purpose of touring the church and studying the architecture of Borromini. But someone is praying there; so, out of respect for the worshipper, he withdraws.

In the modern world there are divisions of such experiences as the aesthetic, the moral/religious, and the rational. We find ways of giving each its due without there being much conflict, although, as Vattimo reports, the aesthetic tends to take over many times (except when he is polite enough to leave Sant'Ivo). After all, in the contemporary world, Sant'Ivo is perhaps more important for its aesthetic or, to disparage somewhat the notion of aesthetics, its "touristic" than its religious status. Vattimo writes about the "trend towards specialization and the separation of distinct spheres of existence by virtue of which art too became isolated in a domain entirely separate from those of truth, moral values and concrete social existence."[49] For him, the project of modern philosophy is to reintegrate these realms, to achieve something beyond what he calls "standard hermeneutic theory." Or to put it somewhat differently, how do we get truth back into art?

Vattimo observes that hermeneutics challenges the notion of aesthetic experience separated from questions of truth, but he wonders whether – or how – that works. Kant saw beauty as a symbol of truth or morality, but with the development of the concept of disinterestedness, there seemed to be no ground for establishing a commonality between truth and art. Schelling, Hölderlin, and Hegel wanted a new "System-Programme" that would replace religion with something else, a religion of the senses. Where once was religion, now will be art, but with the same complex philosophical and moral issues as religion. Is such a thing possible? Could this new mythology of art ever dissever the attraction between art and religion?

Benedetto Croce referred to a dialectic of the distinct;[50] that is, in the modern era, aesthetics has insisted more and more on a hygienic division, a clear distinction, between art and religion. Vattimo comments that "the relation of art to religion remains 'constitutive,' at least in the sense that it is primarily, indeed exclusively, with religion that art has had to avoid being confused in order to affirm its own specificity and exercise its own function in the history of Western culture."[51] The same force that propels art to distinguish itself from religion draws it right back to where it came from. When considering Lukács's attempt to free art from religion only to put it in the service of party and class, Vattimo observes that the bond between art and religion "continues to operate all the more powerfully the less one wishes to recognize it."[52] Because baroque art largely springs from religion and because one necessity of rhetoric is to sermonize, we can easily enough see that art is and has been steeped all the way down and all the way around in the Roman Church and its rhetoric.

Vattimo's hermeneutic project gets caught up with the excruciatingly problematic bond, correlation, or disassociation between the modern and postmodern. In short, and this is David Ferris's analysis, if the postmodern were to be founded upon the end of modernism, then it would not be postmodern.[53] A philosopher can get tied in knots trying to figure out this problem. Those of us who study the early-modern period in Europe, specifically and for the present purposes roughly 1400–1750, concede the reciprocally contingent relationship between art and religion and therefore may, if we so desire, measure out our days not with coffee spoons but with rhetoric, poetics, and hermeneutics.

3 Giovanni Lorenzo Bernini and Inexpressibility

In St Peter's there exists what amounts to an indoor cemetery strewn thick with statues, sarcophagi, plaques, and magnificent shrines and testimonials, all in marble and bronze. This basilica exists *in fact* but also as a product of imagination – not just the imagination of those who built it, designed it, and decorated it, but the imagination of those who have visited it over the past four centuries or so. It is a virtual universe, a universe parallel to another. It is plenitude and a model of the Christian God's creation.

The philosopher Martin Heidegger argued that "Great Art" is "truth-disclosing," and therefore, following the thinking of Georg Wilhelm Friedrich Hegel, Heidegger asserted that Great Art only existed in the past. Indeed, even Heidegger would have wavered on whether Great Art – or Hegel's "art and the absolute" – survived into the seventeenth century, the time of St Peter's and the baroque. Just the same, Heidegger reasoned that in the modern era Great Art is dead; art may still exist but it is not great. It cannot be great because it is propelled by aesthetics rather than truth. Without truth there is no philosophy of art.[1]

To be true, art must, in Hegel's and Heidegger's terms, be accepted by a culture as a whole. I believe we can say with some certainty that the Catholic world *as a whole* accepted this building and saw it much as worshippers and pilgrims experienced Chartres Cathedral, for instance, in the thirteenth century: it is the Heavenly Jerusalem come to earth.

This particular Heavenly Jerusalem is also St Peter's cenotaph, with Giovanni Lorenzo (or Gianlorenzo) Bernini's *Baldacchino* serving as the grave marker (Figure 3.1). The monument is named after the material that depends from its pelmet – a faux (in this case) brocade whose woof is silk and warp is gold thread – whose name in turn derives from the city

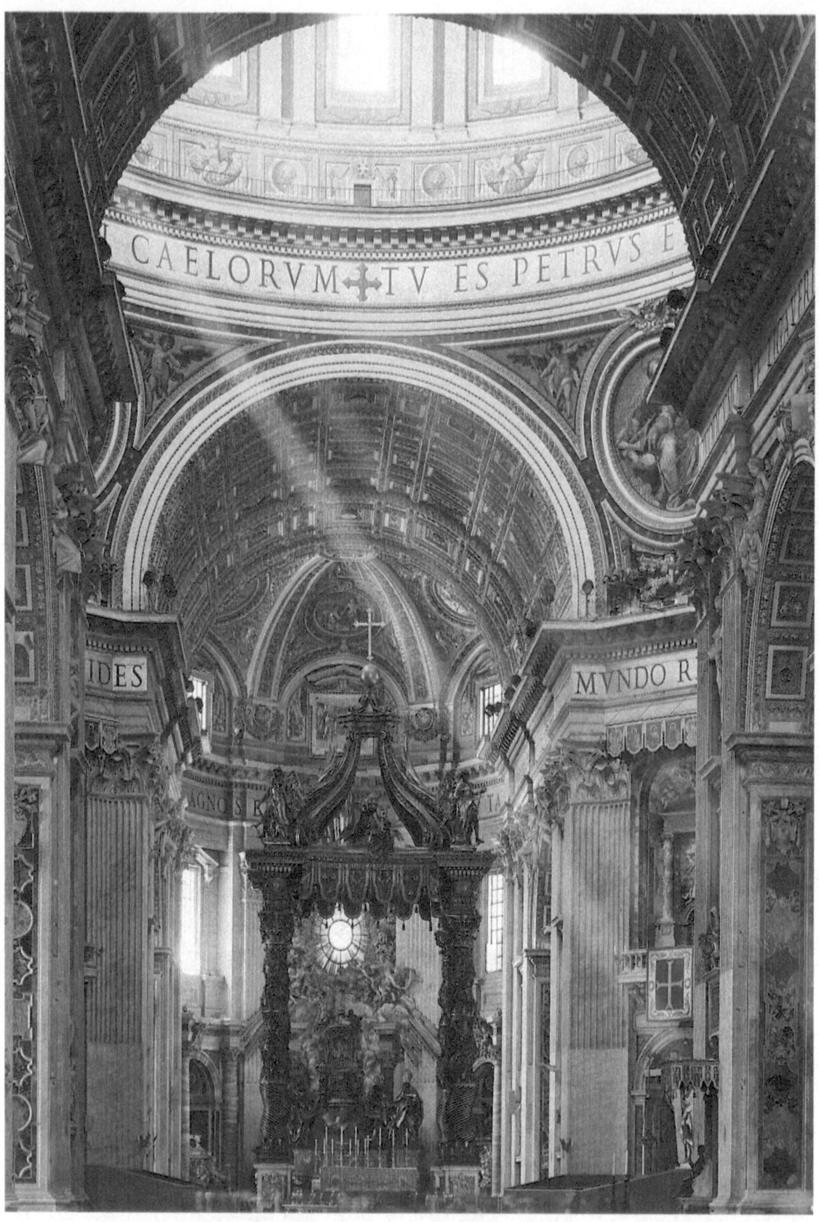

Figure 3.1 Gianlorenzo Bernini, *Baldacchino*, gilt bronze, 1624–33, St Peter's Basilica, Vatican City (Rome), Italy. Photo: Erich Lessing/Art Resource, NY.

of its origin, Baghdad. In addition to marking Peter's tomb, the *Baldacchino* covers the high altar (the pope's altar), scene of Christ's sacrifice to His Father and to humankind. Bernini's use of the Solomonic or helical – that is, spiralling – columns commemorates the presence of similar columns in old St Peter's, now preserved in the reliquaries on the second level of each pier in the crossing; these were thought to have come from the Temple of Solomon in Jerusalem.[2]

Fearful of the malaria sweeping Rome and sweltering from their confinement in the Sistine Chapel, the College of Cardinals elected Maffeo Barberini pope on 6 August 1623. He took the name Urban VIII, and as W. Chandler Kirwin has demonstrated in his indispensable text *Powers Matchless*, the new pope saw the Office of the Propagation of the Faith (*Ufficio di Propaganda Fide*) as the best instrument for empowering the church. Trumpeting and defending Catholicism throughout the world became the universalist task of a universalist pope.

A story told by Gianlorenzo Bernini's son Domenico takes place on the day of the pope's election. Urban called the 24-year-old Gianlorenzo into his presence and intoned, "It is a great fortune for you, O Cavaliere, to see Cardinal Maffeo Barberini made pope, but our fortune is even greater to have Cavalier Bernini alive during our pontificate."[3] Narrating the story in this manner owes as much to older hagiographic writings awash in such tropes (the great leader recognizing a young and quasi-divine hero) as it does to historical fact; just the same, there is no question about Urban's favouring of Bernini. Within days of Urban's election, Bernini was on the Vatican payroll as superintendent of the papal foundry and waterworks. It was not long before his attentions turned to the canopy for the high altar of St Peter's.

To hear Urban's panegyrist Lelio Guidiccioni tell it, the pope hoped to have a ciborium over the Holy Sepulchre in Jerusalem that matched the one he planned for St Peter's grave.[4] Having named himself after the pope who started the first Crusade (Urban II, 1088–99), Urban most likely did have a baldacchino in mind for Jerusalem. In his many religious, institutional, and artistic plans, Urban was determined, pious, vigorous, proud of his accomplishments, and zealous in his promotion of the church.

Bernini's *Baldacchino* stands about 95 feet tall and contains roughly 50 tons of bronze. This, the crowning feature of the apostle's tomb, is Bernini's most monumental work as the architect of St Peter's and introduces us to devices of baroque visual rhetoric. Bernini's biographer Filippo Baldinucci wrote,

> What appears to the viewer is something completely new, something he had never dreamed of seeing. From this I draw the conclusion that for the eye alone and not the ear is reserved the merit of being able to render a complete judgment. Indeed, I will go even further and say that the eye itself at first sight is not capable of conveying it all to the imagination, such is the abundance of sublime ornament offered at one time to the eye. A very clear indication of this is that there is no one, no matter how judicious or expert he may be, whose spirit is sufficiently satisfied by the first sight to form any concept other than that of complete wonderment.[5]

Baldinucci introduces the topos – that is, the topic, or more generally, figure of speech – of inexpressibility: "it is for the eye alone and not the ear," he writes. Topoi first appear as dramatic and telling devices in classical rhetoric under the rubric of invention. One of the most famous examples in the Italian tradition of such an extended metaphor as inexpressibility is Dante's description in the last canto of *Paradiso*, where he tells his readers that with God's help he will attempt to capture in his words the ineffable, even if his language is but a tiny spark of the divine light (*una favilla sol della luce*), a luminosity of such potency it might annihilate him.[6] Forswearing Dante's ambitions to write what the eye can see – at least *un poco* (as Dante puts it) – Baldinucci simply says it cannot be said. He uses words paradoxically; that is, in *words* he says what *words* cannot say. Interestingly enough, the eye (although it too is overwhelmed at first) *can* comprehend what words cannot express, what the ear cannot hear, which both sanctions and commends such a gargantuan work of *visual* art. When inexpressibility is used in literature – "words cannot express ..." – one senses just below the surface (as an affect, in other words) frustration and failure, because we are after all speaking animals – *homo loquens*.[7] But Baldinucci (and by extension Bernini) must have derived some satisfaction from this adynaton, this impossibility stratagem. If visual thinking can exceed verbal expression, then painting, sculpture, and architecture may lay claim to a supraliterary power.

When the pope celebrates mass at the papal altar, set beneath the *Baldacchino*'s great canopy, his eye as he looks up comprehends the *visio Dei*, the image of God. Well, almost. The *Baldacchino* does provide a view upward and slightly outward through Michelangelo's dome and cupola to the refulgence of Dante's tenth heaven, as it were.

In the middle of the ceiling of the *Baldacchino* itself hovers an image of the Holy Spirit, which as the third person of the Holy Trinity mediates between man and God, human and divine. The Paraclete guides the pope so that he does not lead the church into error.

What Baldinucci signals is that we stand mute, almost as if in a trance or dream, before a divine presence. We are in a state of wonderment, seeing something we had never dreamed of seeing, experiencing a moment that is holy, one that hearkens back to the awe of that first moment of manifestation, of vision: "And God said, Let there be light'" (Genesis 1:3). When we are awestruck, we are dumbstruck. In a state of awe, one is open to a vision, has a rapport with it, but more often than not avoids – in fact, is incapable of – analysis.

Rudolf Preimesberger has recorded comments on the grandeur of St Peter's interior that date from the earlier part of the sixteenth century. Not only did those who beheld the rebuilding of St Peter's employ such terms as *grandioso, stupendo, magnificentissimo,* and *meraviglioso,* they observed the emotional charge carried by sheer scale, as if the new St Peter's were built by giants. One is stunned, stupefied, overwhelmed, rendered inarticulate by the basilica's sheer size and splendour. Preimesberger is right to see all these conceits as precursors to the topos of the sublime.[8]

Immanuel Kant wrote that when one enters St Peter's in Rome, "he has the feeling that his imagination is inadequate for exhibiting the idea of a whole, [a feeling] in which imagination reaches its maximum, and as it strives to expand that maximum, it sinks back into itself, but consequently comes to feel a liking [that amounts to an] emotion."[9] The emotion to which Kant refers is the substance of the sublime.

When standing before the *Baldacchino*, we allow Bernini's magnificent structure to *disclose* itself: *it* has to do the work. At least at the beginning. Finally, "we" – more than an individual – enter into or inhere somehow in the work. But it takes time, as Baldinucci warns. We are, in Heideggerian language, "preservers" of the work.[10]

By their presence, intellection, and conception, Heidegger's preservers bring a work into being; they stand "within the openness of beings that happen in the work."[11] Openness in this sense is related to revelation or *meraviglia*, as Baldinucci uses the word. Heidegger goes on: "this 'standing-within' of preservation, however, is a knowing. Yet knowing does not consist in mere information and notions about something. He who truly knows what is, knows what he wills to do in the midst of what is."[12] Here the preservers experience altered states of being, heightened awareness, and profound spirituality. Having gained such enlightenment, the preservers know what to do: they complete the work and pass it through history. Heidegger's "preservers" seem to be immune to inexpressibility, are capable of grasping "the extraordinary awesomeness of the truth that is happening in the work."[13] The comments of Heidegger on the role of "preservers" of a work of art (Heidegger of course wrote generally, making no reference to St Peter's) taken together with Kant's more specific use of St Peter's for illustrating his concept of the sublime call upon a certain *intentionality* to the work of art, which invokes Paul de Man's framing of an intentionality that leads to a "'struggle with meaning,' of which all criticism ... should give an account."[14] We art historians are those preservers; we should indeed give an account of the struggle for meaning.

Ernst Robert Curtius characterizes the root of the inexpressibility (or unspeakability) topos (*Unsagbarkeitstopos*) as an "emphasis upon inability to cope with the subject,"[15] which, though not a very felicitous phrase, strikes close to the core of many traits as well as denunciations of the baroque as a rhetorical mode. There are degrees and varieties of our "inability to cope" with St Peter's as a whole and the *Baldacchino* in particular, and this has to do, at least in part, with our sense of the sublime.

The sublime famously took shape as product and artistic phenomenon of the eighteenth century, when it was written about by Edmund Burke and Immanuel Kant, among others. But the old rhetorical manual written by Longinus, *Perì hýpsos* – usually translated into English as "On the Sublime" – was indeed known and studied in the 1600s. The Greek title can also be translated as "On Grandeur of Thought and Expression," which puts the text squarely in the ancient traditions of Greek and Latin rhetoric. Longinus wrote about epideictic oratory, the highest of the three rhetorical classes.

When Baldinucci states, "che l'occhio stesso di rappresentare alla fantasia sì gran copia di specie sublimissime,"[16] one can understand it somewhat differently from Catherine Enggass's translation "the eye itself at first sight is not capable of conveying it all to the imagination, such is the abundance of sublime ornament offered at one time to the eye." Baldinucci refers to an abundance of sublime *appearance*, as form or shape. *Specie* is not just about ornament, as one usually thinks of it; rather, the eye sees a sublime appearance, a species in the sense that it stands in for something else (*sotto le specie del pane e del vino*, for example, when describing the Eucharist).[17] In scholastic terminology, species is not what is known but how – or the vehicle through which – something is known. Furthermore, the sentence (Enggass's translation) "one must, therefore, come and come again, see and resee, and always that lofty temple is rediscovered in its whole and in its every major part" seems not to have the strength of Baldinucci's original "onde pur gli abbisogna, o voglia o no, il tornare e ritornare, il vedere e rivedere e sempre quell'eccelso tempio ritrova e nel tutto, ed in ogni sua parte maggiore di se stesso." "Abbisogna" takes care of the "must," but "o voglia o no" does not get translated by Enggass. Baldinucci asserts that we have no choice, we must return "o voglia o no" – *whether we want to or not*. Baldinucci's "o voglia o no" is part of the rhetoric of insistence, closely related to the usually misunderstood English "willy-nilly" (originally meaning "unwillingly"). The sense that God may be the one standing behind this insistence is underscored by the seventeenth-century British writer William Gouge, who wrote that "God's will, will we, nill we, shall be accomplished."[18]

Therefore, referring to the *Baldacchino* as a most sublime species grants it a profound role and power in the revealing of (or access to) visibility and spiritual knowledge. This revelatory expansiveness may lead one beyond normal limits of human comprehension and expression. That is why one is *compelled* – it seems to be beyond our will to resist, as I have stated (*o voglia o no*, "willy-nilly") – to return again and again to see this extraordinary, sublime (*eccelso*) temple and its furnishings.[19]

We would be wrong, of course, to assume that Baldinucci is Bernini's mouthpiece or in some sense makes the sculptor's intentions manifest. Neither we nor Baldinucci knows those intentions. That is not why I have looked at his language; rather, Baldinucci provides evidence for how Bernini was perceived and received, at least by one highly articulate and deeply interested (as biographer) artistic cognoscente. Baldinucci also gives voice to the language of epiphany, conceit, and the marvellous – in short, the baroque as an absolute art.

Our inability to understand the sublime or cope with the absolute is also a hint of its undoing: magnificence, like magnanimity, stands always on a precipice, ready to crumble. Romans had their ruins to remind them of a great civilization's mortality, of the inexplicableness of existence, its exigencies and fallenness. Existential crises did not escape Bernini's patron Urban VIII, who wrote in his sonnet 32: "Dalle ruine di Roma antica si riconosce la poca stabilità delle cose terrene" – the ruins of ancient Rome remind us of the instability of things terrestrial.[20] Things celestial endure, and we stand speechless before them.

4 Death and Dying in St Peter's Basilica: Part 1

Papal tombs populate St Peter's in greater abundance than any other multi-figured sculptural ensemble. Gianlorenzo Bernini's tomb of Urban VIII, sculpted 1627–46 (Figure 4.1), stands among Bernini's best known and, in terms of its meaning, among the most complex, not to mention problematical, works of baroque art.[1]

In the new St Peter's, two papal tombs precede Urban's, one by Guglielmo della Porta for Paul III (Figure 4.2, about which I will have more to discuss later) and the other largely by Prospero Antichi (or Bresciano) of Clement XIII. Antichi's tomb was replaced in the eighteenth century by a newer tomb that was entirely of marble (much of the earlier tomb remained in stucco). These tombs have a common ancestor in Michelangelo's Medici tombs in the Medici Chapel of San Lorenzo in Florence, and before that the Renaissance tomb, which is perhaps best represented by Bernardo Rossellino's tomb of Leonardo Bruni in the Franciscan church of Santa Croce, Florence's "pantheon" of illustrious men. In the later arrangement of (specifically papal) tombs (i.e., beginning with Michelangelo), the deceased sits above a sarcophagus, which is flanked by allegorical figures. In his dazzling iconographic reading of Bernini's tomb of Urban VIII, Irving Lavin makes the shrewd observation that this particular arrangement – of a seated portrait of the deceased syncretically or heterogeneously joined with abstract moral, theological, or cosmogonic beings – "is a political allegory rooted in the Petrarchan tradition of allegorical triumphs."[2]

There is a belief that one's soul is protected if buried *ad sanctos*, that is, near the remains of a saint, and here we have the greatest saint of them all, Peter. Maximus of Turin wrote, "The martyrs will keep guard over

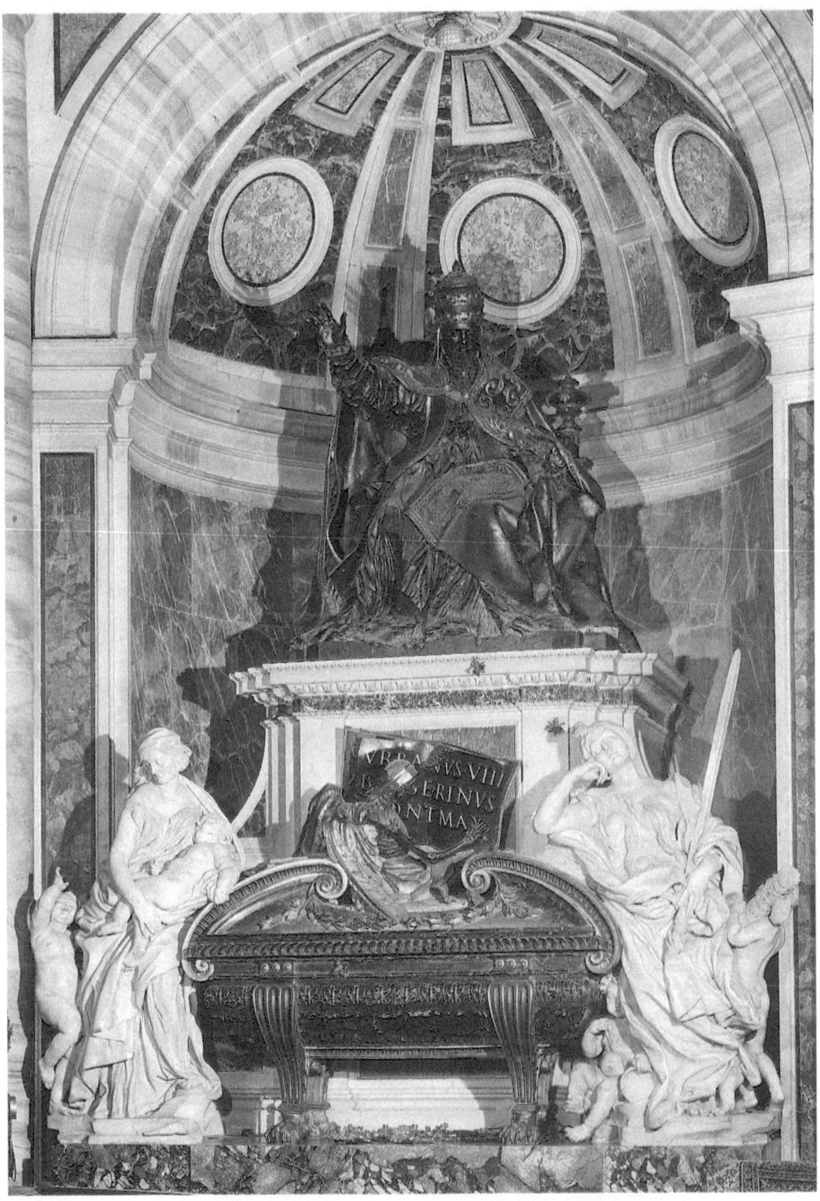

Figure 4.1 Gianlorenzo Bernini, *Tomb of Urban VIII*, gilt bronze and marble, 1627–46, St Peter's Basilica, Vatican City (Rome), Italy. Photo: Scala/Art Resource, NY.

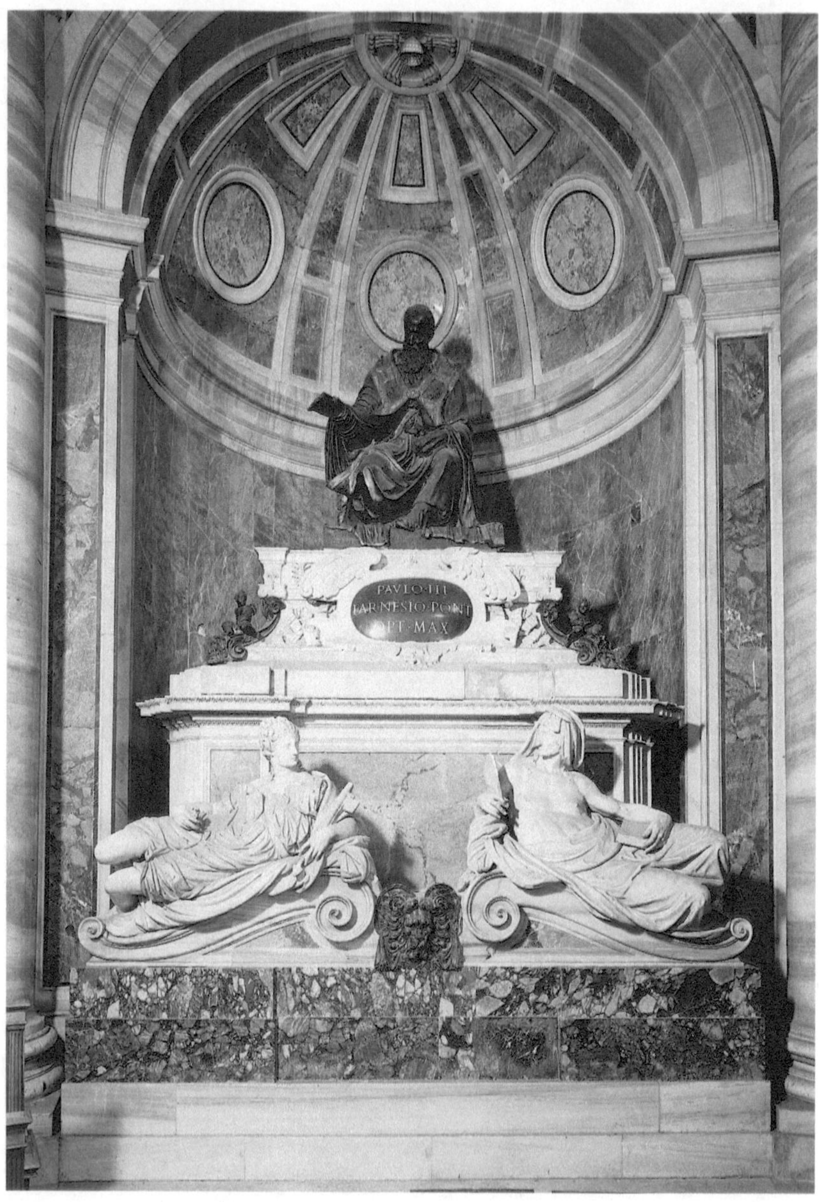

Figure 4.2 Guglielmo della Porta, *Tomb of Paul III*, gilt bronze and marble, 1549–75, St Peter's Basilica, Vatican City (Rome), Italy. Photo: Scala/Art Resource, NY.

us, who live with our bodies, and they will take us into their care when we have forsaken our bodies. Here they prevent us from falling into sinful ways, there they protect us from the horrors of hell. That is why our ancestors were careful to unite our bodies with the bones of the martyrs."[3]

A eulogy is a speech or poem in praise of someone who has died. Gaston Bachelard describes the eulogized place (a felicitous space, a cosmic space) as a *topophilia*, a place that, in effect, feels good, is consoling and pleasing.[4] The eulogy when written – or in this case enacted/performed by the parts of a sculptural complex – specifically on the occasion of death, is an elegy, which brings comfort. The mood of an elegy is sentimental, soothing, and tender. There is an emotional, sensate, or felt presence of the absent Holy Father.

The eulogy/elegy consoles the one who mourns the passing of the Holy Father. We are also reminded, but in encouraging terms, of the phrase *Sancte Pater sic transit Gloria mundi* ("Holy Father, thus passes the glory of the world"), as the master of ceremonies says to the newly elected pope while the pope is being borne on the *Sedia Gestatoria*, which is his throne. The pope knows that his office will be passed on, that he is more an apostolic successor than an absolute monarch. As heir to St Peter, he is, in effect, a headmaster of the church, the one who administers his institution. Christ sends His popes to transmit the living magisterium, the church's traditions and teaching authority, an idea reasserted and powerfully emphasized by the Council of Trent.[5]

Gianlorenzo Bernini stands for many things in the history of art. For one, he impressed upon the visual arts new ways of representing "Early Modern Catholicism." The Council of Trent vigorously repudiated the Protestant Reformation: where Protestants found authority and truth exclusively in the Bible, Catholics insisted upon the continuing – what they termed "living" – role of the pope as an apostolic successor who in his indefectibility (always under the guidance of the Holy Spirit) continues the teachings of Jesus Christ and the apostles. This is what the Roman Church calls its "magisterium."

Bernini's tomb of Urban VIII especially memorializes the church's magisterium in the person of the pope who, though now deceased, represents eternally a vital link to St Peter, the other apostles, and Christ. Bernini, like his friends the Jesuits, believed in the rhetoric of optimism, praise, and authority. Just as the Jesuits and the decrees of the Council of Trent prescribed, both Bernini and Urban wanted a large audience, which St Peter's was built to provide. Bernini understood the rhetorical idea of *enargeia*, or vividness (from the Greek *arges*, for bright).

There are a sarcophagus, an effigy of the pope, and the figure from the *danse macabre* – the extraordinarily witty image of death rising from the sarcophagus and writing Urban's name. The allegorical figure on our left is Charity/Caritas (or Love), a theological virtue, and to the right is Justice, a Platonic or cardinal virtue.

Christ as Divine Shepherd said to Peter "Feed my sheep ... Feed my lambs" (represented nearby on Bernini's *Cathedra Petri*). The pope as vicar speaks for Christ and leads His flock, which is His Church. This is a point of great importance in how Bernini created and staged the funeral complex of Pope Urban VIII.

The pope's benediction recalls the Roman *ad locutio,* the gesture of authority used by the emperor or Roman general commanding attention. Urban seeks to sway, to give voice to and convey his authority. When in the presence of the pope, no other priest of any rank can offer the benediction. As a blessing, this gesture brings to those who look upon Urban a spiritual or temporal good; this sign therefore also is an invocation.

The skeleton, which gets our attention immediately, is the *figura rerum,* the "shower forth" of things, the one who describes and limns what will be. As Urban's alter ego she (*la morte*) dramatizes what Urban already knows, which are the workings between God and Man, the Second Coming, and the Resurrection.[6] She has all the vitality and mordant wit of one of Hans Holbein's dancing deaths. In simple terms of narrative, does the skeleton inscribe Urban's epitaph on a bronze tablet, which then will be affixed to the tomb, or does she, as Baldinucci tells us, enter Urban's name in Death's registry? Here we run into that problem, thinking back to Heidegger but in a somewhat different vein, of *ontology*. According to Merleau-Ponty and Heidegger, there can be two worlds (two ontologies): the world of the work of art and the world in which the work of art exists. Within the realm of this funeral complex, what level or status of reality does the tablet have? In our reality – which is (supposedly, although I will challenge this notion later on) the world within which the work of art exists – it is bronze and has Urban's name and title – "Pont Max" (Pontifex Maximus) – inscribed on it. But in the tomb's own fictive world, the tablet crinkles like parchment and seems to be a creased page in a book. Another page stands behind, with the letters "CL" (above) and "A" (below) visible, which, according to Baldinucci, signifies Urban's predecessor, Gregory XV. It seems more likely, if we are to follow Baldinucci's logic if not his attribution, that the CL begins the name of Clement VIII and the A stands for Aldobrandini, his family name. These letters appear on the fourth tablet back, which corresponds to the sequence: Clement VIII Aldobrandini (1592–1605), Paul V Borghese (1605–21), Gregory XV Ludovisi (1621–3), and Urban VIII Barberini.[7]

Because Death personified is often an insurgent and an insurrectionist, she simply does not work in the usual coordinates of time and space. Death remains a figure who, in Christian traditions going back at least to Dante, structures providential time and describes, here in literary terms, events.

We who stand before this tomb and those who stood there in the seventeenth century have an existential space within the apse of St Peter's. There is then the physical reality of the tomb, but, as I have mentioned, we are imaginatively in a transfigured space, one saturated with religious meaning – an ontological plenum – and so we tend to read the skeleton, the pope, and the allegorical figures of Justice and Charity as each having distinct realities that differ from ours and from one another's. At the same time we as virtual or literal visitors to St Peter's are caught up with the entire universe of the basilica in the same baroque fold, something I will write about presently.

I am suggesting these rather difficult tasks of imaginative seeing so as to understand better Bernini's rhetoric, his way of persuading us of something profound and truth-disclosing. Justice (on the right) is an agent of elegy; in her swoon she mediates between us and the grim fact of Urban's demise. Hers is a lament, a grieving for that which is lost; she is bereft. She also bears the weight of juridical allegory, praising the pope by intimating the honour, even-handedness, and probity he bore as the Vicar of Christ. She seeks to console us, to palliate our grief, as elegy should always do. Perhaps in her faint, she fears the promise of justice may be torn from this earth by the catastrophic albeit inevitable fact of Urban's demise.

But elegy here is not free of irony. A putto marches out – in fact, into the sarcophagus itself – with the fasces as if he were an elfin or sprightly lictor, a bodyguard to Urban, who then becomes appropriately enough a latter-day (and Christian) magistrate, king of Rome, chief priest, and judge, all of whom lictors accompanied in ancient Rome. Another child looks from beneath Justice's skirts. These figures depart from their *idées fixes* as *innocenti*, which is one more way of breaking the fourth wall – that imagined boundary between viewers and the viewed. The puerile lector awaits, in this period of the *interrex* – the *sede vacante* – for the new king of Rome, the new Roman pontiff.

A niche with its frame separates inside from outside, slow time from fast time, historical time from contemporary time, *fantasia* from reality. But in this instance, Bernini undercuts such classical separation by his sculptural complex contending with his own architectural frame.

Some Comments on Putti

By its very naming "putto" embraces irony. According to the earliest edition of the *Vocabolario della Crusca* (1610), "putto" (because of its use by Dante) has carried the burden of the meretricious – the courtesan, the prostitute.[8] In rhetorical terms the putto can be seen as an antiphrasis, an image meaning the opposite of what it purports to mean. Instead of being innocent and cute, these putti (the two surrounding Justice) are knowing and mischievous. But it is hard to pin down just what a putto is supposed to mean, given its pagan *and* Christian sources. Is it an *amorino* or a cherub? Donatello brought back the *spiritelli* – or sprites – Bacchic figures, as Charles Dempsey calls them.[9] Although the children with Charity are in fact children, those accompanying Justice represent something indeterminate. They pose as demons really, classical gods in miniature; as such, they survive the pagan world, given what Leonard Barkan terms a free pass – a *laisser-passer* – by patristic theologians.[10] They are subject to mutability and metamorphosis. Here Bernini uses them for their rhetorical facility, their insouciant pliability: they are meaning shifters. Gordon Teskey writes of the survival of such pagan demons, "magical talismans surrounding the body of the prince with an aura of power drawn from remote and inscrutable sources."[11] Art historians tend to dismiss putti as being compositional devices, traditional fixtures on tombs – somewhat playful, redolent of innocence – guides to souls making their way to the Heavenly Jerusalem, the Kingdom of God. These oddly sexualized children receive scant attention as rhetorical devices or bearers of transmogrifying meaning. Putti may charm, but let us remember they are demonic, at least half pagan, and not to be trusted.

The allegorical statues of Justice and Charity are upright and active, alive in a sense. Christian Charity, on our left, holds one child who lies back after having been fed from her breast, which, originally uncovered, was plastered over to protect the prudish in the late seventeenth century (just after Bernini's death). Another child screams while trying to get the attentions of his mother, she who looks like one of Rubens's peasants and smiles consolingly at the child. The pope's death sends him into a tantrum.

Despite what I have written about the consolation that seems to radiate from these figures, it is curiously unsettling to see allegorical statues come alive. One cannot help but think of Freud's essay on the uncanny, in which he describes how disconcerted we become when confronted by that which is inanimate while having a sense that it is alive. Because of the ways in which they behave, somewhat according to the script (but not really), these figures might make us a bit uncomfortable. By coming alive they also escape, or at least challenge in the mode of irony their settled or traditional meanings.[12]

In his "Epistle to Con Grande," Dante famously introduced the idea that his *Commedia* is polysemous (or polysemantic), a book in other words with multiple levels of meanings.[13] These strata of distinction are constituted primarily by the literal and allegorical, with the allegorical being further subdivided into the moral and anagogical. The gap between the allegorical representation (statues of Justice, Death, and Charity, but also Urban as Supreme Pontiff) and its meaning constitutes that necessary space of the *arbitrary*, out of which interpretation springs (or is drawn). Bernini's statues of Charity along with her two children (one screaming, the other having just nursed) are, in the Saussurian sense, unmotivated – in other words, arbitrary – as signifiers. The meaning gets underway, becomes *in*scribed or *pre*scribed, when we review the history and conventions of representation and papal tombs, always keeping in mind the slippage between image and meaning, signifier and signified. Bernini's vitalizing of his statues focuses our attention of what Dante refers to as the "digressive" and "transumptive" peculiarity of allegory. To digress is to swerve or deviate; to transume is to make a faithful or legal copy: either way, gaps open, whether by means of diverging or by copying. Although no one can or could have read Bernini's mind, we might, just the same, safely assume that Bernini had an intuitive grasp of the slippage between image and meaning, the *play*, which is a kind of visual paronomasia, between the visual experience of an object and the kinds of meanings that spring to one's mind. The result of word and visual play can be in an aesthetic (that is, pleasurable) sense fortuitous, motiveless, and capricious. Using an anti-semiotic element such as play makes visual language "epistemologically highly suspect and volatile," as Paul de Man assesses wordplay in literary language.[14] Perhaps one would expect a papal tomb in St Peter's to make strong epistemological claims, but Bernini's rascally putti (sculpted by Lazzaro Morelli), dozing and beaming allegorical representations, shifty-looking skeleton, and blank-eyed pope merely underline the uncertainty of meaning in the absence of the supreme pontiff. It is this very "struggle with meaning" that should be at the centre of all art-historical (not to mention literary and philosophical) criticism.

To say that art demythologizes its putative subject matter is in a sense to state the obvious. Art by its nature is *always already* artifice, not truth. That fabled and notorious post-structuralist trope "always already" calls attention to the fact that both visual and literary forms of representation embed themselves in our history, culture, and the ways in which the human mind works. It goes without saying (although a practical or philosophical critic will *always* say it) that neither language nor statues give us truth; neither is declarative; both are rhetorical. Representation separates truth from language, truth from paintings. The *always already* is that which is a given, although not generally acknowledged as such.

Paul de Man's laboured and at the same time elegant readings of critics and their "insightful" misreadings of texts grows out of his rejection of what we may call "practical criticism," the unsystematic, non-hermeneutical approach of the New Critics in literature and what I see as many of the approaches found among art historians.[15] In other words, as I look to those lions of post-structuralism (or deconstructionism) for their insights, I do violence to their enterprise by enlisting their understanding while not necessarily subscribing to the notion that all representation seeks ironic "demythification," that all sculpture or painting, for instance, is inherently, insistently, and forever simulacral, never (ever) truth-disclosing. At the core of post-structuralist critiques is the upending not so much of truth claims but of criticism that is not always already analytical philosophy. Despite my interest in the critical turn in literary criticism a generation or so ago, I (and I believe this is true of many – perhaps most – art historians) remain a practical critic and perhaps must plead guilty to the same crime of which the New Critics were accused by Paul de Man, of never being able to make "major contributions."[16]

Both Walter Benjamin and Gilles Deleuze have commented on the ways in which baroque allegory steals a march on symbolism by reaching beyond an encapsulated idea. Deleuze, from whom we will be hearing about the baroque "fold," characterizes traditional allegorical representations (think of statues of virtues on such an Italian sixteenth-century tomb as Guglielmo della Porta's *Tomb of Paul III* in St Peter's, Figure 4.2) as self-contained symbols within which "we isolate, purify, or concentrate the object; we cut all its ties to the universe, and thus we raise it up, we put it in contact no longer with its simple concept, but with an Idea that develops this concept morally or esthetically." In short, the "concentrated object" is a Renaissance statue of a virtue. In the baroque period, however, Bernini's marble figure of Caritas, for instance, is "broadened according to a whole network of natural relations. The object itself overflows its frame in order to enter into a cycle or a series, and now the concept is what is found increasingly compressed, interiorized, wrapped in an instance that can ultimately be called 'personal.'"[17] The next art-historical stage (the time of Filippo della Valle), an age of *buon gusto*, introduces an allegorical figure whose "concept" (as Deleuze distinguishes it) has been compressed, interiorized, and wrapped to extinction.

Like Justice and Caritas, the dead Urban is so alive we wonder about his status, what he means exactly, how we are supposed to respond to him and read him. Bernini was born into and trained in a Renaissance tradition that valued mimesis, which is imitation based upon a functional knowledge of the human body, a theory of *affetti* or affect – that is, a theory of the expression of the emotions, or as it was called then, the "passions" – and an ideal growing out of *virtù* and *nobilità*, always grounded in a world of harmony and accord of parts. Sculptors learned how to clothe the nude by carving or modelling drapery so that it fit and revealed a canonically proportioned body beneath.

By having the figure of Urban cast in bronze, Bernini achieved a rich and colouristic effect, one that underlines dramatically the pope's presence before us. Then there are the agitated drapery patterns, with deep chiaroscural, coruscating pockets. This irrational or non-rational treatment of drapery does not just increase the visual excitement; here we see not simple baroque exuberance, liveliness, and artistic enthusiasm for the sake of delivering a knockout blow. Bernini in fact goes beyond the normative bounds of drapery so as to create something more than grandeur (as we see, for instance, in Hyacinthe Rigaud's famous portrait of Louis XIV (Figure 4.3), in which "la gloire" is paramount). Instead, it is my contention that Bernini understood the visual metaphor, *in modo affigurato*.

The metaphor was discussed widely in early-modern Italian poetic theory, and its visual associations were made explicit by Emanuele Tesauro, among others. But in what way is Urban's drapery metaphorical, and to what effect? First of all, there is no mistaking the fact that through his skill Bernini creates wonderment, which in and of itself was valued in the baroque age. Tesauro writes in his *Aristotelian*

Spyglass, published in Bernini's lifetime, that "it is not without reason that ingenious men are called divine. Since, just as God produces what is from what is not, in the same way wit produces beings from non-beings."[18] This insistence on the close association between wit and metaphor could be characterized by a rhetorician as "ingenious tropology."[19]

Bernini makes a being from a non-being through his production of *meraviglia*, the marvellous. Both Tasso and Marino loved to make their readers marvel; they derived their inspiration from Aristotle's *to thaumaston* – astonishment – which the Greek philosopher felt worked well in an epic, a story *told* rather than a play *presented* on a stage.[20] Vincenzo Borghini wrote that "all things that cause *meraviglia* please you, because it is not simply to learn a new thing ... but [something] more extravagant and rare."[21] Not just a matter of pleasure, however, the marvellous stupefies and then transports its audience to a higher place. It is part of the sublime.

Urban seems to have, thanks to Bernini, a preternatural aliveness, one which contrasts oddly with the blankness of his eyes. The bronze and its disquieted patterns become something else, a life force, a shining forth or epiphany. It is a *concetto*, as the Italians would have said, a *conceit*, as used by the English metaphysical poets. As *concetto* it is also concept, and therefore the physical reality of bronze and its visual appearance together conceive something else. These great swathes of Urban's cope, contrasted with the furrowed and convoluted alb beneath, certainly have visual drama, which is aesthetic; but his clothing conveys another meaning than simply pleats of brocaded material on a physical body; it is cognitive – that is, an image that describes no literal appearance – by virtue of making visible the invisible, material the immaterial: his eternal soul vibrating through his vestments.

Such agitation of *le pli* – the "fold" – fascinated Gilles Deleuze in his reading of Gottfried Leibniz's (1646–1716) *Monadology*.[22] Like William Blake, Leibniz saw a world in a grain of sand, or, more precisely, in a monad. The monad is a constituent element of metaphysics in much the same way an atom constitutes the physical universe; it is part and parcel of the plenum, and, in Leibniz's imagining, monads are psychogenic, something like consciousnesses but consciousnesses that are apt to lurk in the artistic unconscious. Michael Löwy in his reading of Walter Benjamin's "On the Concept of History" explains that "it is the task of remembrance, in Benjamin's work, to build 'constellations' linking the present and the past. These constellations, these moments wrested from empty historical continuity are monads. That is, they are concentrates of historical totality – 'full moments,' as [Charles] Péguy would put it."[23]

The monad is more implicit than explicit; it is not like a walnut lying beneath a tree but some fundamental force that we sense both hidden and revealed at the same time, something folded over so that we cannot see what it is. The monad is part of the aesthetic, that which gives rise to the obscure pleasure accompanying beauty, the *je ne sais quoi* of Bernini's drapery patterns, Bernini's unconscious *jouissance*.[24] Monads also are pleats that unfold to infinity. Unfolding is neither revelation nor interpretation, as in the unfolding of a mystery or a story: there is no flattening out and bringing to full light an essence. Folding and unfolding in Leibniz's eerie universe are metaphors of the way things are, and they hint at the prospect of meaning and understanding. But they also elude our grasp.

Deleuze matches Leibniz's figurative, allegorical, and metaphorical language in his protracted, vatic, and dazzling reading of the baroque fold. Despite the abstract and non-literal applications of Deleuze's fold, it quite literally can be part of baroque clothing, like the folds of Louis XIV's cloak in Rigaud's painting and the folds in Urban's cope. There is the physical fold – the "pleat of matter" – and the one in our souls. The higher type of fold, the soulful one, "sings of the glory of God"[25] – a delightful Deleuzian notion with which, I can imagine, Bernini would have agreed. The fold unfolds endlessly and the singing never reaches a conclusion, never stops. Just as the entire funeral complex projects from its niche and spills into our world, crossing that crucial ontological divide (what we are apt to call "breaking the frame") between subject and object, so too does that drapery go on to infinity. The baroque fold refuses to adhere to the baroque body, repudiating drapery's supplemental or auxiliary function; it becomes something more than an instance of material, whether the original brocade of the imitated garment or the bronze of the physical statue. Again, we come upon ontological divides. The fold is a trait, a baroque phenomenon, even a symbolic form, a symptom, system, signature, fingerprint, lineament, and characteristic. Deleuze may have been thinking of those fiery angels on Bernini's *Angel with the Crown of Thorns* (Figure 4.4) and *Angel with the Superscription* when he wrote that the sculptor endowed drapery "with sublime form in sculpture, when marble seizes and bears to infinity folds that cannot be explained by the body, but by a spiritual adventure that can set the body ablaze."[26]

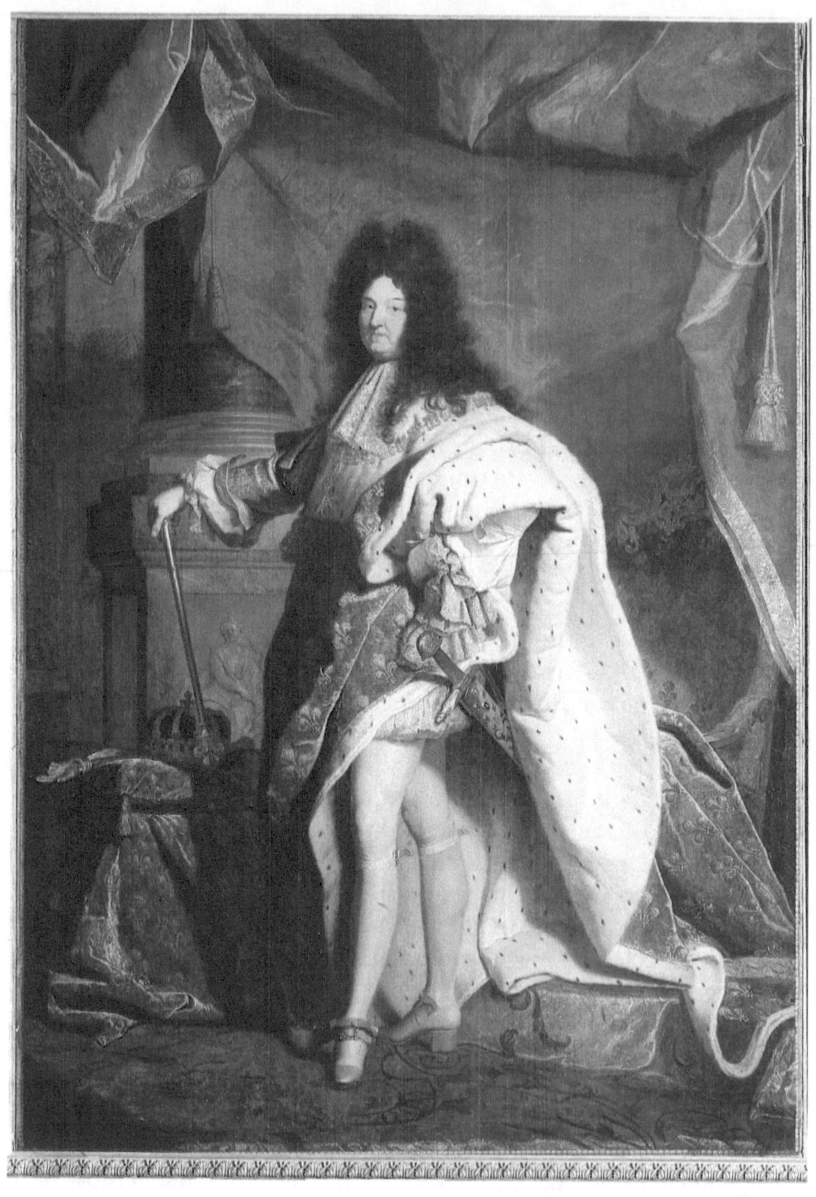

Figure 4.3 Hyacinthe Rigaud, *Portrait of Louis XIV*, oil on canvas, 1701, Musée du Louvre, Paris, France. Photo: RMN–Grand Palais/Art Resource, NY.

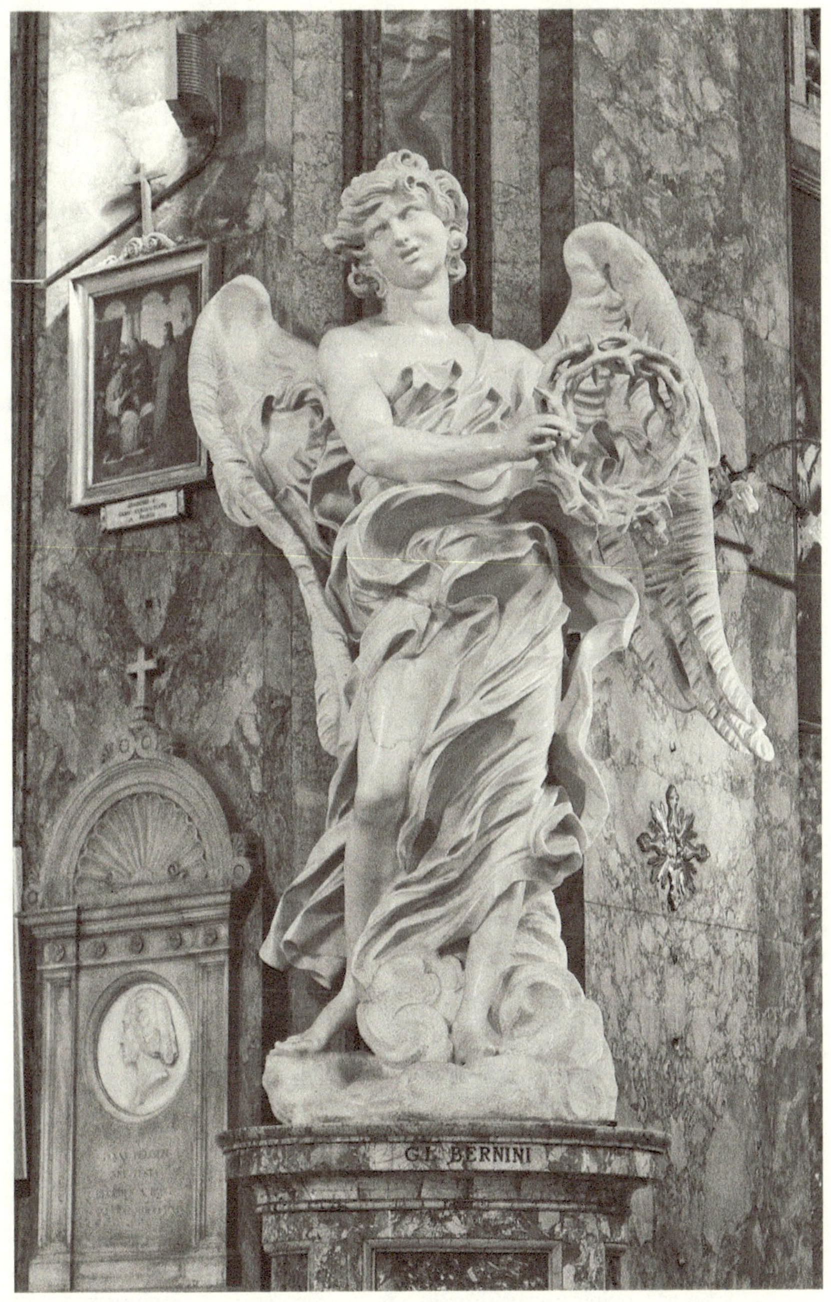

Figure 4.4 Gianlorenzo Bernini, *Angel with the Crown of Thorns*, marble, 1668–9, Sant'Andrea delle Fratte, Rome, Italy. Photo: Author.

Bernini's last work of art is the tomb of Alexander VII (Figure 4.5); it stands above the Porta Sta Marta in the left transept of St Peter's. Giulio Cartari carved the allegories of Truth, Prudence, and Justice; Michele Maglia executed the figure of the pope, and Giuseppe Mazzuoli was responsible for Charity. Bernini supervised the work, providing drawings and working models.

In an early *avviso*, Alexander, his thoughts already on the *ars moriendi*, reveals his interest in composing an inscription for his tomb. The notice begins, "Il Pontefice meditando continuamente la brevità della vita humana,"[27] and then describes his intention to write his own epitaph, which, alas, never materializes. Just as Maffeo Barberini (Urban VIII) had done, Fabio Chigi (Alexander VII) summoned Gianlorenzo Bernini early in his papacy (supposedly the "first day") to plan monuments and artistic projects that would commemorate his pontificate. Alexander immediately requested a skull, which he would keep with him always as a memento mori.

The tomb was finished a decade after the pope's demise. A pious and beseeching image of Alexander kneels on a sarcophagus, while four beautifully conceived and expertly carved statues of cardinal and theological virtues surround the Holy Father. The allegorical representations rest, lean, and incline in a traditionally inert fashion, although Charity turns towards – even seems to petition – the pope. Alexander turns inward to prayer.

It is Death who rockets out of our world and, although almost swallowed by the jasper shroud, shakes the hourglass like a pair of dice. Time is up. Time has been up. Here a truth has been disclosed within the monument's world and within the world the monument occupies – perpetually our world. Bernini represents the organic (a still "living" pope), irony (the Holy Father's "blindness" in prayer and obliviousness towards what is right in front of him), the macabre (insurgent death), and time (the hourglass). The perplexing reciprocation among these players, their attributes and intentions, disrupts the elegiac. Time brings no solace, no rapprochement.

Although delegating much of the execution of Alexander's funeral complex to others, Bernini has not lost his touch. He mastered a rhetorical mode that could shoot through layers of existential space and invade a worshipper's (or tourist's) mind: this skeleton especially has a brute power that goes beyond logic and reasoning. Bernini creates here what a rhetorician might call a *psychalgia* – a dark enchantment of our mind.

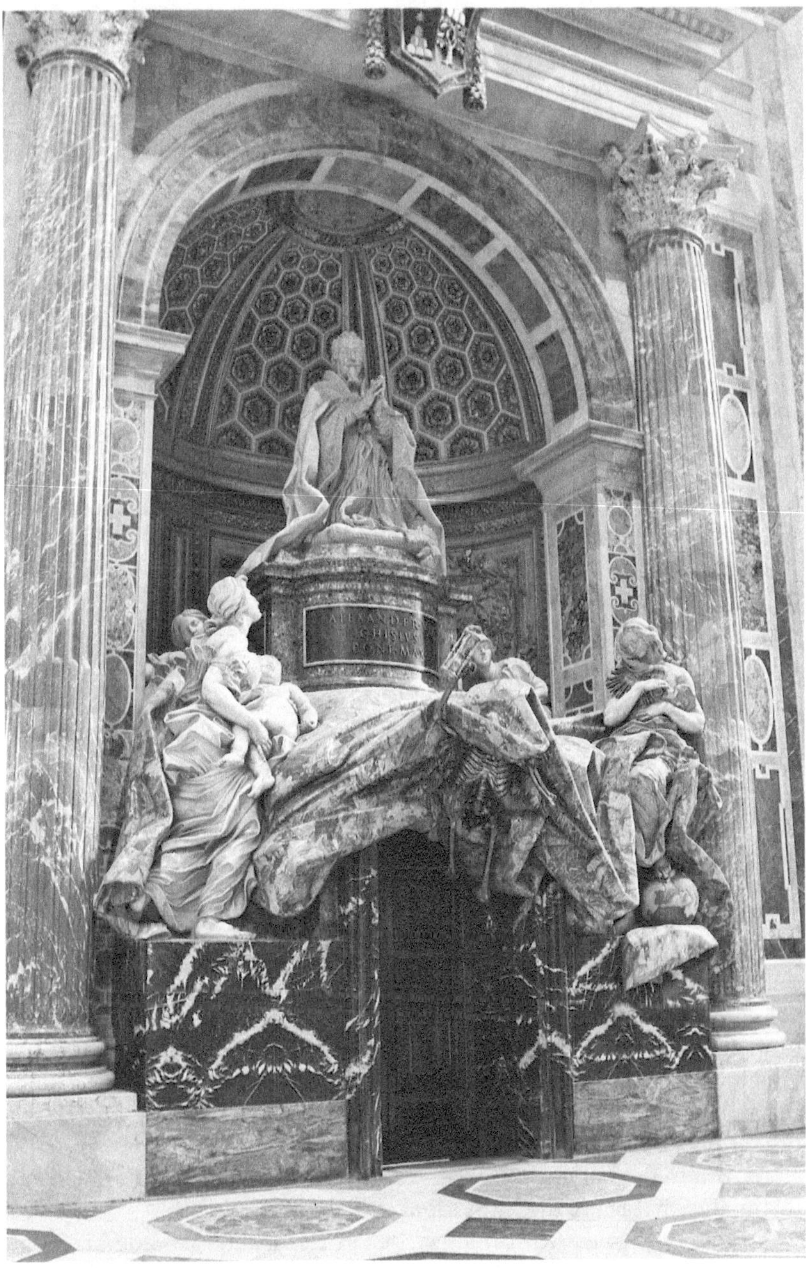

Figure 4.5 Gianlorenzo Bernini, *Tomb of Alexander VII*, bronze and marble, 1671–8, St Peter's Basilica, Vatican City (Rome), Italy. Photo: Author.

The baroque lived on after Bernini's death, at least in its outward appearance as a style. We can see its remains in papal tombs for nearly another century. But in the world outside the Basilica of St Peter's, there were complex changes. The Jesuits, for instance, in their anti-Protestant vehemence continued to promote aggressive forms of decoration and psychologically layered and perceptually challenging religious images set before the faithful's eyes. Yet there was resistance to the Jesuits, their "way of proceeding," their missions, and their control of education throughout the Christian world.

The tradition of Catholic reform antedates the Council of Trent by at least 500 years, and these forces of reform sometimes led to changes in efficiency and strengthening of pastoral commitments – at the parish level – and therefore tended to militate against some of the examples of baroque excitement and grandeur. In France, the Jansenists, who remained loyal to the pope though they were often enough denounced by him, fought against the Jesuits, despite the fact that their theological positions were not so very different, and promoted a new rhetoric (see "Jansenists, Rhetoric, World-Disclosing, and Philippe de Champaigne" in chapter 11). The so-called Port-Royal rhetoric did what it could to undermine Jesuit preaching and rhetoric and in the process confirmed what was happening in the writings of Pascal, Racine, and Descartes.

In the later decades of the seventeenth century a somewhat vague but nonetheless powerful phrase came into common usage: good taste – *bon goût* in French, *buon gusto* in Italian. *Cattivo gusto*, its antithesis, soon enough came to be associated with baroque visual rhetoric. Good taste had many meanings and implications, and it did a lot of cultural "work" in Europe's Republic of Letters and among her connoisseurs, cognoscenti, and dilettantes. It was one of those phenomena that literary and cultural critics often call a discourse. We may not be able to define it, but we can trace its penetrations into institutions and, more generally, into the history of ideas.[28] Because "good taste" arises from human perception and sensation, the concept of "taste" is a nascent idea in the development of aesthetics. For two millennia – at least since the time of Plato – there had been a distrust of the senses, an assertion of the need for a higher intelligence to correct the often-erring passions. But in the later seventeenth century, taste is treated as something instinctive that leads the individual to right reason.

An odd yet powerful organization in Rome, the Accademia degli Arcadi, advocated "good taste" as one of the great engines of reform not just within the church but also in terms of the "Italian nation." Its founder, an ambitious figure by the name of Giovanni Mario Crescimbeni, shouted out "esterminare il cattivo gusto" with all the "gusto" and contumely mustered by Voltaire in his cry, "Écrasez l'infame!" (by which he meant "Crush the infamy [of superstition]"). Voltaire was not so far from Crescimbeni in his sloganeering.[29]

5 Death and Dying in St Peter's Basilica: Part 2

By way of witnessing the devolution of rhetorical norms in Roman sculpture (and the waning of the baroque), I find myself turning again and again to a comparison between Bernini's tomb of Urban VIII (Figure 4.1) and Filippo della Valle's of Innocent XII (Figure 5.1).[1] Something like a century, a mere drop in the bucket of Vatican time, separates them; they are within several hundred feet of one another and of course stand where they have been since being put into place centuries ago.

I am interested in how these tombs as rhetorical structures differ from one another. In some general sense, we can say that the world of the 1740s was not the world of the 1640s, that the Enlightenment and the baroque offer to historians distinct narratives and dissimilar plots. But this is still Rome, St Peter's, a setting – if there ever was one – for *the longue durée.* Nonetheless, the question remains: How long was the duration? My reading is that the baroque does not endure much past the beginning of the eighteenth century.

I suspect that Filippo della Valle's tomb of Innocent XII is not and was not truth-disclosing (or meaningful) in the same way as is and was Bernini's. The baroque master's long shadow is visible but remains but a shadow. Della Valle's attempts at figuration, inherited from generations of Italian sculptors before him – but mostly Bernini – seem not to work up to their allegorical potential. It strikes me that Innocent's benediction, the way his arm collapses and he seems to fall back when raising his right hand, buffeted as by a strong wind, carries a message not unlike what W.H. Auden wrote in the chorus of his Christmas Oratorio, *For the Time Being*: "He is the Truth; Seek Him in the Kingdom of Anxiety." The Age of Anxiety begins with the Enlightenment and the eighteenth century.

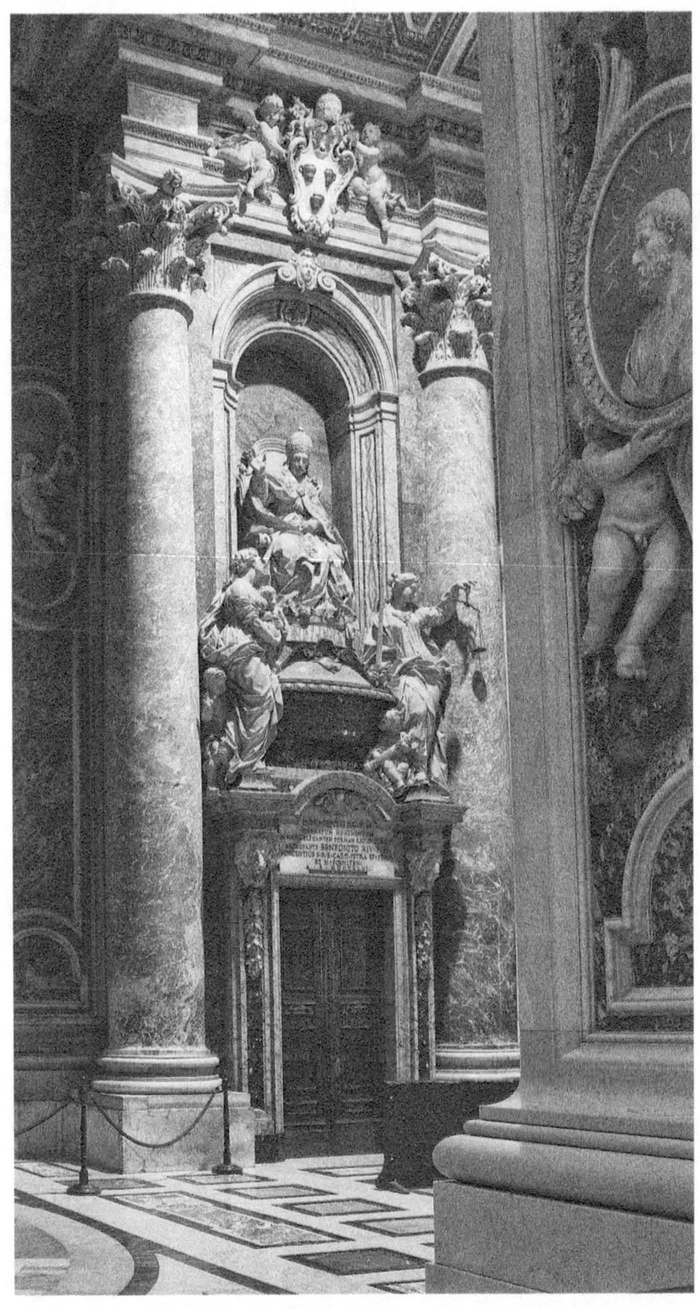

Figure 5.1 Filippo della Valle, *Tomb of Innocent XII*, marble, gilt bronze, and stucco, 1743, St Peter's Basilica, Vatican City (Rome), Italy. Photo: Author.

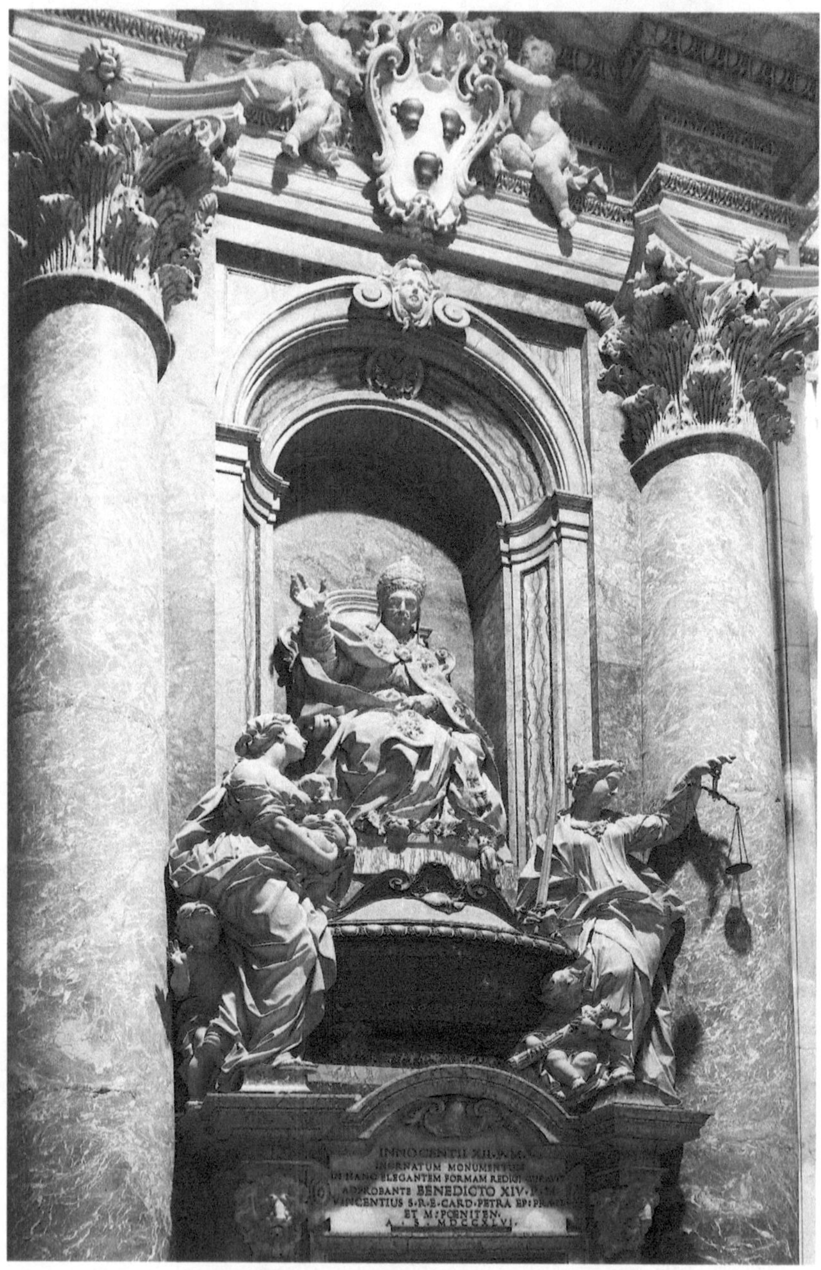

Figure 5.2 *Tomb of Innocent XII*, detail. Photo: Author.

Whereas Bernini's great clumps of drapery create the visible metaphor, della Valle's crinkly patterns are, once again, a shadow of his predecessor's *disegno* and metaphor. Bernini was the strong poet of figuration; della Valle, no less "great" – whatever that may mean – was a stylist, one who handled the chisel with finesse and delicacy, but seemed unsure of narrative, allegory, or figuration in the literary and visual traditions of the seicento. Or perhaps he was a perverse revisionist.

In that della Valle could not have been unaware of Bernini, whom I am positing as the strong poet – using Harold Bloom's language – I sense an anxiety of influence.[2] What Freud calls the Oedipus complex (and in different terms, "the family romance") portrays the artistically filial relationship of della Valle to Bernini. There is in fact a fairly direct filiation between Bernini and della Valle, whose uncle and master, Giovanni Battista Foggini, was the artistic offspring of Ercole Ferrata, who in turn worked with Bernini on the sculptural furnishing of St Peter's.

In Bloom's meaning of the anxiety of influence, della Valle misreads the tradition of putting a pope atop a sarcophagus, anchoring him with allegorical figures to the lower left and right, while sprinkling cherubim about. Della Valle's "clinamen" or "misprision," as Bloom names this version of an archetypal relationship between the artistic father figure and his "son," undermines the father's generation of meaning. In other words, della Valle misinterprets or simply does not "get" – and of course one would posit this as unconscious (or perhaps exquisitely *defensive*) on Filippo's part – how to make art truth-disclosing in Bernini's and Heidegger's sense.

Della Valle, working long after Innocent's death and at the behest of the pope's nephew, chose or had chosen for him a space just above one of the doors in the right aisle of the basilica, directly across from Bernini's monument to Countess Matilda of Canossa. The lines of sight for the memorial, as not infrequently happens in St Peter's, are less than advantageous (Figure 5.2). One's viewing, reception, and *reading* of the monument are obscured, thereby further interfering with one's ability to impute or discover figural, allegorical, or transmutational meaning. Perhaps it is true, as Theodor Adorno argues, that ultimately some artworks are incomprehensible (opaque), while sight is incompetent (or at least inexpert) in its attempt to see the unintelligibility (not to mention the *intelligibility*) of the artwork. Adorno suggests that one "aims" at blindness, which is a way of understanding what we do not understand about the artwork.[3] I find that this modernist view offers an effective critique of della Valle's sculpture.

Also when comparing della Valle's and Bernini's papal tombs in St Peter's, we encounter Aby Warburg's concept *Nachleben*, the afterlife or survival of an earlier style in a later work of art.[4] Della Valle's tomb sculpture is in a sense unintelligible until those anachronistic drapery folds that crinkle throughout the composition come to be illuminated by an awareness of Bernini's folds. One might refer to della Valle's oddly baroque treatment of folds as a "spectral memory," something alien insinuating itself into his art.

Innocent XII's arcosolium hardly deserves the name (at least in baroque terms): it is shallow, has bevelled edges that thematize rather than refute the frame, and is awash with decorations, little cups, swags, lions' heads, and of course putti. Bernini's placement of Urban's tomb enhances transcendence, hallowing of space, and disclosing of truth. Della Valle's tomb, I would argue, succumbs to immanence, artfulness, and aestheticism. And that is just the short list.

Della Valle's statues of Justice and Charity (Figure 5.3) seem lost in dreams of their own past, disinclined to reach for higher meaning. Allegory was dying, after all, by the eighteenth century. The putti are like William Blake's cherub Tharmas, who is a pastoral figure, Theocritan and Arcadian. They are innocent if curious, not self-aware, not self-conscious, always framing narratives through play; never historiated; cute, *carino*. They are in a sense the offspring of God's Angel, the Covering Cherub, whom God "placed at the east of the garden of Eden" with "a flaming sword which turned every way, to keep the way of the tree of life" (Genesis 3:24). Adam had "become as one of us, to know good and evil" and so had to be expelled from the garden "lest he put forth his hand, and take also of the tree of life, and eat, and live for ever" (Genesis 3:22).

In Harold Bloom's artistic myth of the anxiety of influence, the Covering Cherub blocks the way back – not the way forward – for the young poet or artist. Only with constancy, stubbornness, and persistence can the later artist break through and *misinterpret* his forefather. This of course is an old story, one that can be traced back to cosmogonic myths: Saturn devoured his children only to be overthrown by one of them. Bernini dealt with Michelangelo, who in his turn acknowledged Donatello. Filippo della Valle, it seems to me, could not be seen in any sense as one of Bloom's "strong" poets, and therefore his revision of Bernini

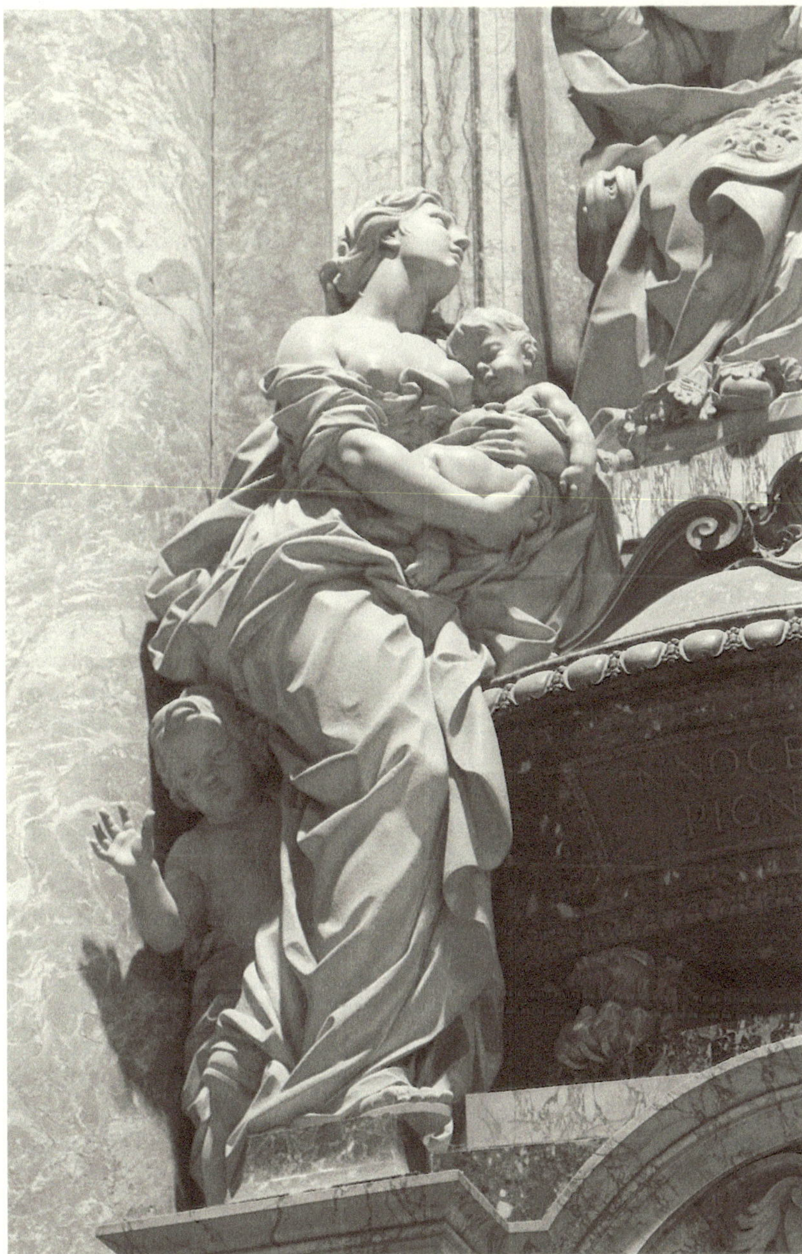

Figure 5.3 *Tomb of Innocent XII*, detail. Photo: Author.

and his misprision of the baroque tradition hardly seems either steadfast or heroic. He does not so much "uncover" the Covering Cherub or defeat him so that he can partake of the tree of life as he dethrones him, turns him into a playful putto, a gynandrous boy musing and flitting about. One can only imagine what would happen if one of Filippo della Valle's putti were to go toe-to-toe with one of Bernini's swarthy, fustian marble children.

When strolling about in Rome's many churches containing eighteenth-century tombs, one is apt to overhear the occasional Italian visitor exclaim, "Come carino!" (how sweet/cute!) when beholding masses of putti gambolling about a tomb – whether hovering on clouds, staring abstractedly at the viewer, or lounging on a pillow and perhaps wiping a tear from his eye. But the dark side of cute and sweet is the uncanny.

Having mentioned in passing Freud's famous essay on the *unheimlich* (uncanny) in relation to Bernini's vital allegorical representations of Charity and Justice, I want now to look again at Freud's remarkable text for its observations on what we might call the aesthetics of anxiety. Freud wrote,

> In the civilization of ancient Egypt, it became a spur to artists to form images of the dead in durable materials. But these ideas arose on the soil of boundless self-love, the primordial narcissism that dominates the mental life of both the child and primitive man, and when this phase is surmounted, meaning of the "double" changes; having once been an assurance of immortality, it becomes the uncanny harbinger of death.[5]

Freud did not have to reach so far back as Egypt to find sculptors working in durable materials representing images of the dead. Perhaps he was loath to cast well-known works of the recent past in terms of the "super-annuated narcissism of primitive times."[6] He need not have worried: we moderns – and Freud knew this – despite our absorption of Enlightenment values and the truths produced by scientific discourse retain our naive and even brutish terror of incomprehensible death. The visible tomb in the early-modern, post-Tridentine traditions assisted the living by reminding them of their departed Holy Father. That is not to say, however, that tombs with their portraits of the deceased, allegorical representations, seraphim, and putti fail to reassure us – the visitors of these tombs – of eternal life.[7] Because they figure our immortal souls, each of these statues represents a *doppelganger*: a double. The double to which Freud refers is, among other possibilities, our soul, which duplicates and represents our living selves as guarantor of immortality. However, with the development of our conscience, which is the superego, we displace or suppress other, more primitive doubles.

In one's primitive self, the double – which is also the putto or cherub – was benign; but when it returns as the repressed, it may be uncanny and frightening. "When I was a child, I spake as a child, I felt as a child, I thought as a child: now that I am become a man, I have put away childish things" (1 Corinthians 13:11). Until, of course, they come back to haunt me. Despite our growing into adulthood and knowing that death is inevitable, we cannot help but deny our mortality.

Freud writes of beliefs surviving from an earlier period being suppressed. Allegorical language, as I have mentioned, had mostly exhausted itself by the eighteenth century, replaced by a Hobbesian search for truth. Richard Hurd's well-known quotation from *Letters on Chivalry and Romance* (1762) both acknowledges the more rational approach of the Enlightenment and laments the loss of allegory: "What we have got by this revolution, you will say, is a great deal of good sense. What we have lost, is a world of fine fabling."[8] "Fine fabling" may not so much be *returning* in della Valle's tomb; rather, it exists as an afterlife, a ghost of its former self. How could one apply the fourfold method of interpretation (literal, allegorical, symbolical, and anagogic) known since the Middle Ages to this odd collection of winged and wingless toddlers, svelte and abstracted young women acting out plays in which they have no particular interest, and a wizened, somewhat feeble old man swathed in fabulous costuming and holding a trembling hand in the position of a benediction? All of this is *heimlich* in the sense of being well known, "homely," and therefore familiar, but is also un*heimlich* – unfamiliar, unhomely, uncanny – in that it simply does not convey meaning in the old-fashioned way, is semiotically occluded, is unreadable in traditional forms of symbolism, and seems dispirited if elegantly, pleasurably aesthetic. Here Paul de Man's "struggle with meaning" (as I mention in chapter 1) seems less like striving and grappling than conceding. Filippo della Valle's tomb exists in the age of art, not in the age of allegory and truth-making. It is the return – or the malingering – of repressed childhood fantasies. And they haunt us.

The uncanny arises because these once meaningful figures return, but do so with a zombie-like curiosity and lack of motivation. This is the tomb of the living dead, with figures wandering aimlessly and listlessly. If Heidegger is right that "beauty is a fateful gift of the essence of truth," then we have to say that in della Valle's tomb there is neither truth nor beauty.[9] Furthermore, there may be aesthetic displeasure rather than aesthetic pleasure. None of this would condemn *Tomb of Innocent XII* to the scrap heap of "bad art." Aesthetic displeasure is still aesthetic, and the uncanny rivets us like no other narrative. Erwin Panofsky wrote of tomb sculpture, "all those who came after Bernini [such as della Valle] were caught in a dilemma – or, rather, trilemma – between pomposity, sentimentality, and deliberate archaism."[10] And no one understood the psychic freight of "deliberate archaism" as well as Freud.

Bernini lived in a world of miracles, spirits, demonic possession, and the power of prayer. A place in which prayer has concrete results is also, as Freud would have it, a time and place of magic, animism, and the omnipotence of thought. Della Valle may have been as devout a Christian as Bernini, but things had changed. Therefore, his tomb carries different intellectual and religious freight than does Bernini's of Urban VIII. We are, I believe, prompted to decode it, read it, in a sense to *receive* it, in a different way.

I find myself in sympathy with Émile Mâle's observation on another of della Valle's statues, this one across the great divide of St Peter's, in the eastern side of the left niche of St Peter's crossing. St John of God (canonized by Innocent XII), the founder of the hospitallers *Fattebenefratelli*, holds a dying man slipping away from him (Figure 5.4). Mâle characterizes John as "the saint of the abandoned sick, of the hopelessly ill. Charity in him had reached a heroic degree surpassing human limitations." And of della Valle's statue, he writes, "[The] saint's eyes seem to look into the distance with an anguished glance, as though he were wondering if his heart were vast enough to take unto itself all the suffering he sees in the world."[11] *This* world may be the heart of darkness, but perhaps death and the world can be redeemed by art and aesthetic experience. Having quoted from Auden, I will turn to one of his contemporaries, Wallace Stevens, who, in *Sunday Morning* observed, "Death is the mother of beauty; hence from her / Alone, shall come fulfillment to our dreams / And our desires."

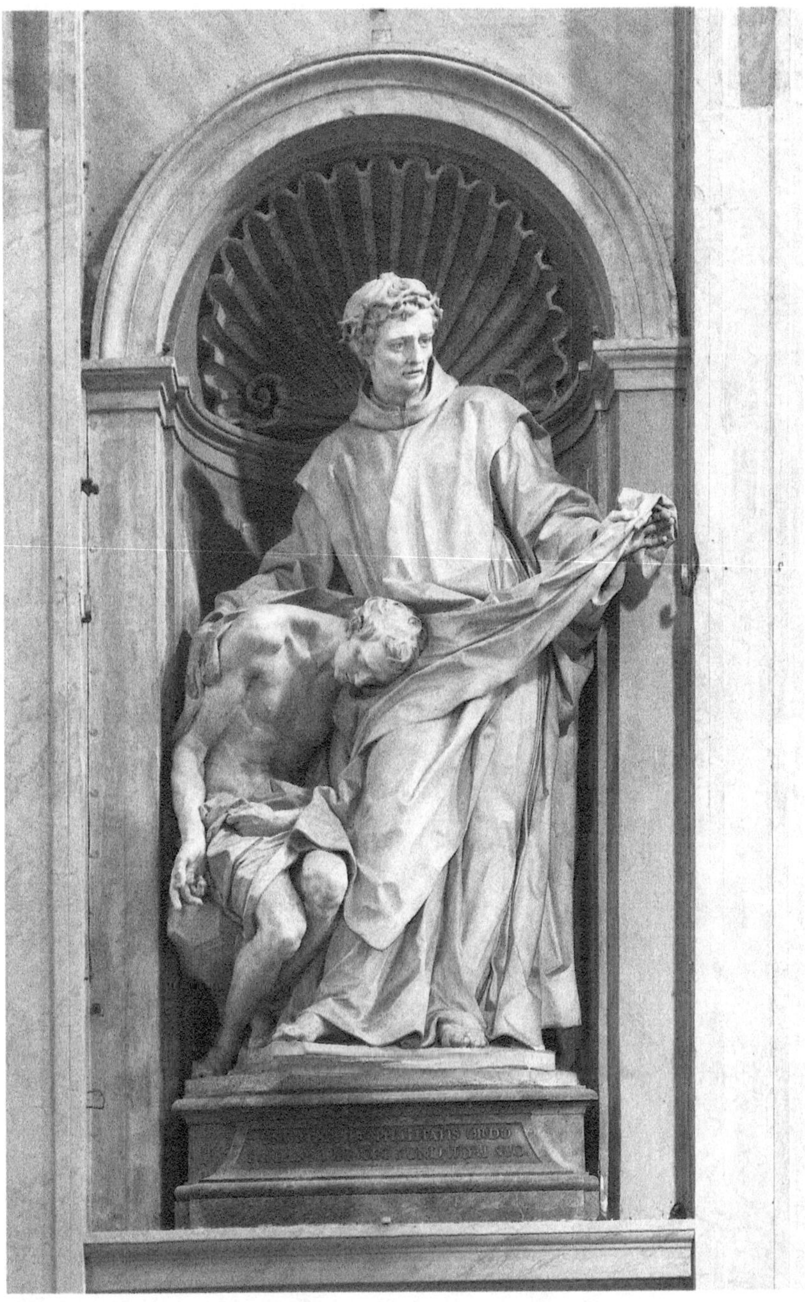

Figure 5.4 Filippo della Valle, *Statue of St John of God*, 1745, St Peter's Basilica, Vatican City (Rome), Italy. Photo: Author.

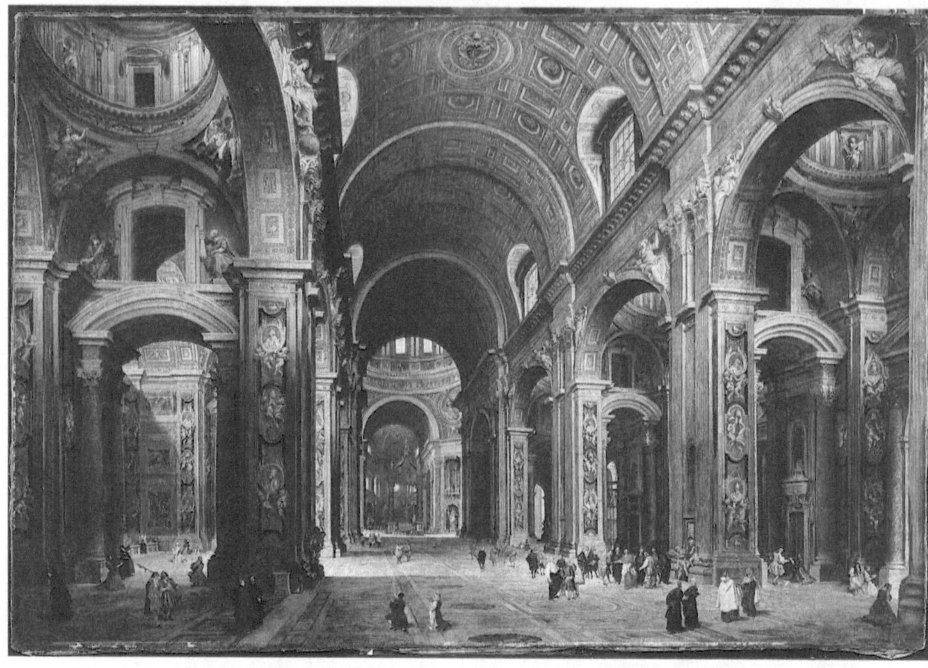

Figure 5.5 Giovanni Paolo Panini, *Cardinal Melchio de Polignac Visiting Saint Peter's in Rome*, oil on canvas, 1765, Musée du Louvre, Paris, France. Photo: RMN–Grand Palais/Art Resource, NY.

We see in Giovanni Paolo Panini's *Cardinal Melchio de Polignac Visiting Saint Peter's in Rome*, a painting finished a few years after della Valle's tomb of Innocent XII was put into place, that something has changed in the great basilica since the time of Bernini (Figure 5.5). It is filled with fewer pilgrims now; grand tourists and Rome's glitterati, enthralled by the beauty and the aesthetic pleasure given to us by the many works of art, have replaced them.

6 Eighteenth-Century Baroque: The Style That Did Not (Quite) Die

Having set up something like a dialectical relationship between Filippo della Valle as the "weak poet" and Gianlorenzo Bernini as the "strong," I have ventured to suggest that Bernini's style had nearly disappeared from the world of large sculptural projects in Rome. But, as anyone who has spent much time in Rome's churches knows, the baroque remained a stylistic choice throughout the eighteenth century, although its rhetorical structure – the ways in which it conveys meaning, in other words – was altered. And it certainly is true that the baroque had a role to play in Romanticism and twentieth- and twenty-first-century art.[1] Styles, considered as rhetorical structure, have an afterlife; they do not just disappear because the circumstances that helped create them in the first place vanish. There are far fewer styles than there are historical moments; it is impossible to imagine that every style reveals its and only its age. But people have a way of bearing grudges against certain styles, too.

Livio Pestilli demonstrates that, despite a certain disdain for Bernini after his death, he was neither forgotten not utterly repudiated.[2] Pestilli succinctly and elegantly states that "the implication that Bernini's appeal had evanesced as early as 1700 is inaccurate and our perspective is flawed by historical hindsight."[3] He wishes to counter an attitude that is pretty much taken for granted in some of the histories of Roman sculpture in the later seventeenth and early eighteenth centuries. For instance, Pestilli quotes Bruce Boucher's comment on the Lateran project (see chapter 7) and makes what at first glance is a not unreasonable observation that this commission "reveals the extent of Bernini's unpopularity by 1700."[4] As a counterpoint, we have Robert Enggass's observation that "Bernini remained fully within the limits of the mainstream of the Italian tradition. His figures are generalizations and idealization of the real, highly dynamic to be sure, overlaid here and there with a few flourishes of drapery that are not fully rational (as in Hellenistic art), but real nonetheless in overall effect, empirically based, then made larger in expressive power."[5] Despite Enggass's situating Bernini within larger stylistic currents (his comments come from a chapter titled "The Style" in his text on early eighteenth-century sculpture in Rome), one is reminded that, as often happens in the annals of art's history, enmity may grow as much from resentment as artistic judgment.

Pestilli goes on to explain the usual take on artistic culture in the third quarter of the seventeenth century, a period marked especially by Giovanni Pietro Bellori's influential *Lives of the Modern Painters, Sculptors and Architects*, in which Bernini's name is not even mentioned.[6] One finds in later seicento Rome shifting attitudes, growing more dismissive and negative as time goes on, towards specific artistic personalities (Bernini, Borromini, Pietro da Cortona) and the growing influence of what can be called the "Greek ideal," or more generally the "classical."[7]

What was at stake counted for more than the popularity of artistic modes, although styles came and went in the seicento much as they have throughout the centuries and in almost every culture. First of all, in Rome there appeared during the papacy of Urban VIII (1623–44) a diffidence on the part of a few towards those artists favoured by Urban – Bernini and Pietro da Cortona (among others in a relatively small group). When one clutch of artists grows rich and receives accolades while another soldiers on in relative obscurity, there is bound to be resentment.

The commitment to a "Greek style" in Rome during the earlier decades of the seventeenth century did not arise simply from enmity and jealousy, although matters of personal empowerment undoubtedly played some role. Nicolas Poussin, for example, may have seen the Greek ideal as a path for foreigners to follow, perhaps because of his background in Lorraine, France. Poussin possibly had some sense of what was going on at the Sorbonne and the reaction of Augustinians before then (one may think of Michael Baius and anti-Molinist, anti-Pelagian thinkers). Poussin and François Duquesnoy as French and Flemish outsiders in a Molinist, Tridentine, Jesuitical city like Rome could be using the Greek style to gain their own kind of presence and power. This is not to say that either of them was simply opportunistic; their commitment to the Greek ideal had deep theoretical, rhetorical, and meditative significance.

But before glancing at our scorecards and noting all the players on the scene in early-modern Rome, we need to take stock of art-historical methodologies current in the twentieth century in order to make some sense of the ways in which we study stylistic shifts (such as that between Bernini and della Valle). I will attempt here an overview of some key matters in the history of art history that bear upon how we write and think about style and history, who were the major players and who the minor, and as I have been doing throughout this text, how broadly and how closely one can *read* works of art. Then I will return to Livio Pestilli's important article.

Denis Mahon (1911–2011), publishing soon after the Second World War his *Studies in Seicento Art and Theory*, considers at length the stylistic categories of classical and baroque. Mahon relies upon late nineteenth- and early twentieth-century German studies in *formpsychologie* and especially the writings of Heinrich Wölfflin (1864–1945), who had turned to the discipline of psychology for his perceptually centred language when writing about the classical and the baroque. And not unlike his contemporaries – those American literary giants who practised New Criticism – Mahon subjects Roman art from the middle decades of the seventeenth century both to close reading and to a search for (he may have been reading some Northrop Frye, too) visual archetypes. That is where Wölfflin comes in.

Mahon values Wölfflin's distinctions and the terminology he introduces, sensing that the classical and baroque are "perennial" oppositions or paradigms. He points out that in the art of the sixteenth and seventeenth centuries, the classical and the baroque exist simultaneously in most works of art, with one usually predominating. This is a similar position to one followed by Jennifer Montagu, who argues for a "baroque classicism" when writing about the sculpture of Alessandro Algardi.[8]

Classical and Romantic (or baroque) have become almost like keys in music; it is as if we are looking for a harmonic centre. The analogy of course is approximate, and perhaps not useful, other than to suggest that there is something representative and exemplary about these categories.

Early on in Mahon's career (he was the son of a banker and the grandson of a marquess, and so came to art history not just as a scholar but also as a collector), Kenneth Clark referred him to Nicholas Pevsner, then at the Courtauld Institute. It was through Pevsner that Mahon first came into contact with Giovanni Battista Barbieri (1591–1666), known as Il Guercino ("The Little Squinter"), a remarkable painter from Cento, not far from Bologna. Mahon studied Guercino's change in style, the cause of which he laid at the door of theory. He observes that Giulio Mancini's *Trattato* (c. 1620) reflects on the differences between Michelangelo Merisi da Caravaggio and Annibale Carracci. Mancini uses terms like "unnaturalism" (in Mahon's translation) when describing Caravaggio's light and notes a dependence on the model at the expense of the idea.

Mancini preferred the art of the Carracci family, finding their style noble and serious and even more "natural" when compared to that of Caravaggio. Then there was the Bolognese writer Carlo Cesare Malvasia (1616–93), who exploited the contrast between Annibale Carracci and Caravaggio as a way to promote his native city. The painter and author Giovanni Battista Passeri (c. 1610–79) associated Guercino with Caravaggio, thereby criticizing Guercino for too close an adherence to nature. Mahon concludes that Mancini, Malvasia, and Passeri were essentially classical theorists and that they, along with Joachim von Sandrart, noted the change in Guercino's style as a result of his move to Bologna in 1642, where and when he came under the tutelage or influence of that offspring of the Carracci Academy, Guido Reni.

But according to Mahon, the real reason Guercino changed his style was Giovanni Battista Agucchi's (1570–1632) idea of beauty: *l'Idea della Bellezza*. The court of the Bolognese Pope Gregory XV (r. 1621–3) and Gregory's nephew Cardinal Ludovico Ludovisi, the ones who attracted Agucchi to Rome, also drew Guercino there. So Mahon sees the change in Guercino's style as occurring during his Roman years, when and where he arrived as a rather naive young painter. He discovered a well-developed style and theory in Rome, and through his association with Agucchi probably wanted to update his own artistic identity and credentials by making his painting more fashionable, noble, and ideal.

The Caravaggio/Carracci opposition is antinomian and a prelude to the classical/baroque distinction. But before that there is another (but short – if not evanescent) chapter in the classical/baroque opposition, this one taking place in the Accademia di San Luca. It is the so-called Sacchi/Cortona dispute, which calls to mind Aristotle setting the epic against the tragic, faulting the epic if it went on too long, thereby losing its unity and sense of *eusynopton* – manageable scale and modest structure. We really do not know very much about the debate in the Accademia, even though Melchiorre Missirini, writing in the early nineteenth century, played it up considerably (not to mention undoubtedly doing some handsome embroidering along the way). There is no contemporary record of the dispute, but it seems clear that, as Ann

Sutherland Harris observes, Sacchi objected to Pietro da Cortona's "over-populated" compositions and to his rather indifferent attitude towards *disegno*, something which should have interested Cortona, given his indebtedness to such artists as Raphael and Annibale Carracci.[9] The larger issue is one that falls into the classical versus baroque discourse and therefore has a bearing on baroque visual rhetoric. Assuming that Missirini had a source for his information – what he writes is to an extent borne out by the actual paintings of Sacchi and Cortona – we can understand and believe that Sacchi probably would have said something along the lines of (in Missirini's words) "it is better to produce fewer but more nearly perfect paintings than many mediocre ones." Sacchi, as we can imagine, preferred (again quoting Missirini) "severe countenances, magisterial attitudes, elegant draperies with a few large folds, disdaining the miniscule."[10] Missirini does cast the Sacchi-Cortona debate in terms of tragedy versus epic, which are old antinomies, that is (in this case), styles that are in themselves reasonable (such as classical and baroque) but which contradict one another and seem unlikely to be reconcilable, although they probably were the opposite sides of the same coin.

In Italy ideological purity in matters of style was not observed too closely in the later years of the seventeenth and earlier eighteenth centuries, except perhaps in terms of literary style, where Giambattista Marino, now long dead, still bore the cross of bad taste. *Concettismo* was generally recognized as being in a mode modern literary historians would call baroque, while the style of Pietro da Cortona, for instance, must have been seen as something simply in the past. There certainly was, however, an awareness that Cortona had prospered during the Barberini papacy, was close to Bernini, and, in general, preferred the epic (and epideictic) mode, especially for his large ceiling paintings.

Now we return to Livio Pestilli's demonstration of Bernini's style and its survival into another generation. Pestilli points out that Giuseppe Mazzuoli, who was a contemporary of and collaborator with Bernini, reveals his stylistic affiliations to his master Gianlorenzo in the statue of St Philip for the *Apostles* series in San Giovanni in Laterano (Figure 6.1). Although I will discuss narratology in the *Apostles* series in the following chapter, there is an opportunity here to follow Pestilli's argument for the persistence of a powerful stylistic mode. As a way of establishing a link with the next section, I also will go beyond Pestilli's comments and explore some of the narrative implications of the late baroque style.

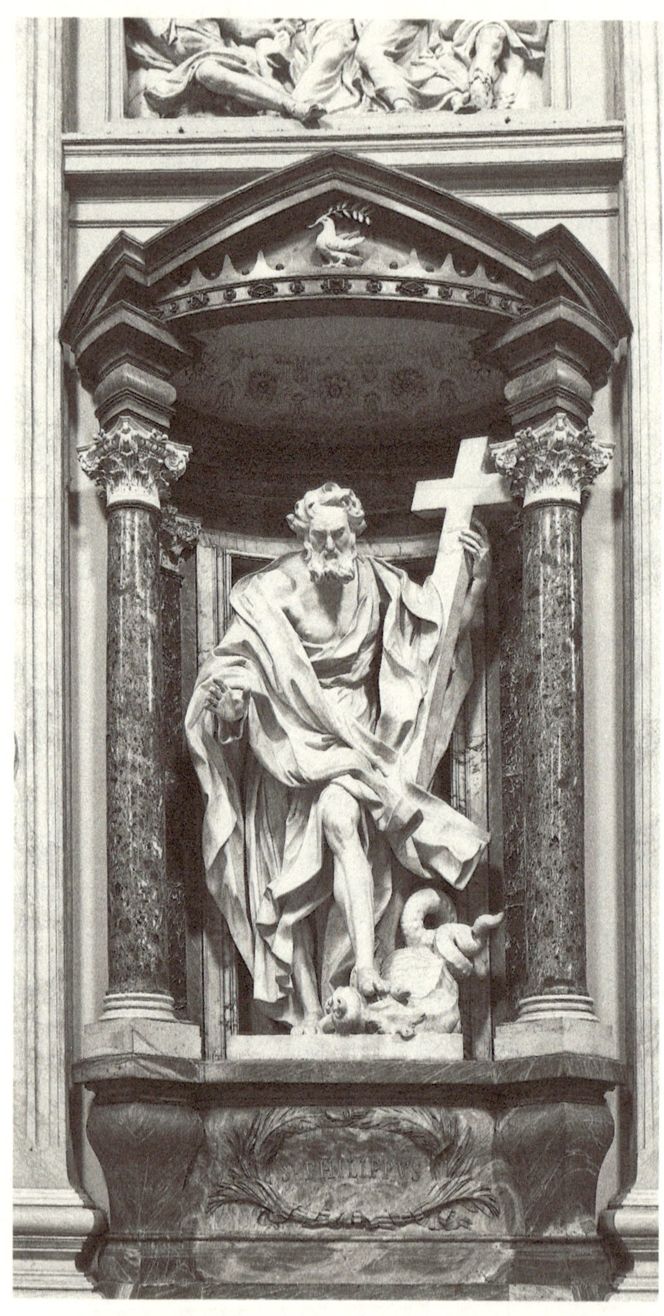

Figure 6.1 Giuseppe Mazzuoli, *St Philip*, marble, 1703–12, San Giovanni in Laterano, Rome, Italy. Photo: Author.

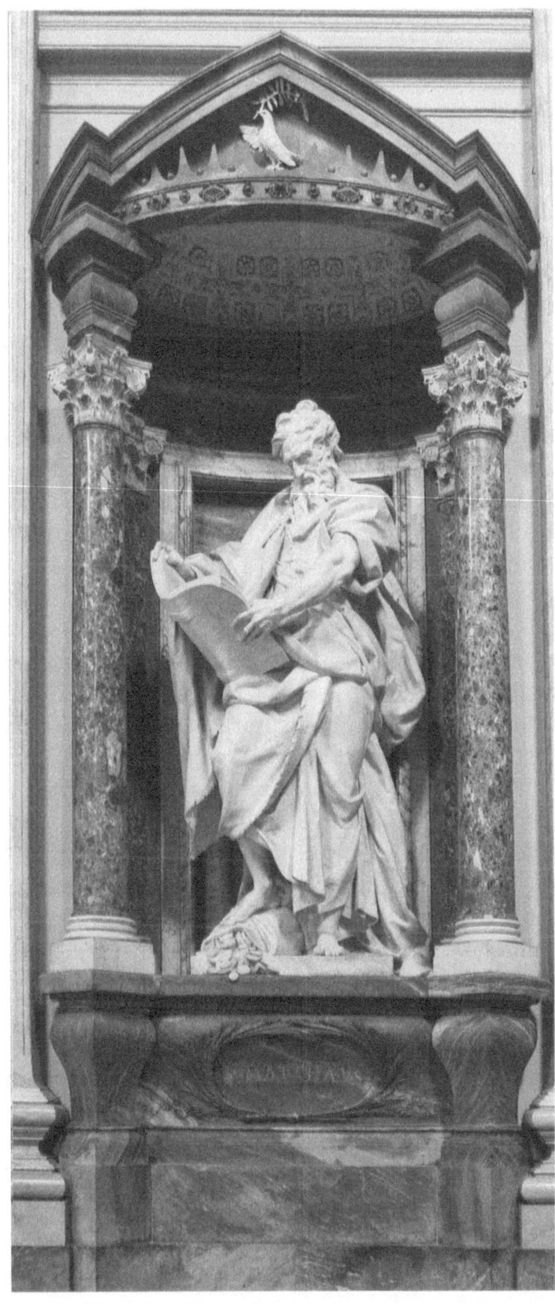

Figure 6.2 Camillo Rusconi, *St Matthew*, marble, 1715, San Giovanni in Laterano, Rome, Italy. Photo: Author.

St Philip treads on a dragon who has just emerged from the Temple of Mars in Hieropolis (it all comes from a story told in the *Golden Legend*). With the assistance and stability of his cross, which seems to be a large peg driven into the ground, Philip convinces this twisting and slithering reptile to betake himself into the desert and return no more – to go away and stay away. As we know from the representation by Filippino Lippi in the Strozzi Chapel of Santa Maria Novella, Florence, the stench of the dragon, which Lippi renders as brownish exhalation, has sickened the people and killed the son of the priest of the Temple of Mars.

Philip's cautioning hand and downturned mouth give evidence of reek and miasma, while his foot urges the dragon on its way, the apostle's heel pressing with enough pressure for the dragon's mouth to open and twist, his tongue to loll. The lenticular, biconvex drapery folds that shudder around St Philip strike one as so much starched muslin loosely twisted about his body. The sheer cottony material billows slightly backward and to the viewer's right side, then spirals into vortices that echo the coiling and uncoiling of the dragon's tail. Perhaps a more apt metaphor would be that Philip's drapery is in fact a blast shield absorbing the beast's deadly, hellish stench. Coming from the netherworld – he has broken out of the basement of the Temple – the dragon represents the world upside down, evident from his writhing tail rising far above his head.

In the Western tradition, the dragon's inversion – he represents, as I have suggested, an inverted world – means that he stands for vice rather than virtue, descent rather than ascent, death rather than love and life, chaos as opposed to order, hell not heaven. The dragon lives in a liminal world of metamorphosis and masks. Filippino Lippi shows a fetid cloud; Mazzuoli, erecting a sculptural group rather than painting a picture, uses the arrangement of figures, the gestures and expressions of Philip, the dishevelled drapery, the deeply drilled beard and locks of hair to reveal the apostle's titanic struggle. The V-shaped composition, with its point on the dragon's head and the cross driving into the ground just behind the beast, stands for victory over the Devil. It is not just Bernini's manner, which this statue at best approximates rather than captures, that is at stake here, but the rhetorical devices such an exclamatory style can command. And they are legion.

Livio Pestilli characterizes the style of Camillo Rusconi's *St Matthew* in the *Apostles* series (Figure 6.2) as "academic late Baroque." This is fairly typical terminology for Roman sculptural styles in the early to middle decades of the eighteenth century. Robert Enggass, who describes

Mazzuoli's *St Philip* as "not like anything else in the group [of those who contributed to the *Lateran Apostles*]," treats Rusconi more or less the same way Pestilli does, as a sculptor cleaving to Carlo Maratti's dictates (see following chapter), which Enggass embraces with the word "classicism."[11] Pestilli goes on to write that Rusconi's *St Matthew* "created an image in which psychological intensity, figural design and dynamic treatment of the garments do not stray far from Bernini's more stylized, sculptural idiom."[12] Again, the point here is not to measure out minutely calibrated degrees of stylistic classicism with its hints of baroque dynamism, which tells one only so much, but to explore some of the possibilities and nuances of baroque visual rhetoric. As already mentioned, Mahon rightly asserted that baroque and classical usually coexist in a single work of art. Which of these two dominates depends, to a certain degree at least, upon what the art historian expects to find.[13]

I choose one further example of the survival of Bernini's baroque into the age of *buon gusto:* the tomb of Pope Benedict XIII in the Chapel of San Domenico of Rome's Santa Maria Sopra Minerva (Figure 6.3). Carlo Marchionni designed the overall tomb complex and made the sarcophagus relief representing the Council presided over by Benedict XIII Orsini in 1725.[14] Pietro Bracci carved the kneeling image of Benedict and the allegorical representation of Purity (also referred to as Religion) with her unguent jar; Bartolomeo Pincelotti carved the figure of Humility with her lamb and a crown trampled under her right foot.[15]

On what was surely a hot August afternoon in 1737 the Dominicans of Santa Maria Sopra Minerva unveiled the newly erected tomb of Benedict on their patron's feast day. According to the Roman newspaper *Diario ordinario d'Ungheria*, published by Caterina Chracas, ornaments hung in the chapel, music burst forth, and, as Chracas was wont to observe, the entire complex had been executed "with all the best design and good taste" (*con ogni ottimo disegno, e buon gusto*).[16] She enthuses over the precious marbles and the gilt bronze, singling out the "four very expensive [*di gran valore*] columns of *verde antico*." The statue of the pope, the newspaper judges, was "brilliantly worked from nature."

There certainly is here an unusual emphasis on verism, with the pope's sternohyoid (neck) muscles standing out sharply from his receding flesh, while the "frowning" muscles – the *depressor anguli oris* – pull the corners of his mouth down towards his lower jaw (Figure 6.4). Benedict's "Elvis muscle" – the one that allows us to snarl (*levator labii superioris alaeque nasi*) – has gone slack, creating the crescents on either side of his nose to descend in an arched curve to a point outside his

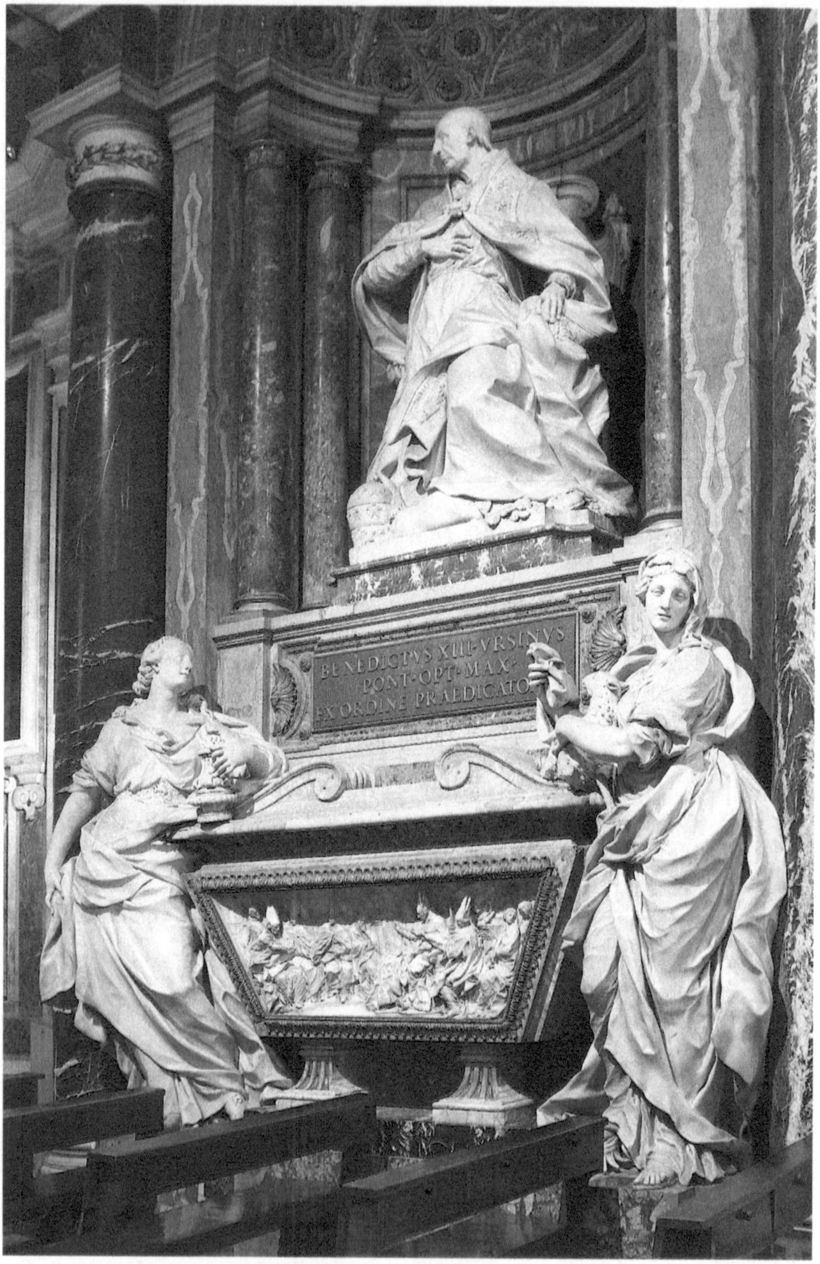

Figure 6.3 Pietro Bracci, Bartolomeo Pincelotti, and Carlo Marchionni, *Tomb of Benedict XIII*, marble, c. 1737, San Domenico Chapel, Santa Maria Sopra Minerva, Rome, Italy. Photo: Author.

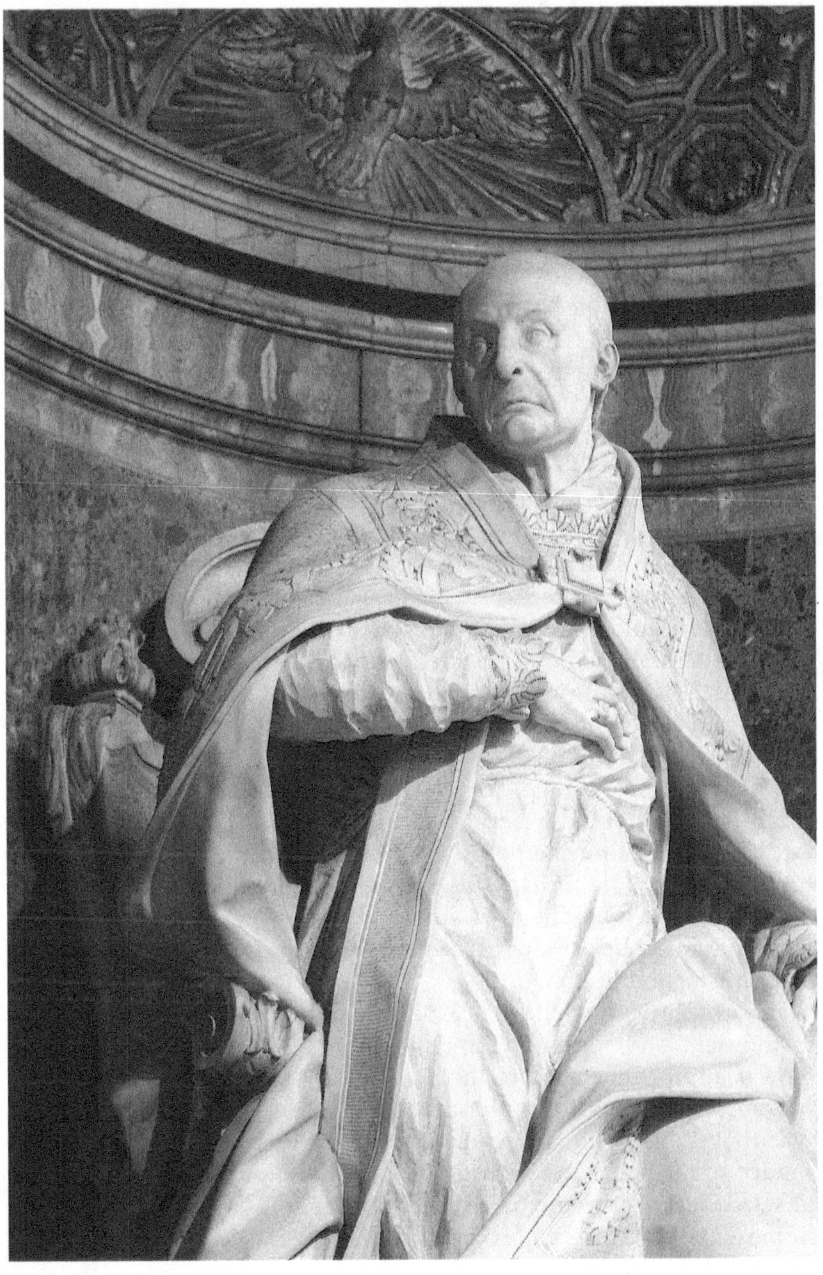

Figure 6.4 *Tomb of Benedict XIII*, detail. Photo: Author.

downturned lips. The elevating muscles of the upper eyelids – *levatores palpebraes superioris* – struggle to keep the eyebrows arched, giving the elderly pope, because of the extra effort needed to sustain the stretched, aging skin of his eyelids, a surprised expression. I use Latinized anatomical language to describe what is one of the most striking faces in eighteenth-century Roman sculpture, a superb example of late baroque verismo.[17] Benedict XIII's glabrous head and venerable homeliness are storied and, I believe, heroic.

When the Dominicans unveiled his tomb, the pope's remains lay in a temporary vault in the nearby Chapel of the Magdalene. Once Marchionni finished the marble version of his relief of the Council of Rome (he also provided the general design for the statue of the genuflecting Benedict), the chapel celebrated its definitive dedication on 28 February 1739 and Benedict's remains came to their final resting place in the Chapel of San Domenico.

One can infer from the pope's image that Bracci, who grew up in Rome, knew something of Benedict's papacy and character. Renowned for his humility and piety, Benedict – born Pietro Francesco Vincenzo Maria Orsini – suffered from a disorder common to the intensely spiritual: an innocence about and ignorance of human treachery and deceitfulness. Benedict entrusted papal finances to Cardinal Niccolò Coscia, a notorious thief. The scandal of Coscia's larceny rocked Rome and led Benedict's successor Clement XII to excommunicate and imprison him. Benedict's guileless, almost childlike face, despite the depredations of age, looks off to the side as he meditates on (one can imagine) the sufferings of the poor, to whom he was particularly dedicated, and the perfidy of human existence. In his contempt for the worldly, he forbade bishops and cardinals from wearing the peruke. His own baldness – with the barest fringe of hair circling his head like a halo behind his ears – must have been a source of considerable satisfaction to him.

Bracci's particular version of a mimetic ontology, his verismo, extends to the details of the pope's mantum that is clasped under his chin by a beautiful morse. Here the starkness of Benedict's face contrasts oxymoronically with the glorious detail of brocade and metalwork. One may think of the baroque veristic tradition represented by Alessandro Algardi and his portrait *Olimpia Maidalchini* (c. 1646–7; Rome, Palazzo Doria-Pamphili) or his large bronze effigy *Innocent X* (1645–50; Rome, Palazzo Conservatori); neither of these can be thought beautiful. Both are clearly baroque.

My way of characterizing the mimetic ontology of Benedict's head does not hold for the rest of his drapery, which cascades and explodes violently, especially when viewed from straight on in this fairly narrow chapel. Here the baroque comes back with a vengeance, creating the kinds of folds and pleats worthy of Leibniz's most esoteric meditations or Bernini's most inventive moments.[18] The patterns are abstract and filled with visual excitement, creating a remarkable counterpoint to Benedict's beautifully plain head.

Livio Pestilli goes on to demonstrate the ways in which Bernini remained an important figure in eighteenth-century Rome. For instance, the Accademia di San Luca often used Gianlorenzo's statues as models for students to follow, a practice which continued for decades after his death. Bernini's last pupil, Antonio Valeri, became director of the Accademia in 1726. One finds praise aplenty for Bernini up to the time of Winckelmann. It is not until about a century after Bernini died that his legacy and style definitively lost the general admiration of Rome's cognoscenti. However, it is not my point here to follow Bernini's declining aesthetic fortunes (they revive of course eventually) but to acknowledge some of the stylistic possibilities open to sculptors and not worry too much about trends, which have more to do with the history of taste than with the ways in which works of art can generate meaning and how we can *read* them, excavate them for their ontologies and narratives, and give them their due, not just as aesthetic objects but as bearers of meaning.[19]

7 Narrative and Symbol in the *Apostles* Series, San Giovanni in Laterano

Not much had been accomplished in Rome's Cathedral of San Giovanni in Laterano for half a century after the extensive architectural works carried out by Borromini during the papacy of Innocent X Pamphilj for the *Giubileo* of 1650. Having seen to the financing of the interior, Innocent also set aside money to give the ancient building a new façade, establishing a fund to which his grand-nephew Cardinal Benedetto Pamphilj later on also contributed. There appears to have been some reticence about rebuilding San Giovanni's façade before finishing the work on its interior.[1] It was not until the reign of Clement XII (1730–40) that Alessandro Galilei's design won the competition for the new façade. Francesco Borromini's grand, beautifully articulated tabernacles for statues along the nave had stood empty since the middle of the seventeenth century (Figure 7.1). In a sense, then, the planning for the Lateran statues had originated in the glory days of the baroque, when Innocent X reigned (1644–55) and employed both Bernini and Borromini. But it was not until the early eighteenth century that the statues finally were commissioned.

Clement XI Albani (r. 1700–21) appointed a "congregation" headed by Cardinal Benedetto Pamphilj, archpriest of the Lateran, and advised by Carlo Maratti and Carlo Fontana to finish the project. Monsignor Curzio Origo, Don Orazio Albani (the pope's brother), and Count Giulio Bussi also served on the congregation.[2] Maratti and Fontana settled on the size and placement of the statues.

Michael Conforti points out that after the death of Bernini (in 1680) there were no sculptors with sufficient *auctoritas* to dictate designs for papal commissions, which is why we have a painter, Maratti, and an architect, Fontana, supervising the sculptural project. Conforti writes

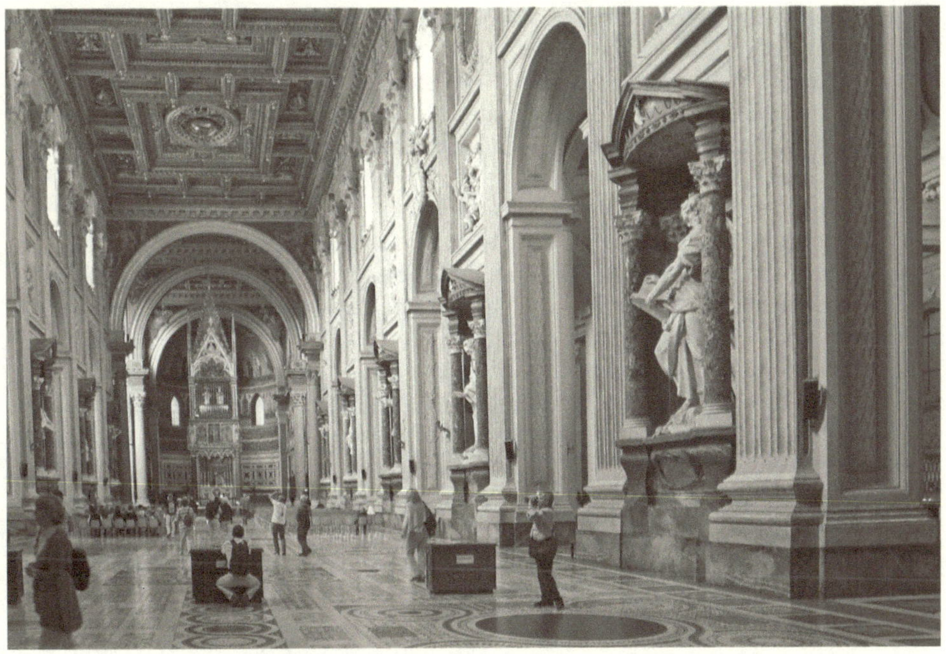

Figure 7.1 San Giovanni in Laterano, View Along Nave, Rome. Photo: Author.

that "no sculptor had the experience and the respect of either of these two powerful personalities, thus their positions were never challenged."[3] However, after Maratti's and Fontana's deaths, in 1713 and 1714 respectively, sculptors themselves did take over the supervising and completion of the series.

Carlo Maratti was taught by Andrea Sacchi and appeared in Giovanni Battista Bellori's hand-picked pantheon of artists of the seicento. Scion of the classic strain in seventeenth-century painting, Maratti prepared drawings for the statues that were to form the *Lateran Apostles*. One of the first sculptors he hired was Camillo Rusconi (1658–1728), a dominant figure in Roman art who also served as president of the Accademia di San Luca. He was entrusted with four statues for the *Lateran Apostles*: St Matthew, St James Major, St Andrew, and St John the Evangelist. Rusconi, more than the late baroque Giuseppe Mazzuoli, fit Maratti's expectations and preferred style.[4] Frank Martin observes that "from the very inception of his Roman career Rusconi found himself attracted to that circle of artists surrounding Carlo Maratti distinguished by their pursuit of classicism."[5]

Domenico Fontana supervised the statues' scale, which is approximately 13 feet high without the pedestal.[6] Rusconi's statue of the Evangelist St Matthew tries to wring as much drama as possible from a standing and reading figure.

Anthony Grafton tells us that the usual practice in the early-modern period was to read aloud. He summarizes the advice of the Milanese humanist Angelo Decembrio: "The good reader would work through his text sentence by sentence, parsing every verb and solving every difficulty, pronouncing the words as he read to promote … memorization."[7] Matthew, I suppose, did not need to memorize his own text, although one wonders why he reads it, silently or otherwise. Indeed, he focuses on his message for its own sake; he thematizes, in other words, his act of communication, his *poetic* function. Matthew insists on the tangibility of his gospel, its form, rhetoric, and structure. We read him as and while he reads himself. One thing any reader does – which can only be intensified when studying one's own text – is in some very general sense and especially in this case to query the relation of *his* word to *the* world. "What have I written that means something to the world?" is a basic question of linguistics and poetics, one which has pertinence for Rome's cathedral and the importance of the gospels and apostles to the Christian faith. Matthew's pose and act of self-reading have profound narratological reverberations. One indeed needs strong arms to sustain such puissance, such poetic power, truth value, and influence.

Matthew's gaze – his *sguardo* – communicates a passionate concentration with hair blowing forward and beard spreading out like a splayed octopus. The apostle's garments appear to respond to wind from another direction, as if fictional meteorological vortices occur in the basilica. Matthew becomes for us an internal focalizer, one whose perspective – his own point of view, which Rusconi amplifies through this fierce expression – emphasizes the gospels and especially *his* gospel. A narratologist would assert that the *Lateran Apostles* have variable focalizers, as many as there are statues it seems. But here we concentrate on the book and the act of reading, just as Matthew does.

The book appears to be a full folio, although represented of course more than life-sized. One assumes that the "signatures" – the gatherings of pages – have been sewn through the hinges, visible on the exterior of the binding. Matthew's drapery constitutes both a tunic and a cloak, fairly standard for an apostle and certainly *de rigueur* for classical garb in the eighteenth century.

The cloak has a fringe, giving his garments a sense of luxury and refinement, showing that Matthew chose well-made attire. He was a tax collector, after all, which is indicated by a bag spilling money at his feet. Luke 5:27 describes him as "sitting at the receipt of custom," and here the custom is generous.

That Matthew has to hold a heavy book at arm's length almost suggests he suffers from presbyopia and also has not thought to bring along a lectern, which would provide a suitable support for such a heavy text. Just the same, the pose creates a powerful equilibrium, with Matthew's right thigh helping to support the cumbersome tome and his brachioradiali, his forearm muscles, astonishingly tensed and thickened.

Rusconi's other Evangelist, St John (Figure 7.2), looks upward for inspiration. His quill pen hovers above the eagle, showing his readiness to record what he breathes in, *inspires*. John's book appears more manageable than Matthew's: he cinches the text against his left hip, which emphasizes his wide-stance contrapposto and springy balance. Ludovico Antonio Muratori, one of those early Arcadians who became a schismatic in 1711[8] (certainly known to Cardinal Pamphilj and other members of the original committee supervising the *Lateran Apostles*), discovered what has become known in biblical scholarship as the "Muratorian Canon," a document dating anywhere from c. 190 to 350 CE. The Canon brings together the Johannine texts, which are his gospel, his three epistles, and Revelation. Even before that, Justin Martyr in the mid-second century identified the apostle with the author of Revelation.

In his 1723 book on the Lateran basilica, the archpriest Alessandro Baldeschi describes the statue of St John the Evangelist in the following terms:

> The next statue is of St. John, one of the titulars of the basilica. The Apostle looks to the heavens: he has in his right hand the pen, in the left the Bible, and the eagle at his feet; from which is manifested the sublime elevation of his mind in its contemplation of the Sun of Justice [Jesus Christ], described in his *Apocalypse* [the woman clothed with the sun and the moon beneath her feet – that is, the Church of Christ], and in his Gospel in a manner superior to all others. The work is by the same Rusconi and equally admirable [in comparison to the statue of St Andrew, which Baldeschi had just described].[9]

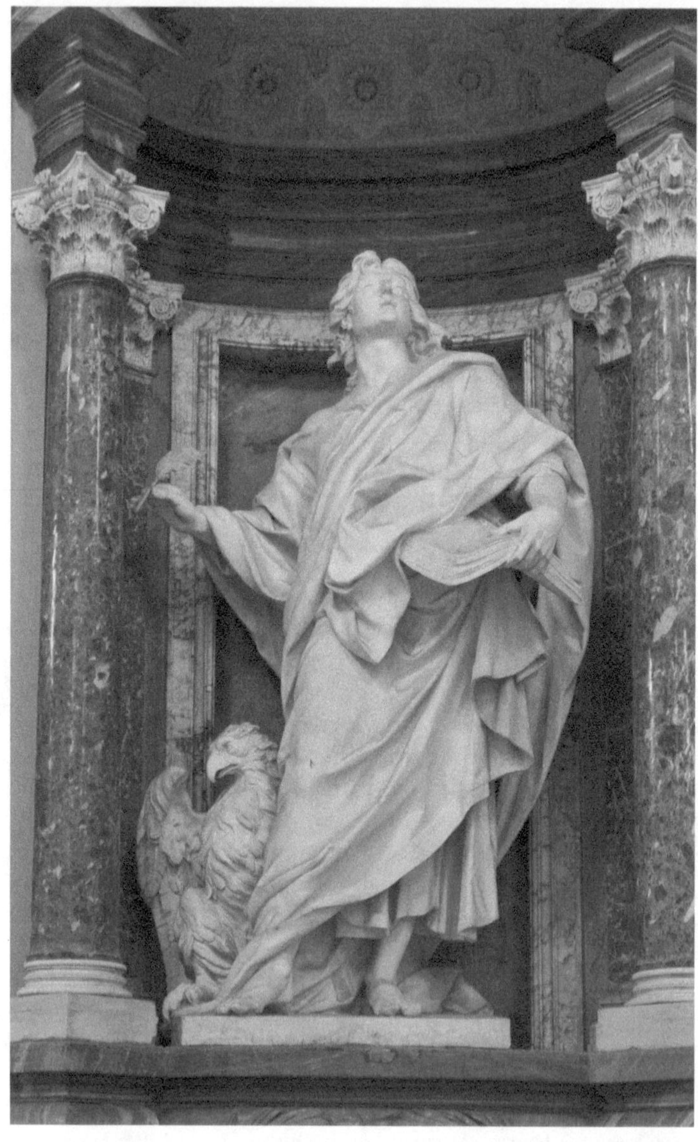

Figure 7.2 Camillo Rusconi, *St John the Evangelist*, marble, c. 1709–12, San Giovanni in Laterano, Rome, Italy. Photo: Author.

The Evangelist Mark presents John as part of Jesus's inner circle: "And [Jesus] suffered no man to follow him, save Peter, and James, and John the brother of James" (Mark 5:37). John also went with Peter and James up into a high mountain when Jesus was transfigured, and of course John was present, if asleep along with Peter and James, for Christ's agony in the garden.

John's upward gaze relates to the visionary John, to his paradisal view, "the time that is at hand." John's recording of his apocalyptic vision reveals God's hidden plan, which John writes for us, as in fact he wrote for the "Seven Churches of Asia." Rusconi presents John still in the grasp of mystical union, listening to the sounding trumpet and witnessing the beatific vision, all on the Island of Patmos. John hears and sees through the mediating angel, who becomes another object of his gaze: the Revelation of Jesus Christ that "he sent and signified by his angel unto his servant John." What Rusconi must thematize here is indeed vision and revelation, which, among other things, foretell a time of crisis, apocalyptic eschatology, the end of the world, Christ's coming, His judgment, His rewarding of the righteous and punishment of the wicked. Rusconi's contemporaries, as indicated by Baldeschi's description of the statue, certainly knew the narrative well, their heads filled with extraordinary images of the seven seals, war, famine, plague, disasters, victory in Heaven, the Antichrist, false prophets, the beast, the seven bowls of God's wrath, the Whore of Babylon, the Last Judgment, and the Descent of the Bride. The book of Revelation admonishes those in the Seven Churches of Asia to guard against their lives falling into sinful ways.

His face calm, nose that of a classical Greek statue – forming nearly a straight line from the top of his forehead to the tip of his nose – John is more apollonian than god-fearing. His hair cascades down his neck and onto his shoulders like twists of loose yarn. If we are looking for pugnacity, someone who seems to have girded himself for the sea of troubles John witnesses, we need look no further than the eagle standing next to him.

Scowling towards the congregation, his feathers blown like flames across his wing and chest, this aquiline piece of marble stands as no witless icon taken from Cesare Ripa's *Iconologia*. He appears ready to join forces with or perhaps take arms against the creatures in what Gilles Deleuze calls "The Book of Zombies."[10] The eagle, a symbol in ancient Rome of victory and strength, appeared on the standards of the Roman legion, later becoming a Fascist symbol. The eagle plays a more active role as a character in Revelation than does John. He is the fourth beast of the Apocalypse and provides the wings for the woman "clothed with the sun, and the moon under her feet, and upon her head a crown of twelve stars" so that "she might fly into the wilderness" and escape the dragon.

Aldous Huxley (1894–1963) once made the amazing (for the precision of his undoubtedly conjectural estimate) and at the same time obvious comment that anyone who paints or carves drapery does not do so mimetically; in other words, about 90 per cent of drapery patterns are invented, executed purely at the artist's discretion: "Artists, it is obvious, have always loved drapery for its own sake – or, rather, for their own."[11] He goes on to estimate that for the "average ... Apostle the strictly human, fully representational element accounts for about ten per cent of the whole." Art historians all too often treat drapery (with the rare exception being those who write about Bernini) as ancillary decoration, something interesting but not especially meaningful beyond whatever it is the drapery represents (such as status, a particular type of dress, or class, for example) or something that has to do with formal analysis (how the drapery along with its colouring and highlights affects a composition or contributes to its colour).

The classical garb worn by St John encases his body. The drapery functions as a narrative frame in the sense that it allows one to organize and understand the fictiveness of setting – the sense of the past as timeless, biblical, classical, even eternal – with John and the book of Revelation thematizing the eschatological, the alpha and the omega, the first and the last. Drapery establishes some of the conditions of meaning in the *Lateran Apostles*: as I suggest here and elsewhere, Derrida's meditation on the frame leads to one's thinking about interiority and exteriority, body and clothing.

The parergon plays a role in and is narratively related to Derrida's discussion of *différance*. The architecture of the Lateran tabernacles establishes its reality and its ontology in terms of the difference between sculpture and architecture, between Rusconi and Borromini, and ultimately between body and drapery.

The Renaissance conceit of the "clothed nude" addresses the ontological issues – the topics for discussion, in other words – on which I am trying to draw a bead. Both inside and outside, body and drapery defer to one another. Our understanding of the two together must take account of their mutual and reciprocal relationship.

Giorgio Vasari (1511–74) advised sculptors on how to make small clay models of nude figures and then drape them with cloth dipped in a kind of muddy water like a "slip" to see how clothes should fit a nude figure.[12] In a sense then, the final clothed figure "defers" (a favoured Derridean term) to the naked body. At the same time, of course, Rusconi had discretion – if we are to believe Huxley, at the rate of 90 per cent – on how to swaddle and envelop John.

We can see how John's inner garment falls about his calves and shins as linenfold (*lignum undulatum*), a stylized form Ruscone may have known from wainscoting.[13] The undergarment then is enfolded by broadly conceived, windswept, puckering, and undulating swathes of heavy garments that angle up from lower left to upper right like rising and spiralling jets of water issuing from a baroque fountain. The heavy wool then circles John's body and passes over his left shoulder.

Although no Roman (he was born in Jordan), John wears the Roman toga, a garment known throughout the ancient Mediterranean world and a logical choice for artists representing biblical figures. The garment underneath this *toga virilis*, the one with the linenfold, is a tunic. Now one may want to reassess Huxley's granting to Rusconi a 90 per cent exemption from description – since in fact the sculptor has to represent a specific garment. Just the same, Rusconi reclaims his artistic freedom through his treatment of folds and rippling cloth.

If John had no pen in his hand, he would be an *Arringatore*, one who gestures towards – haranguing or addressing – a crowd. Such a voluminous toga would be, if laid out, an elliptical piece of wool with rounded ends, the whole thing perhaps extending 15 to 18 feet, which is typical of a Roman imperial toga – or at least double that, given John's 13-foot height.[14] The rhetorical function of a toga would have been well known to literate Romans of the early-modern period. Quintilian in his *Institutio oratoria* wrote at length on the importance to the orator – which merges with John's profession as a writer – of the toga.

Comments from just one section of Quintilian's detailed deliberation on the toga suggests that Rusconi and Maratti were familiar with the ancient orator's exhortations:

> The other fold which passes obliquely like a belt under the right shoulder and over the left, should neither be too tight nor too loose. The portion of the toga which is last to be arranged should fall rather low, since it will sit better thus and be kept in its place. A portion of the tunic also should be drawn back in order that it may not fall over the arm when we are pleading, and the fold should be thrown over the shoulder, while it will not be unbecoming if the edge be turned back. (11.3.140)

The toga conveys authority and authorship, as here, with John penning Revelation, and although its incommodious bulkiness made it go out of style by the second century CE, for an early eighteenth-century artist who may have known that Virgil referred to the Romans as *gens togata*, the appeal of voluminous and dramatic drapery must have been powerful.

Rusconi's creation of deep chiaroscural pockets under John's left arm and right sleeve – not to mention the shadows flickering in the tabernacle – brings us back to the positive and negative spaces articulated by Derrida as appearing in any discourse, which has to do with the complication and predicament of deferral.

I need not dwell too long on Derrida's *différance* to make my point about the narrative situation in the *Lateran Apostles*. The drapery becomes a sign of the deferred presence of John's body, just at the quill pen and book become signs of the deferred presence of Apocalypse both as text and event. I insist on the invisible body here because hidden deep within the "Greek style," as understood by those in the Roman circle of Nicolas Poussin several generations before the time of the *Lateran Apostles*, is the sculpted Greek rather than Roman body expressed by subtle contours and what Estelle Lingo characterizes as "bodily presence."[15] The Greek style stands for the modern art-historical term "classical," which has been applied consistently to the *Lateran Apostles*. Rusconi could not carve John's toga without deferring to John's body; if he had, he would not have achieved the status of an early eighteenth-century Roman sculptor in the sense that art historians understand that designation. Vasari enshrined the clothed nude and made it part of the post-medieval, pre-"modernism" (art of the twentieth century) world. The body leaves a trace in the drapery, while the drapery leaves its traces on the body. In narratological terms, the biblical text leaves its traces on John, as does Rusconi's marble statue of John leave its traces on his architectural narrative domain – the tabernacle and so on throughout the Lateran basilica. While reading these "texts," we unearth the *différance* within and among the other apostles, which is a postmodern way of knitting together a narrative.

When reading Rusconi's and the others' narratives, one also has to consider Borromini's restructuring of the Lateran's interior, the shape and placement of the niches, and how they help to establish a narrative domain. Borromini successfully countered the sprawling spaces typical of huge basilican interiors with his niches, decoration, and plastic handling of piers and walls. He created a sense of *enclosure* in the nave, as if one enters an exhibition gallery. Michael Conforti writes about the 45-degree canting of the corners at the back of the nave and by the entrance, as well as other manipulations: "Borromini's efforts seem directed towards containing the interior space, and this corner resolution along with the convexity of the niches, facing themselves in the interior, all enhance this goal."[16] I refer to the nave of the Lateran as if it were an "exhibition gallery," which is misleading, of course, since one visited and viewed princely collections of art in palaces. Indeed, Conforti characterizes Borromini's niches and piers, projections and recessions as constituting a grand and palatial "salone."

This gives us some idea of the overall "frame" for the *Apostles* series, the cognitive or intellectual ordering of a particular reality, an existence that guides our perception and understanding of the series. One needs to keep in mind the metaphorical and ontological implications of a cathedral, of the Heavenly Jerusalem, the Gates of Paradise, Christ's apostles, and a princely *salone*.

The original intention probably was to fill the tabernacles with Fathers (or Doctors) of the Church and the Evangelists.[17] By the early eighteenth century, however, the idea of presenting the 12 apostles had established itself.

One finds also by the early eighteenth century a belief that the 12 niches stand for St John's vision on the island of Patmos of the 12 gates of Paradise, the Heavenly Jerusalem.[18] Alessandro Baldeschi and Giovanni Mario Crescimbeni in their text *Stato della SS. Chiesa papale Lateranense nell'anno MDCCXXIII* associated the Lateran basilica primarily with the Apocalypse and secondarily with Eden as the earthly paradise.[19] There is the paradisal passage in Psalm 23:2: "He maketh me to lie down in green pastures: he leadeth me beside the still waters." And from Luke 23:44: "Jesus said unto him, Verily, I say unto thee, today shalt thou be with me in Paradise." Then in the book of Revelation we read that the Heavenly Jerusalem

> had a wall great and high, and had twelve gates, and at the gates twelve angels, and names written thereon, which are the names of the twelve tribes of the children of Israel. On the east three gates; on the north three gates; on the south three gates; and on the west three gates.
>
> And the wall of the city had twelve foundations, and in them the names of the twelve apostles of the Lamb. (Revelation 21:12–13)

The niches as gates in which each of the apostles rather than an angel stands lead us into a mythical and imaginary garden, one that is "outside"

Borromini's *Salone*, although perhaps in some way coextensive with it, albeit on a different plane of existence.

Taken as a whole, the *Apostles* inhabit and constitute a "possible world," that is, a realm in which the overall truth value of the series is taken for granted. Rome's San Giovanni in Laterano constitutes a model of the Catholic world, which of course is not necessarily the world those who visit it today and have visited it before deem to be the real world. But for the sake of narration, one worries less about contrasting the subtending realms of interpreter, worshipper, or tourist with that of the "possible world" – the "complete state of affairs ... a set of individuals ... together with their properties" – of the *Apostles* series.[20]

Narration requires setting, placement, sequence, and actors. The setting literally is the nave of San Giovanni in Laterano, Rome; in a more detailed sense, it is the arrangement of marble statues within tabernacles, which is a spatiotemporal circumstance. Allegorically, the environment figures or stands for the Heavenly Jerusalem, which is Paradise. Placement has to do with the nature of the niches and the sequence of carvings within this series of containment vessels. The narrative is essentially achronic; in other words, there is an absence of temporal connection. Although the apostles had overlapping lives, the narrative in the Lateran basilica does not rise to the level of a story in the sense that we have a beginning, middle, and end. One obtains, in other words, a sylleptic narrative, which is spatial rather than chronological. The sequencing of statues comes about in part because of the peregrinating viewer, the archetypal pilgrim traversing great distances to receive an apostolic indulgence. In more recent times, the viewer is likely to be a tourist.

A niche is often treated as an isolating cell, a space set aside, a product of framing that separates inside from outside. Near the beginning of "Parergon," Jacques Derrida writes of "all the rigorous criteria of a framing – between the inside and the outside – carrying off the frame (rather its joints, its angles of assembly) no less than the inside or the outside, the painting or the thing (imagine the damage caused by a theft which robbed you only of your frames, or rather of their joints, and of any possibility of reframing your valuables or your art-objects)."[21] Derrida's vexatious questioning and implicating of property with understanding coincides with Carlo Fontana's decisions on the relation of inside to outside, statue to space, and how things should be displayed in the *Apostles* series.

As I argue later, when critiquing the Lateran basilica's Corsini Chapel, Derrida upends our "usual" sense of inside and outside and the separation brought about by traditional architectural frames, such as the aedicular tabernacle, the pediments and framing columns, Borromini's giant white pilasters, and indeed the entire basilica.

Above the apostles are *edicole* (shrines) with stucco reliefs representing scenes from the Old Testament (on the left, facing the altar) and New Testament (on the right); these were largely designed and executed by Alessandro Algardi in 1650. These reliefs were to be turned into bronze, a project never carried out. At the very top are oval paintings of the prophets (c. 1718).

Borromini's gargantuan white pilasters introduce a large field of white between the richly coloured tabernacles. This abstract, non-emblematic whiteness of the pilasters and the statues radiates through the narrative of the *Lateran Apostles*. Whiteness in most cultures associates itself with sunrise, life, and birth, connecting us with the cosmic and divine. White is the colour of milk, innocence, and the *Immacolata* – the Blessed Virgin Mary. White light embraces all colours (black is their absence); white flowers absorb no colours and so reflect white. White washes over and through each of the Seven Sacraments. For the statue of St Bartholomew in the *Lateran Apostles*, Lorenzo Corsini demanded that Pierre Le Gros choose the whitest marble from the best quarry at Carrara.[22]

Fontana thought one should see Borromini's spaces as *tabernacoli*, not *nicchie*.[23] He seemed to argue, in other words, that there is more here than, as Derrida puts it, "joints" and "frames." The individual tabernacles constitute a relatively small discursive space, a kind of temple: one that has been brought down to size, not quite so small as an altar tabernacle, which is a ciborium containing the Host, but just the same smaller than a "real" temple. Fontana is right, of course, to call this space a tabernacle: it has the shape of a baldacchino, is enclosed and framed, and has a tent-like covering, which relates to the origin of the word "baldacchino."

By occupying tabernacles, statues become ostensive; that is, they display themselves, are blessed and honoured like the Sacrament. To put it somewhat differently, the statues function anagogically: they represent human action as ritual and become figures instantiating the powers of nature. And because the pilgrim promenading through San Giovanni in Laterano sees them serially, we have multi-person narrative developing from individual and minimal narrative: Matthew reads a book;

Paul holds a sword and gives the gesture of *adlocutio*, associated with ancient Roman generals haranguing their troops – and very similar to the Christian blessing.

A convex, broken pediment, with the Pamphilj dove with laurel branch firmly gripped in its beak – set behind a serrated form of castellation like a crown – caps each of these oval tabernacles. The doves vary in presentation. Some, such as the one above Monnot's St Peter, have outstretched wings. Several face the altar, while others do not. Below, mounted on a sarcophagus motif, a cartouche made from the palm branches of martyrs bears the name of each apostle.

Within each tabernacle behind the statue stands an empty three-sided frame of *giallo antico* which in turn is embraced by slightly concave pilasters of *fior di pesco* and attached Corinthian columns of *verde antico*. These monumental, energetic, gesticulating apostles in lavish, chiaroscural, deeply modelled tunics and cloaks pose on marble pedestals, dazzle us, and like actors on display command our attention as if they are about to be mustered for a parade.

I refer to the individual tabernacles as discursive spaces; they may also be called, individually, "narrative domains." In narratological terms, a domain operates figuratively rather than spatially, but the metaphoric connection to space remains powerful and constant. A narrative domain, in other words, refers to a character's potential range, the things that are possible or likely for him or her to do, to accomplish, to act out. What is fictional and abstract in a literary text is physical and even ponderous in the *Lateran Apostles*. These architecturally miniaturized kingdoms provide the ground or enclosure for men who comport themselves or do some of the things literary characters do in a written text.

There is in the *Lateran Apostles* a "story logic," a sequence between and among the free-standing men.[24] In a sense the *Apostles* are metatheatrical actors in search of a narrative and an author. With arms cast out, hands raised, eyes focused every which way, faces revealing intense inner lives, their "authors" legion – seven separate sculptors, two overall directors – many of the *Apostles* hail one another and passers-by from their individual and isolating niches, or they absorb themselves in some self-contained occupation, such as Matthew reading his gospel, Andrew adoring his cross, John gazing upon his angel and revelatory signs. They are like Pirandello's characters seeking a single author in order to finish their individual stories, which are, in a sense, adumbrated, suggested more in outline than elucidated in a lengthy text or theatrical presentation. The 12 *Apostles* form a mythic montage, a juxtaposition of religious figures frozen in time.

The arrangement and placement of the *Apostles* depended upon how Maratti and Fontana gauged the importance of each apostle. Peter begins the series to the left of the altar as one faces it, because he was the Prince of the Apostles, and, of course, the left side is for the Gospels.[25] The right is for reading the Epistles, which means one begins with St Paul in the right niche nearest the altar. After that, figures arrange themselves between the two walls of the nave in a criss-cross pattern based on their descending importance, or, if little is known about them, the sequence of their feast days.

St Bartholomew

I will consider one further statue in the *Apostles* series – *St Bartholomew* by Pierre Le Gros the Younger (Figure 7.3) – by way of exploring an example of the uncanny and also in order to conclude the overall narrative and ontology of this colossal undertaking.

As a young man, the Parisian Le Gros worked at Versailles, where his father produced garden sculpture. At the age of 24 he arrived in Rome as a pensioner of the French Academy, after which successes came quickly for the precocious young sculptor. He lucked into the richest commission in town, the building and extraordinary outfitting of the Chapel of St Ignatius at Il Gesù, a project that involved not just the Jesuit Andrea Pozzo but also Pozzo's adviser, Carlo Fontana, who would remember Le Gros when it came time to choose sculptors for the *Apostles* series.

Although there had been a move afoot to involve Giovanni Battista Foggini for the statue of St Bartholomew (Cardinal Corsini – the future Pope Clement XII – probably favoured him to begin with), Le Gros was in place (Foggini was otherwise very busy in Florence) and certainly acceptable to Corsini, who was paying for the statue.[26]

At this time in Rome the most famous image of St Bartholomew was the one painted by Michelangelo for his fresco of the *Last Judgment* in the Sistine Chapel (1536–41). There Michelangelo, as modern legend has it, portrayed himself in Bartholomew's flayed skin.[27] Paul Barolski, one of the few dissenting voices, observes that we *cannot* recognize a portrait of any sort in the skin Bartholomew carries in his left hand like a long-forgotten, flea-bitten costume.[28] Although Le Gros adopts Michelangelo's merciless representation of the martyred saint's empty

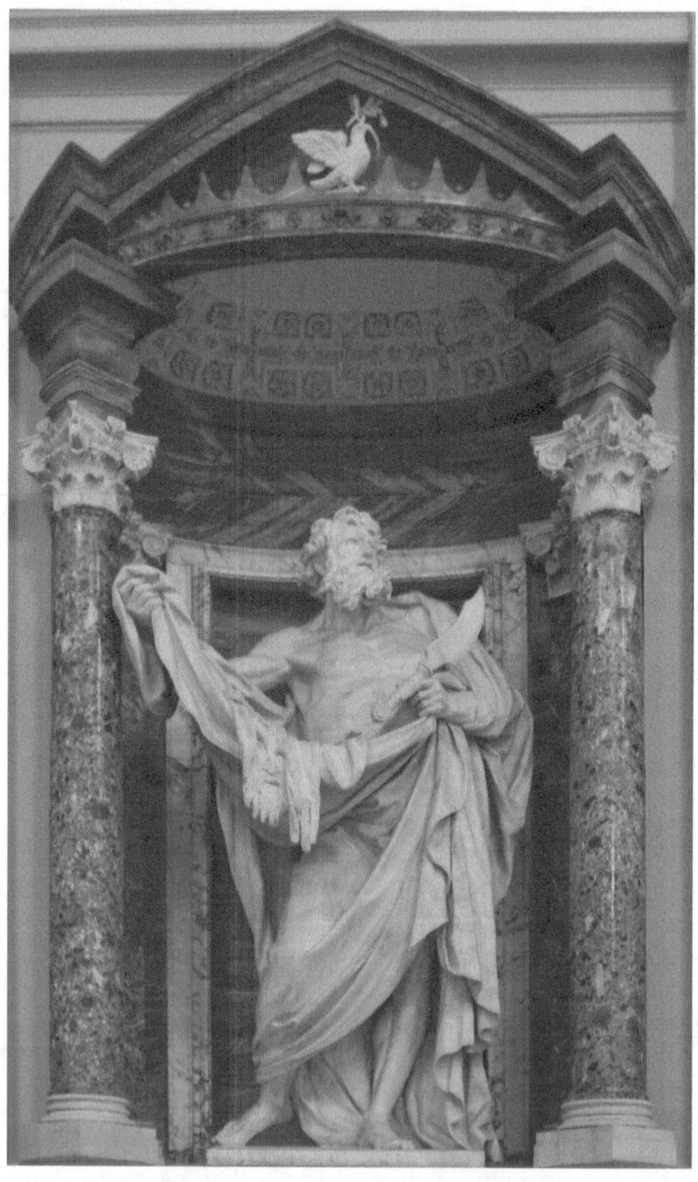

Figure 7.3 Pierre Le Gros the Younger, *St Bartholomew*, marble, 1705–12, San Giovanni in Laterano, Rome, Italy. Photo: Author.

husk, he gives no hint of representing himself (other than implicitly as author) in his rendering of the saint's deflated face. Nonetheless, a red-chalk drawing of Pierre Le Gros shows the artist pointing with his chisel to the statue of St Bartholomew.[29] In psychoanalytic terms, the "double" refers to a representation of the ego in various forms, such as a portrait or a shadow, mirror image, or twin. In other words, Bartholomew's double is his skin; furthermore, Bartholomew and his double together become Le Gros's double.

Alessandro Baldeschi, archpriest of the Lateran basilica, offers only a few words of description here: "The fifth [tabernacle] contains the statue of St. Bartholomew, sculpted with great distinction by Monsieur Le Gros, Frenchman, with his [Bartholomew's] own skin in his hand, which reflects the painful martyrdom suffered by the saint when he was, because of his faith, skinned alive."[30]

In the *Golden Legend*, Jacobus de Voragine, undoubtedly Le Gros's source, cites conflicting reports of Bartholomew's death: St Dorotheus states he, like Peter, was crucified upside down; St Theodore claims Bartholomew was flayed; others report he was beheaded. De Voragine combines all the accounts with his summary: "he was crucified, then, before he died, taken down and, to intensify his suffering, flayed alive, and finally had his head cut off."[31] Le Gros opted not for the standard image of Bartholomew simply holding a knife but chose instead Michelangelo's grisly image of Bartholomew shown twice, once intact and holding a knife rather gingerly, the second time a mere bundle of skin held like a sheet between the saint's hands. Bartholomew's skull-less face depends from its scalp like a tragic mask affixed to a clothesline. Next to the face hangs what appears to be a flayed hand, looking for all the world like an empty glove.

This eerie statue rivets visitors today much as it has undoubtedly done since it was installed. To see an image of an intact man, twice life-size, holding his own skin – when in fact he has yet to be flayed – both bewilders and repels us. How can he have his skin and not have it? How can he show us himself intact and at the same time skinned alive? To be flayed is to be tortured, and yet he appears triumphant. It is not that we are incapable of "getting" the point, but the repellent nature of his martyrdom disgusts us; we suddenly are uncomfortable in our own skins.

The standing Bartholomew proudly shows us his double, the epidermis of his martyred self. Seeing the two Bartholomews casts us first of all into the weird universe of prolepsis, the rhetoric of (in this instance) *horrific* anticipation, a place and time where both we and Bartholomew confront a thing existing before it does.

As I have suggested, this creepy doubling invokes for the modern viewer Freud's essay on the *"Uncanny," Das Unheimliche*, or the "unhomely." The "homely" is the familiar (home) and the quotidian; but here Bartholomew and we find ourselves far from home. A Galilean, Bartholomew died, according to legend, in Armenia, vilified, humiliated, and tortured. He cradles his "other" in his cloak, which he has unwrapped from his shoulder, revealing his muscular chest and torso that both will be, and in a certain sense already have been, flayed. He grasps the instrument of his torment, a Turkish clip-pointed dagger, between thumb and forefinger: with this knife he will be divided; he will be doubled.

As Otto Rank first observed, one's ego in various forms becomes the double, especially in the narcissistic time of childhood, constituting an "energetic denial of the power of death."[32] Both Rank and Freud understood the double as, first of all, one's immortal soul, which is the saint's flayed skin. Bartholomew as apostle and martyr would "see" his skin as indeed a guarantee of immortality; he has "witnessed" his faith.[33] The Father (God) lives on in the embryo of his Son (Jesus) who lives on through the apostles and the martyrs. Because of the nature of Christianity, none of what we see here would appear uncanny to Bartholomew – statue, saint, or martyr – but the viewer cannot escape unscathed. The observer and visitor to the Lateran, whether an eighteenth-century cognoscente or pilgrim (the implied viewers) or a modern scholar/tourist, experiences a *frisson*, a shudder.

I as a professional critic am not deducible from the narrative: Le Gros could not possibly have anticipated a twenty-first-century art historian snooping around his statue looking for clues of interpretation. But I am, just the same, just as shaken as anyone else when I behold St Bartholomew looking fixedly towards Heaven.

Conclusion

Vladimir Nabokov observed that "when we concentrate on a material object, whatever its situation, the very act of attention may lead to our involuntarily sinking into the history of that object."[34] And that of course is what I have been doing with the *Apostles* series – sinking into the history (and the interpretation) of objects and their fictive sequence. In more general terms, what Nabokov describes is what art historians do, of course. But I take his quotation from Bill Brown in his article "Thing Theory" in order to get back to the "thingliness" of the visual arts and how that bears on the ways in which one looks at narrative, whether within a single object or as part of a series.[35] Narratologists usually examine written, projected, and video texts, although, as I hope I have demonstrated, narration is as deeply invested in the visual as it is in the literary arts.

8 Fear and Trembling in Francesco Borromini's Sant'Ivo alla Sapienza

One reads in Francesco Borromini's church of Sant'Ivo alla Sapienza (Figure 8.1) in Rome above the altar: *INITIUM SAPIENTIAE TIMOR DOMINI* ("The fear of God is the beginning of Wisdom" [Psalm 111:10 and Proverbs 1:7]).[1] See Figure 8.2. This fear is submission or obedience to God: submission takes the form of dread, wonder, respect, and amazement. The building itself is a metaphor for divine wisdom, a place whose architecture instantiates an exegesis.

In his exposition on Psalm 33:8 ("Let all the inhabitants of the world stand in awe of Him"), St Augustine writes that "not of the terrors of men, or of any creature, but of Him let them stand in awe."[2] One stands mute in the presence of God.

Hans Ost and Pierre du Prey have reminded us of Borromini's complex symbolism in the church of Sant'Ivo, much of it deriving from the Wisdom tradition, including the writings of Solomon.[3] Borromini's ground plan, preserved in the Archivio di Stato, has in his own hand a transcription in Latin of the first two verses in the ninth chapter of the Proverbs of Solomon: "Wisdom hath builded her house, she hath hewn out her seven pillars: She hath killed her beasts; she hath mingled her wine; she hath also furnished her table."

Borromini's architecture functions rhetorically and Solomonically not simply because it persuades but also because it provides a formal rather than a linguistic interpretation, although the two are not necessarily separable. Du Prey makes a persuasive case for seeing the form of Sant'Ivo's ground plan as the "Seal of Solomon."[4] It is, as I have intimated, like all baroque visual rhetoric, a metaphor of an argument as well as a symbolic form. Ernst Cassirer's *Philosophy of Symbolic Forms* extends Kant's writings on aesthetic and sublime sentience, responsiveness,

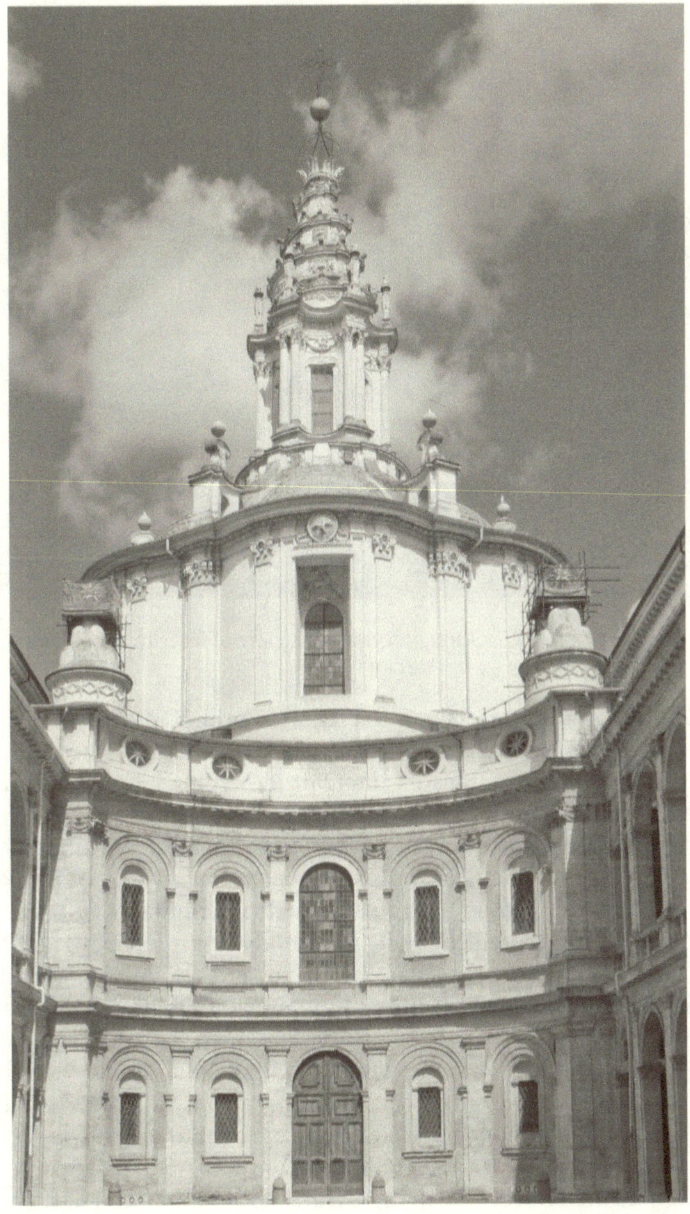

Figure 8.1 Francesco Borromini, *Sant'Ivo alla Sapienza*, 1642–60, Rome, Italy. Photo: Author.

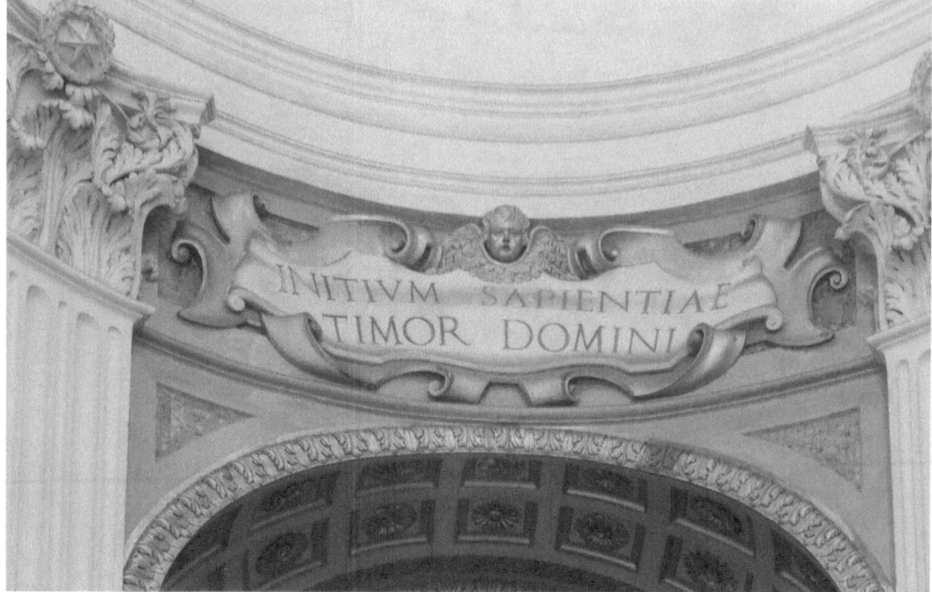

Figure 8.2 *Sant'Ivo alla Sapienza*, interior with view of inscription. Photo: Author.

perceptions, and experiences into Hegel's world of revelatory symbols. Like Kant, Cassirer understood that one's perception of the world carries with it not just raw sensory data but something more. For Kant that something more could be the pleasure of beauty and complexity that arises from the sensory and synaesthetic overtones of the sublime. *Sapientia*, with its etymological roots in *sapor* or "taste," is, not unlike the sublime, *affective*.[5] Cassirer stipulates that concomitants of perception constitute "forms," which in turn embody comprehensive attitudes towards reality.[6] In other words, art, myth, and religion are archetypes that wring from nature something human. Sant'Ivo literally gives non-discursive form to a religious reality, one anchored in, among other things, early-modern, post-Tridentine beliefs. In so doing, the church also instantiates through concrete forms an architectural entelechy, which Aristotle understood to be a thing brought to full self-realization. Both worshipper and tourist see in Sant'Ivo a symbolic form, a cosmos of religious belief pregnant with architectural inspiration and contrivances. The church becomes its own "universe of discourse," carrying with it ancient myths and rituals.

Noam Chomsky has said that when we speak a language we know things we could not have learned.[7] His reference is to the complexities of grammar mastered by a typical four-year-old, ones that seasoned linguists struggle to define. Language embodies in many ways a symbolic form we are wired, especially when young, to grasp with little conscious effort. Seeing and feeling, too, are cognitive and synaesthetic activities for which we are predisposed. Immanuel Kant saw no need to *teach* taste or aesthetic response, for he assumed that such things also come naturally enough.

Craig Dworkin has written about poets "dreaming architecture"; in our current example, I believe, we have an architect dreaming poetry – poetry of the sublime.[8] If any church can inspire in its visitors the experience of trepidation and astonishment, it is Sant'Ivo. Although the inscription was not chosen by Borromini (it originated with Sixtus V, who placed the phrase at the entrance to Pirro Ligorio's cortile), nor was the dedication to St Ives, who represents wisdom, really sorted out until the eighteenth century, the substance of wisdom had been present from the beginning and always informed Borromini's plans, whether in their first phase for Urban VIII (1641–4) or in the subsequent work (especially the spiral tower) during the pontificate of Innocent X (1644–55), along with the completion of the drum and its supports under Alexander VII (1655–67).

The effect of walking into the precincts of La Sapienza, pausing in the courtyard and observing the spiralling *tempietto* at the very top – which ends in the blaze of a laurel crown, filaments of iron, a globe, a dove, and finally a cross – is quite literally awesome (Figure 8.3). The church, a hermeneutic statement in stone and mortar, looks like it wants to corkscrew itself into the Heavens.

Being an architect with a deep commitment to the principles of *disegno* – and all the implications that term carried in early-modern Rome – Borromini began with the simplest and in many ways most adaptable (for architects) of Euclidian forms, the equilateral triangle. The basic ground plan, more easily understood if the visitor looks at the great cornice, appears in Borromini's first known drawing for the project.[9] Although there are a number of interpretations of how Borromini conceived of his plan, the simplest and most convincing is given by Joseph Connors, who sees the original drawings of varying and superimposed triangles, from smaller to larger sizes, as "triangle-plus-apses-minus-angles."[10] The image of a bumblebee, the design of a star hexagon, and a star of wisdom – interesting emblems one and

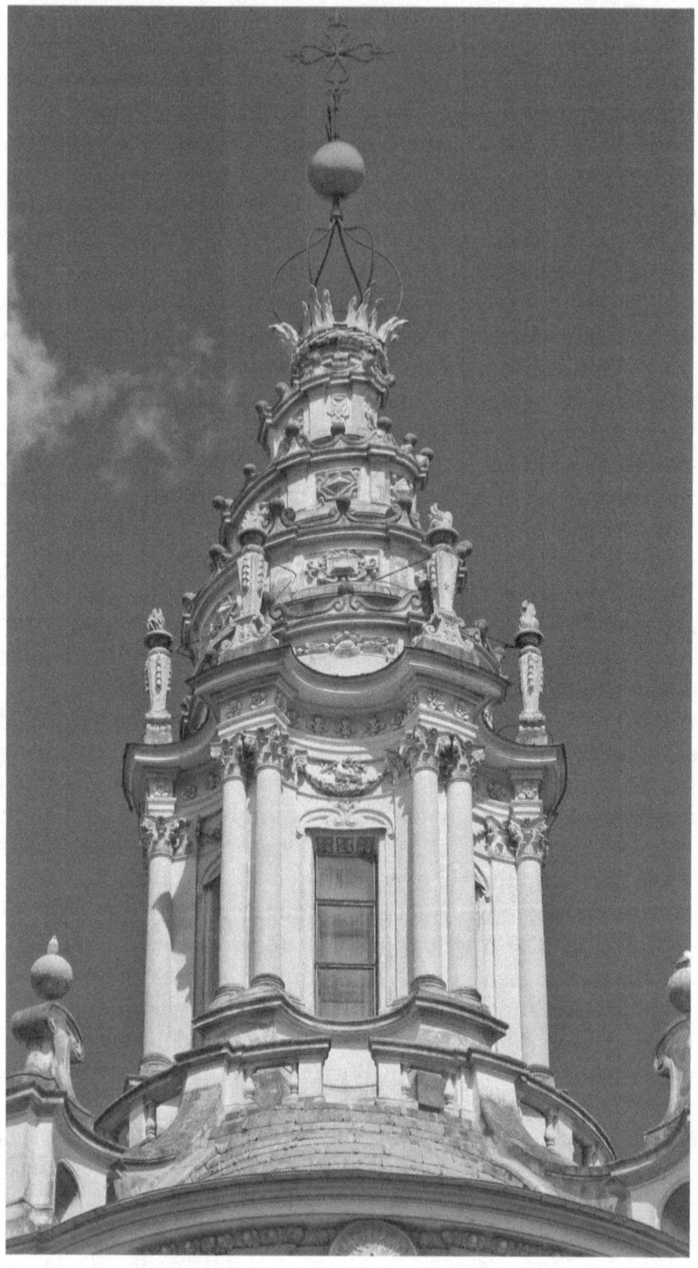

Figure 8.3 *Sant'Ivo alla Sapienza*, exterior, "Tempietto." Photo: Author.

all – Connors puts on hold, arguing that they were *not* there at the beginning. It was only when Fioravante Martinelli described the Sapienza chapel in his *Roma ornate dall'architettura, pittura e scoltura* (1660–63) that the recognition of a Barberini bee in the ground plan had apparently become common currency. What was there in the ground plan at the beginning was pure geometry. Thanks in part to the innovations and infamy of Galileo, mathematics and geometry were important areas of study at the Sapienza, carrying with them large coefficients of authority and, indeed, sapience – and by extension, fear and trembling.

St Paul admonished the Philippians (2:12): "Wherefore, my dearly beloved ... with fear and trembling work out your salvation." The Council of Trent decreed that when one's acquiescence to God's law arises from fear of His authority, then one obeys out of trepidation; yet that dread, constituting an act of "attrition" rather than genuine contrition, is just the same a "profitable sorrow" and prepares one for grace.[11]

Insofar as fear constitutes a fundamental and noble (according to the Tridentine decree) part of the human imagination, we may be able to see this fear and trembling (in Northrop Frye's terms) as participating in an "iconography of the imagination."[12] The analogy I then want to draw is between the putative "messages" emblazoned on the wall above the high altar and Borromini's complex and fearful symmetry. The beginning of wisdom in fear may lead to "a gift of God and an impulse of the Holy Ghost."

As Borromini was finishing the spiral *tempietto* during the pontificate of Innocent X, near the top of the lantern on the inside he painted stucco clouds and a blue sky and attached a carving of the Holy Ghost – the same image as the Pamphilj Dove – to the end of a rod slightly more than two *palmi* in length. Connors gives a lovely description of what it must have looked like before the Holy Spirit fell to earth in the nineteenth century: "The swift-moving Paraclete was placed slightly off center so that the clouds would look as though they were trailing behind Him. It was a dazzling theatrical effect."[13]

Before Cardinal Francesco Barberini with Gianlorenzo Bernini's support and Urban VIII's authority appointed Borromini architect at the Roman Archiginnasio, the position and circumstance of the Chapel of La Sapienza was more or less in place. At the very end of the sixteenth century (1597), Giacomo della Porta wrapped the cortile with his two-story exedra, which became Borromini's lower façade for the chapel of Sant'Ivo.

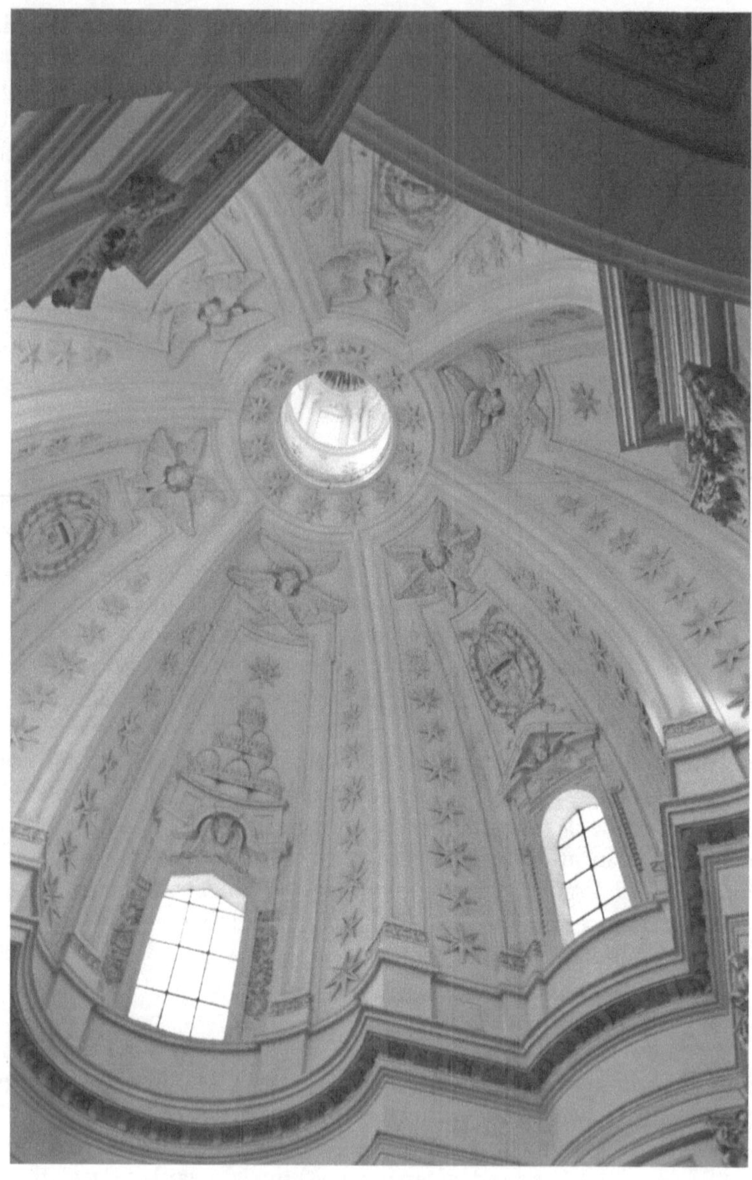

Figure 8.4 *Sant'Ivo alla Sapienza*, interior, view into dome. Photo: Author.

Forgoing the three-dimensional columns that he used at San Carlo, Borromini articulated the interior wall surfaces with razor-edged, fluted, Corinthian pilasters. As has often been pointed out, the precise sides and edges of the pilasters, those *arrises* (the outermost fillets) lead the eye from the floor to the entablature of the lower wall, which then is the base of the tent-like, pumpkin-shaped (Connors's characterization) dome (Figure 8.4). The eye easily ascends into the dome and finally to the perfect circle that forms the base of the lantern. All complexity seeks resolution. The baroque, if I may reify this idea, both plumbs the depths and ascends to infinity.

Having acquired the lower zone of his façade from della Porta, Borromini, who seemed to revel in the constraints he inherited at a building site, encased the subjacent part of the dome in six convex lobes, which counteract the broad concavity below. Here he was not reflecting the structure of the interior dome; rather, Borromini worked in part at least as an engineer bent on using the projections to absorb the outward thrust of the inner dome at a critical point. Simultaneously, he engaged in his usual formal play with projections and recessions.

Borromini was freer to create intricate architectural forms in the "roof," which is realized as a pyramid with ribs buttressed by miniature triumphal arches. These in turn are capped by motifs similar to those employed by Michelangelo at the Porta Pia.

Unlike his contemporary and sometime rival Gianlorenzo Bernini, Borromini was a pure architect, not particularly interested in the *bel composto* of painting, sculpture (although his carved and modelled angels are remarkably provocative), and architecture. For him, *disegno* always remained a concept of forms, geometry, proportion, and products of his compasses, which, like Michelangelo, he carried in his eye.[14]

Martin Heidegger wrote in his *On the Way to Language* that a poet may "come to the point where he is compelled to put into language the experience he undergoes with language."[15] Heidegger's insight applies equally well "on the way" to architecture. Borromini put into architecture the experience he underwent with architecture. The intricate and wildly varied use of buttressing devices, finials, swags, ribs, astragals, torches, *fleurs-de-lys*, rosettes, egg-and-dart moulding with tiny heads of seraphim, composite capitals, shell motifs, volutes, and spirals – not to mention the basics of Euclidian geometry – invites a comparison to a modernist poet like Mallarmé and his "fascination with words and letters of the alphabet, and their endless combinatory possibilities, [which] is at the core of a poetic venture that can only be called an 'experience with language'" (Figure 8.5).[16]

Figure 8.5 *Sant'Ivo alla Sapienza*, exterior, angels' heads. Photo: Author.

With an anticipatory repudiation of Adolf Loos's assertion that "ornament is crime,"[17] Borromini essentializes ornament, making it the very stuff, the syntax, of his rhetoric and experience, the elements of his style and the scaffolding of his hermeneutics. Ornament *is* architectonics. For Borromini ornament never becomes something external or peripheral, never the icing on the cake. He uses architecture to theorize architecture, as Robert Harbison has himself theorized in his "case for [baroque] disruption."[18]

Rudolf Wittkower reads the interior arrangement of architectural spaces in Borromini's San Carlo alle Quattro Fontane as poetic metre.[19] He uses niches, mouldings, and groupings of undulating bays as if he were scanning accented and unaccented syllables or rhyme schemes in poetry. Wittkower certainly knew that patterning in metrical verses originated in classical prosody and the traditions of Western poetry. In his writing on Borromini he sees language as architectural and architecture as essentially linguistic, as when he employs the term "caesura" – deriving from *diaeresis* in classical rhetoric – to describe a break or rupture in the metrical pattern of architectural forms. Wittkower gives no indication that he feels he has borrowed these terms from another discourse or medium, that his reading somehow is metaphorical. He does, however, move on to a metaphor in the form of a simile when he "likens" (his word) Borromini's "overlapping triads" to the "warp and woof of the wall texture. In musical terms the whole arrangement may be compared to the structure of a fugue."[20] In Sant'Ivo one listens to the argument of the eye, doing so in a visceral manner, one that I have already characterized as awe.

Wittkower's scansion of San Carlo and its architectural isochronism suggests that something syntactical and almost phonological operates in Borromini's language, with its "sounds" articulating the fundamental components or elements of a visual language, a communicating system – or, as it is sometimes referred to, "architecture as frozen music."[21] Wittkower makes certain decisions about what Borromini's architecture means by employing scansion, even though the rhythms themselves are not precisely the meaning. Just the same, by choosing and developing his scansion Wittkower infers Borromini's semantic (and architectural) decisions. First one understands San Carlo's sense and then determines its metre.

Having introduced Gilles Deleuze's reading of Leibniz's fold when assessing the ontological adventures of Bernini's drapery patterns in his bronze statue of Urban VIII, I would like to bring back the fold now as a figure for architecture and how it leads to the infinite and sublime.

Both Deleuze and Gottfried Leibniz can be understood as allegorists: they instantiate abstract ideas in physical forms. Instead of producing an allegorical representation of Temperance, for instance, as Cesare Ripa does, Deleuze works with the stupendous and stupefying fold-producing baroque.[22] The concept of the baroque is not a stop along the way in the history of ideas but rather a *thing*, a kind of Hegelian *geist* that makes its appearance from time to time (think of ancient baroque, medieval baroque, early-modern baroque, contemporary baroque). In his figural and reifying language, Deleuze writes that the fold is not an essence but an "operative function" or a "trait" of his personified or manifested baroque.[23]

I would go further and suggest that in fact the fold can constitute a kind of essence, a baroque visual archetype. Fairly early in the seventeenth century Bernini and Pietro da Cortona elevated curved shapes and space to a higher power of expressivity. In Cortona's frescoes and Bernini's drapery patterns, lines, planes, and shapes subtend one another, forming creases, bends, turns, pleats, and tucks. In the baroque, certain shapes can become symbols pointing towards a conceit or transcending image, such as an angel or a burst of light and energy. Both Bernini's agitated drapery and Borromini's convexities and concavities achieve heightened significance.

Indeed Deleuze's claims achieve a metaphysical drama when he writes of matter that it "offers an infinitely porous, spongy, or cavernous texture without emptiness," a baroque and anti-Cartesian plenum within which the curving caverns contain other caverns.[24] There seems to be a force in the universe that twists and spins matter, leading to an essentially curvilinear notion of space, which, according to Einstein, results from flat (or straight) space-time being disrupted by the gravitational forces of mammoth objects, such as stars. For Deleuze, who knew his Einstein, parts of matter "form little vortices in a maelstrom."[25]

All this curving and twisting strikes anyone familiar with baroque art and architecture as an appropriate assessment of baroque movement, especially of Borromini's façades and interiors. Every monad, according to Leibniz, has both an elasticity and resistance; therefore, everything impinges on and rebounds from everything else. Fluids within the folds lubricate all of this throbbing, while the fluids themselves are in turn constituted by other liquid substances between their parts, and so on regressively *ad infinitum*. Deleuze sees both the inside and outside of a baroque church as "thrust[ing] the other forward," although "the monad is the autonomy of the inside, an inside without an outside."[26] The relation of inside to outside is, to say the least, uneasy. Just as one can see from a side view of a baroque church that façades often do not relate very clearly to what lies behind, one can understand how Deleuze would say that a baroque church's interior is a monad, "an inside without an outside." Furthermore, there is the sense, as Gregg Lambert characterizes it, that "the fold of the inside is at the same time, on another surface, the unfold of the outside and vice versa."[27] In Deleuze's conception of Leibniz's monadic fold there tends to be a reciprocal relationship between inner and outer. That is to say, because Deleuze opposes the discriminating of ontologies, the existences of inside and outside cannot in Leibniz's universe of monads be utterly alien to one another. Deleuze describes Leibniz's allegory of the "baroque house" with its two floors, identifying the lower floor as the façade of a church and the upper as the church's windowless chancel, its *fuscum subnigrum*.

A careful reading of a façade – think of Borromini's for the Oratorio of the Filippini in the Piazza della Chiesa Nuova, Rome – does not tell us much about what is inside; there is little correlation, in fact, between the segments of Borromini's façade for the Oratorio and the rooms it covers. Deleuze does not help us much by adding that the inside of a baroque church, its "cell" or monad, is "the metaphysical principle of life," while the outside is "the physical law of phenomena."[28] Perhaps one can conclude that the inside discloses truth, while the outside bears architectural meaning.

As we know from the example of a butterfly beating its wings in Japan and a monsoon boiling half a world away, the nature of a plenum is that anything happening anywhere in the physical world influences everything else; here, in a sense, is a concomitant to chaos theory. Therefore and by extension, despite Deleuze's separation of a baroque church's interior from its façade, everything finally binds itself together, and so the inside and the outside act upon one another, each pushing the other ahead of itself, folding and unfolding. In the spirit of an ambivalent and thus worried relationship between interior and façade, one can say that a visitor or worshipper *exits* Borromini's façade in order to enter his church or oratorio.

As obscure and fanciful as such an image may be, Borromini's architecture seems up to the task of problematizing inside and outside, even turning the outside into something it is not. Simply by giving up the pure tectonics of the architectonic, Borromini, with his pulsing surfaces, his bending and twisting, pushing and pulling, concaving and convexing, lends to his buildings the character of a flexible membrane, the enveloping of inside with outside, the systolic and diastolic – the beating of a folding and unfolding heart. The astute critic of baroque art Giulio Carlo Argan observed that the curved plane – a fold, in other words – is the essence of Borromini's understanding of architectural space.[29]

Collegio di Propaganda Fide

Borromini's façade for the Collegio di Propaganda Fide, in Rome, takes advantage of the restricted point of view born of a narrow street (Figure 8.6). An observer approaching from Piazza di Spagna by

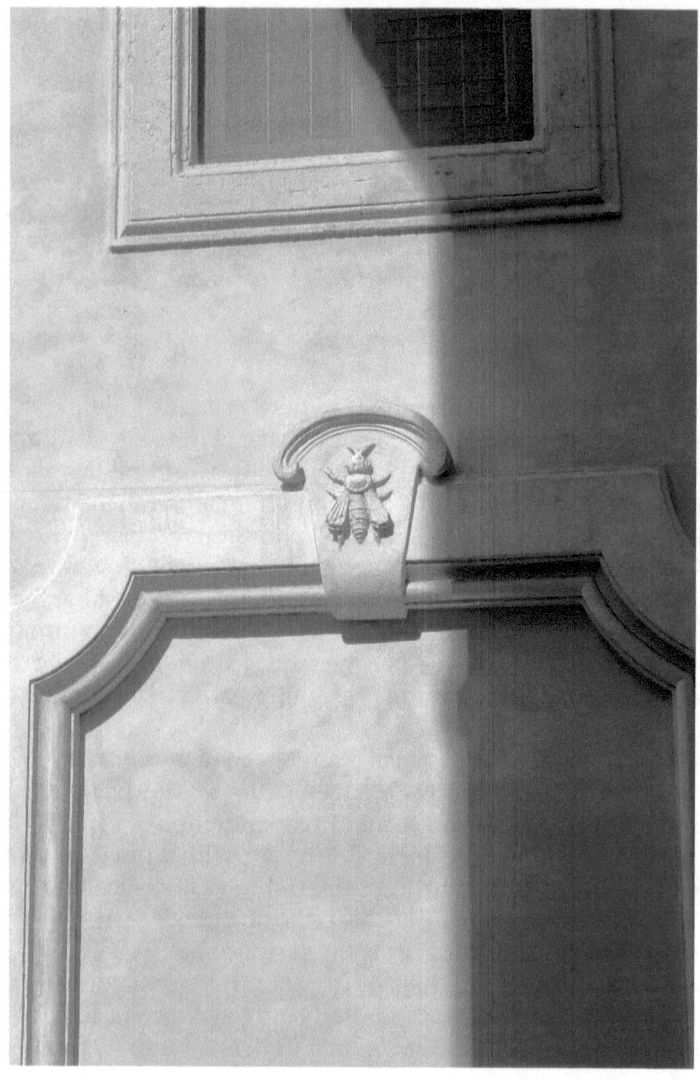

Figure 8.6 Francesco Borromini, *Collegio di Propaganda Fide,* Rome, 1654–67, detail, left side of Borromini's façade. Photo: Author.

way of Piazza Mignanelli notices, attached to the façade facing Via di Propaganda, first of all a wide – considerably more expansive than one's outstretched arms – flat, unfluted pilaster that cants outward like a projecting stage wing (Figure 8.7). Next comes a series of bays separated by the same unfluted pilasters, although now they lie flat, projecting less than a foot from the façade. Within the space of each of these bays is a ground-level blank door surrounded by jointed frames constructed with both curved and straight edges. Each of these empty frames features a crowning strapwork keystone bearing the Barberini bee.

The real interest is in the next story up. One might call it the *piano nobile,* although what lies behind bears little relation to what Borromini signals in the front. Before one can even take in the grand window spaces carved out of the wall (there is in fact a flat surface behind this superimposed, undulant sculpted face), one's attention is arrested by the deeply projecting cornice, with its razor edges first thrusting forward and then bowing inward over the entrance bay (Figure 8.8). Supporting the cornice are compound modillions in complex arrangements with rosettes and other leaf/petal forms of the *patera* sprouting between them. Things get busier in the central bay with both convex and concave elements. Here the strolling art historian is apt to give up the anamorphic approach – coming in from the side – by swinging around and backing up so as to apprehend and then more slowly comprehend the entrance.

I defer to Filippo Baldinucci and his comment on Bernini's *Baldacchino* that it is for the eye alone and not the ear to take in the whole and its parts. It is not that an architectural historian or critic runs up against the rhetorical wall of an adynaton or impossibility stratagem: after all, the critic can turn to Anthony Blunt's brilliant but, from my rhetorical perspective, *unreadable* description.[30] Sometimes parsing a Borrominian architectural unit is not worth the candle – or, in our parlance, the electricity that runs our computers.

I am reminded of Michael Baxandall's cleverly capricious anecdote on ekphrasis: "In every group of travelers, every bunch of tourists in a bus, there is at least one man who insists on pointing out to the others the beauty or interest of the things they encounter, *even though the others can see the things, too* [his emphasis]."[31] Baxandall's rhetorical assertion that we art historians "are that man" hits home. Just the same, he grapples with the difficulties of what he calls "the basic absurdity of verbalizing about pictures"; the matching of words to shapes, be they painted

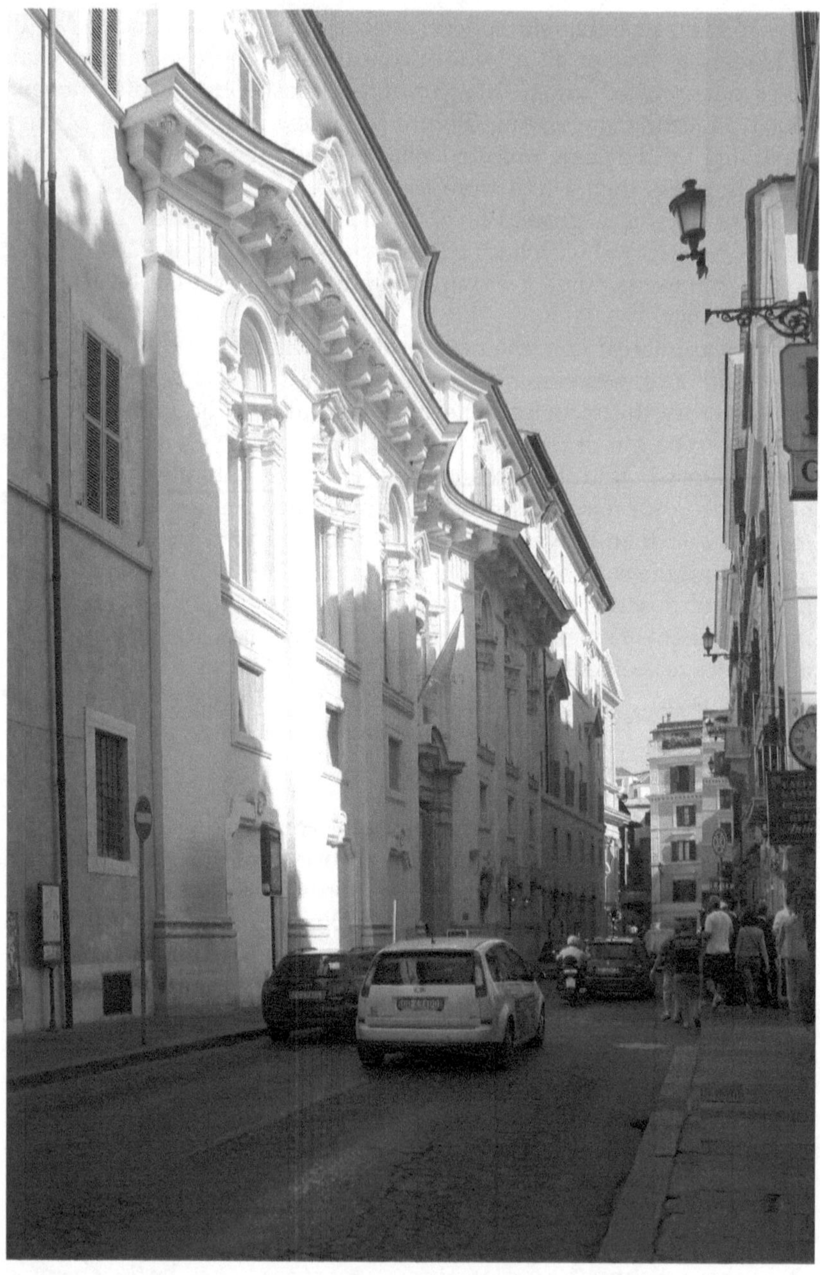

Figure 8.7 *Collegio di Propaganda Fide*, view of entire façade. Photo: Author.

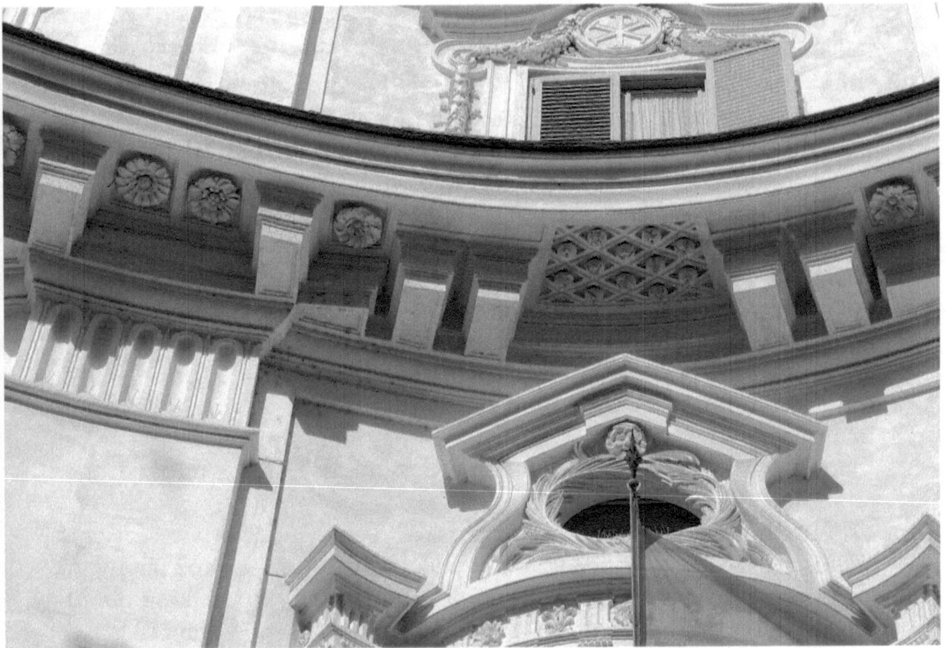

Figure 8.8 *Collegio di Propaganda Fide,* detail of central façade. Photo: Author.

or built. I wonder, is it equally absurd to verbalize texts, even though pretty much everyone can read them?

Baxandall concedes that there is a long and estimable tradition of art criticism, so, of course, it can be done. His approach, one that he successfully pursued for several decades after the appearance of this essay, is what he calls "inferential as to cause."

Despite my plea for some quiet time in the contemplation of the central bay at the Collegio di Propaganda Fide, I now return to Borromini's church of Sant'Ivo and resume the discussion on how the church assists the mind on its sublime road to God. The word "sublime" was used often enough in the seventeenth century by such British writers as Milton, Cawdrey, Herbert, and Dryden and, as we have seen, by Bernini's biographer Filippo Baldinucci. Although still a somewhat inchoate rhetorical concept, the sublime as an episteme – a cluster of ideas creating a form of knowledge – was coming into its own. In the eighteenth century, Edmund Burke and Immanuel Kant articulated and greatly expanded upon the sublime experience. Despite the clearly *aesthetic* substratum to Kant's *Critique of Judgment*, the truth-disclosing attributes of the sublime remain intact.

Kant writes about how we conceive of a quantum, or finite quantity, through the acts of apprehension and comprehension. Apprehension comes quickly enough; standing outside and looking towards the stars, for instance, demonstrates that we can see – that is, apprehend – nearly to infinity. Kant writes that comprehension "becomes more and more difficult the farther apprehension progresses, and it soon reaches its maximum, namely, the aesthetically largest basic measure for an estimation of magnitude."[32] After that there are diminishing returns; the more the comprehension exceeds its grasp, the less the imagination can conceive. Finally, the imagination relinquishes more than it acquires. And that is when we are in awe, in the midst of the sublime.

Kant shows the importance of perspective, or point of view: if one stands too closely, then the whole cannot be apprehended; too far away, and necessary details fade into atmospheric mist. By walking about within the church of Sant'Ivo, thereby creating a *moving* point of view, as we saw for the "outside" of the Propaganda Fide, the pilgrim or cognoscente increases his or her excitement and aids his or her imagination. This can lead to exhaustion, not because of the sheer size of Sant'Ivo but by reason of its architectural complexity. One's comprehension attempts to fit together architectural elements, to see how one group relates to another and how they all combine to create a conceptual, architectonic whole. The fact that things curve, bow, and recede creates the irrational notion that what is solid and immobile is liquid and moving. The mind boggles. It is this Kantian interaction of the visitor's sentience with Borromini's world that gets one into such desperate but pleasurable straits. The effect can become dizzying, which suggests that the maximum response to the sublime is reached, and, as when an engine's revolutions per minute hit the redline, components start to break down. This threatened collapse occurs in the mind of the perceiver.

Sant'Ivo alla Sapienza overwhelms because complexity transforms to perplexity. Kant tended to think in terms of sheer size, however, as we have seen with St Peter's, whose dimensions, giving rise to what Kant characterizes as a "liking" or "emotion," constitutes the pleasure in the experience of the sublime. Pleasure springs from our inadequacy, just as one's fear of the Lord marks and reveals human insufficiency, making us aware of the distance between human and divine. This comprehension of that gap promotes fear and pleasurable trembling, the beginning of wisdom: "Blessed are the poor in spirit [literally the ones who fear the Lord], for theirs is the kingdom of heaven" (Matthew 5:3).

9 Baroque Conceits: Domenichino and Baciccio

Domenichino (Domenico Zampieri, 1581–1641) painted an image of St John the Evangelist in Rome's Sant'Andrea della Valle on the pendentive of the crossing (Figure 9.1). Here is a superb example of baroque metaphorical sophistication expressed as a visual conceit.

Supporting Domenichino's *concetto* is an awareness that various pigments applied to fresh plaster can rise to the level of representation or mimesis and coalesce into something recognizable and identifiable on several levels. This miraculous instance of metaphor and recognition happens simply because one's optic nerve and brain do the really complicated work.[1]

The intricacy of visual conceits can and should put the viewer into a state of awe, which finally is what draws us into the heart of the matter, leading one to the pulse that sustains the experience of the work of art. The awe, which is part of wonder (and therefore *meraviglia*), creates astonishment and respect. There is a moral element to knowing something in the manner of awe: fear and joy associate themselves with the awesome; the fear of the lord, as we have just seen, is the beginning of wisdom.[2]

In Domenichino's spatiotemporal and contrived world, an image of St John, angels, and putti lies within the spherical triangle of a pendentive, which simultaneously supports a dome, becomes a "canvas" for painted images, and functions metaphorically as open sky. John, youngest and handsomest of the Evangelists, shows off curly hair, his *cappelli capricciosi*, and spreads his arms in a gesture of receiving and embracing divine inspiration. Giovanni Pietro Bellori wrote that John's head in this artwork is a copy of an ancient bust of Alexander the Great, who invariably was represented looking upward and slightly

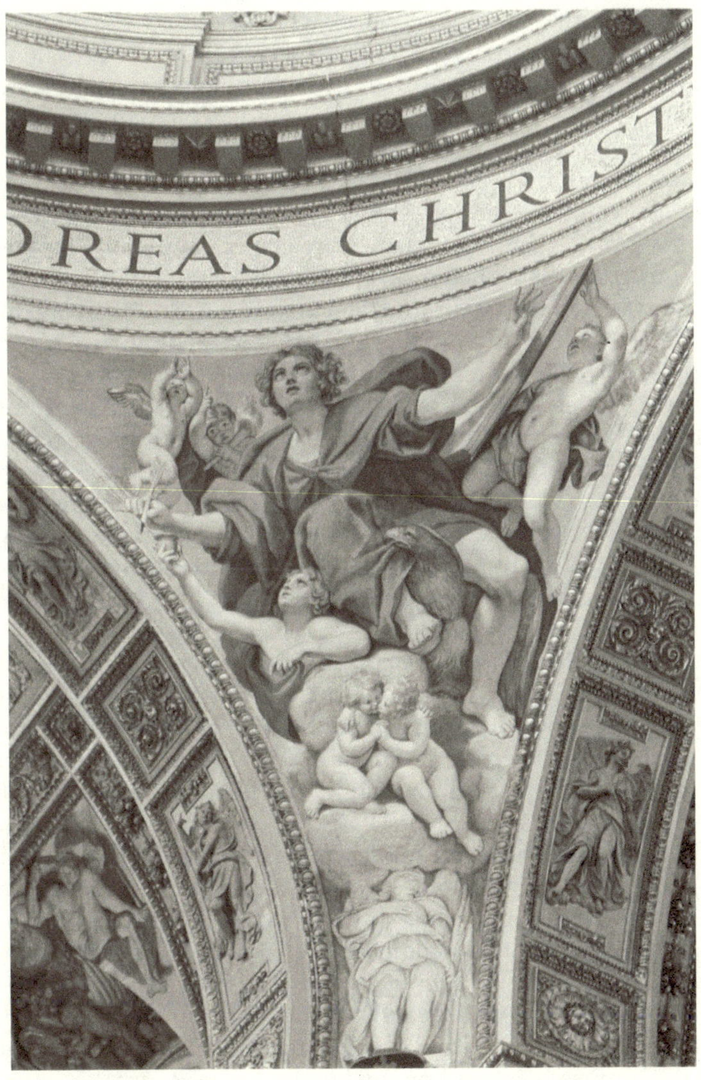

Figure 9.1 Domenichino (Domenico Zampieri), *St John the Evangelist*, fresco, 1623–6, ceiling, Sant'Andrea della Valle, Rome, Italy. Photo: Author.

to his right, perhaps owing to a neck wound.[3] A Catholic saint and the "great" conqueror come together as archetypes, one a witness to the life of Christ, the other a vanquisher; one a contemplative and visionary, the other a man at arms and unifier. Alexander commanded the Greeks to worship him, claiming his descent from Egyptian gods.

In his Alexandrian pose, John's eyes and head turn towards an epiphanic realization or appearance (perhaps referring to John's other great book of the Bible, Revelation), which is represented by the light of God filtering through and past lantern windows, in turn framed by Francesco Borromini's sculptural and architectural designs, and also by way of the windows set into the base of Carlo Maderno's dome. A narratologist may call my reference to the light *outside* the fresco as extradiegetic. In other words, I connect the work of art to its environment, not restricting its narrative to that which goes on inside the frame, which employs feigned egg-and-dart moulding following the outlines of the pendentive. A literary text would seem to have less relationship to where or how a book is held – in one's hands, in a library, or by way of an electronic medium, for instance – than to the world of the text itself, or, in slightly different terms, "the fictional world of the story" as David Bordwell describes it.[4]

The light, both represented *and* real, washes across John, leaving his fictive neck in a penumbral region. Our existential perception of John's image requires physical light, but our reading of the shadow across his neck relies upon metaphor and mimesis. The real light floods the other figures, simultaneously illuminating the pendentive and the lower regions of the church.

One putto points upward to the source of light, while bearing in his left hand a lesser source of radiance – a flaming torch.[5] He looks straight at us, eyes wide, cupid's lips parting, capturing the viewer's attention, seducing one into a fictional game of to-and-fro, a kind of winking acknowledgment of artfulness and play-acting. Like one of Leon Battista Alberti's "speaking figures," this putto undermines narrative absorption by catching our eye, engaging in a kind of apostrophe, like invoking a muse – except here he invokes us as if we were the poet/artist, thereby keeping himself from settling into an actor's role.[6] Yet to describe him as a "speaking" presence belies his infancy. All putti shown as babes share a certain role with the infant Jesus: speechlessness. St Augustine made the witty observation that God let the "word" become incapable of speech as it passed to the infant Jesus. *Infans* in Latin means unable to speak.[7]

Another putto, gazing heavenward, thrusts out his hands in an attempt to shield his eyes from the blinding light. Then there is the angel proffering a pot of ink for John's quill pen, leaving the saint's left hand free for rhetorical exclamation.

An eagle, another emblematic conceit, emerges awkwardly and provocatively from between John's legs. A visual narrative is an all-at-once phenomenon rather than something unfolding in time, although one does *read* – it is not simply a matter of "looking at" – a picture. And this takes time. Working in the restricted space of a pendentive, Domenichino had few choices of where to put the necessary emblem of an eagle; but surely he could have been less phallic in his choice. The saint's spread legs create both a perceptual and conceptual frame for the eagle. According to tradition, it was Jerome who associated John with the eagle because of the soaring language at the beginning of his gospel: "In the beginning was the Word, and the Word was with God, and the Word was God."

A third angel supports the folio-sized text of his gospel. Hovering within layers of dense meteorological puffs, suggesting a level of the firmament, are two clutching and affectionate putti, enacting a prosopopoeia of Cupid and Psyche and probably also suggesting John's so-called "gospel of love."[8] Lower in the empyrean (at least in terms of literal altitude within the church) stands a foreshortened stone angel, confronting us with yet another ontological realm: his right hand touches his heart as if he were pledging fidelity, while he holds in his left the martyr's palm leaf. What does he mean? Why is he "stone" rather than "flesh"? Why does he turn up on three out of four of the pendentives?

John's hands both break the triangular frame, as does the crown of his head, all of which thrusts him into a higher realm, one where he figuratively exceeds the speed of light as he moves into hyperspace. In Christian and Greek cosmologies this sphere is the empyrean, the highest heaven, the realm of fire, a dominion in which Euclidian geometry no longer exists.

John was at Gethsemane and before that at the Transfiguration. No stranger to profound struggles, he held Mary at the Crucifixion. Inspired by the Holy Spirit and assisted by the heavenly hierarchy, here in his ethereal world he will write his gospel and the book of Revelation. This "empyrean" is, as we have seen, the pendentive built by Carlo Maderno. But it is also the church designed by Maderno and Giacomo della Porta, which in turn was protected by Cardinal Alessandro Peretti di Montalto and controlled by the Theatines. Each of these realms I am enumerating has a diegetic claim on Domenichino's fresco and our – the viewers' – attention. These spatial-temporal worlds are nesting ontologies.

Insofar as I am discriminating levels of ontology as realms within realms of representation, I could be framing this discussion with Peircian semiotics and Gérard Genette's diegeses. Doing so suggests that on the one hand, Peirce's that is, I might be distinguishing between and among icon, index, and symbol; on the other hand (Genette's), I could discriminate the homodiegetic from the heterodiegetic or the extradiegetic, and so on. For my purposes, however, I am not drawing such fine demarcations: Génette's more basic reference to "spatio-temporal realms" strikes me as adequate for my purposes (although there are many shades and nuances within these realms). Also, I can avoid the problem of the author/artist's narration, something to which both Plato and Génette pay close attention. Here is what Plato said (by way of the *Oxford English Dictionary*, which I use for its succinctness): "Although Plato and Aristotle use *mimesis* to refer generally to the imitation of nature in art, both also use the term more specifically. Plato contrasts two types of speech: the author's own narrative voice (*diegesis*) and the 'imitated' voice of a character (*mimesis*). Aristotle extended this use to encompass imitative action as well as speech." Obviously there is narrative in painting, but the authorial voice may be a phenomenon more appropriate to literary than visual narration. There is still the matter of personal style in painting, of course, something with which I will deal later on.

But first comes a digression on a fairly elementary if important point about the baroque visual conceit. A conceit behaves metaphorically, both visually and, as the name implies, conceptually; at the same time, the conceit is both sensuously and intellectually rhetorical. Domenichino's tropological mélange of a fictive marble statue – along with hugging putti, angelic assistants, and hovering cherubim – operates like some occult process, not just as ornament.

Beginning with the Arcadian critics and their insistence in the latter part of the 1600s and early part of the next century upon *buon gusto*, the baroque phenomenon – referred to alternately as *concettismo* and *secentismo* – tended to bear the brunt of dismissive attitudes that treated metaphor as adjunctive (like an adjective, something added on and therefore demoted to a subordinate status) and "merely" ornamental. As Jacques Derrida defines the *supplement*, it is an addition, a "subaltern instance."[9] But the process and function, both as province and undertaking, of the baroque conceit was anything but so much fluff or icing on the cake.

Domenichino's conceit extends to the four pendentives supporting the dome (each with its own evangelist) of Sant'Andrea della Valle and then moves outward towards the vault and downward to the wall surfaces of the apse, all of which are covered with events in St Andrew's life.

Just down the street (the modern Via Vittorio Emanuele, roughly comparable to the early-modern Via Papalis) from Sant'Andrea della Valle is another early Counter-Reformation and post-Tridentine church, the Jesuit basilica of Il Gesù, 1568–84. If one goes straight to the crossing and looks up at the pendentives, painted by Giovanni Battista Gaulli (Il Baciccio) in the 1670s (Figure 9.2), he or she finds similar rhetoric to that deployed by Domenichino at Sant'Andrea della Valle. Here is one more Counter-Reformation church with figures painted on pendentives. The difference of course lies with Baciccio, working with Gianlorenzo Bernini's advice and assistance, creating much denser visual worlds, ones in which *all* the Evangelists (on the southwest pendentive) pile into the same somewhat warped triangular space, gesturing and looking every which way.[10] Baciccio carries off a metaphysical conceit, showing himself as ingenious, as one who achieves a *difficulté vaincue*. He practises sprezzatura, in other words, with his apparently effortless execution of a difficult task, thereby drawing attention to his poetic skill and painterly élan. These witty, ingenious, inventive images exist in a heavenly realm, which, when seen represented on the pendentive, coalesce in one's mind as cunning and many-layered signification.

Baciccio shows us a teeming world of four evangelists in a readily apparent painterly universe, one that seems to exist. Of course the fictive world's existence depends upon Baciccio's ability to create it; at the same time, once fashioned, the artist's imagined world gains independent status.[11]

As I have suggested, there is not enough room for everyone, so Luke gets pushed to the back while angels and evangelical attributes crowd in as best they can, adding to this sense of highly coordinated rumble-tumble. Matthew has his angel; Luke his painting of the Blessed Virgin Mary; the curly-haired John, pen in hand and book at the ready, gestures broadly and looks to heaven (Gaulli undoubtedly studied Domenichino's fresco); and finally Mark, right hand on his heart and left holding a page of his gospel (his faithful lion just glimpsed looking off into the background), inclines his head and smiles at us below in a universal gesture of good will and familiarity. Although both physically

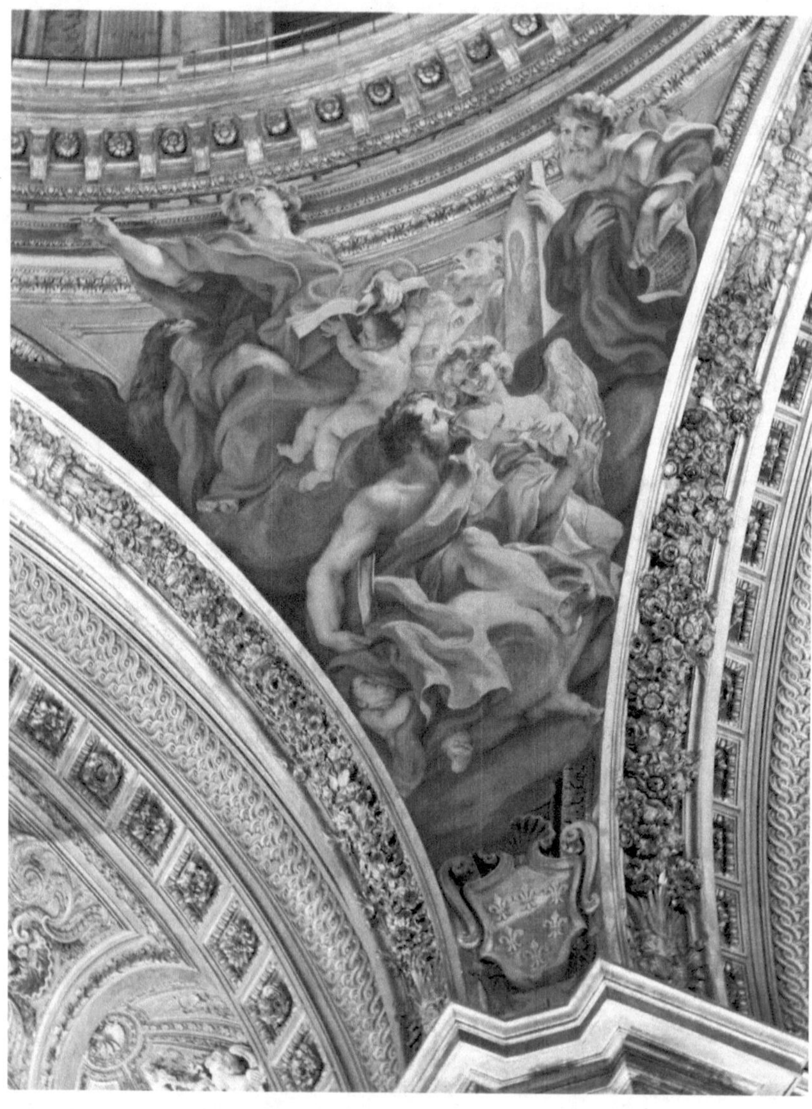

Figure 9.2 Giovanni Battista Gaulli (Il Baciccio), *The Evangelists*, fresco, 1672, ceiling pendentive, Il Gesù, Rome, Italy. Photo: Author.

and conceptually joined in a single pendentive space, the evangelical apparatuses, these emblematic conceits in other words, constitute a different ontological realm from the one in which the evangelical figures find themselves. In fact, John's quill pen, while not literal, is three-dimensional and casts a physical shadow on the moulding of the drum supporting the dome. Although Baciccio paints the emblems with the same degree of verisimilitude as he does the evangelists, they live in another world.

One confronts rippling and oscillating drapery, fully modelled and intensely expressive faces, active subordinate figures, and various kinds of angels. These powerfully alive figures live *their* world, which is not ours but is one filled with being and time, its own spatiotemporal world, one awash in visual conceits.

We know that what lies outside this realm belonging to space-time is the microworld of Il Gesù, but *where* exactly are the evangelists? Merleau-Ponty addresses this difficulty of locating images that have no location, like the animals in the caves as Lascaux: "my gaze wanders within it as in the halos of being. Rather than seeing it, I see according to, or with it."[12] Images are part of the visible, are made of the visible, but somehow elude us; Merleau-Ponty writes of a visible to the second power. But there is and always has been a relationship of the space or world of the artwork and ours. It is precisely that relationship that holds us in thrall.

We as art historians often look at paintings in terms of *being* rather than time – they exist, having persisted *through* time, which is, I suppose, why assigning them a fairly precise date has traditionally been important to art historians. That is not to say we are indifferent to narrative, the *istoria*, which is an arrangement of figures suggesting action, movement, and change. Yet we tend to concentrate more on theme and subject matter, not to mention documentation, than on the *world* within the narration and the painting. As I have just suggested, these figures by Baciccio and Domenichino have their worlds, and so we can and should impute their being and time, attempting to uncover and explicate the various kinds of fictional narratives.

Because we live our times, not just live *in* them, Heidegger has put being and time together.[13] Being, in other words, is not the essence *in* or *of* things but is becoming. It seems to be especially true of baroque painting – and Baciccio embraces the essence of *secentismo* – that the *affetti* of the *dramatis personae* have a higher coefficient of vitality, that baroque art somehow comes alive in ways we do not see in preceding centuries. Therefore, these paintings are not outside of time, despite their apparent lack of *istoria*, of narrative in other words.

The evangelists live their fictional being and their fictional time in the imaginary narrative pendentive space fashioned by Baciccio. This is obviously true in the sense that on one existential level the paintings are so many pigments aging on plaster (as I also pointed out with Domenichino's pendentive fresco); but in their imaginative reality they exist as in a clearing or opening (Heidegger's *Lichtung*), which frames their narrative and constitutes their spatiotemporal world. This *Lichtung* does not require the presence of brilliant light but functions more as a place of enabling, of lightening and lifting, assuaging and alleviating, which creates a buoyant sense of an imagined world like the one we have here in Il Gesù. Heidegger's opening can be set against a background or horizon of culture, where there are rules and expectations generally shared by a community, which here are the Jesuits, the faithful, and the intellectuals – the cognoscenti – then and now.

First of all, these paintings are ontic, entities with facts about them, the basic stuff of art history; but they are also *Sein* – "Being" itself. One cannot exist without the other. We can launch an ontological study of the frescoes with their narratives, which puts us a step beyond the ontic (things that *are* or *happen*, as well as facts about them), and query the Being and the fictional existence of these dramatis personae.

I will switch my language somewhat at this point, having declared my Heideggerian allegiances, to something narratological, specifically the diegetic, while keeping in mind *being* and imagined presences. The almost crushed putto struggling to hold up the cloud into which Matthew seems to be sinking, as if into a plush chair; the winsome angel ticking off points with his fingers; and the chunky child doing the best he can as John's desk – all these flesh out and comment upon the heavenly scene. Like marginalia in medieval manuscripts, these angelic creatures are not the primary actors; however, their peripheral narration, their supplementarity in other words, both subverts and controls the primary *allegoresis*.

The angels can also be thought of as subsidiary focalizers who draw our attention to the embedded narrators, the evangelists. The narratives created by Matthew, Mark, Luke, and John become rooted in the larger narrative painted by Baciccio and create their own diegetic worlds or world-concepts, ones with which the putative viewers of the pendentives already have some familiarity.

The rough-hewn Matthew, tax collector and host to Jesus when He sat with publicans and sinners ("I am not come to call the righteous but sinners to repentance" – Matthew 6:13), apparently relies on a gorgeous wavy-haired blond angel with beatific smile, eyes the size of plums ("The eye is the lamp of the body; so then if your eye is clear, your whole body will be full of light" – Matthew 6:22), and beautifully articulate fingers counting off the points of Matthew's gospel (descent, birth, and infancy of Jesus; Galilean ministry; mission of the apostles, and so on). Matthew's bronzed, muscled arm contrasts with the near whiteness – a pale gold translucence – of the angel. The acknowledging angel gazes at us, breaking free of the absorption often required by narrative. We as viewers occupy an indeterminate zone outside the fictional world. We see the angel; he (Thomas Aquinas refers to angels as masculine) in turn spots us. The angel is in a place somewhat above and behind Matthew; he also has a body, although the angelic nature, as Aquinas tells us in the *Summa Theologica*, is insubstantial. Our angel assumes a "physical" presence, in other words, so that he can have a place and make eye contact with us.[14] His presence is epistemic in the sense of the visual knowledge we infer from Baciccio's fictive realm, which dwells within the spatio-temporal world of a frescoed pendentive in Il Gesù.

Baciccio does not, at least in my reading of the scene, make clear whether Matthew knows there is an angel next to him: the Evangelist seems to look past the angel and towards the light, a source or place of inspiration, ignoring the one who in fact should be his guiding light. The overlooked angel strikes me as acting a bit conspiratorial, as if he and we know something Matthew does not. Baciccio wittily subverts, in other words, the evangelist's status. Tesauro describes *argutezza* – wit – as the divine offspring of intelligence (*ingegno*).[15] Despite his eyes wide open, our witty angel "winks" at us: "Matthew doesn't know I'm here, but you do; and we both know he needs my help," we might imagine him saying. One need only think of the "*analfabetico*" (illiterate) Matthew in Caravaggio's "first" St Matthew in the Contarelli Chapel of San Luigi dei Francesi (Rome). Although rejected for (one assumes) its lack of decorum, the painting calls attention to Matthew's low status (he was a tax collector) and lack of learning (although historical evidence suggest a highly literate Matthew). Baciccio indulges in a certain degree of persiflage or bantering, a bit of flippant intertextual communing with a long-dead brother-in-arms and fabulist.

Thomas Aquinas's explanation for why angels assume a body is that they do it "not for themselves, but on our account; that by conversing familiarly with men they may give evidence of that intellectual companionship which men expect to have with them in the life to come."[16] Aquinas's explanation may persuade us that our tousle-haired angel is "conversing familiarly" with us as well as the shades of our ancestors.

At the bottom of Baciccio's fresco, where the empyrean clouds fade away and the celestial sphere comes to its end, a bit of the "firmament" obscures the corner of a scalloped ridge framing the Farnese coat of arms. Cardinal Alessandro Farnese, who trumpeted on the church's exterior frieze his foundational role in the construction of Il Gesù, finds here his heraldic representation, with six *fleurs-de-lys*, marginally obscured. The Jesuits, we know, loved heraldry and emblems, publishing as many as 600 titles in 1700 editions. In a witty and small gesture of disruption, Baciccio with a wedge of plaster and the illusion of a shadow metaphorically puts his thumb over a corner of Cardinal Farnese's religious propaganda and personal identity.

I can think of no greater challenge to a diegetic (or ontological – by which I mean much the same thing) reading of a baroque image than one confronts when standing beneath Baciccio's *Adoration of the Holy Name of Jesus* on the main vault of Il Gesù (although Andrea Pozzo's *Mission of the Jesuits* is not far behind). One's sense of the fictional spatiotemporal realm reels at the prospect of sorting out the artist's multiple worlds (Figure 9.3).

The Copernican and Galilean cosmology informed by a superhuman (perhaps even angelic) "eye" – the *cannocchiale* (telescope) – allows us to see a plurality of worlds subject to the uniformity of circular motion and put them into an infinite space rather than restricted spheres. Baciccio pictures his worlds as uniformities in an immeasurable realm.

John Donne wrote,

And new philosophy calls all in doubt,
The element of fire is quite put out,
The sun is lost, and th'earth, and no man's wit
Can well direct him where to look for it.
And freely men confess that this world's spent,
When in the planets and the firmament
They seek so many new; they see that this
Is crumbled out again to his atomies.
'Tis all in pieces, all coherence gone,
All just supply, and all relation;

Prince, subject, father, son, are things forgot,
For every man alone thinks he hath got
To be a phoenix, and that then can be
None of that kind, of which he is, but he.

– "The First Anniversary,"
An Anatomy of the World (1611)

While Donne laments the new cosmology and sees its danger as tied to the Jesuits, I would imagine Baciccio welcomed it and that he, too, saw himself as a phoenix.[17]

Leon Battista Alberti's perspectival "window," which he seems to have introduced into his writing for heuristic reasons, is a relatively simple metaphor about artistic space compared to what happens on Baciccio's ceiling, where there is no vanishing point, no orthogonal, no horizon.

The one who has done the best at sorting out the scenes and spatial development of the great vault of the Gesù is Robert Enggass, whose 1964 monograph on Giovanni Battista Gaulli remains an important reference. I rely on him for identifications and placement of scenes.[18]

Once he finished with the pendentives in 1677, Baciccio turned to frescoing the great vault of the Jesuits' mother church. By the end of 1679 the scaffolding was down, and according to the diary of Paolo Ottolini, on the last day of the year a mass was celebrated and people – *"che fu in gran numero"* – rushed in to see the new fresco, enjoying it with *"gran plauso."* The crowds returned on New Year's Day.[19]

Here was Baciccio's opportunity to allegorize in monumental terms the name of Jesus, drawing upon Paul's letter to the Philippians: "Wherefore God also hath highly exalted him, and given him a name which is above every other name: that at the name of Jesus every knee should bow, of things in heaven and things in earth and things under the earth" (Philippians 2:9–11). Paul also asseverates that "every tongue confess that Jesus Christ is Lord." The name of Jesus overwhelms the people of the earth, as Baciccio's fresco overwhelmed those Romans who saw it then and still does those who see it now.

But the significance of the Philippians passage that Baciccio illustrates may not just be a matter of asserting the epideictic mode of rhetoric so as to astound the visiting crowds and the worshipping congregation. In other words, despite what one remembers about Pope Nicholas V's phrase "We build to impress," there may be here something more than a baroque tendency to overpower with visual artifices.[20]

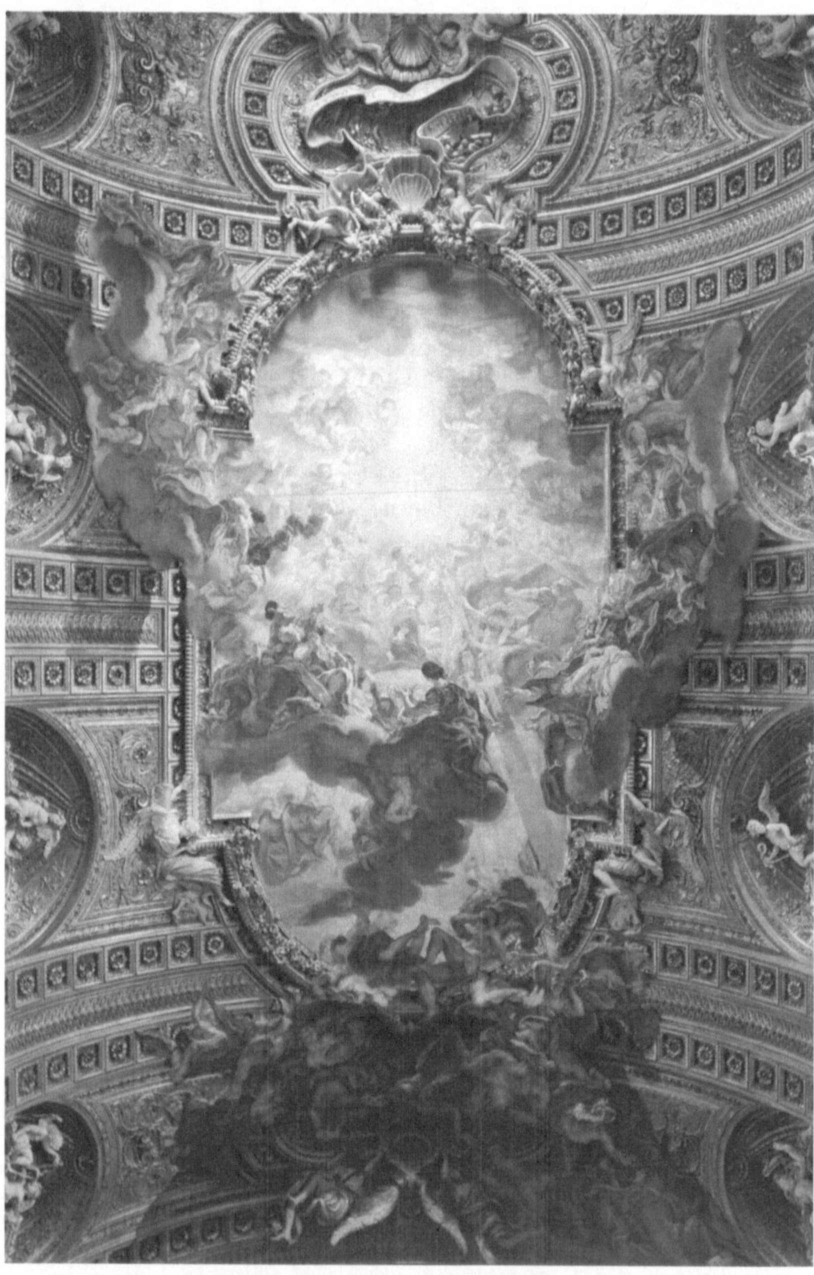

Figure 9.3 Giovanni Battista Gaulli (Il Baciccio), *Adoration of the Holy Name of Jesus*, fresco, 1672–85, Il Gesù, Rome, Italy. Photo: Author.

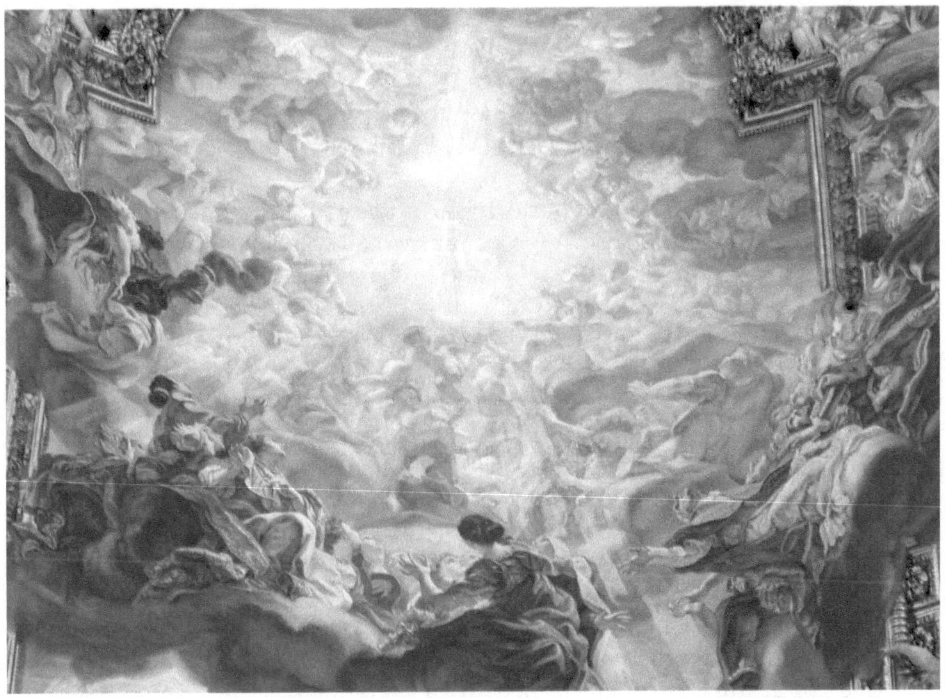

Figure 9.4 *Adoration of the Holy Name of Jesus*, detail of "IHS." Photo: Author.

Just as we find in Philippians, there is exaltation over every knee bending and every tongue confessing at the name of Jesus, and therefore of the Jesuits, who almost certainly chose the passage and determined its meaning for their specific church and mission. We know that from his prison cell Paul attempted in his letter to the Philippians to refute a rival gospel proposed by "Judaizing Christian itinerants"[21] who had appeared in Philippi, an ancient town in Macedonia. His letter therefore falls into the category of deliberative rhetoric; that is, he appeals to the better nature of the Philippians, relying on praise and optimism to reprove his friends. As a good *rhetor*, Paul (in the words of Duane Watson) "must avoid the impression of being abusive or proud, yet refer to his good faith, recite his acts of service, and present himself as struggling against difficulties and misfortunes. Also, he can make it clear that he addresses the audience out of a sense of duty to friends and because of a serious moral consideration."[22] By the time Paul reaches the "exemplification," in which everyone bends his knee at the name of Jesus – the scene represented by Baciccio – we have an appeal to humility. "We" Philippians, in other words, when marvelling at Baciccio's ceiling, bend our knees in meekness at God's power, Jesus's grace, and the Jesuit mission. Then comes verse 12: "Therefore, my beloved, as you have always obeyed, so now, not only as in my presence but much more in my absence, work out your own salvation with fear and trembling." We have seen in our discussion of Sant'Ivo alla Sapienza that fear and trembling is a "profitable sorrow" and prepares one for grace.

Baciccio's scene comes in the middle of the six verses (2:6–11) read every Palm Sunday and Good Friday in the Catholic liturgy. This passage is called the "*kenosis* hymn," which has to do with emptying or being obedient, which Jesus did when living his human life. Then of course comes the triumph of Him and His name.

Within the fresco itself there are several zones. First of all, the letters "IHS" – the monogram for the Holy Name of Jesus – hovers in the centre of the empyrean (Figure 9.4). Enggass prepared a drawing superimposed on a cross section of Il Gesù that shows in approximate terms what it might look like to study Baciccio's illusionistic space from the side. The blessed – according to our quasi-schematic rendering, our "depth" chart – occupy a cone-like space (the widening part of an upside-down funnel), with the angels lodging in a heavenly cylindrical or tube-like area where they sing "Hosanna in excelsis Deo" – praise to God (actually Jesus) in Heaven (Figure 9.5). It is what the crowds sung before Christ's Crucifixion. And then arranged outside the device framing the central part of the fresco are images of the damned being cast into hell, out of the light and into John Milton's "darkness visible."

Before bearing down on Baciccio's various ontological divides, I will comment on how he sets up his special effects and creates the illusion of a heavenly realm within and, in illusionistic terms, outside Il Gesù. It was fairly short work for Baciccio to create an ornamented vault with three-dimensional coffers upon which stucco figures, many of them angels by Antonio Raggi and Leonardo Retti, were attached at various points on the ceiling and the window surrounds. We have, therefore, the three-dimensional reality of the sculptural figures, the three-dimensional coffers of the ceiling, and then figures painted in true fresco technique on plaster moulded to represent the clear air of Heaven, as well as various clouds bearing the damned into hell.

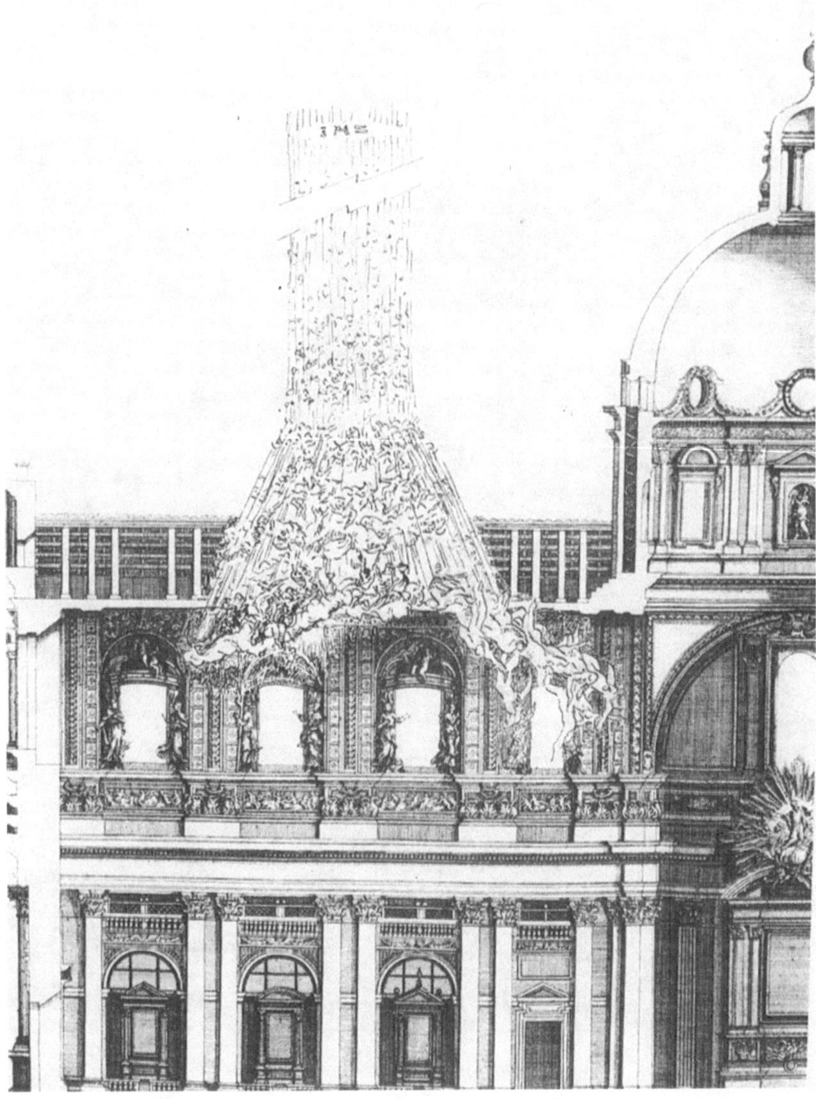

Figure 9.5 Longitudinal representation of a section of the nave of Il Gesù, Rome, Italy. Photo: Glenn Ruby.

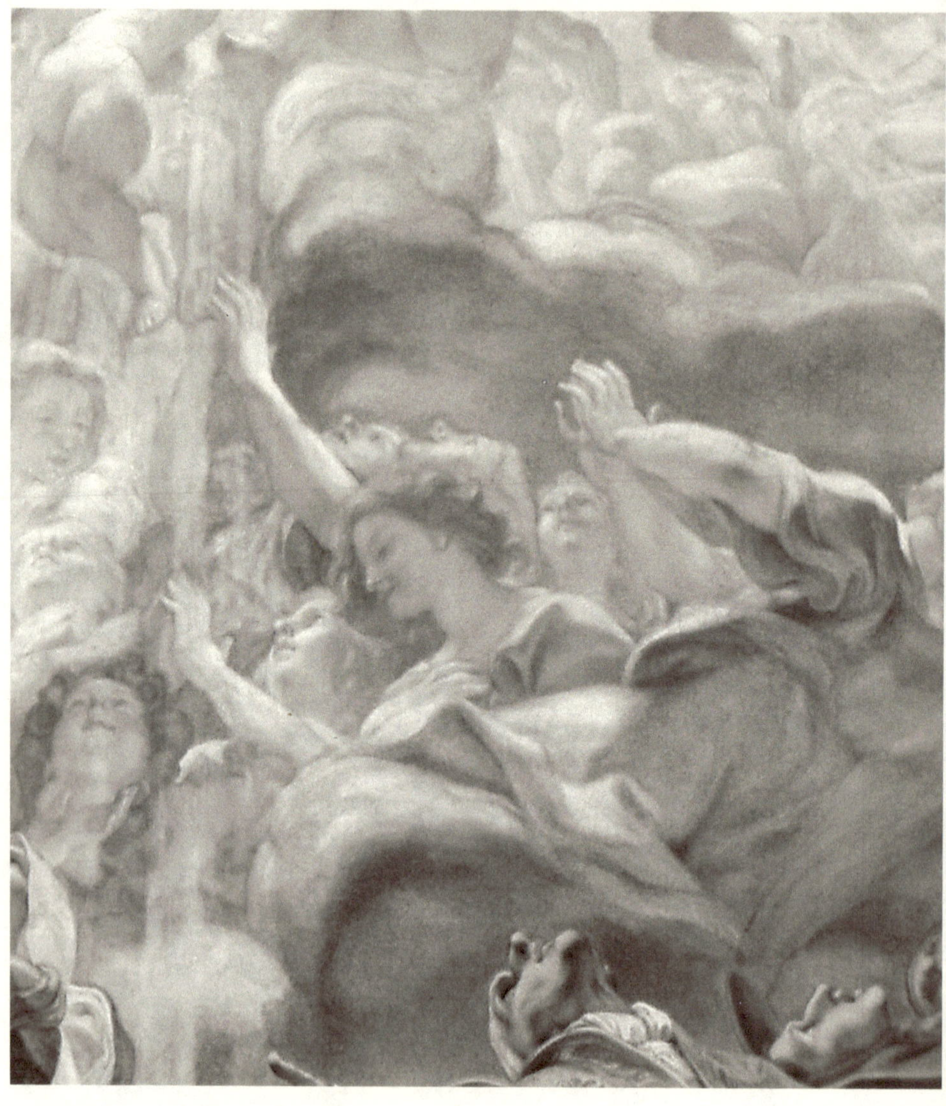

Figure 9.6 *Adoration of the Holy Name of Jesus*, detail of angels. Photo: Author.

This of course is truly one of those experiences in which words do not adequately express what is going on. Rhetorically speaking, my statement that "words cannot express" is an adynaton – an inexpressibility stratagem; but, in fact, the statement *really is* prosaically true. You *really* have to be there.

The naked cherubim and seraphim tumble about in the empyrean realm (Figure 9.6); larger (frequently smiling) angels arrange themselves in ranks a bit farther out from the refulgence of the monogram IHS (the first three Roman letters of the *Greek* word for Jesus).

Angels are mentioned in Scripture, and even the numbers of their wings are enumerated in Isaiah 6:2 and Ezekiel 1:6. Their ranks had pretty well been established since the Fourth Lateran Council of 1215, when the church determined that angels were created before humankind. Next came Thomas Aquinas's disquisition on angels, which was taken as an article of faith.

Aquinas relied upon, among other texts, Pseudo-Dionysius the Areopagite's angelology for his "Treatise on the Angels" in the *Summa Theologica*. Pseudo-Dionysius the Areopagite, author of the *Celestial Hierarchy*, was in all likelihood a Syrian Neoplatonist who lived in the late fifth or earlier sixth century CE, although in the seventeenth century many (especially the Jesuits) believed he was the man whom Paul converted when he preached in Athens: "So Paul, standing in the midst of the Areopagus, said: 'Men of Athens, I perceive that in every way you are very religious'" (Acts 17:22). Already by the fifteenth century, Lorenzo Valla had called into question the identity of the author of the *Mystical Theology* and the *Celestial Hierarchy*.

One of Aquinas's "Questions" (52) considers how it can be that an angel relates to a "place," something that bears upon my discussion of a painting's fictional or diegetic world. Aquinas, whom of course the Jesuits studied closely, wrote this:

> It is befitting an angel to be in a place; yet an angel and a body are said to be in a place in quite a different sense. A body is said to be in a place in such a way that it is applied to such place according to the contact of dimensive quantity; but there is no such quantity in the angels, for theirs is a virtual one. Consequently an angel is said to be in a corporeal place by application of the angelic power in any manner whatever to any place.[23]

The aptly named "Angelic Doctor" invokes the virtual world and, as an afterthought almost, adds that angels can appear anywhere they like.

He reviews Dionysius's hierarchies in his own Question 108. Agreeing that there are such orders, Aquinas then concludes, "the nature of a hierarchy requires diversity of orders."[24] Those closest to the Supreme Being are the seraphim, cherubim, and thrones; the next hierarchy contains dominations, virtues, and powers; principalities, archangels, and angels populate the lowest hierarchy. Scriptures give us only three angelic names: Raphael, Michael, and Gabriel (sometimes Uriel is added). Although John Milton added a throng of new angelic appellations, we cannot point to any specific names among the heavenly host in Baciccio's ceiling. There may be a few historical figures represented, although their identities remain uncertain.

The highest rank of angels, those childlike bodies flitting about in the heavenly maelstrom – this etheric whirlpool – are, as we have seen, the cherubim, seraphim, and thrones, who, according to Dionysius, dance immediately around God, or in this case, the emblematic representation of the name of Jesus.

The monogram of Jesus fashioned by the Jesuits is the IHS, which had been adopted by St Bernardine of Siena in the fifteenth century and then in the seventeenth century was taken up by Ignatius of Loyola as part of his personal seal. Afterward it became the emblem for the Society of Jesus, often shown with a cross raised above the horizontal bar of the "H," as shown in Baciccio's fresco. Some of the naked and therefore innocent angels sprout wings, while others do not, perhaps relating to rank or responsibilities. Some may be "attending" angels as opposed to those who dance about God's refulgence.

The early Jesuit Jerónimo Nadal wrote in in his *Apologia pro Exercitiis S.P. Ignatii* (1554) that Ignatius's *Spiritual Exercises*, based upon the Jesuits' "way of proceeding" (in prayer), to some extent depended upon Dionysius's writings in their development of the three stages of "purgation, illumination, and union."[25] Even well into the seventeenth century, as I have mentioned, nearly all Jesuits believed Dionysius to have been the one to whom Paul preached and who then converted in Athens.

This sixth-century Syrian was not so much an imposter as he was a philosopher who enacted a rhetorical figure known as the *declamation*.[26] Baciccio's frescoes assisted the Jesuits in their prayers and owed much to Dionysius's *Celestial Hierarchy*. As John O'Malley observes, "The correlation of the *Exercises* with the 'ways' of Dionysius served ... two purposes: it further validated the evangelical origins of the *Exercises*, and it broadened their scope beyond the month of retreat to a more general design for a person's spiritual journey throughout life."[27]

An interesting footnote to Dionysius, one that indeed may have some bearing on baroque *zeitgeist*, is that Jacob Bronowski in his *Origins of Knowledge and Imagination*, quoted from Dionysius:

> God's love is universal; it infuses the whole of nature, and it therefore infuses every piece of matter. And, therefore, not only does God's love draw every piece of matter to him, but every piece of matter must be drawn to every other piece.

Bronowski sees a little of Dionysius in Sir Isaac Newton's theories of gravitational attraction between two bodies.[28]

Dionysius begins his writing on the *Celestial Hierarchy* with a quotation from the Gospel according to St James (1:17): "Every good endowment and every perfect gift is from above, coming down from the Father of lights."[29] Dionysius's understanding of what is above and what is below springs from his passion and fixation on hierarchy, which informs his mystical theology: "If one talks then of hierarchy, what is meant is a certain perfect arrangement, an image of the beauty of God which sacredly works out the mysteries of its own enlightenment in the orders and levels of understanding of the hierarchy."[30] The word "hierarchy" itself is probably a neologism coined by Dionysius.

In the anteroom of divinity, the topmost angelic beings – shown as tumbling, somersaulting, pitching, plunging naked infants in Baciccio's fresco – experience primal theophanies, carry warmth with them, are innocent of earthly imaginings, immediately surround Jesus and God, and overflow with incandescence.[31] Cherubim possess wisdom along with the power to know and see God. Thrones always are "upward bearing," climbing infinitely beyond the sky into the purist ether. The dominations, virtues, and powers (also sometimes translated as dominions, authorities, and powers) are in charge of the next rank down; their characteristics are masculine, suggesting control, courage, and authority. The lowest rank of angels constitutes those who have communication and association with both humans and their nations. This rank consists of the principalities, archangels, and angels. As a group they tend to be guardians who assist people and convey visions to humankind. They help sustain the material world. Dionysius also writes that "all angels bring revelations and tidings of their superiors."[32]

The Jesuits had a clear and detailed understanding of Dionysius's *Celestial Hierarchy*. There were many editions of his writings in the seventeenth century alone. Bernini's own *Cathedra Petri* (see chapter 10) reflects a deep and abiding interest in the celestial as well as ecclesiastical hierarchies. Just the same, trying to read Baciccio's *Adoration of the Holy Name of Jesus* as a detailed and faithful illustration of the *Celestial Hierarchy* can be misleading. First of all, no work of art can be exhaustively interpreted by reference to a single text: that, as we know, is not how critical discourse works. There are other reasons, too, why one needs to be cautious when reading, interpreting, and applying the *Celestial Hierarchy*, which does not easily lend itself to visual representation. Dionysius insists on the *via negativa*, the back door to the divine, when he explains,

> High-flown shapes could well mislead someone into thinking that the heavenly beings are golden or gleaming men, glamorous, wearing lustrous clothing, giving off flames which cause no harm, or that they have other similar beauties with which the word of God has fashioned the heavenly minds. It was to avoid this kind of misunderstanding among those incapable of rising above visible beauty that the pious theologians so wisely and upliftingly stooped to incongruous dissimilarities, for by doing this they took account of our inherent tendency toward the material and our willingness to be lazily satisfied by base images.[33]

And second, the iconography is, before anything else, related to the Jesuits, their mission, and – to a certain but limited extent – Ignatius's *Spiritual Exercises*. Nonetheless, I believe that much of the sense of Baciccio's work at Il Gesù is rooted in the kind of ecclesiology and Christian mystical Neoplatonism represented by such a text as the *Celestial Hierarchy*. Also, I am trying to draw an analogy between and among these numinous spiritual traditions and baroque art. And in this essay, I am exploring what I have called the diegetic and the ontological, which are evident in Baciccio's techniques for establishing several levels of reality or "world-concepts."

Before attempting any of these critical investigations, I need to continue pointing out in the most literal way I can what is recognizable in Baciccio's frescoes and the stucco work carried out under his direction on the great vault.

As we leave behind the cherubim and seraphim swimming about in the centre of the ceiling, representing Dionysius's first triadic grouping, we see several of those gorgeous angels who seem to have more to do with guardianship and therefore are part of the bottom triad, the grouping of principalities, archangels, and angels. Because they have direct contact with us, these angels appeal to our love of beauty, which is our aesthetic sense. And that is perhaps why Baciccio and other artists of the early-modern period make them so lovely and why they often smile beatifically.

Just below the rosy-cheeked custodian angels there is a group of blessed souls, those who already have joined the ranks of the elect. We read them as outside Baciccio's physical frame; therefore, they appear to be hovering within the confines of the church itself, phenomenal figures in an ontic space. Enggass refers to them occupying "the great arc of the blessed" and writes that they "retain the customary attributes of human form: the sense of weight, mass, clarity of outline, clearly articulated anatomy – in short all the qualities necessary to give the illusion of their immediate and tangible existence."[34]

Women gather in the centre, while men spread to the outer zones. On the side farthest from the damned tumbling into the dark abyss are the three Magi, and on the other is a figure of a pope with his arms spread, a prototype of St Ignatius, as Enggass observes.[35] Furthermore, there are a king and a cardinal, "then an aged cleric with a white beard, perhaps Cardinal Alessandro Farnese, offering up to heaven a model of the church of the Gesù."[36]

The greatest drama occurs at the opposite end of the fresco, where the blinding light emanating from the Sacred Monogram of Jesus thunders to the edge of the frame and casts the damned into darkness, created simply by a shadow, a gloaming that spreads menacingly over the cursed, doomed souls (see Figure 9.3). Two fully modelled, powerful angels struggle to sustain Baciccio's parergon (frame); they share glances with one another as if calculating the struggle and commiserating over the strain of such a superhuman (nearly super-angelic) feat. They are half in the hellish shadow, half in blessed radiance. Neither the shadow nor the light we see here exists in the real world of Il Gesù; it owes its existence to Baciccio's trickery and illusion. In narratological terms the viewer – and I mean the viewer in the church, not the one looking at a photograph – undergoes a deictic shift. For those who study visual and literary narratology, a deictic shift occurs when the viewer (in our case) relocates his or her space/time coordinates to those created by the artist. We put ourselves, in other words, into a cognitive structure and location – a "storyworld" – created by Baciccio.[37] In this one there seems to be much fear and general trembling.

Bare-breasted women and naked swarthy men twist like anguineous creatures (Milton's "infernal serpent"?) pummelled by "super-essential winds" (a phrase used by Dionysius) as they fall almost on our heads, roiling our atmosphere and barrelling down into the pit of Hell. The "what" of Baciccio's story is the power emanating from the monogram IHS; the "how" is the style, the anguish, the *narrating* of the story, the whole passion and presentation, the energy and vortices, grief and gnashing of teeth, the ecstasy followed by the agony – the telling of the story, the sections and layers of its (not *our*) world.

Ignatius famously told his exercitants, those who followed the *Spiritual Exercises*, to hear the screams of hell, smell the sulphur, feel the heat. Baciccio and Bernini read his book.

Walking into Il Gesù to see this fresco already puts one into a controlled and, for many, unfamiliar environment, one of great scale with its own poetics of space, its own existential feel. So, in a sense, one may be doubly disoriented and doubly enfolded into the storyworld, this dramatic, baroque, fictive experience.

The angels struggling to maintain the margins of heaven – those who are caught in two different lights as they bear up the contours of Heaven, while miraculous light spews the damned into hellish darkness, all by way of justifying the ways of God to men – maintain the boundary between Heaven and Hell. Simultaneously, other angels – graceful, baroque, and unlaboured – work as stage managers holding the rest of the frame in place.

The stucco coffering, painted in gold and blue, echoes ceiling treatments in Roman churches going back centuries. In other words, it appears as something eminently Roman and not particularly remarkable, until, of course, we see what Baciccio has done with it. The context of the frame surrounding and giving way to the river of damned souls is not in the same context as is the frame that opens the rest of the ceiling to a heavenly vista. Those stucco angels who hold the frame at a distance from hellish disturbance while Heaven disgorges sinners and some fallen angels (the occasional cherub finds himself in the maelstrom) seem buoyed by the task, basking in their own super-essential winds.

The wind pushes an angel's hair forward from a cowlick low on the back of his head and at the same time creates eddying patterns in his long, diaphanous gown. The puckered and agitated stucco, feigning, as I suggest, lustrous garments, are fiery (metaphor) or fire-like (simile – but one still part of the metaphorical discourse) patterns. "Visual conceiving" for Bernini and Baciccio often demands visual metaphor.[38] The undulating double and triple vines in the background, patterns of Baciccio's gilded and stuccoed ceiling, combined with the rosettes set into the blue background panels framed by egg-and-dart mouldings are not simply standard decorative motifs but work efficiently as a whole creating the fiery setting of Dionysius's heavenly hierarchy. The importance of light is, as we have seen with Dionysius's introduction to the *Celestial Hierarchy*, about "The Father of lights." "We must lift up the immaterial and steady eyes of our minds to that outpouring of Light which is so primal, indeed much more so, and which comes from that source of divinity."[39]

What we can be sure of is the need by Jesuits and every other sort of person occupying Rome in the later seventeenth century for storytelling, for making of their existence and their lives an imaginative narrative. Their motivations were pious as well as related to power and social position. Who gets to tell and show the greater narrative controls meaning and shapes the way to ultimate truth and, being simply human, tries to make sense of the wholeness of his existence along with his "storyable" place within the cosmos, world, and time.

10 Bernini and the Metaphor of the Fiery Angel

In the apse of the Roman Catholic Church's greatest basilica, Gianlorenzo Bernini and his patron Pope Alexander VII Chigi created an altarpiece unsurpassed in scale and richness and unparalleled in ecclesiastical and celestial meaning. The *Cathedra Petri* (Figure 10.1) is at once a summation of the millennial relationship between art and religion, a complex of signs, symbols, and metaphors that brings to mind a wealth of associations and meanings sometimes older than the church itself, and a *concetto* for a mystical theology that provides the mind's road to God.[1]

Although the empty throne, an image of divine power, is the centre of the composition and a potent symbol, I suspect that Bernini was more interested in the angels, those holy and fiery messengers whose convulsive drapery patterns, especially on the two flanking the throne, led to a style that most expressively plumbs the depths of his religious consciousness. It seems to me that an interpretation of the angels requires more than the traditional iconographical analysis. Bernini's angels achieve the rhetorical status of visual metaphors.

One of the texts that informs this monument is Dionysius the Pseudo-Areopagite's *Celestial Hierarchy*, which figures prominently in my chapter 9. Dionysius's *Celestial Hierarchy* appeared in more than 100 editions throughout the seventeenth century.[2] In this text, which provides an anagogical method for achieving mystical union with God, the believer ascends by contemplating signs and fixing his attention on the archetypes or ideas that lie behind and above them. Dionysius's two hierarchies (clearly represented in the *Cathedra*) enable the worshipper to ascend through the agency of the clergy, the sacraments, the angels, and the light of God, which Bernini renders as a "cascade of illumination" (Dionysius's phrase) – a dynamic, flowing visual text.

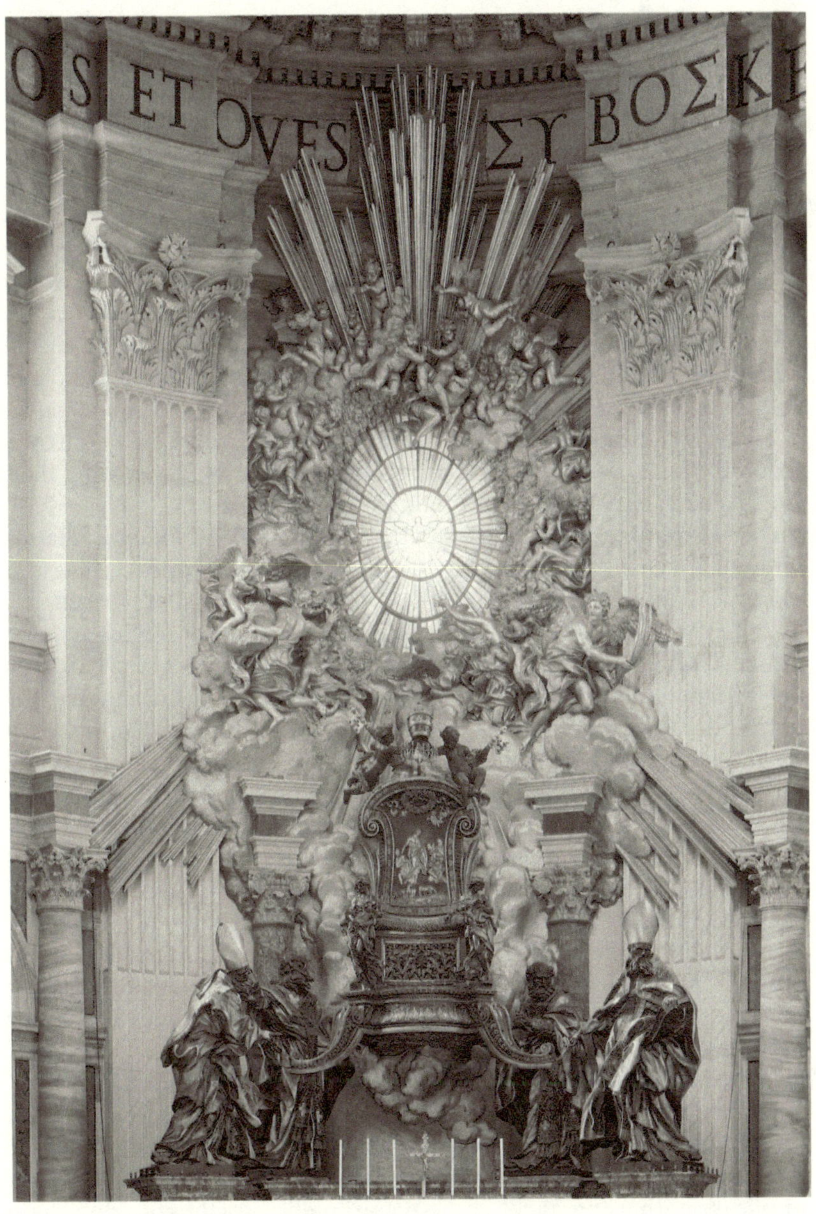

Figure 10.1 Gianlorenzo Bernini, *Cathedra Petri*, gilt bronze, marble, and stucco, 1624–33, St Peter's Basilica, Vatican City (Rome), Italy. Photo: Scala/Art Resource, NY.

The *Cathedra* is not connected with the whole mystical experience itself but provides a Dionysian path to a particular mystical moment where the I/Soul meets God beyond the sensory.

Dionysius writes of the fiery likeness of angels and asserts the appropriateness of fire as simile: "I think then, the similitude of fire denotes the likeness of the Heavenly Minds to God in the highest degree," for fire is pure, immaterial, and of hidden essence.[3] That Bernini does not have the figures merely holding torches – although someone saw fit to add candelabra, doubting perhaps the efficacy of Bernini's visual metaphor – but instead finds a way to have them *express* fire, results in their becoming active agents in the process of religious consciousness.

These angels as celestial attendants (hence no wings) demonstrate that the "Godly wise ... depict the celestial Beings as fire, sharing their Godlikeness, and imitation of God so far as attainable."[4] The axis of each of Bernini's angels describes a long, sinuous, flame-like "S." Hands without bones undulate like vapours of heat. Bernini varies outline and pattern between the two: on our left, the angel's silhouette breaks up as twisting lengths of material are filled with air and coil away from arm and hip; the other's garments remain closer to his body. Currents of air seem to blow the drapery across the abdomen of the angel on the left, under a stabilizing arm, and unexpectedly back again, between his legs, to fan out, held there by some "super-essential" wind. Wind, as Dionysius maintains, "bears a likeness and type of the supremely Divine energy."[5] Edges of folds form striations that reinforce the feeling that a current is invisibly moving about the angel and is warmed by his heat. Between the ridges of cloth run deep rivulets, filled with shadows that set up flickering patterns of light and shade. On the other angel, the drapery folds are flatter, the sense of movement less nervous. All the same, the long curving lines of material move like flames; both are empyrean, fiery creatures. Fire is a conceit (*concetto*) because Bernini never shows flame. In effect he reveals the angelic essence – an incorporeal mind – both as bodily form, which is its mortal "mask," and through metaphor: the fire. By making the fire allusive rather than descriptive, the sculptor can also suggest that angels are present almost more immanently than spatially: we have the visual evidence, through implication, that the angel is there spiritually. Strictly speaking there can be no physical proof of spiritual existence, except (in this case) through metaphor.

Bernini's use of the angels' robes to portray fire is consistent with Dionysius's remark on the sacred garments: "the shining and glowing raiment, I think, signifies the Divine likeness after the image of fire."[6] Dionysius compares the angels to several materials, one of which, brass, has the "likeness of fire." Bernini gilded the bronze, as he had done to all the stucco angels in the glory, to emphasize this quality.

With this metaphor – the fiery drapery – Bernini shapes the identification between artistic object and mystical idea. The throne below, as an outright symbol, has specific, traditionally established meanings: the chair of St Peter, a bishop's chair, the throne of God, the throne of Christ, and the throne of power. The throne instantiates various universal ideas, but it does so in no very active way. The metaphorical presentation of the angels, on the other hand, creates a dynamic interaction between how we see them materially and how we see them in our mind's eye. There is a tight bond between these two ways of seeing. The symbolic translation arises already from the handling of the drapery, which in turn is the result of its being shaped by the sculptor. What I take to be a primary conveyor of artistic meaning, and simultaneously religious meaning – the currents and folds of drapery – appears in a very unclassical light. Drapery, after all, is an aspect of *disegno,* which in the Renaissance tradition calls for the orderly arrangement of garments over the armature of an ideal nude. Vasari, Dolce, and Pino in the sixteenth century gave unambiguous prescriptions for drapery: the artist, whether painter or sculptor, should show the body and garments as separate entities although simultaneously visible, and thereby create the so-called clothed nude. In the rational, normative sense of *disegno,* the drapery may not cling unnecessarily to the body (*attacato alle carni,* in Dolce's words) but must exhibit a logical sense, *senza confusione,* so that an anatomical and proportional rendering of the human form is not obscured.[7] Of course Bernini had other ideas.

His highly expressive and non-classical drapery patterns do not permit a comparison of ideas as if they were similes or allow the figures to stand merely as substitutions or inert signs for other ideas; rather, they function as metaphors in the sense that Max Black conceives of metaphor: two thoughts together – in this case angelic image and angelic idea – inter-illuminating each other.[8] A literal substitution or comparison process, such as having the angels hold torches to signify "the likeness of the Heavenly Minds to God," in the terms of Dionysius's language, would give rise to a transfer from image to idea that could easily be explained away. The torches could vary in shape, size, or placement and not materially affect the meaning; the form of the work of art would not be relevant to its meaning. As Black explains the process,

> interaction metaphors are not expendable. Their mode of operation requires the reader [in this case the viewer] to use a system of implications ... as a means for selecting, emphasizing, and organizing relations in a different field. This use of a "subsidiary subject" to foster insight into a "principal subject" is a distinctive *intellectual* operation ... demanding simultaneous awareness of both subjects but not reducible to any *comparison* between the two.[9]

Bernini's sense of mystical baroque form, if we follow Black's reasoning, creates a new insight: we have a "simultaneous awareness" of Bernini's angelic form, Dionysius's mystical conceit (fire), and the relationship of the angels to God. The logic or sense informing Bernini's angels is somewhat alien to the classical-humanist tradition of art theory: the interpenetration of modes of thought and visualization creates a new symbolical form in which a work of art refers as strongly to itself as it does to a religious idea. The handling of the work is the vehicle of meaning giving the immanent new power in relation to the transcendent.

Since antiquity, for instance in the *Olympic Discourse* of Dio Chrysostom, one naturally assumed that sculpture could not represent such an intangible element as fire.[10] Similarly, in the seventeenth century, when asked by the painter Cigoli to express his views on the *paragone* – comparing the relative merits of painting and sculpture – Galileo replied that "sculpture imitates more that which is tangible in nature and painting more that which is visible."[11] But he also remarked that "the further removed the means of imitation are from the thing imitated, the more worthy of admiration the imitation will be."[12] Galileo articulated here a sentiment not unlike Domenico Bernini's statement that "art consists in everything being simulated although seeming to be real."[13] The simulation is an illusion that masks the essential dissimilarity between the medium and the image to which it gives rise. In the Aristotelian sense of finding similarity in dissimilarity, Bernini gives us a metaphor. The sculptural illusion of fire, a *difficulté vaincue*, both deceives the worshipper and calls attention to itself as a *meraviglia*. And yet Bernini's achievement is not one of gratuitous stylishness; his shaping of drapery patterns to achieve identification between angel as statue and angel as idea is metaphorical, and by its very nature the metaphor is transcendent and destroys any possibility of an autotelic moment.

11 Blaise Pascal, Jansenists, Jesuits, and the *Lettres Provinciales*

Because the Jansenists and the Jesuits play a significant role in the culture of Rome in the later seventeenth century and throughout the eighteenth, this essay provides some prefatory remarks for the reading of Philippe de Champaigne's paintings that will follow, as well as a discussion of the art of the Roman eighteenth century. I mention here, by way of introduction, what really is a primary "problem" that I wish to consider: the role of Jansenism not only in general culture but in the rhetoric of the visual arts and the arrival of *buon gusto*, or good taste. In his study of Rome in the eighteenth century, Hanns Gross wrote that "a great deal of what happened in Rome during the ancien régime can only be explained in terms of the Jansenist controversy. Even areas beyond the strict confines of theology were shaped by events and thought patterns that on the surface had little to do with the confrontation of Jansenists and Jesuits, but which were still couched in those terms."[1] In my own study of the artistic, religious, and political culture of carly settecento Rome, I made the same assertion, also without providing much evidence, leaving that task for another time.[2] This, then, is that other time.

Acceding to demands and responding to disputes that had reached fever pitch long before his own reign, Pope Clement XIV published on 21 July 1773 his brief of Suppression (*Dominus ac Redemptor*) against the Society of Jesus. The Jesuits, he wrote, from their earliest days "bore the germs of dissensions and jealousies which tore its own members asunder, led them to rise against other religious orders, against the secular clergy and the universities, nay even against the sovereigns who had received them in their states."[3]

As a result of the Suppression, which was revoked in 1814, what had been combative and vociferous in Jesuit rhetoric now grew quiet, with those fathers who wished to continue in the Society fleeing to Prussia and Russia, where the pope's brief was not promulgated. Otherwise, the Jesuits were vanquished; when the dust settled in Rome, the once mighty Society of Jesus was no more. Its buildings, charitable monies, influence, and schools were – all of them – gone. For the purposes of this essay, the most telling of those "dissensions and jealousies" borne by the Jesuits were fomented more than a century earlier by the Jansenists.[4]

The rise of Jansenism played out against the distant background of the Protestant Reformation. Not unlike Luther and his reliance on St Augustine as the one who got orthodoxy right and knew how to calculate the weight of human sin, Cornelius Otto Jansen turned to the Bishop of Hippo to find his religious centre.[5] The story begins in Paris around 1607 when the Fleming Jansen and the Basque Jean du Vergier de Hauranne found themselves locally in opposition to some of the members of the Sorbonne (the Theology Faculty of the University of Paris) and more widely sceptical of Molinism, a Pelagian school of thought on matters of grace and free will developed by the Spanish Jesuit Luis de Molina. The Molinist position, sanctioned by the Council of Trent (and promoted by the Society of Jesus), posited a free will unimpaired by original sin, one that paradoxically for some rested comfortably with the causality or determination of grace. It was not so much the subtlety and fastidiousness of this position that affronted them, although it may have rankled a bit, as it was the effect of such an outlook, one that granted penitents the benefit of the doubt all too often. Though they almost certainly understood the danger of seeming too close to Calvinism, De Hauranne and Jansen desired a religion like that of the early Church Fathers, in particular St Augustine; unlike the Protestants, they had no desire to break with the Roman Church.

In the Sorbonne one heard the usual discussions on Aquinas and Scholasticism, which De Hauranne and Jansen must have felt were empty gestures and tactical moves in an endless theological board game. Nor were they any happier when, as classmates in Louvain, they listened to Justus Lipsius and his Neo-Stoic philosophies. The Jesuits they came to abhor.

The two young men eventually went their separate ways, with Jansen returning to Louvain. There he spent decades on his pièce de résistance, the *Augustinus*, completed in 1638, which was also the year of his death.

It took another two years for the text to be published in Paris, with backing from his friends.

In a short time the book became a sensation, igniting reformative zeal generally but especially at Port-Royal, where Jansen's old friend De Hauranne had become abbot in 1623. The Abbé de Saint-Cyran, as De Hauranne was now known, had been effecting reform with his reliance upon the Augustinianism he and Jansen had been discussing for years. Now he had Jansen's book and the opportunity to foment a revolution in the master discourse of his age – Christian theology.[6]

Because there was no order of Jansenists as there was a Society of Jesus, "Jansenism" and "Jansenists" have become terms of art – rather than descriptions of a tangible organization – used by historians to recognize a period and an episode in history, generally understood to be in France in the middle to later decades of the seventeenth century, with repercussions continuing well into the eighteenth century. Making the followers of Cornelius Jansen and Port-Royal a kind of sect and an "ism" (*Jansénisme* in French, *Giansenismo* in Italian) allowed the Jesuits, who were early promoters of those words, to paint Jansen's followers with the broad brush of the condemned "Five Propositions" (which I discuss briefly next) and, through linguistic allusion, to associate them with "Calvinism" and "Calvinists."

Even if there was no "Society of Jansen," there was indeed a reform movement, one that arrived with a remarkable swiftness, manifesting itself first of all at Port-Royal. Saint-Cyran brought in members of the Arnauld family, led by Antoine, *Le Grand Arnauld*. His sister, La Mère Angélique, who had been at Port-Royal since childhood, became abbess of the convent in Paris. Their father, also Antoine, had done his best – and with some success – to have the Jesuits driven out of France in the last years of the previous century. There were those who referred to this as the "original sin" of the Jansenists, although it predates the *Augustinus* by nearly half a century. The younger Antoine and several of his brothers became "hermits" attached to the old convent at Port-Royal des Champs outside of Paris, while La Mère Angélique continued as abbess at the convent's new location in the capital. In addition to the solitaries in the valley of the Chevreuse and the sisters at the Parisian convent and chapel, many leading writers and intellectuals were part of the community, including Blaise Pascal and Jean Racine. They all found that Jansen's inspired text carried a rare form of excitement that could change peoples' lives. But a religious reform springing from the fertile soil of popular devotion, and one that may have seemed too close to Protestantism, did not meet with approval at the highest levels of government or of a church that already considered itself reformed.[7]

In 1567 Michael Baius (Michel De Bay, 1513–89), who was something of an Augustinian forerunner of Jansen, had 79 of his statements on original sin condemned by Pius V. The same fate awaited Jansen's text: Nicolas Cornet – a French Jesuit-educated theologian, friend of Richelieu and Mazarin, and syndic of the Sorbonne – presented to the Sorbonne's assembly "Five Propositions" derived from the *Augustinus* (originally there had been seven, but two were dropped), along with letters from Antoine Arnauld. Many at the time (most prominent among them Arnauld, much to his misfortune) observed that the assertions ascribed to Jansen, heretical though they may have been, indeed were nowhere to be found in the *Augustinus*; others believed that they might logically be extrapolated from Jansen's claims. The Sorbonne, with its mix of Jesuits and numerous but sometimes timorous Jansenists and Jansenist sympathizers, did not desire or was unable to take a firm stand; finally, the propositions were sent to Rome and in 1653 duly condemned by Pope Innocent X in *cum occasione*. Both with excitement and under the cloud of censure, "Jansenism" was born – and almost immediately politicized.[8]

Arnauld suggested to the nuns at Port-Royal that they split hairs by acceding to the pope's findings on the heretical nature of the Five Propositions while questioning his infallibility in "findings of fact" – the fact, that is, of whether or not these propositions really had anything to do with Jansenism.[9] In the early years of the controversy, the Jansenists may not have understood all the political implications of their beliefs, especially with regard to the French crown, from which, given Louis XIV's support for Gallicanism (and therefore against the absolute primacy of the pope in choosing bishops), they might have expected sympathy and support. But they misplayed their cards and never gained the king's backing.[10]

Nor did the early Jansenists divine the repercussions of their anti-Jesuit stance, which to begin with was not so much against the Society as hostile to theological and moral positions identified with the Jesuits. It must be said, however, that before long the Jansenists, and especially Blaise Pascal, so identified the Jesuits with their stance on grace that it was the Society and not just their ideas that they attacked, almost exulting in their condemnations of the "mystic hydra" – the Jesuits and the many heads of their probabilism.[11] There was, too, a French tradition that the *Loyolites* had been introduced by the Spanish as a way of overthrowing the Most Christian Kingdom of France.[12]

In their opposition to the laxity of morals in the church of their time, the Jansenists naturally saw the Jesuits as their enemies. In turn, the Jesuits, very much part of the Tridentine reform movement, appealed to the masses, were optimistic in their vigour and rhetoric, believed in the efficacy and curative effect of frequent acceptance of the Sacrament of the Eucharist, and certainly avoided being excessively judgmental in their view of piety and human character. Jansenist pessimism naturally became a thorn in their collective side.

For all the fuss, talk, and wrangling that went on in France and Italy – and it lasted for more than a century – the putative issues, the central ideas and beliefs, were relatively simple if profoundly important. First of all, one should remember that politics in the seventeenth century concerned itself more often with the eternal life of the soul than with life on earth.[13] Therefore, the following questions were not just religious; they had to do with the way things had been, were, and ever should be. What is human nature? What is sin? What is salvation? What are the implications of Adam's Fall? Which is more real, freedom or destiny? What even is the nature of time – has it, paradoxically enough, by now occurred? In other words, is grace prevenient – anticipatory, already accomplished? Does a confessor consider circumstances or individual cases of conscience (i.e., casuistry, an early-modern form of situational ethics) when forgiving sins? Is there probable cause (probabilism) for doing so? Is our contrition owing to fear of damnation or to the love of God? If only the former, can we be saved? Finally, there is the ineffability of grace and the mystic relationship with one's Saviour and one's God.[14]

We must recall, too, that in order to fulfil religious obligations, Catholics were compelled to take communion at least once a year at Paschal Time. The Jesuits argued for more frequent communion, Arnauld for keeping communion to a minimum.[15] In order to receive the Sacrament of the Eucharist, one had to confess. Observance of the central rituals of the church was important to one's standing in the community and one's identity as a Christian. Therefore, questions of sin and grace were not just personal and spiritual; they were also social.

Shortly after the publication of Innocent X's Bull, the diffidence of those at Port-Royal, and the somewhat timid acquiescence of the theology faculty at the Sorbonne, Blaise Pascal weighed in with his *Provincial Letters* (*Lettres Provinciales*). A few years earlier, he had undergone a night of fire and been swayed by the Jansenists into becoming a follower of their teachings.[16] His sister Jacqueline preceded him at Port-Royal, and his niece experienced a miraculous cure there.[17]

In the *Provincial Letters*, one of the issues seems to be logic – or the use and misuse of terms – rather than just theology. With characteristic brevity and clarity, Pascal, in his defence of Port-Royal and his friend Antoine Arnauld, whom the Sorbonne had condemned for his assertion that the Five Propositions were not to be found in the *Augustinus*, contracts the questions separating the Jansenists and the Jesuits:

> In a word, then, I learned that their difference concerning sufficient grace consists in the fact that the Jesuits claim that there is a grace given generally to all, so subject to free will that this makes it efficacious or not as it chooses without any fresh assistance from God, and without anything more being needed for it to act effectively; which is why it is called *sufficient*, because by itself it is sufficient for action. The Jansenists on the contrary will not admit the existence of any actually sufficient grace which is not also efficacious; in other words, all forms of grace which do not determine the will to effective action are insufficient for action, because they say that we never act without *efficacious grace*. That is where they differ.[18]

Then with brilliant satire, mordant irony, and feigned confusion, Pascal moves close to the absurd as he reports on a Dominican's attempt to steer a middle course between the Jansenists and Jesuits. "N.," a friend of the "provincial" to whom Pascal addresses his letters, is to all appearances the source of Pascal's information.

> He went on to tell me about the doctrine of the neo-Thomists. "It is very odd," he said, "they agree with the Jesuits in admitting a *sufficient grace* given to all men, but yet they maintain that men never act through this grace alone, and that before they can act they need God to give them an *efficacious grace* really determining their wills to action, and not given by God to all men."[19]

And so it goes. The Thomists wanted to have their cake on grace and eat it too. Pascal and, one assumes, most of his readers, except of course the Dominicans – the "Thomists" – found it somewhat difficult to distinguish between sufficient and effectual grace.[20] In short, if sufficient grace is not sufficient without effectual grace, then there is no such thing as sufficient grace. But in many ways that is beside the point; it is the infernally slippery positions taken by the personages, excepting the modest Jansenist, in Pascal's world (and by some in the real world, for that matter) that capture and hold our attention.

Pascal's dialogue recapitulates the debates of a papal congregation called by Clement VIII at the end of the preceding century. The *Congregatio de auxiliis* allowed the Dominicans and the Jesuits to put forth their contrasting notions of grace, with neither side receiving the blessing of the Apostolic See. Both were permitted to promote their views; neither was allowed to attack the other.

As if "sufficient" and "effectual" were not enough to confuse the pious mind, next in the *Provincial Letters* comes a disquisition by a "good" (and fictional) Jesuit father on "actual" grace, which boils down to a bad case of casuistry, as Pascal and his Jansenist friend put it. "We claim that God gives actual grace to all men on the occasion of each temptation, because we maintain that, if on every occasion of temptation you did not have the actual grace to refrain from the sin, whatever sin you committed could never be imputed to you."[21] This position soon leads one to other fine points distinguishing between sins of commission and omission, ignorance of fact, ignorance of law, and finally to the myriad problems in establishing an awareness of right and wrong. Certainly the logic is not easy to follow, no matter who is arguing. The point Pascal makes, of course, is that the Jesuits are soft on sin, and although it is not their policy to corrupt morals, "their sole aim is not to reform them either."[22]

Pascal makes a strong case for a Jesuit rhetoric that is more than tinged by hypocrisy and sophistry. At a certain point, in response to Pascal's comment that a certain Jesuit casuist's opinions were contrary to those of the Church Fathers, the Jesuit father responds, "You do not understand much about it. The Fathers were good for the morality of their time; but they are too remote for the morality of ours."[23] This puts into rather crude terms and therefore belittles what is, in a more sophisticated sense, a rhetorical "way of proceeding" (*noster modus procedendi*) employed by the Jesuits. Mark Fumaroli sees the Jesuits' casuistry as based upon a rhetoric that construed St Augustine, for instance, in terms of his context and his own rhetorical "nuances." The Jesuits' circumstantial approach took into account such things as "time, place, propriety, context, and semantic structures."[24] In other words, the Jesuits interpreted; they did not see old texts as monolithic and lifeless, forever set in their meaning and never debatable. In short, the Jesuits were not "strict constructionists."[25]

These debates on sin and the proper use of ancient texts, most notably St Augustine's, were implicated in contemporary debates on textual criticism. French and Italian intellectuals of the day were often deeply interested in humanist philology and a desire to treat early sources, especially the Church Doctors, with care and attention to what the scholars believed to be those texts' "original" meanings.

In the late seventeenth and early eighteenth centuries, there was in Europe something of a revolution in the writing of history, especially ecclesiastical history. Claude Hercule Fleury's 20-volume *Histoire ecclésiastique* (1690–1720) nudged and then soon enough gave a good hard push to the paradigm of ecclesiastical history only recently established by the Venerable Cesare Baronius (1538–1607), who, like Eusebius before him, was known as the "Father of Ecclesiastical History." Baronius's *Annales Ecclesiastici* was written as a corrective to the famous Protestant tract *Centuries of Magdeburg*,[26] which in turn had been produced to demonstrate that the Roman Church had veered from the true path, which was only regained by Luther and the Protestant movement. The search for truth in history through the establishment of textual authority was often enough motivated by polemical, dogmatic, and institutional requisites. Fleury made it clear that he supported Louis XIV and absolute monarchy; he also attacked the Jesuits and their role as Europe's most powerful and ubiquitous teachers. Fleury's impact in Rome, especially in the circle of Cardinal Domenico Pasionei (a Jansenist sympathizer, or philo-Jansenist) was immediate and fervent. The cardinal called for an Italian *storia sacra* written "according to our system, just as [Fleury] in his discussions put into relief those [points] which make his case."[27] But we are getting ahead of ourselves here; I will return to the Italian connection with the Jansenists after commenting on Pascal's own rhetoric and the possibilities of, in a more general sense, Jansenist rhetoric, especially as one perceives it through Philippe de Champaigne's paintings for Port-Royal.

The effect of Pascal's *Provincial Letters* was to keep the heat off Arnauld; for a short time it worked. Pascal also achieved at least a pyrrhic victory post-mortem because, by the end of the century, many of the Jesuits' casuistic and probabilistic practices, although not the Jesuits themselves, were condemned by Pope Alexander VIII.[28]

Arnauld provided Pascal with Jesuit tracts, which Pascal dutifully read and then portrayed in mocking terms. Certainly one cannot condemn Pascal for making up his accusations out of whole cloth. He may have been selective in what he chose to quote and attack, but he was usually if not exclusively meticulous in his characterization of ideas and reproduction of citations. This, however, is not the place to defend or condemn penitential practices of the early-modern period. What I am trying to do is characterize the dynamics of a particular religious controversy of the period and then to show how a number of the issues embedded in that controversy also play out in rhetorical and therefore artistic terms.

My sense of rhetoric encompasses but is not restricted to the history of rhetoric as oratory. I am drawn to Aristotle's statement that rhetoric's function "is not so much to persuade as to find out in each case the existing means of persuasion."[29] This statement applies not just to the one who wishes to move an audience and therefore must plot the most fitting, expedient, and advantageous rhetorical strategy, but also to the critical historian who attempts to comprehend the means of persuasion in the past and then to convince his or her own audience of the efficacy of this knowledge.[30] In other words, the critical historian attends to the "means" of the artist, architect, poet, pamphleteer, or author; these means are not just matters of style or "ways of proceeding" – the Jesuit catchphrase – but something more complex. One must take into account the objectives of various discourses, concepts, and constructs, what were the political, theological, and philosophical underpinnings, and what were their goals.

Pascal's own way of proceeding offers an introduction to what can be called Jansenist rhetoric. In an authoritarian culture, one dominated by absolute monarchs in both the political and spiritual realms, a grass-roots movement with metaphysical and theological claims – one that is traditionalist, rigorist, and hearkens back to the "purity" of the early church – can lead to sectarianism and potential insurgency, or at least that would have been the fear of religious and civil authorities (both Richelieu and Mazarin were wary of the Jansenists). The ensuing debates in the Sorbonne, intervention of the papacy, and opprobrium of the monarch, whose confessors were Jesuit, along with the Jesuits pulling out their big guns to go after Pascal, probably came as no surprise to the Jansenists in the early years of their movement.

Pascal's counter-attack was wily and artful. He knew the dangers to an author who took on entrenched and powerful forces, so he chose, with some success, anonymity, rendering himself less expugnable. As fallacious as *ad hominem* arguments may be, authors often did not then – nor do they now – fare well when taking up risky positions in defence of strict observance and demanding religious practices.

Although, as Wallace K. Ferguson has observed, most French Catholics were not likely to have followed the rigorous practices of the Jansenist few, Jansenism's ability to raise the ire of the Jesuits and others in power made the movement dangerous.[31] Pascal therefore wrote from a position of anonymity and succeeded in shifting the focus from the "author function" to the text itself, of which he was the master.

The epistolary form served him well, too, because it makes the discussion familiar, as if one were merely corresponding with a friend, a provincial one at that. Pascal can therefore invoke the old topos of country versus city, of the honest, plainspoken countryman on the one hand and the sophistic, oftentimes corrupt urbanite on the other. We know that the narrator is on the side of the provincial because the letters have the effect of the informal, anecdotal, and easily communicable. Pascal's language is that of the friend, unpretentious and yet gossipy (he is, after all, something of the *faux naïf*) as he tells of his meetings and conversations with the denizens of the metropolis. One reads the first dozen or so letters with ease, as if from a position of *otium* and reflection, enjoying the exchanges and the obvious wit of one's correspondent.

The tone of the letters shifts when Pascal turns away from his provincial pen pal and engages directly with the Jesuits in general (Letters XI–XVI) and finally with one in particular, Reverend Father Annat, the king's confessor (Letters XVII–XVIII). In the end, Pascal's easy-going banter and genial wit evaporate as he turns angry and scornful, parrying the Jesuits' aggressive thrusts, bitter accusations, and what he calls their "extravagant opinions."[32] He lashes out at the Society's stance on sin and defends his own indignant mockery (*raillery*) in the following terms:

> For do we not find God both hating and despising sinners, so much so that at the hour of their death, the moment when their condition is most deplorable and wretched, the divine wisdom will add mockery and derision to the vengeance and wrath which condemn them to eternal torments: "I also will laugh at your calamity: I will mock when your fear cometh" [Proverbs 1:26]. And the saints, acting in the same spirit, will behave in the same way, since, according to David, when they see the punishment of the wicked: "The righteous also shall see and shall fear and shall laugh at him" [Psalms 52:6]. And Job says the same: "The innocent shall laugh them to scorn" [Job 22:19].[33]

Rarely has scorn and laughter been turned to such vitriolic and dark purposes, revealing the deeply pessimistic side of Pascal's own wit and Jansenist theology. He was a fundamentalist and, like other Jansenists, tended "towards the permanent establishment of martial law in divinity."[34]

Pascal goes on to defend his rhetoric of disdain, laughter, derision, and ridicule as appropriate and deserved, for there is much in the Bible, he claims, to support the mordant and derisory. In the same letter he defends the simplicity of his (Jansenist) rhetoric, as opposed to the deceit of the Jesuits, while asserting his hatred of duplicity:

> the spirit of piety always leads us to speak with truth and sincerity, whereas envy and hatred employ falsehood and slander: "*splendentia et vehementia, sed rebus veris*" [splendid and vehement in words, but true in things], says St Augustine. Anyone who resorts to falsehood is acting in the spirit of the devil. No amount of directing the intention can justify slander; and even if it were a question of converting the whole world, it would never be permissible to traduce innocent persons, because we should not commit the least evil to promote the greatest good, and "the truth of the Lord hath no need of our lies," according to Scripture. "It is the duty of those who defend truth," says St Hilary, "to advance only those things that are true." So, Fathers, I can say before God that I detest nothing so much as the slightest injury to truth, and that I have always been particularly careful not only not to falsify, which would be repugnant, but not to alter or in the least way distort the sense of any passage.[35]

We do not know enough about Pascal's early education (he was homeschooled by his father, Etienne) to say with any certainty that he learned the rudiments of rhetoric in a formal way. What we do have are his texts, and these are evidence enough.

Pascal chose the pamphlet format, allowing him to bypass permissions, censorship, and scrutiny outside the text.[36] In other words, by not seeking the *privilège*, Pascal frustrated extraneous investigations, once again forcing his readers, both sympathetic and antagonistic, to pay attention to his words. At the same time, it is no coincidence that he created a tempest of speculation on the author's identity simply by withholding it.[37] It was not until 1659, three years after the first of his *Provinciales*, that his identity became generally known. By then, the furore had calmed down some, and he was quit of the project, having moved on to the *Pensées*.

Port-Royal sponsored readings in Parisian salons before each of the letters appeared, further intensifying the reading public's anticipation.

There was real danger in what Pascal and his printers were attempting because, had he been found out, he would have in all likelihood landed in jail. By no means was Pascal oblivious to the danger. When Pope Alexander VII promulgated his bull *Ad sanctum sedem* in the spring of 1657, with its blanket condemnation of Jansenism, Pascal saw that his situation had become tenuous and the forces ranged against him powerful. He suspended his *Provinciales* in the middle of Letter XVIII, never to return.

The first three letters show the putative author to be open-minded, easily captivated, and not infrequently politely disputatious. He seems willing to listen and be convinced, which was hardly the position of Pascal himself, who had bones to pick with the Jesuits from early on.[38] Things become less peaceable beginning with Letter IV, when the format switches from a primary speaker or letter writer introducing and summing up an argument to that of a lively dialogue between the amiable but misbegotten Jesuit father and the somewhat more wary and dubious authorial voice. Pascal never lost sight of the fact that the Jesuits had a rhetoric that was celebratory, inventive, and oftentimes eulogistic; he just saw it as empty.

From Letter X to the end, there is no more dialogue, just Pascal – or at least a voice that is very close to Pascal's own – brooking no compromise with his adversaries. Where the Jesuits accuse him of lacking charity, Pascal, a genuine traditionalist, stands firm in his moral absolutism and accuses them of the very same sin. He is by turns obdurate, testy, accusatory, denunciatory, and recriminatory. His rhetorical strategies are relatively straightforward, patient, and methodical, building his arguments (*gradatio*) and using the Jesuits' own words against them when he can. At the same time he may be illogical, periphrastic, insinuating, and tautological.[39] He often employs *le style coupé*, which is characterized by vehemence, discontinuity, and fragments (a style employed with skill in his *Pensées*). No slave to brevity, he asserts in Letter XVI, "I would have written a shorter letter, but I did not have the time." Pascal uses whatever ammunition is at hand, although he avoids prolixity (not necessarily the opposite of brevity) and what he would have believed to be the language of the Jesuits, whom Marc Fumaroli ironically describes as "extravagantly baroque preachers."[40] Fumaroli of course is repeating an old prejudice, one with which he vigorously disagrees. Blaise Pascal was a Jansenist follower defending Jansenism in what is recognizably a Jansenist style.[41]

Descartes

When one historian conjectures what Cartesianism has to do with Jansenism, his answer is "not much and plenty."[42] Many Jansenists rejected Descartes's dualistic philosophy; others embraced it, while the philosopher himself left no indication of his attitude towards them or their movement.[43] There is a tradition, Stephen Nadler brings up, that some close and almost inevitable association existed between Descartes and the Jansenists.[44] Marjorie Grene writes that "Cartesianism became, we are told, up to a point the official doctrine of Port-Royal."[45] In fact, to be at Port-Royal was *not necessarily* to read Descartes. With the significant exceptions of Arnauld and Robert Desgabets, a Benedictine from Lorraine, Jansenists as a whole beat a retreat from Descartes, convinced that his emphasis upon "extension" as the essence of matter was anathematic to the doctrine of transubstantiation in the sacrament of the Eucharist.

Christian orthodoxy insists that once bread is consecrated, it may retain the extension, shape, texture, colour, smell, and taste of bread, but its essence has changed. Cartesian philosophy maintains that what is real about something is not surface, colour, smell, and so on, which are accidental elements, but extension, which is the displacement of space. For a Cartesian, then, there is no essence other than extension; the essence of Christ's body cannot be in the Eucharistic bread essentially unless it is there extensionally. Descartes tried to work his way around this problem by saying that what remained of the bread after consecration was merely accidental; that what stayed behind was nothing more than "the surface that is common to the individual particles of the bread and the bodies which surround them."[46] But the problem remained: where is the body of Christ, if it does not take on the shape or dimensions of the bread? Descartes, in his communications with Arnauld on this very issue, invoked the position taken by the Council of Trent that one cannot explain in words how it is that the body of Christ is in the bread, for it is beyond the capacity of human reason or language to understand transubstantiation, and indeed Descartes explicitly exempted questions of grace from his philosophy.[47] Both Arnauld and Descartes sought solace and exception from explanation in the Tridentine position (although of course it did not really solve the problem). Arnauld remained a supporter of Descartes, arguing against the other Jansenists by asserting that one could accept him both theologically and philosophically. Arnauld's *Port-Royal Logic* is, in Stephen

Nadler's words, "permeated by Cartesian principles."[48] Arnauld conceived of Descartes as a Christian philosopher, one whose philosophies actually supported and advanced Christianity. Descartes's mind-body dualism proved, for Arnauld, the immortality of the soul. But Arnauld's great champion, Pascal, in his *Pensées* (no. 78), wrote, "Descartes – useless and uncertain [*inutile et incertain*]."

Descartes got into trouble because his philosophy of the essence of matter as extension seemed to be at odds with the Council of Trent's declaration that Christ is "really and substantially" present in the Eucharist. Certainly everyone wanted to avoid the Calvinist position that the body of Christ was present in the Eucharist only spiritually.[49]

René Descartes did not take sides in the Jesuit-Jansenist controversy. He had enormous respect for the leading Jansenist Arnauld but at the same time was no enemy of the Jesuits, having studied at the Jesuit *La Flèche*, one of the most prestigious schools in France. He hoped that the Jesuits would alter their *Ratio Studiorum* at his alma mater by incorporating his philosophy and physics. He wrote to the Jesuit Etienne Charlet, a teacher at *La Flèche*, "I venture to hope that [the Jesuits] will find many things in it [his *Meditations*] which they will think true and which may readily be substituted for the ordinary views, and serve effectively to explain the truths of the faith without, moreover, contradicting the writings of Aristotle."[50] Although Descartes himself did not think his philosophy new, there were those in seventeenth-century France who would indeed see his *Meditations* as a departure from Aristotle's natural philosophy, which was supported by the Jesuits, and would therefore associate it with Jansenism. Despite his attempt to chart his own course with a kind of point-to-point navigation, others had difficulty conceiving of Descartes's philosophy outside of contemporary politics and religion. The Jesuits, despite the fact that many individuals in the order admired Descartes's philosophy, saw to it that the *Meditations* were placed on the *Index*. The Jansenists who protested Descartes's science and even his notion of the progress of science found themselves on the side of the Jesuits. The irony was not lost on them, of course, but they very much needed *not* to be associated with Calvinism and therefore undoubtedly thought it highly prudent on this occasion to agree with their enemies.

The writers who responded to Jansenist theology and practice brought about a sea change in European literature. At or near the intersections of various institutional mandates and interests, one finds an efflorescence of literary activity. Between and among the papacy, its injunctions and pronouncements, competing parties in the Sorbonne, Richelieu's and Mazarin's executive tactics and schemes, the persuasive power of and widespread resistance to the Society of Jesus, Port-Royal, the salons and *salonnières*, disquisitions on *goût* ("taste"), and the discourses of "French Classicism," there arose a recognizably Jansenist literature. In addition to Jansen's *Augustinus*, one finds early on Saint-Cyran's and Mère Angelique's *Lettres spirituelles*. Soon afterward came Arnauld's *De la fréquente communion*, Arnauld and Pierre Nicole's *Port-Royal Logic*, Le Nain de Tillemont's *Histoire ecclésiastique*, Pascal's *Provinciales* and *Pensées*, much of the writing of Nicolas Boileau (the so-called Lawgiver of Parnassus) and La Rochefoucauld's *Maximes*, not to mention the writings of Bossuet and La Bruyère. Molière with his emphasis upon *honnêteté* also responds to the element of restraint, self-possession, and integrity that undergird Jansenist piety.

Jansenists, Rhetoric, World-Disclosing, and Philippe de Champaigne

A vexatious question in the discipline and practice of art history has to do with an artist and his or her context and identity. My purpose here is not to review, construct, deconstruct, or interrogate "context," something already done with remarkable brilliance by Mieke Bal and Norman Bryson.[51] I do, however, wish to revisit and reconsider the ways in which Philippe de Champaigne may be thought of as a Jansenist painter, while dancing as carefully as I can around the question of a "Jansenist style," opting instead for a critique of his painting as both "world- and truth-disclosing."

Pinning down and fleshing out an artist's or author's identity occupies the critical historian as biographer, a role somewhat burdened by troublesome and even annoying questions such as "what is an author?"[52] I am willing to settle for a more-or-less Foucauldian understanding that authorial identity is a symptom or concomitant of the author's text or work. That is not to say, however, that when assessing and conjecturing an authorial identity one avoids the usual recounting of who, what, where, when, and why. When it comes to Philippe de Champaigne, Jansenism figures in each of these "w" questions and is the subject to which I shall once again turn, before taking account of the artist himself.

The discourses of art and rhetoric have to make sense of the interrelation of artist and his or her cultural context, an undertaking that in the early-modern period was fraught with questions of personal and national identity, taste, pastoral duty, papal authority, contentious religious organizations, piety, dogma, a pared-down rhetoric, and the history of ideas.[53] As Richard Parish has stated, Jansenism and "the ethos of Augustinian pessimism ... dominated a significant part of French thought and writing in the later part of the seventeenth century."[54] The same could be said for Italy.

Philippe de Champaigne and the Jansenists

When still in his teens, the Brussels-born Philippe de Champaigne (1602–74), acknowledged as a precocious talent from his earliest years, went with his master Jacques Fouquier to Paris.[55] He arrived in 1620 as a young Flemish painter who, if not yet entirely formed, was already imbued with the "habitus 'flamands'" (the Flemish style or manner) which would continue to shape his art throughout a long life.[56] Louis Marin distils and typifies this *habitus* as a product or *mélange* of prevailing artistic fashions and techniques then current in Flanders, from what he calls mannerism, academicism, and baroque. These general styles and attitudes, along with his Flemish upbringing, Marin maintains, provided Champaigne and his paintings with vision, imagination, sensibility, a strident sense of colour, sensuality, expansive scenography, tactility, and the capacity to capture in his portraits a density of soul (or "creatureliness") in faces, gestures, and postures.[57] This of course is one critic's fictive, if powerful, reading of a young painter and his artistic being. Marin's characterization is neither right nor wrong; it is, rather, a depiction, an interpretation. What one cannot avoid here, however, is that Marin has one thing indubitably right: Philippe de Champaigne's artistic identity was already, or at least to a large extent, shaped by the time he started his career in Paris.[58]

Philippe was called back to Flanders to marry Charlotte Duchesne, the daughter of one of his patrons, and when the couple returned to Paris, he almost immediately found work with the Queen Mother – Marie de' Medici – and her son Louis XIII. Later on, during the minority of Louis XIV and the regency of Anne of Austria, he painted scenes from the *Life of the Virgin* for the Palais-Royal. From his early days Philippe de Champaigne was well connected and well launched on an artistic career.

It was Charles Augustin Sainte-Beuve, who, in his mid-nineteenth-century text on Port-Royal, wrote of Champaigne's art as calm, sober, serious, and restrained, thereby conjoining the painter and the Jansenists.[59] Ever since, a debate has turned on whether or not Champaigne's art has within it something we can call Jansenist and, if so, in what manner and on what grounds one can make this claim.

In all likelihood, Philippe de Champaigne did not become an important part of the Jansenist community until after the death of the Abbé de Saint-Cyran. The abbé was imprisoned by Richelieu in 1638, not to be freed until shortly before he died in 1643. It seems unlikely Champaigne and Saint-Cyran had an opportunity to make one another's acquaintance, but we do know that soon after Saint-Cyran died, his closest followers pressed Champaigne to paint their great friend and leader's portrait. Saint-Cyran's nephew Martin de Barcos, who succeeded him as the Abbé de Saint-Cyran, is quoted in 1660 by Le Maître de Saci (in a letter to La Mère Angélique) as having said "que si Monsieur Champaigne eût connu feu Monsieur de Saint-Cyran durant sa vie, il ne fût jamais mort" – insofar as Monsieur Champaigne knew the late Saint-Cyran in his life [which he in effect accomplished by painting Saint-Cyran's portrait, albeit post-mortem], he is never dead.[60] In this only apparently paradoxical statement, we have the rhetoric of praise. Champaigne's powerful art makes the absent present, the dead alive again, just as Cicero said friendship could do.[61] This may be a well-worn trope, but it has its force and certainly bears witness to the Jansenists' admiration for the Flemish painter.

Perhaps with the help of Martin de Barcos and Hardouin de Péréfixe, Archbishop of Paris, Champaigne (now a widower) commended his two daughters, Catherine and Françoise, to the educational care of Port-Royal as *pensionnaires*.[62] He decorated Port-Royal's chapel in Paris, painted the portrait of La Mère Angélique and Le Grand Arnauld, then produced the frontispiece for the twelfth edition of *De la fréquente communion*. His daughter Françoise died at the abbey in 1655; the surviving child, Catherine, took the habit in 1657, probably as a result of her sister's death. In 1660, La Mère Angélique asked that Champaigne make a portrait of Antoine Le Maître from a death mask, perhaps prepared by her.

In the early 1660s, the solitaires were vacillating over the signing of Alexander VII's formulary.[63] Finally in 1664, those at Port-Royal placed their trust in Philippe de Champaigne by sending him to plead their case, unsuccessfully as it turned out, before the archbishop of Paris, Hardouin de Péréfixe, the same man who had in all likelihood sponsored Françoise and Catherine's entrée into Port-Royal years earlier. When Champaigne died, the *Nécrologe de l'abbaye* for 12 August 1674 commented on the painter's skill, his piety, the affection with which he was held at Port-Royal, and his willingness to support and represent Port-Royal in all its dealings, even before the great men of the world.[64] These are the bare bones of the story connecting Philippe de Champaigne and Port-Royal.

Painting, Contemplative Seeing, Tears, and Identity at Port-Royal

The surviving daughter of Philippe de Champaigne took the habit on 14 October 1657 with the name Catherine de Sainte-Suzanne. To mark her entry into the community of Port-Royal, Champaigne painted and gave to the solitaires of the convent two pictures, *St Mary Magdalene* (Figure 11.1) and *St John the Baptist* (Figure 11.2), in Catherine's name. These paintings of more-or-less identical dimensions were placed in the church choir of the *religieuses* at Port-Royal, Paris, where they remained until the abbey was closed in 1665.[65]

John the Baptist was the first to publicly identify Jesus as the Christ, and Mary Magdalene was the first to see Him arisen. John and the Magdalene are also saints of penance: John said, "Bring forth therefore fruit worthy of penance" (Matthew 3:8), and the Magdalene, the greatest of all penitential figures, washed out her sins with her tears of sorrow.

It was the Fourth Lateran Council of 1215 that established the need for confession in order to receive Holy Communion, which must be taken at least once a year. The Council of Trent reasserted the importance of penance as a sacrament preceding and indispensable to communion. Antoine Arnauld in *De la fréquente communion* admonished his readers, who were the intellectuals of modern France, not in Latin but in the vulgar tongue, to follow the Fathers and the early church, treating communion as something to be approached in the language of St John Chrysostom and St Augustine with awe and trembling. Is it better to communicate often or seldom? Seldom, argued Arnauld, believing in genuine "contrition," which requires more time and soul-searching than the "attrition" he associated with Jesuit laxity.

The lives of the penitents at Port-Royal were what the church calls contemplative. The nuns, inspired by prayer and penance, would present themselves to the priest, who heard their confession and pronounced absolution. The practice of confession "was not conceived of as a repetitive individual routine except among monks and unusually pious laymen,"[66] according to Thomas Tentler in his history of penance before the Reformation. Although Tentler does not take into account

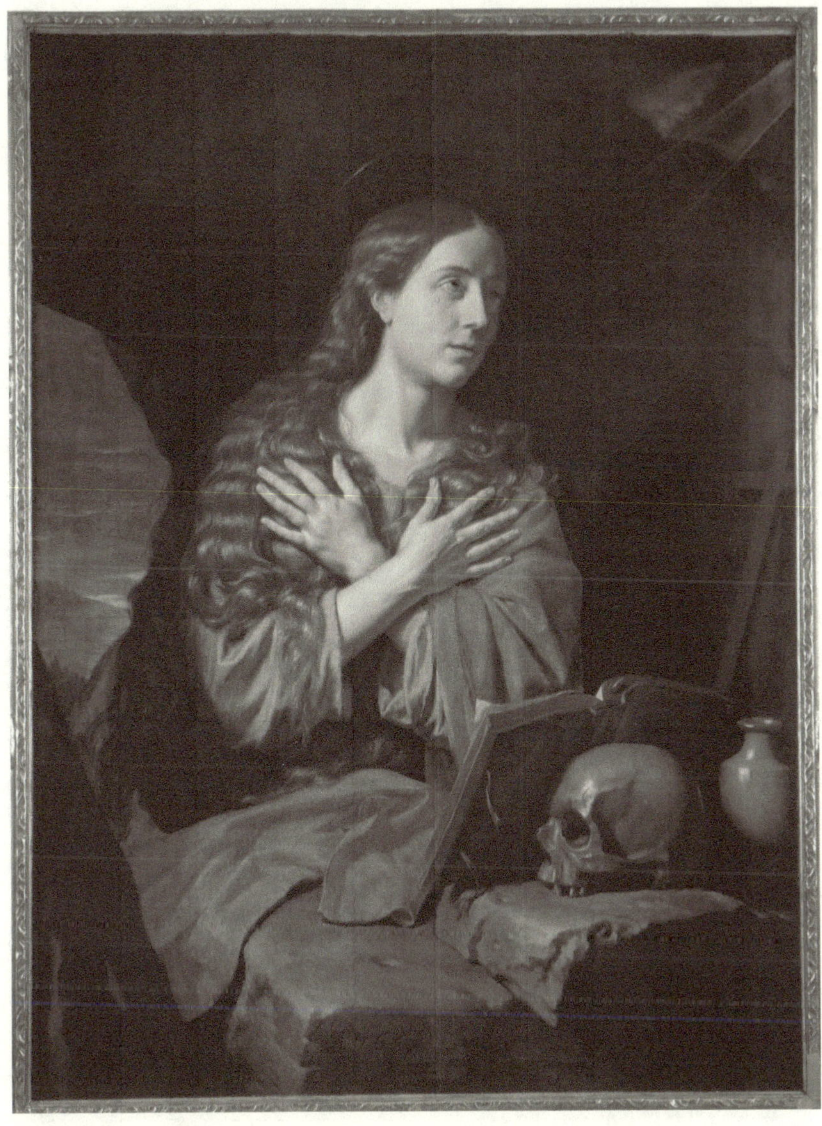

Figure 11.1 Philippe de Champaigne, *St Mary Magdalene*, oil on canvas, 1657, Musée de Beaux-Arts, Rennes, France. Photo: RMN–Grand Palais/Art Resource, NY.

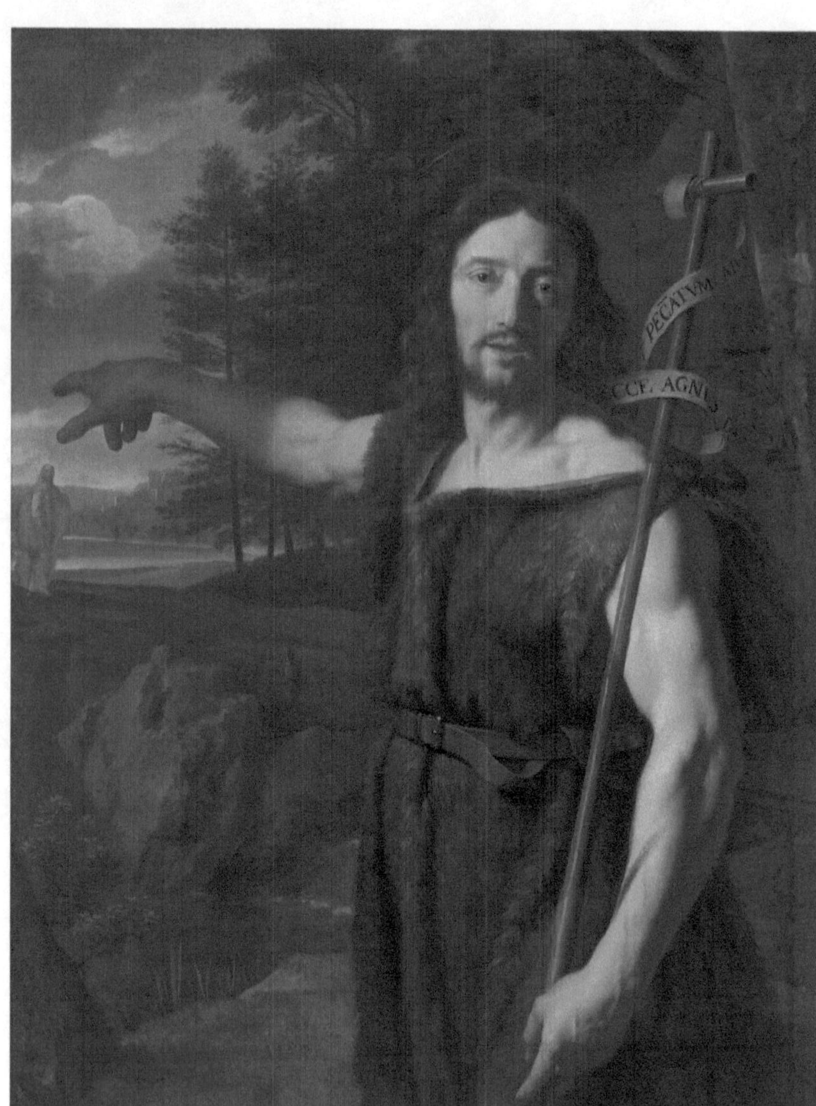

Figure 11.2 Philippe de Champaigne, *St John the Baptist*, oil on canvas, 1657, Musée de Peinture et Sculpture, Grenoble, France. Photo: Musée de Grenoble, France, Secrétaire de l'Administration.

Jansenist practice, his observation on the likelihood of recurring cycles of the four stages of penance – confession, contrition, satisfaction, absolution – would have held true for the solitaires at Port-Royal. Following in the spirit of Le Grand Arnauld, they probably performed the sacrament of penance far more often than that of Holy Communion.

According to the Council of Trent, Session XIV, Christ

> then especially instituted the sacrament when, after being risen from the dead, He breathed upon His disciples, and said: "Receive ye the Holy Ghost, whose sins you shall forgive, they are forgiven them, and whose sins you shall retain, they are retained" [John 20:22–3]. The consensus of all the Fathers has always acknowledged that by this action so sublime and words so clear the power of forgiving and retaining sins was given to the Apostles and their lawful successors for reconciling the faithful who have fallen after baptism.[67]

In Champaigne's *Mary Magdalene*, the penitent saint in her cave in the wilderness near Marseilles kneels before a crude altar made from thrown-together rocks; the skull, her ever-present memento mori, supports the Book, which she has been reading.[68] The visible rays of divine emanation, directed towards the Magdalene's upturned face, signal her mystic union with God. Crystalline tears, not unlike those once painted by Rogier van der Weyden, wash down her cheeks, recalling Peter Damian's words that "tears, which are from God, rise up confidently to the divine tribunal, pleading immediately, and trusting in the immediate remission of our sins."[69]

The contemplative life, commented on by St Augustine and St Thomas Aquinas but associated strongly with the "Mellifluous Doctor," St Bernard of Clairvaux, is the vocation most strongly associated with Mary Magdalene, who had given up all in her reclusion, a solitude without community. Her devotion to the Word of God was one of loving tenderness, the emotion she displayed so ardently with Jesus when she washed His feet with her tears and anointed His body after His Crucifixion. Here she is in a state of adoration and self-abnegation, consumed with those occupations of the contemplative – prayer and penance. Because she is in a cave, a natural cell, her eremitic withdrawal is, if anything, greater than that of the solitaires at Port-Royal. Nonetheless, they too lived the life of contemplation, which is in many ways a sublime act.

Indeed, as rhetoric goes, this image by Philippe de Champaigne is sublime by virtue of that with which it engages. The most primitive of emotions is awe (as I have suggested in relation to Sant'Ivo alla Sapienza), and in this painting the solitaires saw the Magdalene's theophanic moment, comparable in its awe(fulness) to the gesture that began all things: "Let there be light" – the same light that washes over her face.[70] The moment is holy: the solitaires' "seeing" of this painting, as they meditated on it in their prayers – just like Mary Magdalene's "seeing" of God – would have been contemplative seeing, one constituting a heightened, even an extraordinary, awareness. Mary Magdalene's tears cleanse like the waters of baptism, bringing forgiveness, the Holy Ghost, and sublime grace.

Philippe de Champaigne bestowed on the community this painting, an image whose significance sprang to life as it was consumed by the solitaires in prayer. The painting stimulated and simulated the prayers, penance, and adoration of the Port-Royal community, which now included Catherine de Sainte-Suzanne.

Champaigne paints Mary Magdalene piercingly spotlit and emerging from cavernous gloom. The spectator has a privileged point of view, as if mystically occupying the Magdalene's cave, just on the other side of her stone reading desk. A penitent or solitaire in deep prayer, one focusing specifically on the Magdalene and penance, occupies more or less the same position as the imagined viewer of Champaigne's painting. Deep prayer, like any form of profound meditation, gives rise to images, ones that are not at a distance but are immediate, impinging on the mind of the religious, like a hallucination. The painter's precise Flemish manner accentuates surfaces, crevices, and edges of stone blocks, stressing their obdurate mass. The intensity of his style matches the force or insistence of our, the Magdalene's, the solitaires', and Champaigne's awareness. The chiasmus of the Magdalene's arms pressing into her chest forms a reversed or closed orant gesture, creating a sense of her prayer being directed towards her own heart. Mary Magdalene's meditation is rhetoric turned inward, towards her own stream of consciousness.

This motion of her arms also offers resistance – or at least support – to her forward leaning (and perhaps keeps her heart from "bursting with joy"). Because contemplation, before it is anything else, is *seeing*, she almost leads with her eyes, pulling her upper body into an awkward and painful position. Mary Magdalene's experience of theophany literally illuminates her; she is not necessarily petitioning God, nor does she seek a specific message or receive an explicit answer: she is simply and mysteriously enveloped by wonder. That is what, in their own penitential, contemplative, and prayerful attitude, the nuns at Port-Royal saw and experienced.

In Philippe de Champaigne's other painting for the high-altar chapel at Port-Royal, John the Baptist's eyes brim with tears, which threaten at any moment to cascade down his cheeks. He addresses his beholders – who are Catherine and her sisters (not to mention, in a different ontological key, the "priests and Levites from Jerusalem sent by the Jews to ask him, Who art thou?" in John 1:19) – with parted lips and his familiar pointing gesture, in this instance towards a diminutive Christ in the far background. Perhaps Champaigne was thinking of the text in Psalms 42:3: "My tears have been my meat day and night, while they continually say unto me, Where is thy God?"[71] These tears then would be his "meat," answering those who, when they saw John in the wilderness, claimed that he "came neither eating nor drinking" (Matthew 11:18). And he does indeed point to where his (Lamb of) God is.

When John saw Jesus coming to him, he said to the multitude, "Behold the Lamb of God, which taketh away the sin of the world" (John 1:29), which we see written on John's staff in Latin: *Ecce agnus Dei qui tollit pecatum mundi*.[72] "John bare witness of him, and cried, saying, This was he of whom I spake, He that cometh after me is preferred before me: for he was before me" (John 1:15). The rhetoric of John the Evangelist's language is hyperbatic, not so much in syntax as in temporality: that which is after comes before. This paradox repeats itself in the visual presentation where John, impinging like a giant on the existential space of the beholder and therefore the space of the choir at Port-Royal, visually comes *before* and nearly obscures the tiny Jesus seen *after* and from afar on the other side of a gulch. One is reminded of Svetlana Alpers's comment on Velázquez's *Las Meninas*: "No measure rules here: size and significance are at odds."[73] Jesus looks towards us, as if waiting his turn to come onto the world stage, so as to precede John. We behold; Christ awaits.

In a far-reaching theoretical discussion on Champaigne's *Mary Magdalene* and *John the Baptist*, Eric Méchoulan insists that "these are not simply pictures to admire, but also figures upon which to meditate. In contemplating them (both attentively and inattentively), one undergoes a whole 'theoretical experience.'"[74] He then goes on to consider the paradox of the "after" and "before," as I also mentioned earlier. But it is his use of the phrase "theoretical experience" that interests me here.

In their text on contemplative seeing, Christopher A. Dustin and Joanna E. Ziegler point out that in Anaxagoras's assertion that the purpose of living is to *behold*, the key word in Greek is *theorian* – theory.[75] *Theōria* derives from *thea*, which means showing (hence "theatre"), and *horaō*, "to see or look at something." John Florio in 1598 defined theory as "contemplation, speculation, deepe study, insight or beholding."[76] Theoretical seeing – beholding – is an act of self-surrender, an engulfment or ingurgitation of the viewer, who no longer is a spectator – a term suggesting an apartness or a withholding of active participation – but one fully involved in the event, a performer. The *religieuses* at Port-Royal most likely did not *analyse* Champaigne's paintings; rather, they were in accord with or had bonded with the images. These paintings, even in the relatively few years left to Port-Royal (approximately eight years from the time of the gift to the abolishing of the community and closing of the church), were nonetheless an intimate part of the "horizon-of-experience" of the penitents, who both consumed them and, in a religious sense, surpassed them, as they moved through their penitential stages.

The more traditional language of art history seems too unreligious and unphilosophical when applied to these paintings of Philippe de Champaigne. Although the historical critic does not necessarily turn his or her mind to divine things, those whose acts of seeing I am trying to recreate certainly did. It is my sense – and my argument – that the art-historical critic attempts to open the "world" of the work of art and then to interpret it. What I see in these paintings is something not unrelated to what the solitaires at Port-Royal beheld, and for that we should acknowledge the prayerful attitude of the Jansenist community of penitents.

In its obsessions with "truth of being," Heideggerian language – which is both prophetic and visionary – perhaps can help us to see these images as something beyond stunning historical artefacts or texts that require only "interpretation." In the Heideggerian world, a work of visual art *discloses* itself (as well as Truth and the World), and so we try to come to terms with that disclosure while assessing the work's *presence* – the reality it has for us. Heidegger tries to push against the flow of perception, to find the primordial, the moment of disclosure and presentness. His language is, as I have suggested, more oracular than inductive or epagogic.

The trick, then, is to write in a way that is, in effect, perspectival, dualistic, and rational so as to describe something that is very different. I, the subject, view the object – the paintings of Champaigne and the phenomenon of Jansenism and Port-Royal – objectively and analytically.

But while expressing myself in an apparently positivistic manner, I use a Heideggerian idiolect.

Heidegger's notion of *Dasein* – being there, or being in the world (*In-der-Welt-sein*) – refers to how we occupy space and time and what we feel about it. In the imaginative viewing of works of art, one projects onto the recognizable images and stories of these picture worlds questions about being in *that* world, how one occupies the reality of the picture world, that reality's space and time, and how that space and time "feel" to the viewer. The task for the critic is hermeneutical, which means one approaches what Heidegger called "fundamental ontology," what being in the world – in the present case, the world of Port-Royal in the middle years of the seventeenth century – was like for the solitaires and how they while praying (which is an action more supplicatory than interpretive, something that precedes cognition) apprehended and understood Champaigne's images.

Because of long conditioning by the Renaissance tradition in imagery and modern photography and film, we may easily enough be seduced by the direct mimetic quality of such devotional works of art as these by Philippe de Champaigne. But, as I have just suggested, often enough one feels more than one articulates. Part of the task of the art-historical critic, it seems to me, is to put into words those feelings – that which is not often articulated – I have mentioned and to recreate, so far as this is possible, the horizon of viewing possibilities and expectations of the original viewers.

In their contemplative lives, the penitents at Port-Royal would have viewed these paintings as "events" of truth, incorporating them into their prayers.[77] It is my contention that the nuns did not conceive of themselves as subjects viewing objects but as worshippers who, in their prayers, were already on the path to a theophany (the "mind's road to God"), not unlike the one experienced by Mary Magdalene. The nuns at Port-Royal were in tune with the *event* of art. Champaigne functioned as a poet or intermediary, the angel or interpreter of the ways of his God and his Jansenist experience to men and, especially, the women of Port-Royal. But he did it in such a way that his persona as poet or painter steps aside, out of the spiritual avenue leading from here to there and back again. In a sense nothing came between the solitaires in their prayers and Champaigne's pictures. In the *Origin of the Work of Art*, Heidegger maintained that "[e]verything that might interpose itself between the thing and us in apprehending and talking about it must first be set aside. Only then do we yield ourselves to the undisguised presence of the thing."[78]

Examining these Jansenist works by Philippe de Champaigne through Heidegger's philosophy of presence allows us to see them as if in a clearing. George Steiner in his lapidary prose makes this very point: "Instead of the Platonic 'illumination from outside,' with its archetypal figure of the eye reaching out to an object along an exploratory light-ray, we shall have what Heidegger calls *die Lichtung*, the 'clearing,' in which truth is *experienced*, not perceived, as part and parcel of the 'facticity' (*Tatsächlichkeit*) and historicity (*Geschichtlichkeit*) of man's existence. We must labour not only to reach this clearing but to dwell in it."[79] There is indeed a difference between the traditional aesthetic view of art and what Gianni Vattimo conceives of as searching for a truth that is revealed by the "opening" of a work of art. Vattimo writes that "[a]esthetics, at least from this point of view, can no longer be a reflection on the pure and simple transcendental conditions of possibility of the experience of art and of the beautiful, but must allow itself to listen to the truth that is 'opened' in the work of art."[80] Here he reflects Heidegger's statement that "[t]he art work opens up in its own way the Being of beings. This opening up, i.e., this deconcealing, i.e., the truth of beings, happens in the work."[81] The art-historical critic attempts to "dwell" (using Steiner's language) in the clearing made by the work of art and to imagine or recapture the apprehension of those who may have dwelt there in the past.

Mine has been an imaginary re-creation of a Heideggerian reading of works of art as if they and I were in the church at Port-Royal in the mid-seventeenth century. But of course, since then the world (as Heidegger would put it) has withdrawn from the works and the works have been withdrawn from their original location, that world where they were the "appearing," which is the place within which penance occurred.[82]

Ex-Voto: "In Fulfilment of a Vow"

In 1662 Philippe de Champaigne painted the *Ex-Voto* to commemorate his daughter Catherine's miraculous recovery at Port-Royal (Figure 11.3).[83] Beginning in October 1660 and continuing for about 14 months, Catherine de Sainte-Suzanne, unable to rise or walk, suffered a feverish weakness. We can imagine her father's extreme and protracted worry. A sister at Port-Royal implored Mère Agnes (sister to the late La Mère Angélique and source of our information on Catherine's recovery) to pray for his daughter's healing. The Jansenist sisters employed the novena, a nine-days' devotion, if not for a cure at least for the granting

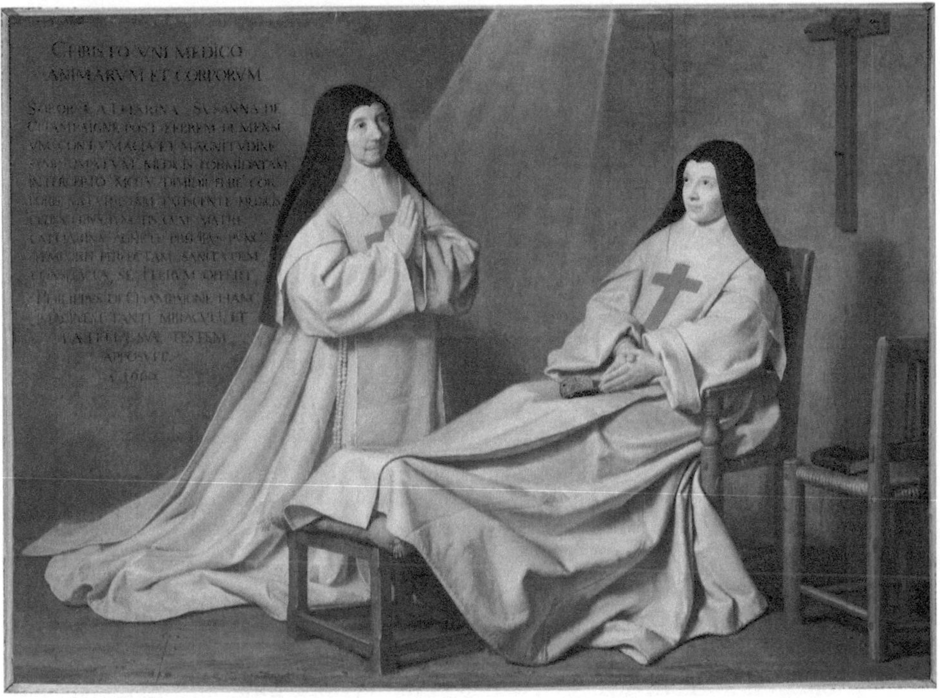

Figure 11.3 Philippe de Champaigne, *Ex-Voto*, oil on canvas, 1662, Musée du Louvre, Paris, France. Photo: Erich Lessing/Art Resource, NY.

of God's grace and the encouragement of the invalid. We read that on the last day of the novena, which was also the Feast of the Epiphany, Mère Agnes sensed the possibility of a cure; the next morning, Catherine de Sainte-Suzanne awoke just as Mass was being celebrated nearby, stood up for the first time in more than a year, and, after some hesitant steps, walked about her room in the chapter house. That same day she attended Mass by kneeling in a tribune above the chapel; then, shortly afterward, she was able to descend to the chapel itself.

Philippe de Champaigne had to conjecture what he could not see; that is, although the nuns at Port-Royal were not in *clausura*, it is unlikely that Champaigne knew his daughter's chamber or even the spaces in which she prayed behind the *corretto* screens. What the painter infers is a room in which his daughter, in a prayerful attitude and seated upon a chair, is placed to the right, with Mère Agnes to our left. However dear the church and convent of Port-Royal were to him, he cared little for exact appearances. Not that he loved Port-Royal less, but he loved Catherine more.

An ex-voto is more object than representation; therefore, our reading of the space operates largely outside of fictive topographies. There are here, of course, characters in a space, Mère Agnes and Catherine de Sainte-Suzanne, with God's grace as a cone of light falling between them. Words as if forming an epitaph appear cut miraculously into the chamber's wall. Roughly translated, they read,

> To Christ, the singular doctor of bodies and souls Sister Catherine Suzanne de Champaigne, after a fever of 14 months that had frightened the doctors by its tenacious character and the strength of its symptoms; with half of her body paralysed, her spirit exhausted, the doctors having given up, and being joined in prayer by Mère Catherine Agnès, in a single moment recovered her health. Philippe de Champaigne offers this image of a great miracle as a testimony of his joy; presented in the year 1662.

We are inside, although our point of reference or perception is somewhat indistinct or un-situated. That is because, I believe, we are witnessing not a narrative but a *hyper euchēs*, that is, a document executed in fulfilment of a vow, which is, at the same time, an "image of a great miracle." The canvas represents more a *frame* for a miracle than a place in which a story is told; it is a wonder accomplished rather than unfolding. First of all it is a gift or token, which "betokens" an unfolding or disclosure. Although all paintings are concrete objects, an ex-voto is *more* concrete object than simulacrum or representation. The emphasis here shifts to the sign rather than the signified; perhaps one could say that the semiosis works backward, focusing (as an index) on the maker and his joy rather than on narrative in the chambers of Port-Royal.

The composition follows nearly to the letter the closed and linear style formulated by the great art historian of *formpsychologie*, Heinrich Wölfflin. The danger for art-historical discourse lies, of course, in identifying this classical style as being somehow congruent, coextensive, or homologous with the principles of Jansenism. If we follow this kind of thinking, we wind up with an inter-art comparison that is merely and exasperatingly homonymic: Champaigne's style is "classical," which is a homonym for Wölfflin's "classical style," which is a homonym for "French literary classicism" of the seventeenth century – and so on.[84]

Jansenist Rhetoric

"Les Messieurs du Port-Royal" (variously identified as Bernard Lamy, Antoine Arnaud, and Pierre Nicole) in *The Art of Speaking* of 1679 argue not necessarily for a classical style in rhetoric – whatever that may mean – but for a "natural" one – whatever that may mean. Chapter 4 of this source makes a case for "less is more"; invoking the *lex parsimoniae*, or law of succinctness, the author (or authors) writes, "so we need no other Rules for speaking Ornately, than the Rules already given for speaking justly." They admire the "perspicuous" and insist that no expression be ambiguous; they abhor "impertinent words" and aver "clearness like a Torch dispels all obscurity, and makes every thing visible." Arnauld and company remark on the importance of concision in sound and a pronunciation that is "fluid and easy."[85]

The author goes on to assert that the best ornaments are those that, like the columns or pillars of a building, provide support. The worst – and most common, it would seem – ornaments are those in which "there is nothing of truth; they do rather perplex and embarrass, and render things more inconceivable than if your discourse were simple and natural."[86] Here we have voiced Cicero's *temperentia*, his invocation of a cardinal virtue, one of sobriety and just measure. Arnauld attacks "great things" by way of belittling human ego, observing how easily we are seduced by the grand because it is "rare and extraordinary."[87] He associates pomposity with grandeur, in other words, and marshals our fear of megalomania by appealing to the simple and the common, something men too often dismiss. Magniloquent epideictic oratory consists of (here Arnauld quotes from Horace) "*Sesquipedalia verba*" – words that are a foot-and-a-half long: "To dazzle and amaze, we need only clothe our Propositions in strange and magnificent Language." We do not understand what is under that opulent cover of verbiage, what the pelmet of Bernini's *Baldacchino* (for instance) seeks to obscure or hide, "because obscurity has some appearance of Grandeur, sublime and exalted things being for the most part obscure and difficult."[88] How is it that ornament has drawn such contempt? Is it because the glorious and resplendent (for which read "fulsome" and "over dramatized" – if we are to follow the spirit of the Port-Royal rhetoric) – embody Jesuit values?

Philippe de Champaigne, Jansenist though he was, cared little for a boiled-down rhetoric unaccompanied by a poetics of catharsis. There is, in other words, more to the story of Champaigne's rhetoric than a

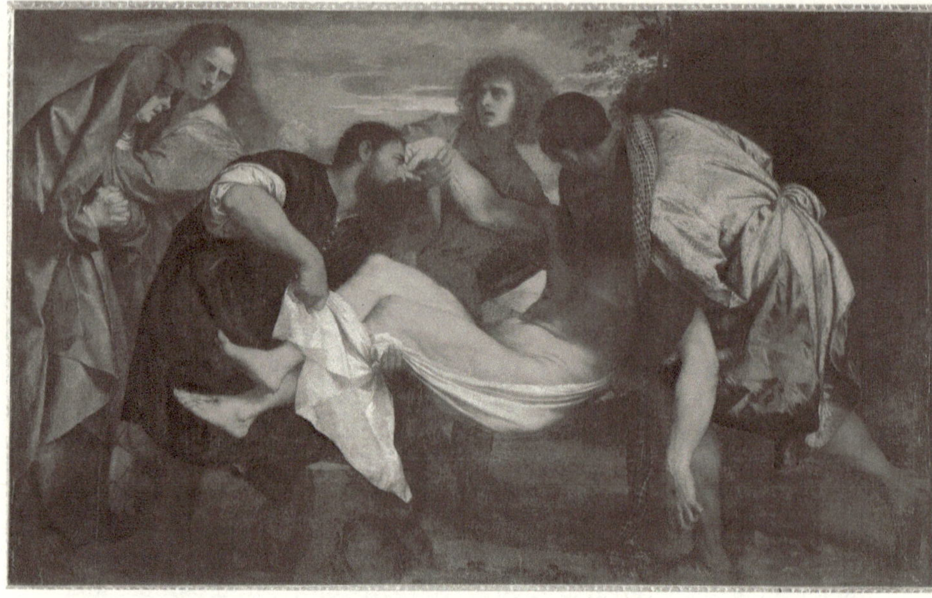

Figure 11.4 Titian, *The Entombment of Christ*, oil on canvas, c. 1520, Musée du Louvre, Paris, France. Photo: Erich Lessing/Art Resource, NY.

"natural" style (whatever that is), smooth planes, cubical forms, even lighting, and precise contours.

The "Conference" on Titian's *Entombment*

We can find out more about Champaigne by listening in on his presentation to the artists of the Académie Royale during one of the famous "Seven Conferences" reported by André Félibien. Here he examined Titian's *The Entombment of Christ* on 4 June 1667, in the king's cabinet of paintings (Figure 11.4). We may consider these comments under the rubric of the acroamatic, that is, as observations on paintings made privately to disciples, like Aristotle's lectures to his closest friends and students (the origin of his *Poetics*).

The *Entombment* originally belonged to the Duke of Mantua, painted in all likelihood for Isabella d'Este or her son Federico II Gonzaga, but was in the king's collection at the time of the conferences. It remains in the Louvre.

Champaigne begins, as Félibien tells us, by assuring his audience that without question this painting is genuine, done in the summer of Titian's years, "before the vast Intelligence he had acquired began to decline."[89] Because just the month before, Charles Le Brun had finished his disquisition on Raphael's *St Michael*, in which he dwelt at length upon matters of contour, lineaments, projections, and recessions – in short, the elements of *disegno* – Philippe de Champaigne moved to the less tangible phenomena of colour, light, and expression, befitting Titian's reputation as a great master of *coloure*.

Dead and shadowed, Christ's body lies limp, heavy, and flaccid, as Champaigne observes. Veins and sinews have retracted, except where the rigor has set in around the nail holes in his hands. Nicodemus partially blocks Christ's face, which is further obscured by shadow – "the better to imprint the character of Death on every member of the Body which Shades and Darkness are a proper Emblem." Here Champaigne comes down on the emotional side of painting, extolling Titian's grand mastery of pity and fear. He reads the actions of John, Nicodemus, and Joseph of Arimathea, along with the very colour of their flesh, as betraying sensations, commotions, and pain. He can see on the Magdalene's face and he can infer from her movement and the colour of her garment that she is torn between supporting Mary and following her Saviour to his tomb: the "Tenderness and Compassion she feels for the Mother of this beloved Spouse, keeps her behind." John, too, "looks back to the Virgin whose distress adds to his own, and raises in him a greater Degree of Affliction." Champaigne identifies with John's suffering, for there is sorrowing "painted" – using the participle metaphorically and literally – on his face. The Flemish artist discerns different coefficients of grief in the expressions of Nicodemus and Joseph of Arimathea, who have not witnessed the love of Christ as had John and Mary Magdalene, have not borne him and raised him from infancy as had his mother.

Félibien reports that some in the Académie found fault with Titian's managing of bodily proportions and articulation of parts; it was generally believed, just the same, that one would do better to concentrate on the artist's strengths than his weaknesses. The implication here is that one who masters the distribution of light and shade and the modulation of colours is unlikely to have Michelangelo's or Raphael's virtuosity in the rendering of anatomy and pictorial structure. A painter, it seems, is either in the *coloure* camp or the *disegno* camp.

Returning to the elements of Titian's colour, "M. de Champaigne" makes numerous admiring observations on the massing of light and shade, which constitutes the balancing of complementary colours and their ability to bring a sense of order and equilibrium to the composition as a whole. These are abstract and somewhat esoteric (acroamatic, as I have mentioned) observations for a select group of listeners.

But then the academicians find themselves following Champaigne's lead by looking again at the faces of the Blessed Virgin Mary, Mary Magdalene, and St John. Félibien comments specifically on how Mary's face reveals her determination to conquer her anguish so she can follow her son's body as it is borne to his grave; everything in her aspect conveys her soul's titanic struggle to stay strong and alert, to witness what must be witnessed – "for her eyes stand out, and her Eyebrows are erect, her Nose and Mouth stretched out as if she was drawn along by the dead Body." Metaphoric, figurative, and tropological, the language of Champaigne, the academicians, and Félibien describes Titian's painting as if one were witnessing a tragedy.[90] The peripety, which is a reversal of fortune, has been accomplished; now all is pathos.[91] The Magdalene's eyebrows are "cast down and half covering her Eyes ... her Hair disheveled and hanging carelessly on her Shoulder; and ... her Action ... has no other Object but the divine Body which is carried to the Tomb." John's face shows his compassion for Mary; we know this by "certain Folds form'd by his eyebrows, by being drawn near to one another, and so raised up at the two Extremeties."

Christ's passion both fits and does not fit within classical tragedy. A tragic hero, Aristotle writes (and I am using him as a spokesman for Champaigne's age – certainly Corneille and Racine so understood him, as did Félibien in the *Conferences*), is one who provokes in us pity and fear, for pity is "directed towards the man who does not deserve his misfortune" and fear "towards the one who is like the rest of mankind."[92] Christ as the Son of God is not like the rest of humankind; Christ as the son of man is. Champaigne clearly reads *The Entombment* in emotional – that is to say, human and dramatic – rather than transcendental and revelatory terms.[93]

Given the ruinous state of his *Poetics* (it is only a fragment of a lecture script, and there may have been a part 2), a full accounting of Aristotle's meanings for pity and fear is not possible, but these are ideas so closely associated in the Western tradition with mythic tales of suffering, death, and loss – and so powerfully evoked by Champaigne's reading of Titian's *Entombment* – that one turns to them when assessing the affective impact of such a great and mournful painting.

Champaigne's sense of pathos informs his every utterance on the painting, and his judicious analysis of the *Entombment* shows how purgation results from our vicarious experiences of pity and fear. Titian's rhetoric inflames our feelings.

As I have already suggested, Champaigne (along with Félibien and the academicians) reads Titian's *Entombment* much as a modern critic would: in figurative terms. For instance, the almost casual reference to "darkness and shadow" as "emblem" could be a typical comment by one schooled in early-modern poetics. We might prefer a term such as "symbol" to describe a certain passage of darkness in a painting as standing for and persuasively expressing something it is not – the "character of death"; just the same, Champaigne's remark is perfectly in line with *figuration*, with the transforming of an idea (death) into an image (shadows). In other words, Champaigne does not describe something we might categorize under the rubric of style; rather, he is evoking the power of images to be poetic constructions that create narrative, pity, and fear. It is not simply that Christ is dead but that death is "imprinted on every member of His body" – the corruptible body of incarnation. Christ in Titian's painting is intensely dead, as if death itself were not an absolute state of being but a power that grows and intensifies until it overwhelms those near to Christ and those outside the picture world, the young men in the Louvre who witnessed Titian's painting while Champaigne spoke.

Summary and Conclusion

Before I attempt to draw my conclusions on Philippe de Champaigne as a "Jansenist painter," I will digress briefly on the ways in which the problem of a Jansenist style has concerned literary historians, especially around the plays of Jean Racine.

Already in the earlier part of the eighteenth century, no less a figure than Voltaire (whose brother was a Jansenist) recognized a Jansenist *Phèdre* by the Jansenist-educated Racine.[94] The fact that Racine broke with the Jansenists seems not to have discouraged those in search of an Augustinian-Jansenist ideology or subtext in his plays. This identification and conjoining of a writer and his Augustinian leanings seemed to strike one as reasonable in the day when, repeated assertions from the papacy that it was anathema notwithstanding, many continued to foment and follow Jansenism in France (not to mention Italy). Since then a veritable industry of literary criticism has grown up around theological biographies of Racine and the search for a Jansenist ethos in his plays.[95] On the other hand, as John Campbell has shown, one treads cautiously these days into the territory of Jansenist themes in Racine's plays and Augustinian pessimism as it issues from the mouths of Orestes, Andromache, or Pyrrhus, Theseus, Hippolytus, or Phaedra.[96] One does not have to look far in order to find Augustinian pessimism in Racine's plays, but then Shakespeare, too, gives us many a character who seems doomed by forces beyond his control and plods through life towards a violent end, one which he can see but cannot seem to prevent. In other words, these are broad themes that one can hardly pin just on Jansenist theology and Augustinian notions of grace. As Campbell writes, there is considerable difficulty in assessing that which is *specifically* Jansenist in Racine's plays rather than simply part of the "literary commonwealth."[97] In short, taking a complex ideology set atop a comprehensive, knotted, and interwoven theology and transposing it, procrustean-style, onto something like Racinian tragedy is not unlikely to fail. In his limpid and vivid prose, Campbell summarizes, "Applied to literature, [Jansenism] becomes so vague as to function only as a synonym for 'pessimistic.' It is a splash of local colour rather than an attempt at accurate delineation, less a brushstroke than a pot of paint spilled on the canvas of meaning."[98]

With this apt painterly metaphor, we turn to Philippe de Champaigne to see about applying "Jansenism" in something other than a synonymic fashion. We can start with historiographical matters: What about the attempts made to yoke Champaigne to Jansenist ideology, theology, texts, practices, and of course Port-Royal itself? I have reported on some of these exercises already, beginning with Sainte-Beuve and his characterization of Champaigne's "sincere brush" and the argument – if it can be so called – for Champaigne's Jansenism growing from one's readings of the piety, affection, sincerity, and sensibility of a movement and one of its adherents.

In Lorenzo Pericolo's judicious reading, Sainte-Beuve's affection for Champaigne becomes the foundation for the myth of Champaigne as the good painter and good Christian, the one who transposes onto the canvas the sensibility of the Jansenists.[99] Pericolo comments on the painter's power as an artistic thaumaturge, who is a performer of miracles. With an inexplicable alchemy, Champaigne knew how to render for disciples of Jansenism their aspirations and questions of heart and soul. But the matter for Pericolo turns on whether or not there is anything one can call an "aesthetic" for Port-Royal. The answer (not surprisingly – although Pericolo works diligently through numerous Jansenist documents before getting there) is *no*: "[I]t appears evident that there never existed an aesthetic of Port-Royal, if one intends by this a coherent system of precepts and prohibitions concerning the practice of painting."[100]

The word "aesthetic" may be anachronistic, but Pericolo's definition clarifies things and puts them into a stylistic context. After all, who would expect Jansenists to come up with a manual of style for painting? They did so, of course, for logic, grammar, and rhetoric; but that is a different story. On the opposite side of the political and theological divide, the Jesuits most certainly understood imagery, although they too failed to theorize it. This is not the place to rehearse all the rules, maxims, and principles that guided, defined, and justified the visual arts in the European (and specifically Catholic) world from the time of Pope Gregory the Great's defending of images at the turning of the sixth to the seventh century through the twenty-fifth session of the Council of Trent, which promulgated its decrees on the "legitimate use of images." But generally speaking there was no (as Pericolo puts it) "coherent system of precepts and prohibitions concerning the practice of painting" as it related to particular religious or theological suppositions. It may be true, for instance, that a painter in New York City in the 1950s, exhibiting in major galleries, would indeed have been aware of and in all likelihood attentive to a coherent system of precepts and restrictions: he or she probably would have been abstract. But such a test does not sit well with early-modern painting within the narrow confines of religious orders. That is not to say there were no "schools" or artistic tendencies at the time. We as modern art historians can classify and analyse, allowing ourselves to be swept up by holistic imprecision, such catholicities and universalities as "classic" and "baroque." But that again is beside the point.

We often mislead ourselves by acting like "hard determinists" when seeking an identity between a visual style and a religious movement. It is as if one were caught up in the sometimes reductive and often limiting discourse of definition, a process that requires us to settle on the necessary and sufficient properties of whatever is to be defined. In art history, that has often enough meant that we look to style as the telling essence, the substance that encodes certain values, such as those of the Jansenists. We are apt to believe that, in order for Jansenist principles to be necessary and sufficient, they should have a particular relation to a specific or idiosyncratic style, not merely be something that is widely diffused. A Jansenist style should be just that, a style peculiar to the Jansenists, *not* one that originates elsewhere and that is sometimes, but not invariably, employed by a painter who produces canvases for Jansenist patrons. Because we identify an artist with his style, we tend to assume that the connection between the artist and, say, a religious organization can be cemented if all the elements of identity fall into place.

But, as I have suggested, Philippe de Champaigne's manner was pretty much fixed by the time he arrived in France. His art may have been congenial to the Jansenists, although there is no evidence that they judged his style to be necessary and sufficient to their needs. But is this really a barrier in developing an argument that Philippe de Champaigne was in fact a Jansenist artist, not just because of his style, not just because he worked for them, but in some more profound way? Our problem may be that we count too much on style to convey meaning, that we have learned too well the old lesson that form *is* content, that the medium is both message and massage.

Louis Marin has used semiotics and linguistics to find rhetorical similarities between Champaigne's painting and Jansenist writing (specifically Arnauld and Nicole's *Port-Royal Logic*), although he remains careful to distinguish, often in complex, searching, and even exquisite terms, between the verbal and the visual, the real and the figural, word and image, the signifier and the signified, the portrait and the one represented in the portrait.[101]

The question remains whether there is something Jansenist we can identify in Champaigne's painting and on what basis we can make that claim. Rather than use the language of the seventeenth century, whether it be in regard to Jesuit or Jansenist rhetoric, the language of criticism used by Giovanni Battista Bellori or the discourses in the Académie Royale as reported by André Félibien, I turn once again to the more nearly contemporary language of ontology, phenomenology, hermeneutics, and specifically Martin Heidegger.

Like Hegel, Heidegger marked the dying away of "great art," art that was borne and consumed by an entire culture of believers.[102] The great age of faith in Europe, the Middle Ages, was in some ways spent, but the church marched on, the squabbling of Jesuits and Jansenists notwithstanding. Painting, sculpture, and architecture conveyed the Word of God – the Logos – by propagating sacred imagery, power, and truth. In the Heideggerian and Hegelian sense, the religious art of the seventeenth century still disclosed truth.

Heidegger's concentration on the "work of art" differs from an aesthetic point of view, one growing out of percipience, mentality, conception, and feeling. The "art work," as he saw it, is the *kunstwerk*, which is an arena for "truth happening" – *Grundgedanke*. Despite the fairly common complaint about the obscurity of Heideggerian language, his understanding of "truth happening" strikes me as a fitting and near approximation of the "event" in much of seventeenth-century religious art. By event, I mean in this instance (following Julian Young) something charismatic.[103] That is, John, eyes moist with tears, points to Christ, while Mary Magdalene – she, too, of the crying eyes – reveals to the true believer God's redemptive love (*charis*) and grace. It is, as St Paul wrote (1 Corinthians 9), the word of faith that comes as a gift.

The happening of truth implies the opening of a world, the world of the work of art as well as the world – the omneity or fullness – of the work's own time and place. Art historians, of course, often enough concern themselves with context, but Heidegger meant something different from context in its usual art-historical sense. For instance, Raphael's *Sistine Madonna*, originally in the monastery and church of San Sisto in Piacenza, was given by the monks in the eighteenth century to Augustus III of Saxony. It now resides in Dresden's Gemäldegalerie.[104] Heidegger remarked that Raphael's painting belongs to the church and monastery in Piacenza "not merely in an historical-antiquarian sense, but according to its pictorial essence."[105] Taken from its home, the *Sistine Madonna* loses its quiddity or essence and becomes an "aesthetic object," one dependent upon connoisseurship.[106] Given his reference to connoisseurship as a privileged and nearly exclusive practice in art history, Heidegger's understanding of this discipline, even into the 1960s, may not have been profound. He seems to have had somewhat limited experience with or sympathy for what had become, even long before then, a sophisticated and often highly intellectual form of critical inquiry. Despite Heidegger's somewhat dismissive phrase, I find it difficult to disagree with his judgment on the change in ontology and meaning when a painting functions as a "work of art" rather than as an icon. It has lost its Benjaminian aura.

Reuniting Champaigne's paintings with the convent and chapel of Port-Royal during those relatively few years in the middle of the seventeenth century before the "persecution," when the painter was alive and Port-Royal was allowed to exist, is at best a highly imaginative undertaking. But only by willing ourselves to do so can we assess his paintings as vehicles and disclosures of truth, of *aletheia*, perhaps sensing that an understanding of Philippe de Champaigne as Jansenist has substance. He was a Jansenist because he, like the sisters in the convent (including his daughter), was *in* the Jansenist world that he disclosed and to which he gave visual presence.

12 The Corsini Chapel: Its Sense of Place and Time

The early eighteenth-century Italian architect Alessandro Galilei (distantly related to the family of Galileo Galilei) instructed the sculptors whom he employed for the building of the Corsini Chapel (1732–5; Figure 12.1) in Rome's basilica of San Giovanni in Laterano not to project their statues or reliefs beyond certain limits.[1] He explicitly forbade, in other words, any hint of *secentismo* – the style of Bernini, Pietro da Cortona, and Borromini. "Do not break the frame!" he (in effect) exhorted the leading sculptors in Rome.[2] Perhaps that departure from baroque majesty and decorum with its projections and recessions led Francesco Valesio (in his early eighteenth-century *Diario di Roma*) to comment that the chapel "has not met the satisfaction of all, being judged too precious and dry [*venendo riputata minuta e secca*]."[3]

Although *secca*, understood as dry, seems fairly straightforward (just the same, what is a "dry" style?), *minuta* – which I translate as "precious" (Elisabeth Kieven uses the word "boring")[4] – may suggest more nuanced stylistic overtones. These may include the fastidious, fine, or even minute in the sense of being small (rather than ostentatious or frame-breaking), and, in a pejorative sense, inconsequential – piffling or trivial, in other words. It is this putting together of fine and fastidious that brings up the precious, which strikes me as close to what Valesio perhaps was trying to communicate. And indeed "boring" it may have seemed to some.

As the modern editors of his *Diario di Roma* suggest, Valesio was a man given to subtle irony, often with a hint of condescension, here perhaps demonstrating an awareness of the velleity – a kind of wan wishfulness – relating to artistic style in the Rome of the 1730s. The style of the Corsini Chapel "wished" for something Tuscan and

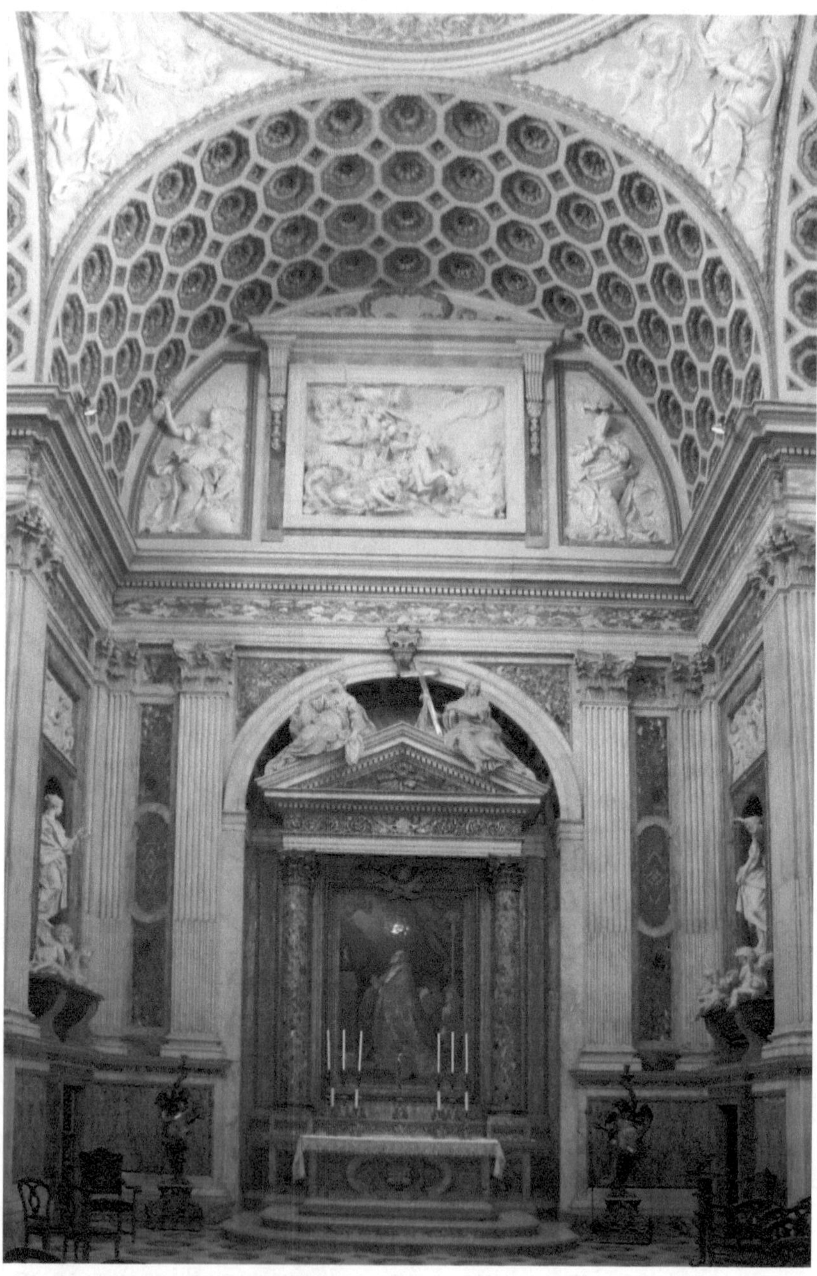

Figure 12.1 Alessandro Galilei, *The Corsini Chapel*, 1732–5, San Giovanni in Laterano, Rome, Italy. Photo: Author.

restrained rather than something Roman and filled with "unnecessary projections."[5]

What Valesio probably did not know is that Galilei in effect issued a restraining order on his sculptors, as we have seen. And Galilei backed up his insistence on a version of classicism with the threat that anyone going over the line would have to fix things at his own expense.

There may be a whiff of mockery, too, in Valesio's description of the dedication of the chapel. He writes that the entire chapter (i.e., those chaplains appointed by Pope Clement XII to the Corsini Chapel) attended the dedication with a "serene and temperate" air, while explosions from no fewer than four *mortaletti* (small cannons) marked the arrival of each cardinal. The dedication seems to have embodied the rhetorical figure of an oxymoron – explosively serene.

Precisely because Alessandro Galilei proscribes and promises punishment for any violation of the frame, whether the traditional aedicular form or the passepartout of the bas-reliefs, he draws the historical critic's attention to Kant's and Derrida's parergon. What Galilei tries to stifle he in fact calls to our attention; his insistence on the separation between sculpture and architecture ensures their reciprocal and problematical relationship. He planned a pure zone of architecture and a separate space for sculpture. It also is my reading of Galilei that he intended for sculpture – which must remain within its frame – to have a supplementary and subordinate relationship to architecture. It is the chapel, after all, that houses the sculpture, the architect who dictates placement and limits.

In his *Critique of Judgment*, Immanuel Kant calls attention to the *parergo* as that which represents the importance in Western metaphysics between inside and outside. He writes of architectural frames (columns and pilasters), sculptural frames (drapery), and frames around paintings. Kantian frames are not passive delimitations but have the active purpose of setting things off: They are repoussoirs, devices that contain and therefore draw attention to something. Kant's *parerga* remain supplementary or adjunctive to the *ergon*, the thing framed; this is especially true of a picture frame, which supposedly is less a part of the painting than are columns a part of architecture.[6]

I will begin with some observations on the parergonal, especially in relation to what I infer to be Alessandro Galilei's intentions. Simply in terms of tectonics, one can look at the Corsini Chapel's frames in light of Galilei's policy not to break them. Robert Enggass has written on the colours of the chapel as if they too were frames. He contrasts the marbles here with the deeper, richer, more saturated coloured stones of the Chapel of St Ignatius in Il Gesù, Rome. For his broad purposes of comparison, Enggass observes this of the Corsini Chapel:

> As we enter the light-flooded interior of this enormous room we are impressed at once by the way in which it combines richness with restfulness and quietude, in sharp contrast to the Chapel of St. Ignatius. Architectural elements for the most part are shallow, slender and symmetrical, and the overall effect of the color is calm and light.[7]

Enggass succeeds in describing that sense of constraint implicit in Galilei's directives on planes and frames. The colours of the Corsini Chapel's marbles and the remarkable intricacy of architectural and sculptural elements, although undoubtedly impressive and rich to the eye of a modern visitor, nonetheless pale next to the Jesuits' Chapel of St Ignatius in Il Gesù (Figure 12.2). In a similar fashion, the sense of that which is discrete (Corsini) seems to be better understood when opposed to that which is conjoined (St Ignatius). In other words, Enggass made his points by comparing a classical style (Corsini Chapel) to a baroque style (Chapel of St Ignatius).

When looking at the altar mosaic of St Andrea Corsini praying before a biblical text and crucifix, we may not immediately notice, because of the plethora of framing devices, the relatively delicate gilt frame into which the mosaic has been inserted (Figure 12.3). Once we observe the picture frame, our eye moves to other framing devices, panels of *alabastro rosso* with columns of *verde antico* in turn flanking these frames. Then as our eyes broaden the visual field we come upon another panel of *alabastro rosso* (which itself is framed by narrow panels of *verde antico*), followed by red and white *breccia*. So far these framing devices have been building from the altarpiece outward as if this were a negative *mise en abyme* – in a sense, a moving away from the abyss, step by step, until one realizes all of this framing is framed by an arcuate form of Carrara marble that is in turn flanked by fluted Corinthian pilasters; as parergon this arch has the ontological status of an aedicular frame. Each frame embeds itself within another. Our ekphrastic efforts begin to flag at this point as framing device succeeds framing device, and we must concede that Galilei's directive on his project seems to hold, although what value that restraint has is not immediately apparent. Multitudinous frames shackled by a somewhat reduced size (at least in terms of relief)

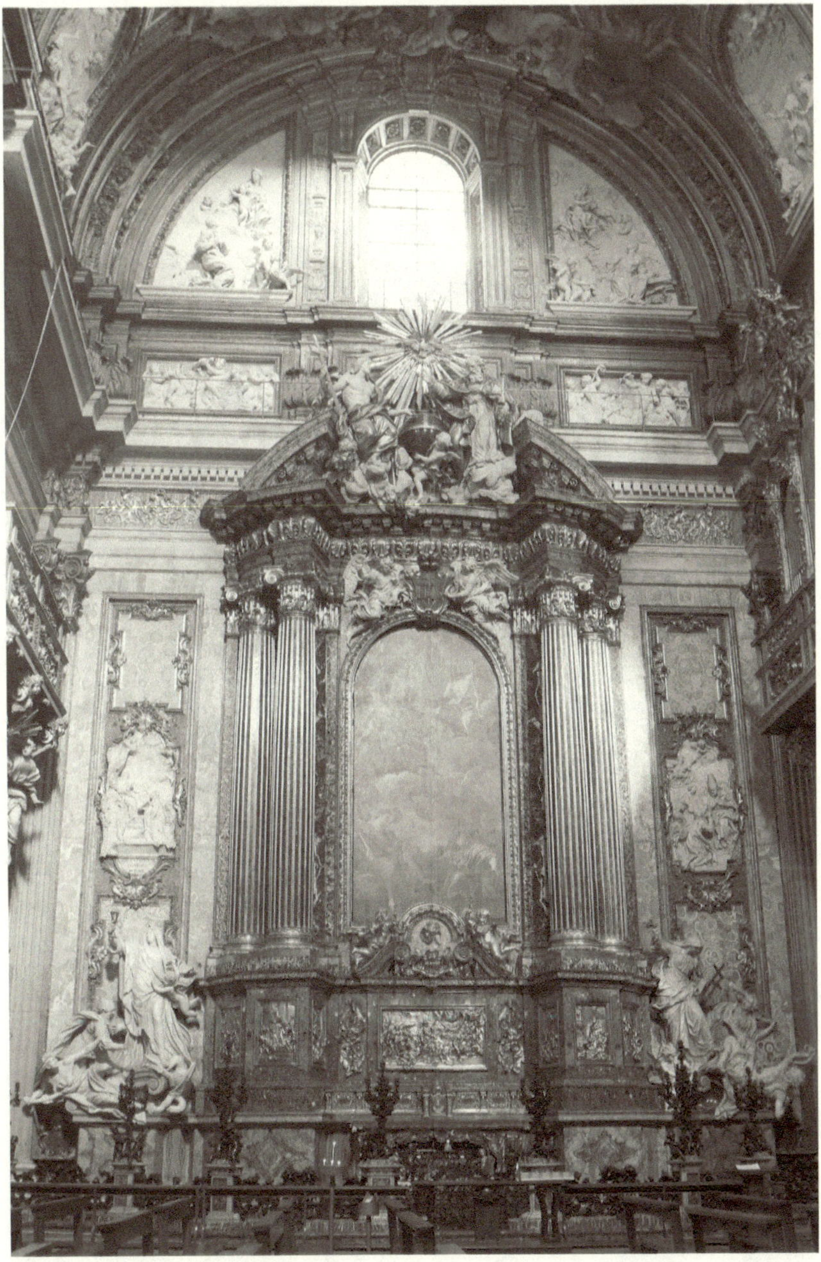

Figure 12.2 Andrea Pozzo (architect), *Chapel of St Ignatius*, 1696–1700, Il Gesù, Rome, Italy. Photo: Author.

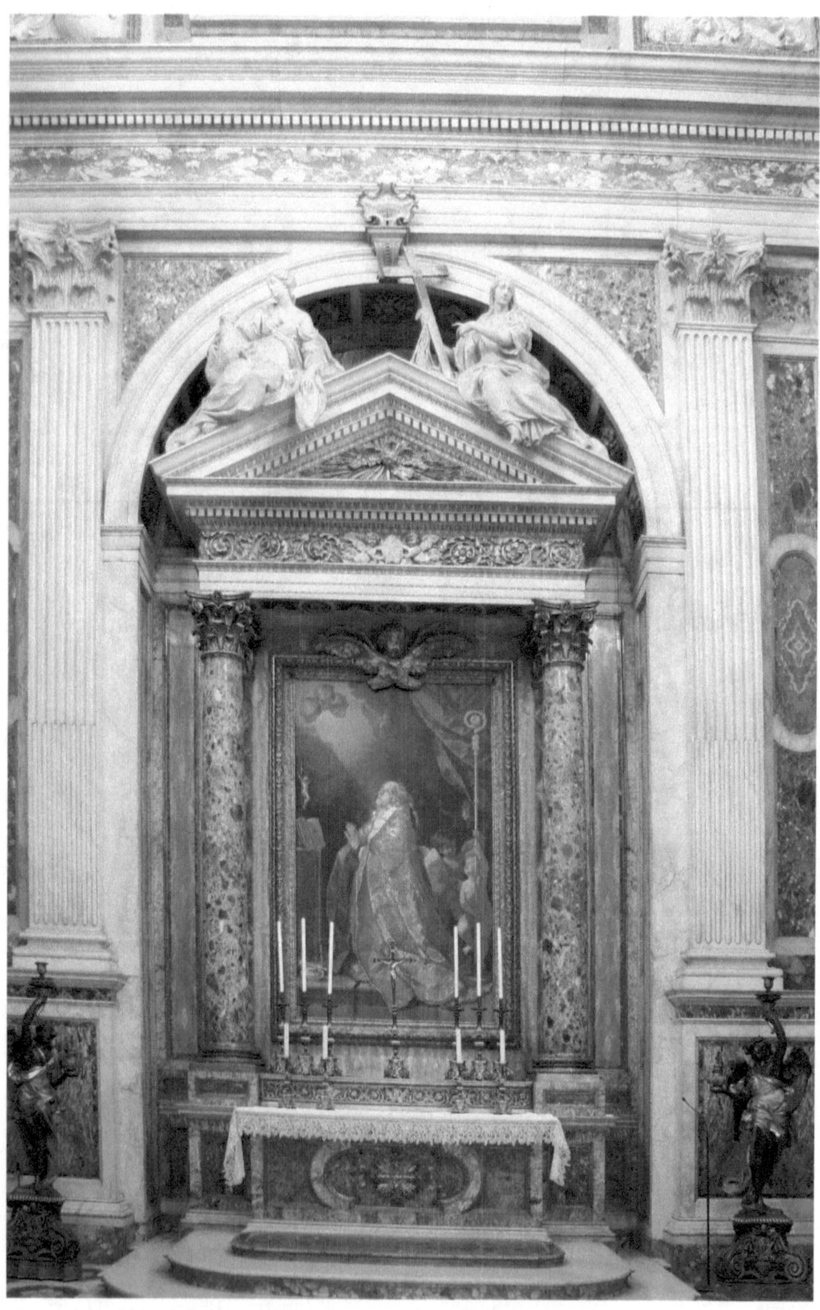

Figure 12.3 Guido Reni, *The Corsini Chapel: St Andrea Corsini*, mosaic (copy of oil painting), 1732–5, San Giovanni in Laterano, Rome, Italy. Photo: Robert G. La France.

dazzle us just the same with their exquisite materials, precise design, and unending detail.

When a critical historian of art grapples with meaning, he or she must at some point come to terms with the *conditions* of meaning, the ways in which meaning can be discussed. And that effort seems to have bearing on what is inside and what is outside the work of art, what is fair game in the struggle over writing about meaning and what seems to be out of bounds. Jacques Derrida tells us in *The Truth in Painting* that the parergon – the frame – is neither "the work (*ergon*) nor outside the work, neither inside or outside, neither above nor below, it disconcerts any opposition but does not remain indeterminate and it *gives rise* to the work."[8] Interiority and exteriority are in dialogue with one another, offering self-reflexive explanations. Furthermore, one understands the architecture of a chapel in terms of its *difference* from the sculpture and mosaic, just as the sculpture is the obverse of the architecture. Instead of binary opposition in the Corsini Chapel, however, there is binary reconciliation and reciprocity. If indeed Galilei hoped for separation and independence, then he in fact managed to accomplish precisely the opposite, which of course does not constitute a failure on his part, except perhaps in his intentions.

The multiplication of "peripherality" is fundamental to the chapel's character, indispensable to its meaning, keeping in mind that the frame is not interior to (inside) the work (chapel and everything in it) – so Derrida says – but is not "extrinsic" to it either. All these parergons – and I intend by that also the coloured stones spanning "zones" (definitely *not* "unmeaning" zones) between and among passepartout and aedicular/tabernacle frames – constitute Derridean "difference," "deferral," and the "supplement." Architecture and sculpture; inside and outside; plane and relief; stones of pink, yellow, white, and green – all of these work together in "metaphysical complicity."[9]

This complicity has to do with *play*, which is a key word for the complex relationship between and among mosaic, sculpture, and architecture in the Corsini Chapel (there is no painting). We do not deny such things as inside and outside, frame and not frame, but we allow the concepts to interpenetrate, to comment on one another, to play with one another, and to pile atop one another. The effect of all this performance and teasing results in a three-dimensional density of *affect*, the complex experience we have of a place and space in which there are contesting aesthetic and epistemological forces.

Derrida points to the intricacy of interrelations and how they come to constitute something we might call meaning:

> *Parerga* have a thickness, a surface which separates them not only (as Kant would have it) from the integral inside, from the body proper of the ergon, but also from the outside, from the wall on which the painting is hung, from the space in which statue or column is erected, then, step by step, from the whole field of historical, economic, political inscription in which the drive to signature is produced ... No "theory," no "practice," no "theoretical practice" can intervene effectively in this field if it does not weigh up and bear on the frame, which is the decisive structure of what is at stake, at the invisible limit to (between) the interiority of meaning (put under shelter by the whole of hermeneuticist, semioticist, phenomenologicalist, and formalist tradition) and (to) all the empiricisms of the extrinsic which, incapable of either seeing or reading, miss the question completely.[10]

Derrida says two things here relevant to the ways in which critical historians of art go about their business. First of all, we art historians need to be careful in our "contextualizing" of art. The nature of our profession suggests (although does not demand) that the work of art is the star of the show, that it is the phenomenon around which we marshal evidence so as to make sense of the world in which the Corsini Chapel (for instance) found itself in Rome in the 1730s or finds itself today. This is part of the "drive to signature," which is not about just the artist but involves a complex array of factors and "senders" that construct an artistic identity.[11] The second point is that we have to "drive" on the "rail" of the frame, and, like circus performers, we do it as if upon a unicycle while juggling countless balls. In other words, art history is a markedly delicate balancing act, a performance we never quite master, a job that is never done.

The parergon or frame, along with Galilei's preoccupation with its boundaries, brings us into a space and a place, leads us into epistemological territory where we do not seek a settled interpretation – something strictly hermeneutic, in other words – but move to and fro with conditions of meaning. Framing devices and the relation of architecture to sculpture bear close scrutiny.

The chapel is closed off from the rest of the basilica by glass (added recently) and densely screened bronze gates that allow one standing outside the chapel to peek at but not quite observe details of the chapel

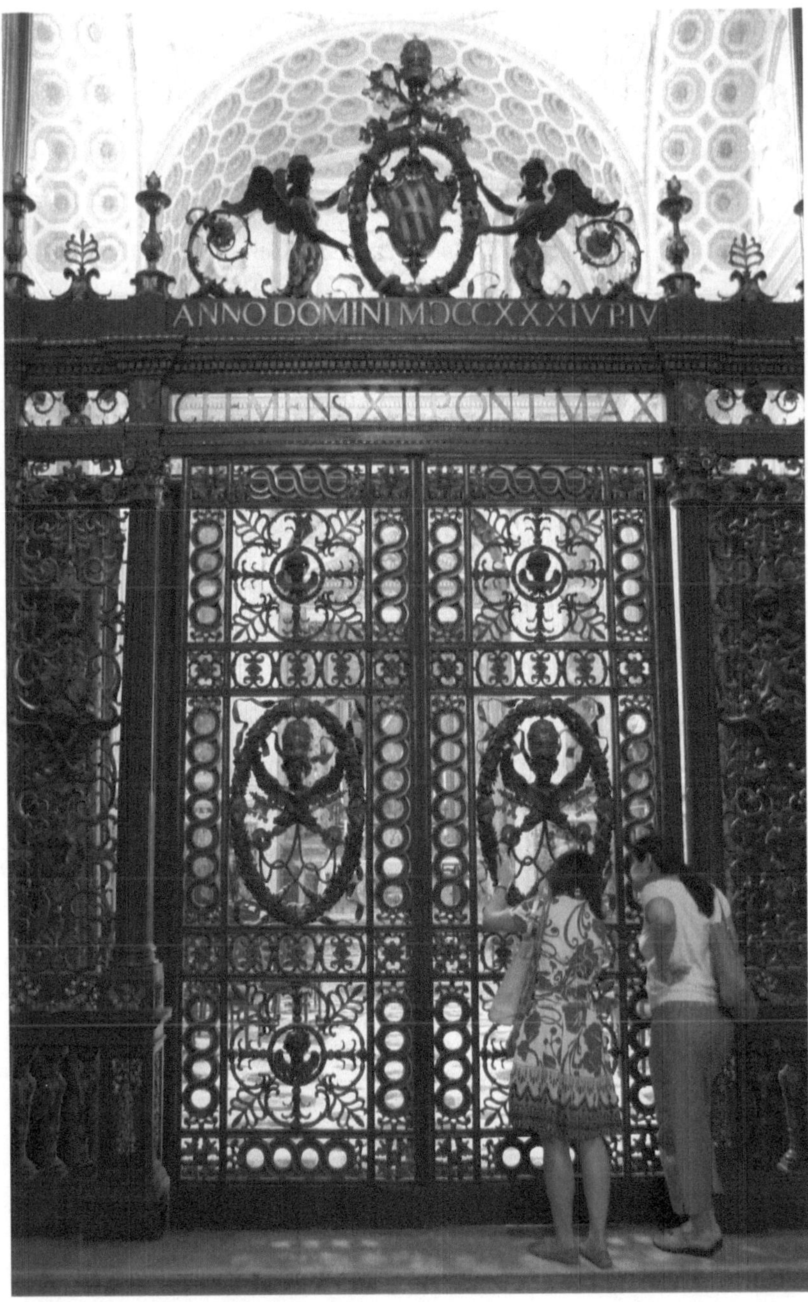

Figure 12.4 Alessandro Galilei, *The Corsini Chapel*, view through gates. Photo: Author.

either closely or with any freedom of vision (Figure 12.4). After negotiating permissions (the chapel is private, remaining in the hands of the Corsini family) and getting into Galilei's space, visitors, now physically inside, attempt to come to terms both with place and space in the chapel. Although the space is anisotropic – that is, there are differing dimensions as one looks from statue to statue, architectural form to architectural form, and surface to surface – nonetheless there is this feeling more of space than place. The Greek-cross plan, the majestic dome (Figure 12.5), and the honeycombed, coffered barrel vaults above the windows, altar, and entrance bays give rise to a sense of cosmic space rather than *genius loci*, despite the fact that we are, by definition, in a place of eulogy – a funerary chapel.

If, like turning the barrel of a camera lens, we twist the focus ring of our minds in the direction of art, we are once again back in a *place*, one that causes a critical historian of art to rub his or her hands in anticipation of getting down to the business of studying myriad details, of considering illusions of space on one side or the other of the great ontological divide between our world of lived and breathed moments and that other, the one through the looking glass (as it were), the artistic realm of silence, imagination, and very slow time. The frames are in our world; the statues and reliefs lead us elsewhere.

But, as I say, one is hard-pressed not to sense before anything else, thanks to Alessandro Galilei's architecture, that the space of the Corsini Chapel is cosmic. On the floor the isosceles trapezoids of orange and black marble with varying floral motifs lead to this micro universe's omphalos – represented by the Corsini coat of arms with a tiara-crowned putto (Figure 12.6).

I say cosmic for a number of reasons. First of all, sacred architecture from time immemorial had been instantiating the divine, bringing the cosmological to the terrestrial, if always in rhetorical terms and physical form. In the Corsini Chapel we are on a spot – off the nave of a Roman church – within the "massive matrix of relations" (as Edward Casey calls it) of an infinite universe.[12] The meaning of this particular piece of ground pales in comparison to God's universe. It is a funerary chapel but is about a memory that is in God's mind, not about physical remains. And, as I have suggested, we moderns have a difficult time holding in *our* minds the sense of space in its sheer infinite grandeur. In fact I, an art historian, care very much about *place* rather than space, and my concerns, representing at least in part the interests and provinces of a post-Enlightenment academic disciplinarity (art

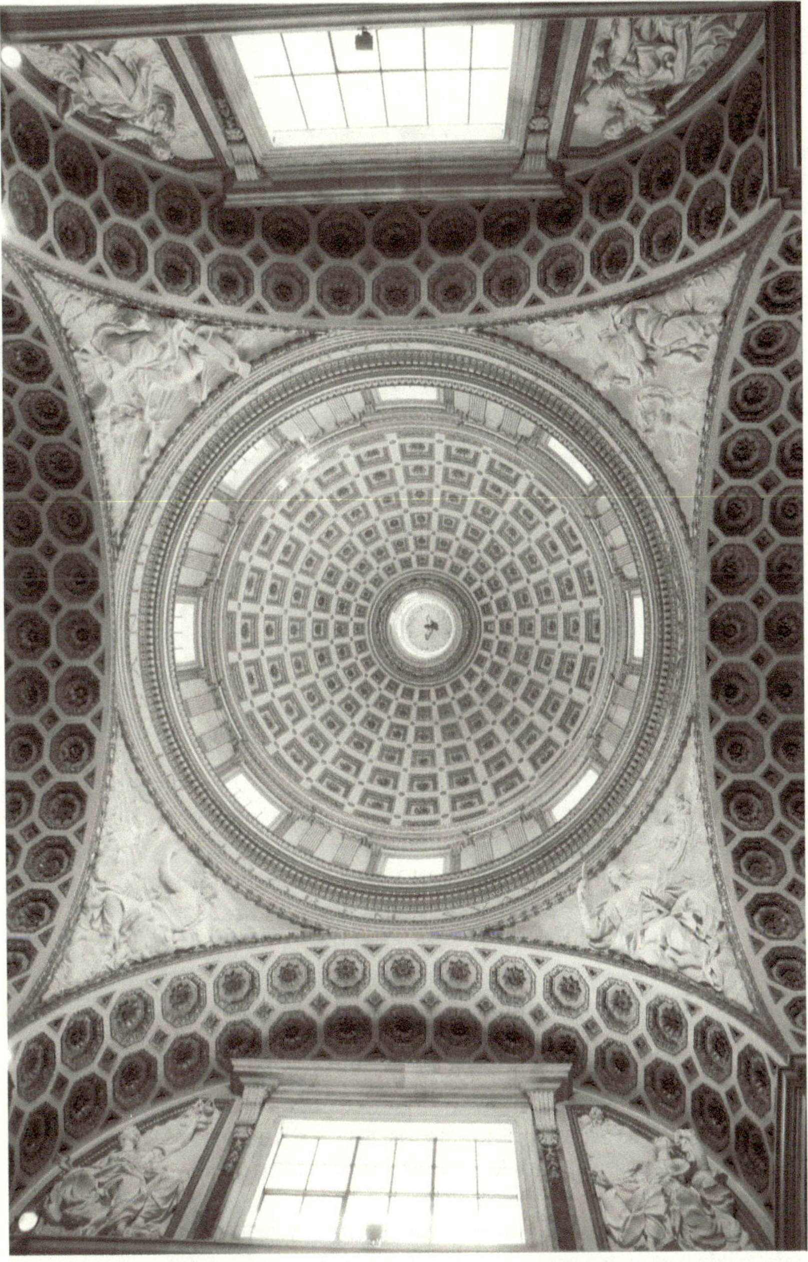

Figure 12.5 *The Corsini Chapel,* interior dome. Photo: Robert G. La France.

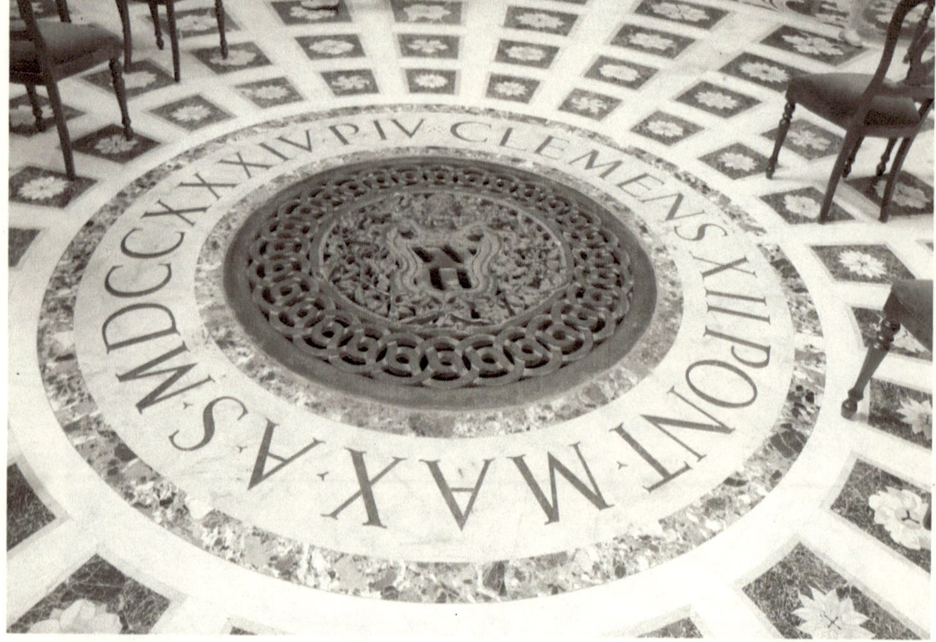

Figure 12.6 *The Corsini Chapel*, view of grating in floor. Photo: Robert G. La France.

history), nearly always take over in the end. But I am getting ahead of myself here and so return to a willing suspension of disbelief in the absence of place.

That brings me back to frames, which introduce measurement into space because they divide space. These parergons – and here I think Derrida would have agreed – create reciprocities in the Corsini Chapel.

The soaring entrance arch, matching Francesco Borromini's arches along the nave, merges on either side with stop-fluted Corinthian pilasters, which are followed as the eye goes outward by another set of stop-fluted Corinthian pilasters, these folded into the corners (Figure 12.7). Above are levels of architrave, frieze, cornice, and finally a barrel vault pockmarked by octagonal, bronze-lined (with egg-and-dart motifs), rosette-plugged cavities. These architectural forms embrace both coloured stones and under the vault two lunette reliefs along with a *corretto* screen (now covered by drapes). One can

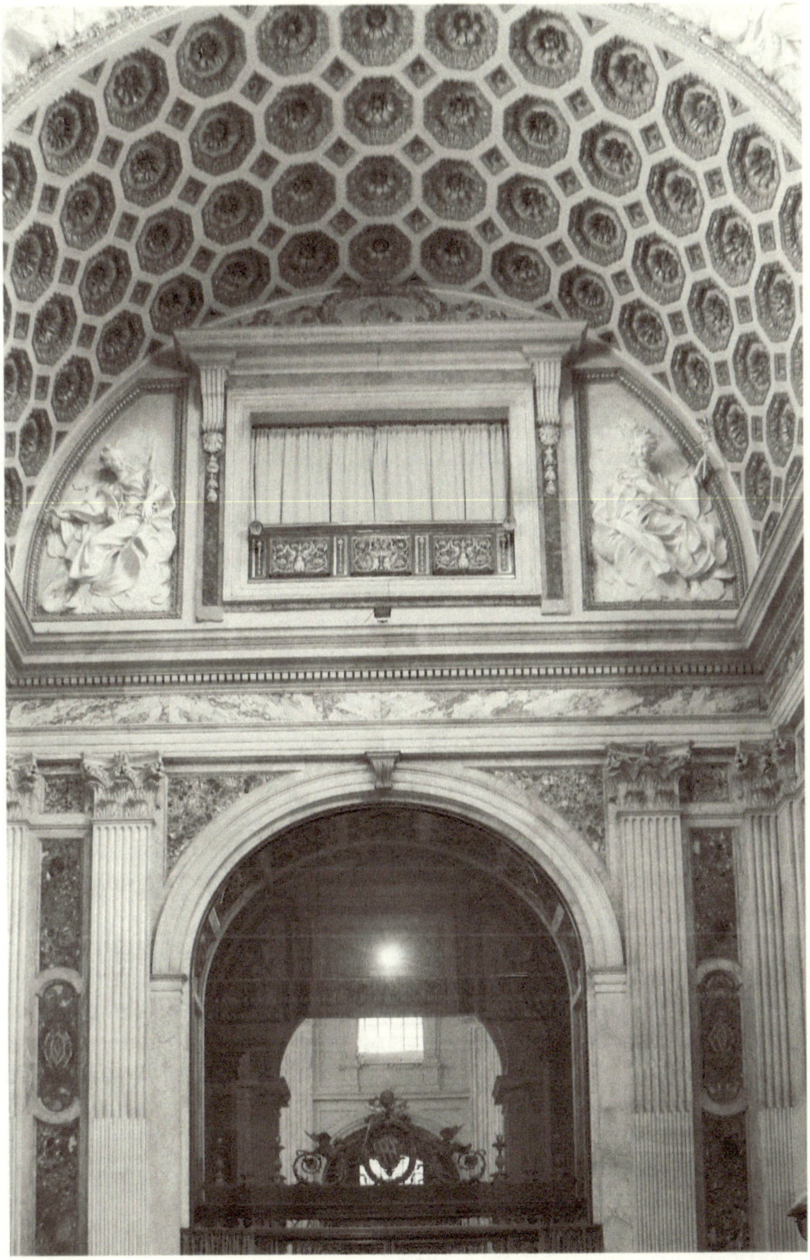

Figure 12.7 *The Corsini Chapel*, entrance bay. Photo: Robert G. La France.

see how Derrida's assertion on the necessity of "weighing up" and "bearing on" the frames here is unavoidable and utterly necessary for our "theoretical practice," for our consideration of what goes on in the Corsini Chapel.

The Corsini's private viewing chamber, or *corretto* as these spaces have been called since the seventeenth century, has a low balustrade across three panels of intricate bronze patterns. Although the purpose of a *corretto* is putatively to allow the Corsinis to view the celebration of the mass below without themselves being viewed, the framing devices in fact turn the invisible worshipper above into a work of art, framed by an upper cornice supported by scrolled modillions from which descend marble acanthus leaves and tessellated pomegranates. What exquisite framing of the (supposedly) invisible worshipper! This rhetoric of magnificent and self-effacing irony is not missed by those below; framing – supposedly an architectural supplement – drives, as Derrida tells us, to *signature*.

It is indeed an interesting ride. Derrida's "signature" is usually seen as authorial, although broadly conceived, it refers us to the one who designed the chapel. Alessandro Galilei has, in Derrida's explication of the parergon, an indexical relation to each and every frame in the chapel. Each of these frames in effect points like an index finger at the architect. The drive to signature in and among frames also can reach back to the one who conceived of there being a chapel here, which would mean both Pope Clement XII and his nephew Cardinal Neri Corsini, the ones who "signed off" on the chapel. And, as Mieke Bal and Norman Bryson understand the artist/architect as "sender" (in this case, not *just* Alessandro Galilei) in post-structuralist poetics, he or she is not so much a person out in the world, one who has stashed a certain meaning into a work of art. Rather, the author is an epiphenomenon of his or her creations, the product of an "elaborate work of framing, something we elaborately produce rather than something we simply find."[13] Here we realize, too, that "framing" has its metaphorical import in human discourse, in language, and in how we construct authorship and meaning, how we posit something, set it apart from people, ideas, and objects around it.

Sir Christopher Wren's tomb in St Paul's, London, the church he designed and built, carries the epitaph *Si monumentum requiris, circumspice* ("if you seek his monument, look about you"). The monument is he, the architect, and therefore St Paul's frames and constitutes the architect's identity and immortality.

The Chevalier de Jaucourt in one of his many entries for the great French *Encyclopedie*, provided the following definition of "monument": "an architectural term, this word means in particular a tomb *quia monet mentem*, because it informs the mind."[14] The monumental tomb informs the mind by making the absent present, in Leon Battista Alberti's terms, through enacting a sculptural and architectural prosopopoeia. We have conflated ideas of a building, a tomb, allegorical figures, and "the drive to signature" – the architect as author.

But we are not done with frames in this particular lunette. Carlo Santardini earned 150 scudi for his reliefs representing the Beatitudes, one on either side of the *corretto* screen. To our left as we look up is "Blessed are they which are persecuted for righteousness' sake: for theirs is the kingdom of heaven" (Matthew 5:10; Figure 12.9).

Santardini's stucco female allegorical figure, who is long-necked and oval-faced with upward-sweeping hair, extends a right arm in a beseeching supplicatory gesture; she rides backward through the billows and the sky as if on a nursery rhyme's cockhorse, careening herself and her invisible (well, not quite: it seems to be a cloud) conveyance across difficult, even agitated, terrain. Her nervous drapery flutters into biconvex and lenticular swirls. Unable to bear witness to the persecution, she turns her head away, her blank eyes sightless. Drapery slips from and uncovers her left breast, now ready to suckle righteous souls rushing into the kingdom of heaven. The palm-branch and sword intertwine to remind these shaken souls of what they have endured and what will be their reward. Santardini's elegantly cut and delicately shaped stucco drapery smothers violence and intimates a near-somnambulant blessedness.

All this prettification stays within the limits of the quasi harpsichord, half-lunette-shaped window, although there is some infringement upon the inner frames. Apparently, Santardini was given a *laissez-passer* for this admittedly mild infraction in the contestation of framing, pitting what is inside against what is outside. It is almost as if the surface itself of the frame, what is traditionally an "unmeaning" zone, functions as a "warning track": You can come this far but no farther.

To the right is "Blessed are the peacemakers: for they shall be called the children of God" (Matthew 5:9; Figure 12.8). This beatitudinous figure rests comfortably on her curling clouds, knees pulled to the side and legs crossed. One glimpses elegant sandals and sees the drapery arranged in puckering, shuddering folds. She turns her head back towards the *corretto* screen, breathes in through parted lips as if about

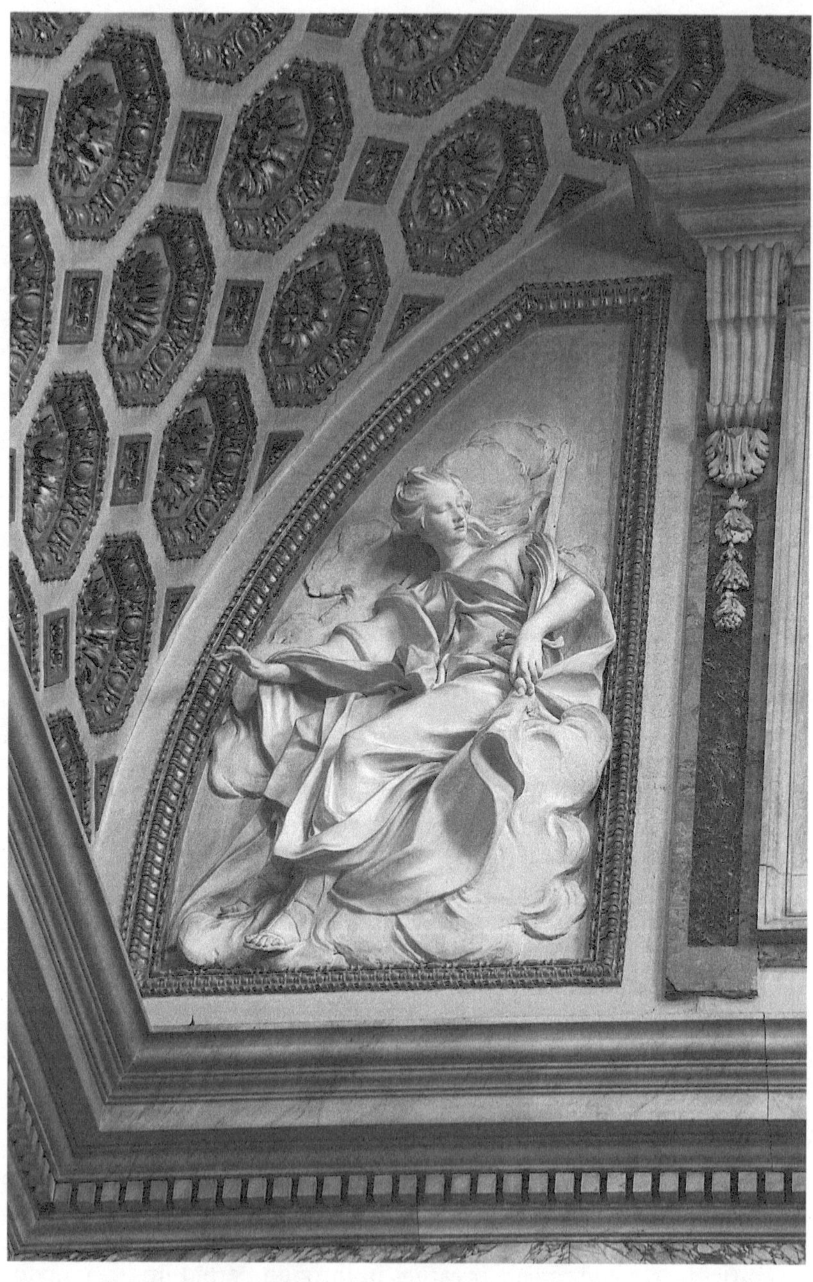

Figures 12.8 and 12.9 (opposite) Carlo Santardini, *Beatitudes*, stucco, Corsini Chapel, San Giovanni in Laterano, Rome, Italy. Photo: Robert G. La France.

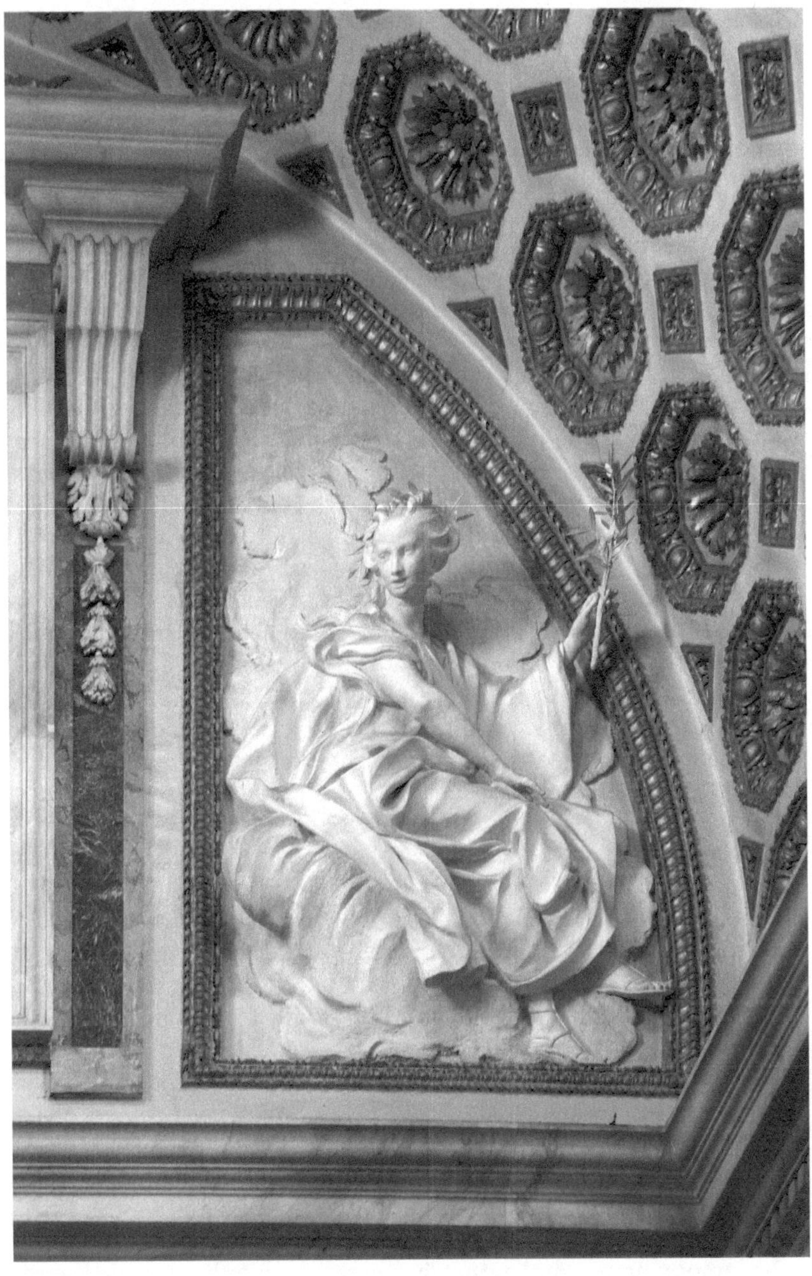

to sing out. Her eyes are focused, their pupils drilled. The peacemakers' Beatitude's hair draws itself into bunches, laurel leaves nestling atop her head and forming a small crown. She daintily holds a sprig of laurel in her left hand, a hand that projects forward somewhat but not so that one sees it as a *scorcio*, a foreshortened frame-breaker. Here again Santardini respects the enclosing nature of the frame while participating in a long tradition of piercing the picture plane, that fourth wall of Alberti's perspective system. But, as I have said, we have no egregious trespassing of ontological spaces. The eighth Beatitude is a prettified woman, one who could have stepped out of any number of etiquette books published in her century (here, the eighteenth).

As St Matthew reports, the final two Beatitudes appear to refer to the church under persecution, just before the Second Coming. Because Giovanni Bottari, the one who dictated symbolism and biblical references within the chapel, stood, along with Cardinals Neri ("Junior," 1685–1770) and Andrea Corsini (1735–95), with the Jansenists, he may indeed have sensed that the church in these earlier decades of the eighteenth century was suffering persecution at the hands of the Jesuits, whom he seems to have loathed. Of course all eight of the Beatitudes are represented within the chapel, so we cannot isolate these final two flanking the Corsini family's room for private worship from the others. In all likelihood, Bottari chose the Beatitudes because Jesus spoke them; they are His words, told and pronounced during the Sermon on the Mount. With their importance to Christian discipleship, they are fundamental to a pope's chapel, for he – Clement XII – is part of the unbroken apostolic discipleship, a successor to the prince of the apostles, Peter.

The Beatitudes are eudaemonistic; that is, they focus on happiness as a just result of virtue, which is represented in the chapel by the seven cardinal virtues. So far so good. But Bottari, attuned to Arnauld and the Jansenists (as well as to Cardinal Passionei and the French Lumières), could certainly have caught more than a whiff of "enlightened eudaemonism." One finds with Kant and other philosophers of the time an awareness of happiness, the just end of a good life, attuned more to modernist notions of pleasure, which are, after all, at odds with virtue as practised by the Stoics. And can we ignore the lushness of life and art in the Corsini Chapel and Corsini Palace? My sense is, then, that Bottari, his cohorts, and the Corsini family were more Epicurean than Stoical: the Corsini Chapel instantiates a sensualist's happiness and pleasure, even though it is funereal. That is not to say the chapel is either amoral or immoral; rather, it is moral in an Enlightenment sense.

The Traditional Approach: Stylistic Categories

The last thing Ludwig von Pastor describes in his account of the life of Pope Clement XII (1730–40) is the Corsini's family chapel.[15] He writes that the "mausoleum of the Corsini bears as eloquent a testimony to Clement XII's artistic feeling as does the Lateran façade – the fruit of one single conception – to the transition then in progress of Italian architecture to classicism."[16] Although a follower of Leopold von Ranke and his commitment to writing about the past "as it really was" (*wie es eigentlich gewesen*), Pastor felt he could improve upon the Protestant Ranke's *History of the Popes of the Last Four Centuries* because he, Pastor, was a Catholic and therefore had a better, almost innate, understanding of the popes, not to mention his expectations of gaining access to the Vatican's *Archivio Segreto*. In a somewhat similar vein, Pastor demonstrates an insider's knowledge of the history of art in his very specific and "connoisseurial" writing about style.[17]

Although much has been considered and debated in Roman art and architecture since Pastor's time, the notion that the Corsini Chapel occupies a transitional zone somewhere between the baroque and a version of classicism has found general agreement. In a detailed study of the Corsini Chapel, Elisabeth Kieven first reviews contemporaneous reactions to the chapel, then moves ahead to see what the next generation of commentators had to say.[18]

The somewhat derogatory observations of the 1730s (see Valesio's remarks earlier, for instance), she discovers, largely fall away by the middle years of the century. Kieven explains this phenomenon in part by positing the architect Alessandro Galilei as being ahead of his time. Several of the early disparaging comments seem to reflect an unflattering and perhaps unconscious comparison between the Corsini Chapel and Carlo Fontana's mausoleum chapel for Sixtus V at Santa Maria Maggiore, which was Galilei's model.

One can perhaps say that Galilei left behind seventeenth-century and even some early eighteenth-century Roman art and moved towards a neoclassical sense of form, one that Kieven demonstrates in her analysis of the architectural elements of the Corsini Chapel. She claims indeed that Galilei's Corsini Chapel was a "forerunner" to neoclassicism. To be ahead of one's time in the 1730s meant, among other things, a turning towards clarity and precise demarcations of spaces, which tends to leave behind a previous generation's valuing of grandeur and monumentality.

Trying to locate the chapel along a continuum from one style to the next is a typical art-historical practice, although it is complicated by a fact Kieven points out, that the architecture has a tense relationship with its own sculpture.[19] Putting aside for the moment that "latent" – in Kieven's words – anxiety, one can see the category of classicism applying itself to the Corsini Chapel in several senses. First of all, "classicism" when used as a critical term in either the history of literature or art refers to a version of the ancient precept of *imitatio auctorum*: imitate the best models and the best masters, which means the art of Greece and Rome as well as of the Renaissance – while avoiding the baroque. The entire architectural vocabulary if not necessarily the syntax of this chapel derives from Vitruvian models. And specifically in art history the term "classical" has come to be associated with the Wölfflinian version of discrete "closed" and linear forms in opposition to the "open," interpenetrating, and painterly ones of the baroque, a conceptualization with which Alessandro Galilei probably would have agreed.

Art history's enchantment with stylistic categories sometimes leads to anomalies. Here one has to say that the chapel is not Renaissance, Mannerist, baroque, rococo, nor even quite yet neoclassical; it seems to be moving along a trajectory between baroque and classical, but precisely where it is one cannot quite determine. What we learn from situating an object on a graduated stylistic scale is not always obvious. This positing of formal categories as a means of decoding or understanding the chapel, in other words, can lead away from its various kinds of meanings as well as the circumstances attending the conception and execution of the work of art. The difficulty may have something to do with the fact that the Corsini Chapel and its decorations appeared at a time when *eruditi italiani* were involved in fevered debates about literary and visual rhetoric and the insurgent notion of *buon gusto*.[20]

It is clear that the early-modern version of style we find articulated by Valesio and his contemporaries is normative rather than descriptive. Valesio acts more like an art critic than a historian when he reports on the chapel's reception as "*minuta e secca*"; rather than ascribing, in other words, a historical classification, one that situates the chapel within and among varying artistic discourses, tendencies, and styles, Valesio gives us his opinion, a quick and dismissive evaluation.

Pastor also makes the somewhat surprising but acute comment that the Corsini Chapel "constitutes a small museum of contemporary Roman sculpture."[21] Although he surely makes here an anachronistic observation, subtly reminding the reader of his own twentieth-century connoisseurship, Pastor's equating of an early eighteenth-century family chapel in one of Rome's great basilicas with the modern museum is appropriate.

In other words, the chapel is not unlike the Palazzo Nuovo on the Campidoglio where Marchese Gregorio Antonio Capponi, under the tutelage of Pope Clement XII, had just overseen the opening of one of Europe's first public museums. The difference between the two is that the Capitoline Museum housed ancient sculpture while the Corsini Chapel is filled with sculpture of the 1730s, although some of the monuments are fashioned out of ancient materials. The objects in this "museum" have through the passage of time and changing of customs and societies lost much of their original "aura," their cult value, while accruing aesthetic and historical interest. At the moment of its unveiling the Corsini Chapel constituted cosmic space and brimmed with religious aura and family prestige; at the same time, it already was taking on a museum-like identity. In philosophical terms, it was becoming, as I have already suggested, more place than space, more a cultural institution than a sacred world.

The Capitoline Museum and the Corsini Chapel, architectural spaces and places with apparently very different intentions, might be seen to share more than one would at first expect. These three observations – that the style of the Corsini Chapel is "in transit" and therefore not quite determinable, although it is in some general sense classical, that the architecture and the sculpture are slightly out of sync with one another, despite (or because of) the architect's directive against baroque sculptural effects, and that the impression of the ensemble is like that of a museum – disclose the uncertain status of the visual arts in the midst of highly controversial debates about taste and poetics in the early part of the eighteenth century. It also reveals something about the way art-historical criticism has attempted to come to terms with an artistic object or ensemble.

Because the modern meaning of the Corsini Chapel is not just aesthetic or religious – one needs to consider how viewers involve themselves within its space – I would like to make certain comments on how a visitor, specifically one who is an art historian, takes stock of the chapel and then critiques it. What, in other words, is my posture as an art historian towards this architectural, decorative, and sculptural ensemble? First of all, how does one *see* and experience the Corsini Chapel in the twenty-first century?

As I have mentioned, the Corsinis still maintain the family mausoleum and do not normally open it to the public except on the feast day of Sant'Andrea Corsini (4 February). After making a request of the proper authorities, an art historian – I am now positing myself as the visitor – may gain permission to enter the chapel for the purposes of "professional" examination. In other words, the historical critic's "being in the world" of the Corsini Chapel is both defined and somewhat confined by an obligation to those in charge, as well as a duty to the profession. From a scholarly position, one may choose to experience the space as if it were indeed a museum of historical sculpture, architecture, marble work, and taste. I as an art historian, although in this instance I have a somewhat different voice than I did when writing about the parergon, will probably try to appraise the chapel, while I have my private tour, in terms that are peculiar to the practices of art history: by putting the chapel and all its decorations into a context or scholarly framework involving stylistic categories and an aesthetic judgment, I will carry out, at least in part, my art-historical responsibilities, giving my experience in the chapel a certain disciplinary focus.

At the same time, I will – largely because of the time in which I live – walk through the chapel as if it were a museum. My visit will be primarily motivated by a desire to see the art, not to contemplate the memory of Clement XII, St Andrea Corsini (Figure 12.10), and other members of the family. Just the same I will be attentive to the artistic representation of death – the sarcophagi and putti who idly wipe tears from their eyes or snuff out a torch – commemoration, identity, power, religion, tradition, and authority. I will be a reader and receiver of – or participant in – certain messages from the architecture and its appointments. As I hope to show, the messages or aesthetic promptings are likely to complicate my art-historical duties. One senses an uneasy tension between attractiveness and transcendental meaning in the Corsini Chapel (or what I earlier referred to as sense of place versus sense of space), an apprehension that coloured much of the discussion of the chapel in the eighteenth century and that lies in the near background of modern commentary. My "existential" space – that is, the world I occupy and in which I walk about – is also the space of the art-world. I am physically within the work of art, although the use of pedestals, a throne, and niches helps to isolate and carve out what Gaston Bachelard calls "eulogized space" for the sculpture and what, as we have seen, Jacques Derrida analysed as the parergon.[22]

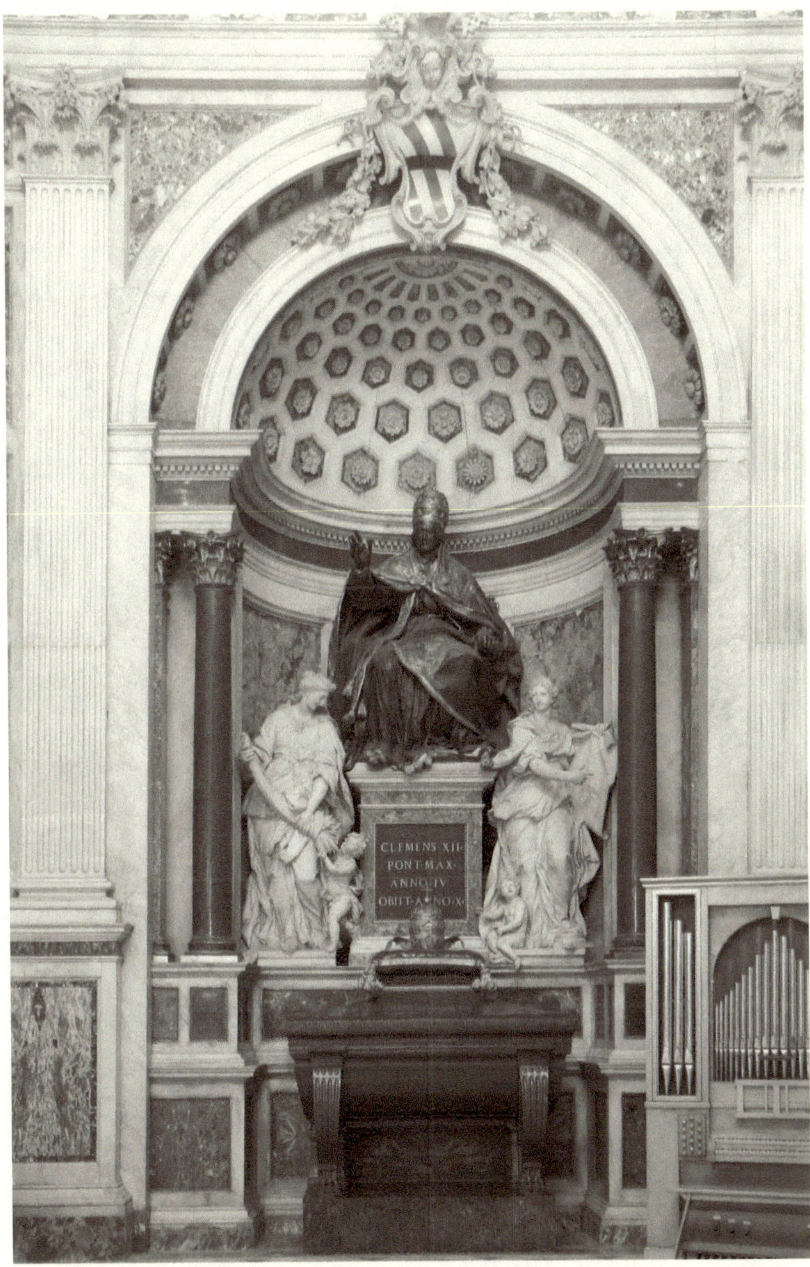

Figure 12.10 Giovanni Battista Maini, *Monument to Pope Clement XII* (allegorical figures in marble by Carlo Monaldi), 1732–5, Corsini Chapel, San Giovanni in Laterano, Rome, Italy. Photo: Robert G. La France.

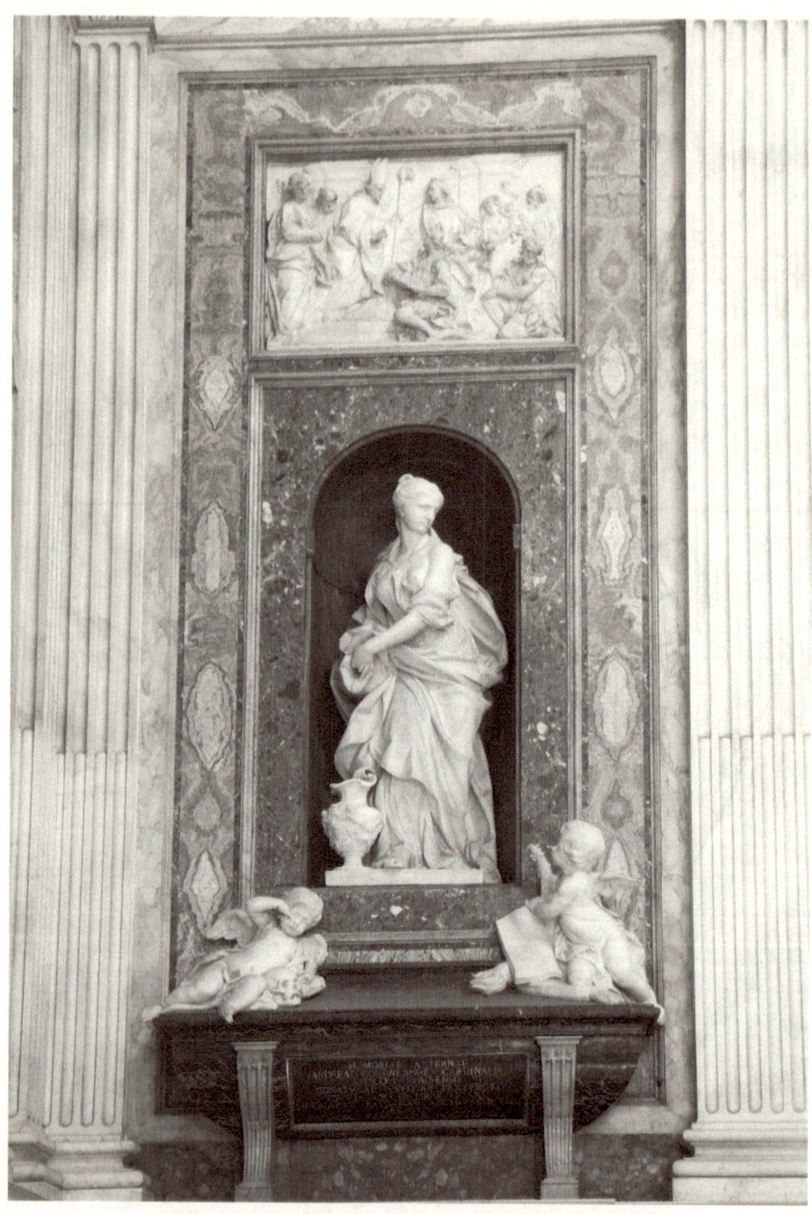

Figure 12.11 Filippo della Valle, *Temperance*, marble, 1732–5, Corsini Chapel, San Giovanni in Laterano, Rome, Italy. Photo: Robert G. La France.

Here I want to shift the discussion once again towards epistemological concerns, which have to do with the conditions of meaning in the Corsini Chapel. What were those situations and environments? To ask a related question, what were the various and often competing discourses in 1730s Rome? That of course is a large question, one that has to do with discursive formations. Michel Foucault, who used the word "episteme" to characterize these formations, defined them as

> the total set of relations that unite, at a given period, the discursive practices that give rise to epistemological figures, sciences, possibly formalized systems ... The episteme is not a form of knowledge or type of rationality which, crossing the boundaries of the most varied sciences, manifests the sovereign unity of a subject, a spirit, or a period; it is the group [*ensemble*] of relations that can be discovered, for a given period, between the sciences when one analyses them at the level of discursive regularities.[23]

In recent years the "discursive regularities" of Rome in the first half of the eighteenth century have been examined in a thorough manner and from numerous points of view.[24] This is not the place, in other words, to attempt a general discussion of all the findings represented by these studies. However, one can restate some of the more general points, which have to do with papal and political politics; the battles between Florentine and Roman sensibilities, especially during the reign of Clement XII, 1730–40; tensions between the supporters of the Jansenists and the Jesuits; the struggle for cultural leadership between the French and the Italians (the French prevailed); and especially the often polemical arguments about taste, whether *buon* or *cattivo gusto*, which in very general and somewhat awkward terms can be seen as surrogates for those conflicts between the baroque and classical styles (classical = good; baroque = bad).

The Corsinis' librarian Giovanni Bottari determined which allegories were to be represented by the various sculptors hired to work in the chapel (Filippo della Valle, *Temperance*, Figure 12.11; Giuseppe Rusconi, *Fortitude*, Figure 12.12; Giuseppe Lironi, *Justice*, Figure 12.13; and Agostino Cornacchini, *Prudence*, Figure 12.14). He chose the four Platonic or cardinal virtues and suggested that the sculptors follow in general terms Cesare Ripa's representations in the *Iconologia*.[25] There are four doors in the bases of the chapel's walls, above which are black marble sarcophagi for the Corsini family. Surmounting these are niches that contain allegorical statues.

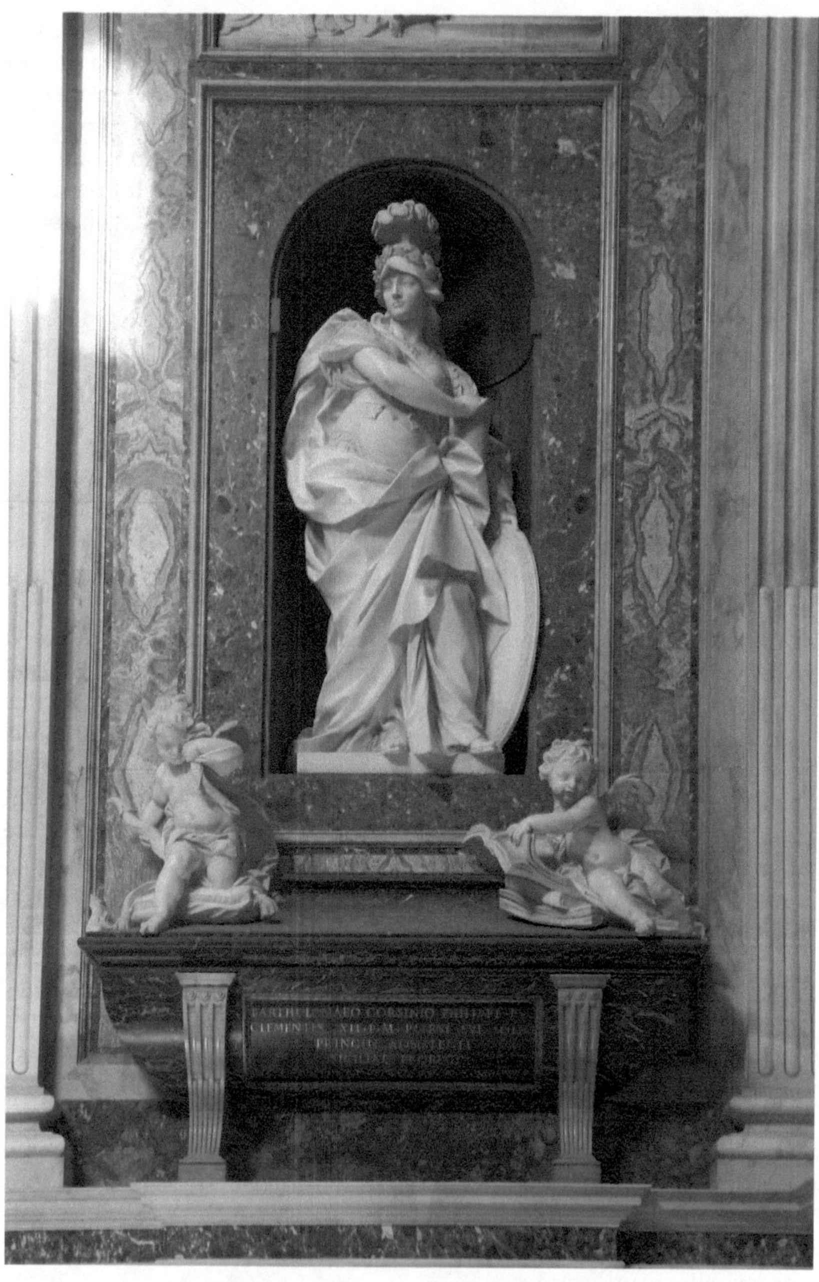

Figure 12.12 Giuseppe Rusconi, *Fortitude*, marble, 1732–5, Corsini Chapel, San Giovanni in Laterano, Rome, Italy. Photo: Robert G. La France.

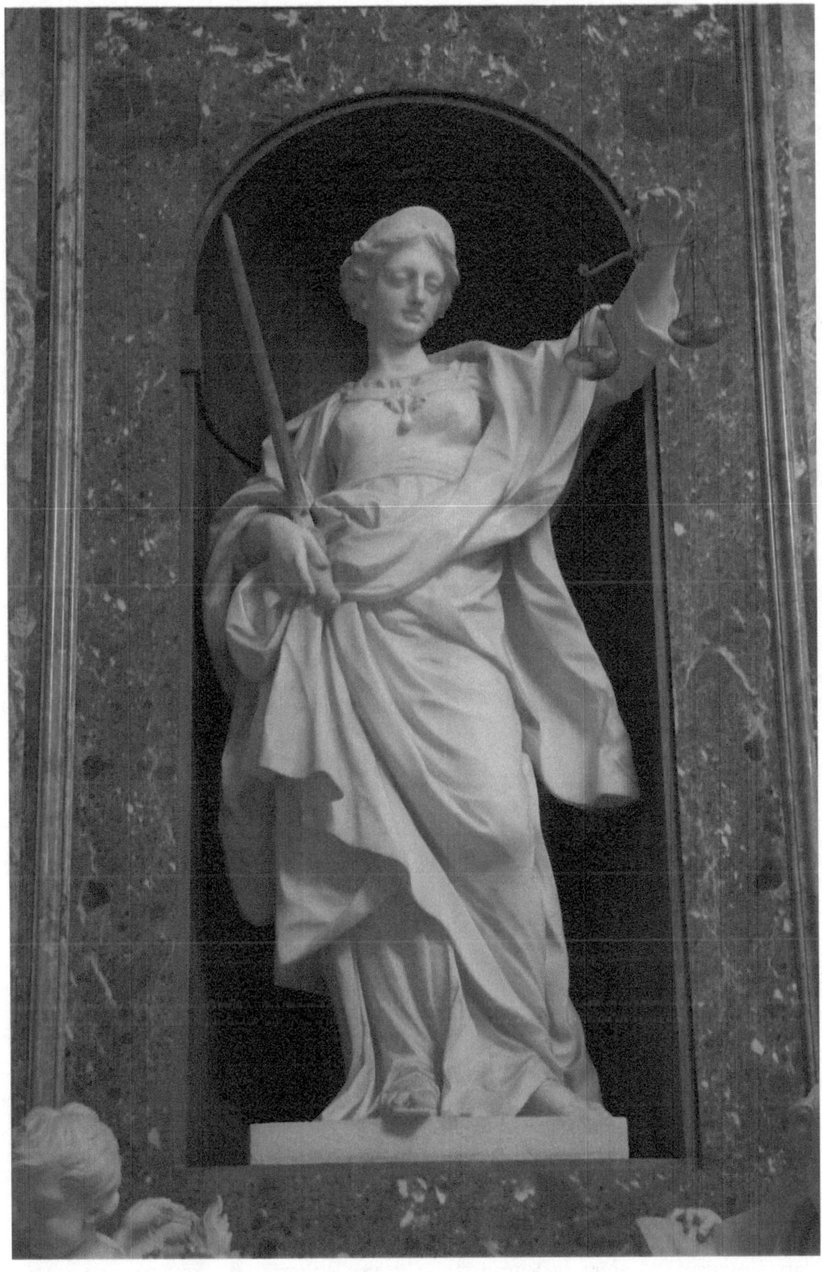

Figure 12.13 Giuseppe Lironi, *Justice*, marble, 1732–5, Corsini Chapel, San Giovanni in Laterano, Rome, Italy. Photo: Robert G. La France.

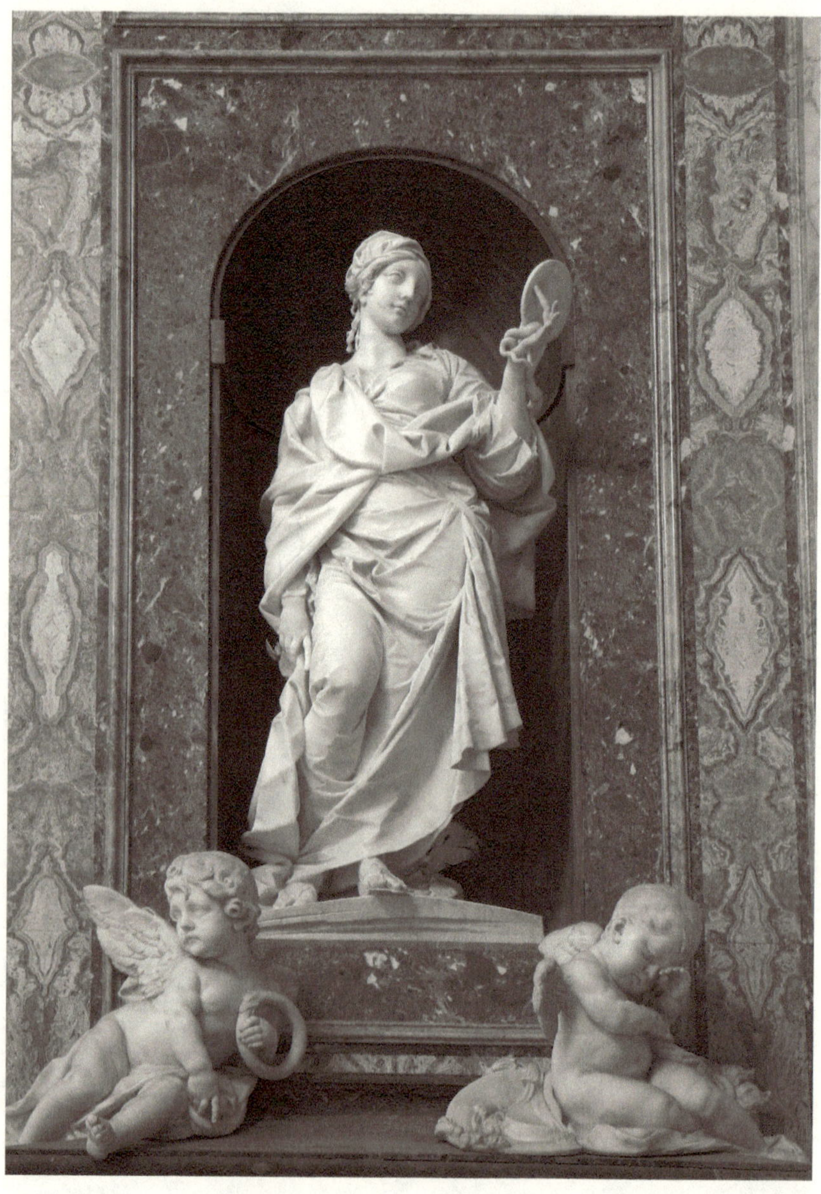

Figure 12.14 Agostino Cornacchini, *Prudence*, 1732–5, Corsini Chapel, San Giovanni in Laterano, Rome, Italy. Photo: Robert G. La France.

As was true of allegorical language in general, representations of virtues, vices, and other personifications in Roman sculpture died a slow death in the eighteenth century.[26] Although there can be no question that these statues in the Corsini Chapel in some way signify the general tradition of the virtues, the signal is weak and given to disruptions. Because I have already introduced the experience of a viewer in the Corsini Chapel, I would like to return to a kind of dialogism here, by which I mean the conversation that goes on between statue and interlocutor. I as a viewer recognize the action of diluting wine (della Valle's *Temperance*) with water as an aspect of *sophrosyne*, the Greek principle of self-control that underlies the Latin, Stoic, and Christian traditions of temperance. It is interesting to point out that despite Bottari's suggestion that the sculptors rely on the well-known book by Cesare Ripa, della Valle chose an action that is not in the text. Nonetheless, it is one sanctioned by tradition and literature.[27] When in the chapel, I also should be able to recognize the attributes of the other allegorical figures, such as *Fortitude*'s shield and armour, *Justice*'s sword and scale, and *Prudence*'s mirror. These attributes certainly assist us in identification, but the degree to which they participate in making the allegorical representation a true hypostatic agent is not clear. I find that the *kinesics* – the placement, gestures, and expressions of the humanized abstractions – deny in some ways the values supposedly instantiated by the figures. They do so because these elements of kinesis with their rhetoric and psychology should in fact convey meanings consistent with the overarching abstraction. Personification is normally treated in rhetoric under the rubric of prosopopoeia, which Aristotle (*Rhetoric*, book 3) saw as adding vividness to a literary or in this case sculptural utterance. But none of these figures vivify those abstractions that Ambrose, Augustine, and Thomas Aquinas found to be of such moment in one's moral life. Indeed, if the cardinal virtues are the very hinges (from the Latin *cardo*) upon which ethical human behaviour swings, why are they expressed in such a wan manner by such listless figures?

Prudence looks for all the world like a mannequin in a store window. It is not that she has a self-contained passivity like the figure of Prudence from Guglielmo della Porta's tomb of Paul III in St Peter's; rather, she uses the mirror not for self-knowledge but more in the tradition of *vanitas*. She has the self-admiring, smug appearance of one who hardly needs to look into her mirror to confirm what she already knows about herself: she is a beauty.

Statues of allegorical figures in the early-modern period have a long history. In the more recent past, there were those stony images, as I have mentioned, that seem detached from any kind of narrative (like those on the tomb of Paul III); and then we have personifications of Death, Caritas, and Justice on Bernini's funereal monument to Urban VIII (St Peter's), who are fully occupied in worldly or one might even say historical activities, while nonetheless making clear their significant "other" – their allegorical duty. Those hieratic images on Paul's tomb seem almost to be empty vessels, ones who are nonetheless efficient conduits for transcendental ideas. Bernini's figures achieve full historicity and anagogical function. But the Corsini allegories maintain a fictional autonomy, as if they were part of the pastoral world that becomes an archetype for Wolfgang Iser's "fictive and the imaginary," the state that is necessary for an aesthetic appreciation of art.[28]

But I am not suggesting that here there is only disinterested pleasure on the part of the viewer. I do believe that the interlocutor of this space and these statues witnesses and participates in an opening onto a world in which a hidden presence lies behind and above the images and the architecture. For all the contrariness of the allegorical figures, one is perfectly aware that they are part of a sequence of images in the early-modern history of Italian and specifically Roman sculpture, and that they are by context and tradition religious. In some manner that is not easy to determine, these statues share in the revelation of truth, are part and parcel of the church's magisterium, which is its traditions and its teachings. We are not, after all, in a museum.

The Accademia degli Arcadi, with its thousands of members and its ability to wrest control of culture from the Vatican and to penetrate every other institution in settecento Rome, in a very real sense manufactured *buon gusto* and made it something to be reckoned with. These statues, and the architecture they inhabit, as niches, aediculae, and chapel, avoid baroque *concettismo*, "excesses" of style, and decorum as grandeur. At the same time, these representations of cardinal virtues invoke a kind of pastoral *otium* that leaves them and us somewhat sceptical, languorous, and – to transfer a psychological state from us to them – self-absorbed, selfish perhaps, preoccupied, more pouty than pious, more precious than proud. The indolent putti who seem only mildly concerned about the deceased trapped within the sarcophagi (flesh-eaters) on top of which they lie, are ready to nap until the Day of Judgment, when they will be obliged to assist the souls of the Corsini on their journey to the Heavenly Jerusalem. But we must remember that this "pastoralizing" (rather than "prosifying") of decorum and rhetoric is the way the Italians wanted it. Trying to pass off this sort of art as rococo or a "little baroque" (the discredited term "barocchetto") creates nothing more than a weak characterization of strong art. When I look at the allegorical statues, I find there an *otium negotiosum,* not an *otium otiosum* (although the putti may qualify for this less inspired state of tranquillity).

Calling the architecture classical creates a directional signpost for style but emphatically does *not* convey a sense of what it is like to stand in the middle of the chapel. Also, Pastor's apparently off-hand characterization of the chapel as a museum of modern sculpture suggests an aesthetic rather than a metaphysical interpretation of the chapel. But we must keep in mind that Christ's incarnation is what makes Christian art possible; the incarnational presence is not absent from the Corsini Chapel, although its presence may be wan.

And speaking of presence, where precisely is the Corsini Chapel? I do not believe we can assert simply that the chapel coexists precisely with its geographical location in an ontological sense. I have suggested here different kinds of sites and readings. Sometimes the chapel seems to exist along a continuum of styles; sometimes it threatens to become a museum, a discursive space of vastly different strictures and possibilities than an Apostolic Roman Catholic chapel. It is a text among other texts; it is an intertext. The Corsini Chapel has one existence when studied through a gate, another when entered. How one dwells with and within the chapel can determine different ontologies. The truth of the chapel emerges from a complex of circumstances and hermeneutic possibilities – several of which I have tried to show here.

Notes

1 Introduction

1 *The Works of Francis Bacon*, ed. J. Spedding, R.L. Ellis, and D.D. Heath (New York: Hurd and Houghton, 1869), 7:289, as quoted in Floyd Gray, "The Essay as Criticism," in *The Cambridge History of Literary Criticism*, vol. 3, ed. Glyn P. Norton (Cambridge and New York: Cambridge University Press, 2006), 271.

2 Harold Bloom, in *The Western Canon* (New York: Harcourt Brace & Company, 1994), 146–68, writes brilliantly and movingly (in the first person) on Montaigne's *Essays*.

3 Francis Bacon, *Essays*, ed. R. Whately (Boston: Life and Shepard, 1868), xxxvii.

2 Critical Perspectives

1 Michael Ann Holly, in *Past Looking: Historical Imagination and the Rhetoric of the Image* (Ithaca, NY, and London: Cornell University Press, 1996), has produced a lucid and extended case for considering art history in post-structuralist (or postmodernist) terms.

2 Wayne C. Booth, "Criticism," in *Encyclopedia of Rhetoric*, ed. Thomas O. Sloane (New York: Oxford University Press, 2001), 182.

3 The word "text," because it comes from the word "texture," suggests an object rather than an abstraction. And one does, I maintain, *read* a painting (building, print, textile, statue, etc.) and not just look at it – at least if one is an art historian. I also agree, however, with Svetlana Alpers and Michael Baxandall that there is such a thing as "pictorial intelligence." See Svetlana Alpers and Michael Baxandall, *Tiepolo and the Pictorial Intelligence* (New Haven, CT, and London: Yale University Press, 1994).

4 Michael Ann Holly, "Interventions: The Melancholy Art," *Art Bulletin* 89, no. 1 (March 2007): 7.
5 Mieke Bal and Norman Bryson, "Semiotics and Art History," *Art Bulletin* 73, no. 2 (June 1991): 184.
6 Walter Benjamin, *On Hashish*, ed. H. Eiland and intro. Marcus Boon (Cambridge, MA: Belknap Press, 2006), 67.
7 Mieke Bal, *Quoting Caravaggio: Contemporary Art, Preposterous History* (Chicago: University of Chicago Press, 1999), 41.
8 François Cusset, *French Theory: How Foucault, Derrida, Deleuze, & Co. Transformed the Intellectual Life of the United States*, trans. Jeff Fort (Minneapolis: University of Minnesota Press, 2008).
9 My references are from the later edition: Paul de Man, *Blindness and Insight: Essays in the Rhetoric of Contemporary Criticism*, intro. Wlad Godzich (Minneapolis: University of Minnesota Press, 1983); de Man's essay on Derrida, "The Rhetoric of Blindness: Jacques Derrida's Reading of Rousseau," can be found on pages 102–41.
10 See Angus S. Fletcher, "The Perpetual Error," *Diacritics* 2, no. 4 (Winter 1972): 14–20; Fletcher is not charmed by de Man's style of writing: "The book is simply too difficult. Its sinuous, argus-eyed, scholastic manner makes it very nearly impossible to read" (14).
11 De Man, *Blindness and Insight*, 123.
12 Ibid.
13 I am perfectly aware that a kind of ennui has fallen on any number of literary critics in the aftermath of post-structuralism. I continue to make references to deconstruction not because it is the latest thing, which of course it is not. Deconstruction has nonetheless joined the philosophical tradition and deserves as much attention as Kant, Freud, or Nietzsche; it forms an important part of the Western intellectual tradition.
14 Louis Menand, *The Marketplace of Ideas: Reform and Resistance in the American University* (New York: W.W. Norton & Company, 2010).
15 Ibid., 80.
16 One need not, it seems to me, openly express "appreciation" in the visual arts. But it should be implied by *how* one writes.
17 Gotthold Ephraim Lessing, *Laocoön or the Limits of Poetry and Painting*, trans. William Ross, (London: Ridgeway, 1836).
18 Clement Greenberg, "Avant-Garde and Kitsch," in *Art and Culture* (Boston: Beacon Press, 1961), 34–9 (originally published in *Partisan Review* 6, no. 5 [1939]).
19 John Summerson, *The Classical Language of Architecture* (London: Methuen, 1963), 30.

20 John R. Spencer, "UT RHETORICA PICTURA: A Study in Quattrocento Theory of Painting," *Journal of the Warburg and Courtauld Institutes* 20, nos. 1/2 (January–June 1957): 26–44.
21 Ibid., 26.
22 Ernst Cassirer, *The Philosophy of Symbolic Forms*, vol. 2, trans. Ralph Mannheim (New Haven, CT: Yale University Press, 1955), 26.
23 Spencer, "UT RHETORICA PICTURA," 36.
24 Frederick J. McGinness, *Right Thinking and Sacred Oratory in Counter-Reformation Rome* (Princeton, NJ: Princeton University Press, 1995).
25 Especially useful on the matter of literary conceits is K.K. Ruthven, *The Conceit* (London: Methuen & Co., 1969).
26 Samuel Johnson, "Life of Cowley (1779–81)," in *Lives of the English Poets*, ed. L. Archer Hind, vol. 1 (London: Everyman's Library, 1925), 11.
27 Aristotle, *The Complete Works of Aristotle*, ed. Jonathan Barnes, vol. 2, Bollingen Series LXXI–2 (Princeton, NJ: Princeton University Press, 1984), 2335.
28 W. Tatarkiewicz, "Mimesis," in *Dictionary of the History of Ideas: Studies of Selected Pivotal Ideas*, ed. Philip P. Wiener, vol. 3 (New York: Charles Scribner's Sons, 1973), 225–30.
29 Frank J. Warnke, *Studies in the Renaissance*, vol. 2 (New York: Renaissance Society of America, 1955), 169; Giovanni Battista Marino, *Opere Scelte di Giovan Battista Marino e dei Marinisti*, 2nd ed., ed. Giovanni Getto, vol. 1, (Turin: 1966).
30 Georg Simmel, *The Philosophy of Money*, 2nd ed., trans. Tom Bottomore, David Frisby, and Kaethe Mengelberg (1907; New York: Routledge, 1990), 475.
31 Emanuele Tesauro, *Il Cannocchiale Aristotelico: Scelta*, ed. Ezio Raimondi (Milan: Giulio Einaudi Editore, 1978), 29.
32 Alois Riegl, *The Origins of Baroque Art in Rome*, ed. and trans. Andrew Hopkins and Arnold Witte (Los Angeles: Getty Research Institute, 2010).
33 Johann Joachim Winckelmann, *Reflections on the Imitation of Greek Works in Painting and Sculpture*, trans. Elfriede Heyer and Roger C. Norton (La Salle, IL: Open Court, 1987); Johann Joachim Winckelmann, *History of Ancient Art*, 4 vols, trans. G. Henry Lodge (1849–72; New York: Frederick Ungar, 1968).
34 David Ferris, *Silent Urns: Romanticism, Hellenism, Modernity* (Stanford, CA: Stanford University Press, 2000), xiv.
35 Heinrich Wölfflin, *Principles of Art History: The Problem of the Development of Style in Later Art*, trans. M.D. Hottinger (New York: Dover Publications, 1950).
36 Heinrich Wölfflin, *Classic Art: An Introduction to the Italian Renaissance*, trans. Peter and Linda Murray (London: Phaidon Press, 1952).

37 Ibid., xv.

38 Ibid., xvi.

39 David Summers, "'Form,' Nineteenth-Century Metaphysics, and the Problem of Art Historical Description," *Critical Inquiry* 15 (Winter 1989): 372–93.

40 Erwin Panofsky, "Iconography and Iconology: An Introduction to the Study of Renaissance Art," in *Meaning in the Visual Arts* (Garden City, NY: Doubleday, 1955), 26–54.

41 Rosalind Krauss, "Poststructuralism and the Paraliterary," in *The Originality of the Avant-Garde and Other Modernist Myths* (Cambridge, MA: Harvard University Press, 1985), 293, emphasis added; quoted in Summers, "'Form,' Nineteenth-Century Metaphysics," 378.

42 Plato, *Phaedrus*, trans. B. Jowett (1892), 251a–251c.

43 Thomas Mann, *Death in Venice, and Seven Other Stories*, trans. H.T. Lowe-Porter (New York: Vintage Books, 1936), 25.

44 E.H. Gombrich, "On Physiognomic Perception," in *Meditations on a Hobby Horse and Other Essays on the Theory of Art* (London: Phaidon; distributed by New York Graphic Society Publishers, Greenwich, CT, 1963), 45–55; W.K. Wimsatt and Monroe Beardsley, "The Intentional Fallacy," in W.K. Wimsatt, *The Verbal Icon: Studies in the Meaning of Poetry* (Lexington: University of Kentucky Press, 1954), 3–20.

45 Summers, "'Form,' Nineteenth-Century Metaphysics."

46 Richard Palmer, *Hermeneutics: Interpretation Theory in Schleiermacher, Dilthey, Heidegger, and Gadamer* (Evanston, IL: Northwestern University Press, 1969), 34.

47 Although one has to be careful with the term "exegesis," as Palmer explains: "Even from the title of the book, one gathers that hermeneutics is distinguished from exegesis as the methodology of interpretation. The distinction between actual commentary (exegesis) and the rules, methods, or theory governing it (hermeneutics) dates from this earliest usage and remains basic to the definition of hermeneutics both in theology and, when the definition is alter broadened, in reference to nonbiblical literature" (ibid.).

48 Gianni Vattimo, *Beyond Interpretation: The Meaning of Hermeneutics for Philosophy*, trans. David Webb (Stanford, CA: Stanford University Press, 1997), 58–74.

49 Ibid., 61.

50 A.A. Bellow, "The Great Chain of Being and Italian Phenomenology," in *Analecta Husserliana: The Yearbook of Phenomenological Research*, vol. 11 (Boston: D. Reidel Publishing, 2012).

51 Vattimo, *Beyond Interpretation*, 63–4.

52 Ibid., 65.

53 David Ferris, "Decrostuzione e secolarizzazione di Sant'Ivo," in *Dopo il Museo*, ed. Federico Luisetti and Giorgio Maragliano, Quaderni di Estetica & Ermeneutica 2 (Turin: Trauben, 2006), 25 (in which Ferris is querying Vattimo's position on the postmodern): "Per Vattimo, l'esperienze di un'arte postmoderna presuppone un'arte non più legata ai gesti di fondazione della modernità." (For Vattimo, the experience of a postmodern art presumes an art no longer tied to the founding gestures of modernity.)

3 Bernini and Inexpressibility

1 I have summarized here Heidegger's position in the 1930s, one that he later altered so that he could include Paul Klee and Paul Cézanne, among others; see Julian Young, *Heidegger's Philosophy of Art* (New York: Cambridge University Press, 2001), and Martin Heidegger, *Poetry, Language, Thought*, trans. Albert Hofstadter (New York: Harper & Row, 1975), 39–78.
2 W. Chandler Kirwin, *Powers Matchless: The Pontificate of Urban VIII, the Baldachin, and Gian Lorenzo Bernini* (New York: Peter Lang, 1997).
3 Domenico Bernini, *Vita del Cavalier Gio. Lorenzo Bernini, descritta da Domenico Bernino, suo figlio* (Rome: Rocco Bernabò, 1713), 24; translation by Franco Mormando, *The Life of Gian Lorenzo Bernini by Domenico Bernini: A Translation and Critical Edition* (University Park: Pennsylvania State University Press, 2011), 111.
4 Lelio Gudiccioni, *Latin Poems, Rome 1633 and 1639*, trans. and ed. John Kevin Newman and Frances Stickney Newman (Hildesheim: Weidmannsche Verlagsbuchhandlung, 1992), 264 (from Gudiccioni's *De Ornato Apostolorum Sepulchro*: "At splendid cost, Urban, you bid the tomb arise, in which the lofty city conceals its twin fathers. What then will you do one day in Jerusalem, if ever the tomb of the Lord is revealed, recovered by the stalwart hand of Christians?").
5 Filippo Baldinucci, *The Life of Bernini*, trans. Catherine Enggass (University Park and London: Pennsylvania State University Press, 1966), 16.
6 Stephan Bemrose, "'Una favilla sol della tua gloria': Dante Expresses the Inexpressible," *Forum for Modern Language Studies* 27, no. 2 (April 1991): 126.
7 For discussions along these lines, see Ann Chalmers Watts, "*Pearl*, Inexpressibility, and Poems of Human Loss," *PMLA* 99, no. 1 (January 1984): 26–40.
8 Rudolf Preimesberger, "Il San Longino del Bernini in San Pietro in Vaticano: Dal Bozzetto alla Statua," in *Bernini a Montecitorio: Ciclo di conferenze nel quarto centenario della nascita di Gan Lorenzo Bernini* (Rome: Camera dei Deputati, 2001), 95–112.

9 Immanuel Kant, *Critique of Judgment*, trans. Werner S. Pluhar (Indianapolis, IN: Hackett Publishing Company, 1987), 109. Kant of course did not visit St Peter's; he merely relied on the accounts of others.

10 Young, *Heidegger's Philosophy of Art*, 51; Heidegger, *Poetry, Language, Thought*, 66.

11 Heidegger, *Poetry, Language, Thought*, 67.

12 Ibid.

13 Ibid., 68. My attention to Heidegger, rather than only to the teachings of the Roman Catholic Church, is necessary, because in my opinion the art historical critic should see the baroque from a critic's rather than from a believer's point of view – while doing one's best to understand the Christian adherent.

14 Paul de Man, "Form and Intent in the American New Criticism," in *Blindness and Insight*, 27.

15 Ernst Robert Curtius, *European Literature and the Latin Middle Ages*, trans. Willard R. Trask (Princeton, NJ: Princeton University Press, 1990), 159.

16 Filippo Baldinucci, *Vita di Bernini scritta da Filippo Baldinucci*, ed. Sergio Samek Ludovici (Milan: Edizione del Milione, 1949), 82.

17 Domenico Bernini also used the word *specie* in his description of the *Baldacchino*. In Franco Mormando's *The Life of Gian Lorenzo Bernini*, the translator and author of the commentary – Mormando – writes, "According to the premodern, Aristotelian understanding of optics, the so-called intromission theory, objects sent forth their likeness of 'species' in the form of rays that are carried through the air and penetrate the eye of the beholder" (307). Here is Mormando's translation of Domenico Bernini's sentence: "However, in this process, with the eye transmitting the species of the structure to the imaginative faculty of the mind, the intellect must necessarily affirm the truth of what the Cavaliere used to remark out of modesty, that is, 'This work came out well by chance.'" While both Baldinucci and D. Bernini used specie as the way in which one sees, they both emphasize what Domenico refers to as the "imaginative faculty of the mind," which aligns the perceptual *specie* with the philosophical and religious *specie*.

18 Paula Kadose Radetsky, "To Will or Not to Will: The Evolution of Willy-Nilly," *Proceedings of the Twenty-Second Annual Meeting of the Berkeley Linguistics Society* 22 (1996): 303.

19 Baldinucci, *Vita di Bernini*, 82: "Segno di ciò evidentissimo si è che infatti nessuno si trova, per giudizioso ed esparto che egli sia, a cui basti l'animo a prima vista formarne altro concetto, che di tutta maraviglia sì, ma in universale; onde puur gli abbisogna, o voglia o no, il tornare e ritornare,

il vedere e rivedere e sempre quell'eccelso tempio ritrova e nel tutto, ed in ogni sua parte maggiore di se stesso."

20 M. Barberino, *Poesie toscane*, ed. A. Brogiotti (Roma, 1635), quoted in Carlo del Bravo, "Sul significato della luce nel Caravaggio e in Gianlorenzo Bernini," *Artibus et Historiae* 4, no. 7 (1983): 77.

4 Death and Dying in St Peter's: Part 1

1 The comments here are a greatly expanded discussion that I first took up in "Filippo della Valle's Tomb of Innocent XII: Death and Dislocation," *Gazette des beaux-arts* 112 (1988): 133–40.

2 Irving Lavin, "Bernini's Bumbling Barberini Bees," in *Barock Inszenierung: Akten des Internationalen Forschungscolloquiums an der Technischen Universität Berlin, 20–22 Juni 1996*, ed. Joseph Imorde, Fritz Neumeyer, and Tristan Weddigen (Zurich: Edition Imorde, 1999), 55.

3 *Patrologia latina*, vol. 12, cols. 427–8; quoted in Philippe Ariès, *Western Attitudes toward Death from the Middle Ages to the Present*, trans. Patricia M. Ranum (Baltimore: Johns Hopkins University Press, 1975), 16.

4 Gaston Bachelard, *The Poetics of Space*, trans. Maria Jolas (Boston: Beacon Press, 1969), xxxi.

5 The church's position on magisterium has evolved, so that in the *New Catholic Encyclopedia*, vol. 13, 2nd ed. (Detroit: Gale, 2003), 778, we find a change from the Tridentine version: "The reference to the traditional doctrine was never denied or lost sight of, but more emphasis was placed on what the Church infallibly teaches today. Too much insistence upon the juridical function of defining, which certainly pertains to the magisterium, brought about the tendency to equate the teaching authority of the Church with the power of jurisdiction. This point of view overlooks the fact that the primary function of the teaching office is the pastoral function of witnessing to the traditional faith of the Church, and that this office is essentially a charismatic gift conferred by episcopal consecration, even though jurisdictional authority is required for its legitimate and efficacious exercise."

6 Erich Auerbach, *Scenes from the Drama of European Literature* (Minneapolis: University of Minnesota Press, 1984), 53: "*figura rerum* or phenomenal prophecy, as a prefiguration of Christ."

7 I am assuming that Bernini (or this skeleton) dropped the name of Leo XI (1605), who died in the twenty-seventh day of his papacy.

8 *Vocabolario della Crusca* (1612): "PUTTO. Add. puttanesco, di puttana. Lat. *meretricius*. Dan. Inf. c. 13. La meretrice, che mai dall' ospizio Di Cesare, non torse gli occhi putti." "That courtesan who constantly surveyed

Caesar's household with her adulterous eyes" (*Dante: The Divine Comedy*, vol. 1, *Inferno*, trans. Mark Musa [New York: Viking Penguin, 1984], 188).

9 Charles Dempsey, *Inventing the Renaissance Putto* (Chapel Hill: University of North Carolina Press, 2001).

10 Leonard Barkan, *The Gods Made Flesh: Metamorphosis and the Pursuit of Paganism* (New Haven, CT: Yale University Press, 1986), 99–101.

11 Gordon Teskey, *Allegory and Violence* (Ithaca, NY: Cornell University Press, 1996), 89.

12 Sigmund Freud, *The Uncanny*, trans. David McLintock, intro. Hugh Haughton (New York: Penguin Books, 2003). Freud takes his somewhat uncanny essay far beyond the issue of a doll (Olimpia) in a story by E.T.A. Hoffmann coming alive.

13 Dante Alighieri, *Dantis Alagherii Epistolae: The Letters of Dante*, ed. Paget Toynbee (Oxford: Clarendon Press, 1920), 160–211.

14 Paul de Man, "Resistance to Theory," in *The Resistance to Theory* (Minneapolis: University of Minnesota Press, 1986), 10; in that same discussion de Man also observes that "we now have to recognize the necessity of a non-perceptual, linguistic moment in painting and music, and learn to *read* pictures rather than to *imagine* meaning" [emphasis in original].

15 I use the term "insight" here as de Man uses it as the title of his essays *Blindness and Insight: Essays in the Rhetoric of Contemporary Criticism*.

16 De Man, *Blindness and Insight*, 20.

17 Gilles Deleuze, *The Fold: Leibniz and the Baroque*, trans. Tom Conley (Minneapolis: University of Minnesota Press, 1993), 12; Walter Benjamin, *The Origin of German Tragic Drama* (New York: Verso, 1998).

18 Emanuele Tesauro, *Il cannocchiale Aristotelico* (Venice: Milocho, 1682), 51; translated and cited by Fernand Hallyn, "Cosmography and Poetics," in *The Cambridge History of Literary Criticism*, vol. 3, *The Renaissance*, ed. Glyn P. Norton (New York: Cambridge University Press, 1999), 448.

19 Ibid.

20 Aristotle, *Poetics*, trans. Gerald F. Else (Ann Arbor: University of Michigan Press, 1970), 65.

21 Vincenzo Borghini in P. Barocchi, ed., *Scritti d'arte del cinquecento*, vol. 1 (Milan and Naples: 1971), 658, as cited and translated in David Summers, *Michelangelo and the Language of Art* (Princeton, NJ: Princeton University Press, 1981), 172.

22 Deleuze, *The Fold*.

23 Michael Löwy, *Fire Alarm: Reading Walter Benjamin's "On the Concept of History,"* trans. Chris Turner (London: Verso, 2005), 95.

24 Véronique Voruz and Bogdan Wolfe, eds., "Preface," in *The Later Lacan: An Introduction* (Albany: SUNY Press, 2007), vii–xvii, write about the ways in which Lacan saw the unconscious as occupied by a pleasure principle – *jouissance* – that must be given up by the analysand in order for the analyst to complete the work of psychoanalysis. Neither I nor anyone else can decode Bernini's unconscious mind post-mortem. Just the same, having spent decades looking at Bernini's sculpture I cannot but see a deep joyfulness, one that can indeed have started in his unconscious mind and become manifest in his "folds."

25 Deleuze, *The Fold*, 3.

26 Ibid., 121–2.

27 Michael Koortbojian, "*Disegni* for the Tomb of Alexander VII," *Journal of the Warburg and Courtauld Institutes* 54 (1991), 268.

28 What I am summarizing here is treated in greater detail in my text *The Death of the Baroque and the Rhetoric of Good Taste* (New York: Cambridge University Press, 2006).

29 Giovanni Mario Crescimbeni, *Storia dell'Accademia degli Arcadi Istituita in Roma l'Anno 1690* (first published 1712; London, 1804), 52.

5 Death and Dying in St Peter's: Part 2

1 See my earlier treatments of this characterization in "The Recollection and Undermining of Allegory in Eighteenth-Century Roman Sculpture," *Storia dell'Arte* 57 (1986): 183–91, "Filippo della Valle's Tomb of Innocent XII: Death and Dislocation," *Gazette des beaux-arts* 112 (1988): 133–40; *The Death of the Baroque and the Rhetoric of Good Taste*, 81–82; *Passive Tranquillity: The Sculpture of Filippo della Valle* (Philadelphia: American Philosophical Society, Transactions Series, 1997), 68–76.

2 Harold Bloom, *The Anxiety of Influence: A Theory of Poetry*, 2nd ed. (New York: Oxford University Press, 1997).

3 Theodor Adorno, *Aesthetic Theory*, trans. Robert Hullot-Kentor (Minneapolis: University of Minnesota Press, 1997), 26.

4 Georges Didi-Huberman, "Artistic Survival: Panofsky vs. Warburg and the Exorcism of Impure Time," *Common Knowledge* 9, no. 2 (Spring 2003): 273–85.

5 Sigmund Freud, *The Uncanny*, trans. David McLintock, intro. Hugh Haughton (New York: Penguin Books, 2003), 142.

6 Ibid., 143.

7 Freud wrote that "our unconscious is still as unreceptive as ever to the idea of our own mortality. Religions continue to dispute the significance of the undeniable fact of individual death and to posit an afterlife" (ibid.).

8 Edith Morley and Henry Frowde, eds., *Hurd's Letters on Chivalry and Romance with the Third Elizabethan Dialogue* (London: Henry Frowde, 1911), 154.

9 Martin Heidegger, *What Is Called Thinking?*, intro. J. Glenn Gray (New York: Harper & Row, 1968), 19.

10 Erwin Panofsky, *Tomb Sculpture: Four Lectures on Its Changing Aspects from Ancient Egypt to Bernini* (New York: Harry N. Abrams, 1964), 96.

11 Émile Mâle, *Religious Art* (New York: Noonday Press, 1970), 174.

6 Eighteenth-Century Baroque

1 See Bal, *Quoting Caravaggio*. And of course there was an ancient baroque – Hellenistic sculpture.

2 Livio Pestilli, "On Bernini's Reputed Unpopularity in Late Baroque Rome," *Artibus et Historiae* 63, no. 32 (2011): 119–42.

3 Ibid., 119.

4 Bruce Boucher, *Italian Baroque Sculpture* (New York: Thames and Hudson, 1998), 203.

5 Robert Enggass, *Early Eighteenth-Century Sculpture in Rome* (University Park and London: Pennsylvania State University Press, 1976), 1:29.

6 See the latest edition with a superb translation and excellent commentary: Giovanni Pietro Bellori, *Lives of the Modern Painters, Sculptors and Architects: A New Translation and Critical Edition*, trans. and ed. Alice Sedgwick Wohl, Helmut Wohl, and Tomaso Montanari (Cambridge: Cambridge University Press, 2005).

7 See Elizabeth Cropper and Charles Dempsey, *Nicolas Poussin: Friendship and the Love of Painting* (Princeton, NJ: Princeton University Press, 1996), especially chapter 1; Estelle Lingo, *François Duquesnoy and the Greek Ideal* (New Haven, CT: Yale University Press, 2007); and Lisa Beaven, *An Ardent Patron: Cardinal Camillo Massimo and His Antiquarian and Artistic Circle: Giovanni Pietro Bellori, Claude Lorrain, Nicolas Poussin, Diego Velázquez* (London: Paul Holberton Publishing in association with Centro de Estudios Europa Hispanica, 2010).

8 Jennifer Montagu, *Alessandro Algardi* (New Haven, CT, and London: Yale University Press, 1985), 1:viii. She is well aware of the severe limitations of such broad and anachronistic stylistic categories as "classical" and "baroque."

9 Ann Sutherland Harris, *Andrea Sacchi* (Princeton, NJ: Princeton University Press, 1977), 35.

10 Melchiorre Missirini, *Memorie per Servire alla Storia della Romana Accademia di S. Luca* (Rome: Nella Stamperia de Romanis, 1823), 112: "il Sacchi era gran coloritore; profondo nelle teorie, ed avea per dettato che il merito di un Pittore consiste non in far molte opera mediocri, ma poche e

perfette: Non ischivò il gentile, ma parve nato pel grande. Gravi semianti, attegiamenti maestosì, panneggiamenti facili, e di poche e larghe pieghe: in tutto sdegnò il minute."

11 Enggass, *Early Eighteenth-Century Sculpture in Rome*, 1:40.

12 Pestilli, "On Bernini's Reputed Unpopularity in Late Baroque Rome," 120.

13 This is as much confession as anything else; it is an old truism that meaning in an artefact is as much produced as it is found.

14 For further discussion of this relief see my entry in Edgar Peters Bowron and Joseph J. Rishel, eds., *Art in Rome in the Eighteenth Century* (Philadelphia: Philadelphia Museum of Art, 2000), 261–2.

15 For Bracci see Costanza Gradara Pesci, *Pietro Bracci: scultore romano* (Milan: Alfieri & Lacroix, 1920), and Hugh Honour, "Pietro Bracci," in *Dizionario Biografico degli Italiani*, vol. 13 (Rome: Istituto della Enciclopedia Italiana, 1971). Bracci did two other portraits of Benedict, one in terracotta (Museo Nazionale del Palazzo di Venezia, Rome), another in the Thyssen Bornemisza Collection, Lugano.

16 Caterina Chracas, *Diario Ordinario*, 10 August 1737, no. 3124, pp. 4–5: "In occasione di solennizzarsi Domenica nella Basilica di Santa Maria sopra Minerva da quei RR PP. Domenicani, con nobile apparato, e Musica la festa del loro glorioso Fondatore San Domenico, dentro la Cappella ad esso Santo dedicate si vide scoperto il nuovo nobilissimo Deposito della santa memoria di Papa Benedetto XIII.; costrutto con ogni ottimo disegno, e buon gusto, & ornato di stucchi, e bronzi Dorati, e di fini, e preziosi marmi, tra' quali Quattro colonne di verde antico di gran valore, oltre di un bassorilievo, e due bellissime statue rappresentanti l'una Umilità, a l'altra la Religione, e la statua del defonto Sommo Pontefice lavorata eggreggiamente al natural; riuscito il medesimo Deposito in tutte le sue parti al sommo bello, e magnifico, e di universal applauso."

17 Carl Goldstein has suggested to me that Bracci may have been working from Benedict's death mask. Although I have, interestingly enough, found the death mask of the antipope Benedict XIII at St Andrews University Museum, I have had no luck discovering the legitimate Benedict XIII's death mask, if in fact there ever was one.

18 See discussion of "the fold" in chapter 8.

19 I consciously adopt John Onians's title for his text on the ancient architectural orders ("Bearers of Meaning") because my interests are as capacious as his, which is to come to terms with how we understand our "relationships to the gods, to each other," and to ourselves. John Onians, *Bearers of Meaning: The Classical Orders in Antiquity, the Middle Ages, and the Renaissance* (Princeton, NJ: Princeton University Press, 1988), 3.

7 Narrative and Symbol in the *Apostles* Series

1 Michael Conforti, "Planning the Lateran Apostles," in *Memoirs of the American Academy in Rome*, vol. 35, *Studies in Italian Art History 1: Studies in Italian Art and Architecture 15th through 18th Centuries*, ed. James H. Ackerman and Henry A. Millon (Cambridge, MA: MIT Press, 1980), 243–55, 257–60.

2 Frederick Den Broeder, "The Lateran Apostles," *Apollo* 85 (1967): 360–5.

3 Conforti, "Planning the Lateran Apostles," 245.

4 The other sculptors are Lorenzo Ottoni (St Thaddeus), Pierre Le Gros (St Thomas and St Bartholomew), Pierre Étienne Monnot (St Paul and St Peter), Angelo de Rossi (St James Minor), and Francesco Moratti (St Simon).

5 Frank Martin, "Camillo Rusconi in English Collections," in *The Lustrous Trade: Material Culture and the History of Sculpture in England and Italy c. 1700–c. 1860*, ed. Cinzia Sicca and Alison Yarrington (London: Leicester University Press, 2000), 50.

6 Michael Conforti, "The Lateran Apostles" (PhD diss., Harvard University, 1977), appendix 4; Conforti, "Planning the Lateran Apostles," 248.

7 Anthony Grafton, *Commerce with the Classics: Ancient Books and Renaissance Readers* (Ann Arbor: University of Michigan Press, 1997), 45.

8 Those members of the Accademia degli Arcadi who left and founded the Arcadia Nuova. See Susan Dixon, *Between the Real and the Ideal: The Accademia degli Arcadi and Its Garden in Eighteenth-Century Rome* (Newark: University of Delaware Press, 2006), and Minor, *Death of the Baroque*.

9 Alessandro Baldeschi and G.M. Crescimbeni, *Stato della SS. Chiesa papale Lateranense nell'anno MDCCXXIII* (Rome, 1723), 14: "La Statua contigua è di San Giovanni, uno de' Titolari della Basìlica. Guarda l'Apostolo il Cielo: ha nella destra la penna, nella sinistra il Libro, e l'Aquila ai piedi; onde si manifesta la sublime elevazione della sua mente a contemplare il Sole di giustizia, dèscritto nella sua Apocalisse, e nell'Evangelio con maniera superiore ad ogni altra. Il lavoro è del medesimo Rusconi, e di pari ammirazione." Rusconi apparently worked from a drawing by Carlo Maratti: Robert Enggass, *Early Eighteenth-Century Sculpture in Rome: An Illustrated Catalogue Raisonné* (University Park and London: Pennsylvania State University Press, 1976), 100, identifies a drawing by Maratti which can be found in the Holland collection in Newcastle upon Tyne (W. Vitzhum, "Sacchi and Maratta at Dusseldorf," *Burlington Magazine* 110 [1968], 362).

10 Gilles Deleuze, *Essays: Critical and Clinical*, trans. D.W. Smith and M.A. Greco (Minneapolis: University of Minnesota Press, 1996), 36 (from the essay "Nietzsche and Saint Paul, Lawrence and John of Patmos").

11 Aldous Huxley, *The Doors of Perception* (New York: Harper and Brothers, 1954), 10: Huxley's riff on drapery takes him into mescalin-induced reveries, such as when he writes, "It is a knowledge of the intrinsic significance of every existent. For the artist as for the mescalin taker draperies are living hieroglyphs that stand in some peculiarly expressive way for the unfathomable mystery of pure being." One can see here the attraction Huxley held for Jim Morrison.

12 Giorgio Vasari, *Vasari on Technique*, trans. Louisa S. Maclehose, ed. G. Baldwin Brown (New York: Dover Publications, 1960), 150–1.

13 For an interesting study of linenfold wainscoting see Nathaniel Lloyd, "Medieval Wainscoting and the Development of the Linen Panel," *Burlington Magazine for Connoisseurs* 53, no. 308 (November 1928): 230–3, 236–7.

14 Shelley Stone, "The Toga: From National to Ceremonial Costume," in *The World of Roman Costume*, ed. Judith Lynn Sebesta and Larissa Bonfante (Madison: University of Wisconsin Press, 1994), 17.

15 Estelle Lingo, *François Duquesnoy and the Greek Ideal* (New Haven, CT: Yale University Press, 2007), especially chapter 3.

16 Conforti, "The Lateran Apostles," 60.

17 Ibid., 61–8.

18 Ibid., 71. In the Latin Commentaries on Revelation, this one by Victorinus, we have the following (on chapter 22): "In that he says there are three gates placed on each of the four sides, of single pearls, I think that these are the four virtues, to wit, prudence, fortitude, justice, temperance, which are associated with one another. And, being involved together, they make the number twelve. But the twelve gates we believe to be the number of the apostles, who, shining in the four virtues as precious stones, manifesting the light of their doctrine among the saints, cause it to enter the celestial city, that by intercourse with them the choir of angels may be gladdened. And that the gates cannot be shut, it is evidently shown that the doctrine of the apostles can be separated from rectitude by no tempest of contradiction. Even though the floods of the nations and the vain superstitions of heretics should revolt against their true faith, they are overcome, and shall be dissolved as the foam, because Christ is the Rock by which, and on which, the Church is founded. And thus it is overcome by no traces of maddened men. Therefore they are not to be heard who assure themselves that there is to be an earthly reign of a thousand years; who think, that is to say, with the heretic Cerinthus. For the kingdom of Christ is now eternal in the saints, although the glory of the saints shall be manifested after the resurrection" (http://www.newadvent.org/fathers/0712.htm).

19 Baldeschi and Crescimbeni, *Stato della SS. Chiesa papale Lateranense.*
20 Gerald Prince, *Dictionary of Narratology* (Lincoln: University of Nebraska Press, 2003), 77.
21 Jacques Derrida, *The Truth in Painting*, trans. Geoff Bennington and Ian McLeod (Chicago: University of Chicago Press, 1987), 18. Derrida here refers to his own 1974 publication *Glas*.
22 Anne Lise Desmas, "Why Legros Rather than Foggini Carved the 'St. Bartholomew' for the Lateran: New Documents for the Statue in the Nave," *Burlington Magazine* 146, no. 1221, Sculpture (December 2004): 805.
23 Conforti, "Planning the Lateran Apostles," 247. Fontana writes, "Tal'uni o per dir molti prendono errore nella denominazione di quei luoghi, dove vanno collocate le statue marmoree dentro la Basilica Lateranense, de nominandole per Nicchie, e pure il composto degl'ornati di essi fanno vedere essere Tabernacoli, mentre, che ordinariamente le Nicchie non hanno un fasto attorno di si belle parti, havendo quel grand'Artefice distributele medesime spaziosamente con eleganza per ricevere nel proprio seno senza angustia la statua per ottenerne un compost correlative a tutto di quei ornati, che vestono pomposamente quelle nobili Pareti replicando, che le dette pareti, che circoscrivono le navate non ammettono parimente Statue grandia à causa della poca distanza, che hanno, onde per sfuggire tall'errore l'artefice sudo dispose l'ornati, che assegnano la misura della statua medema proportionata al godimento di quelle distanze."
24 David Herman, *Story Logic: Problems and Possibilities of Narrative* (Lincoln: University of Nebraska Press, 2002). He writes at the beginning of his text, "story recipients, whether readers, viewers, or listeners, work to interpret narratives by reconstructing the mental representations that have in turn guided their production" (1).
25 Conforti, "The Lateran Apostles," 72.
26 Desmas, "Why Legros Rather than Foggini," 798–9.
27 Although, so far as we know, the legend begins in the twentieth century with two articles that coincidentally and independently made this assertion in 1925: F. La Cava, *Il volto di Michelangelo in Giudizio Finale* (Bologna: N. Zanichelli, 1925), and Charles de Tolnay, *Michelangelo, V: The Final Period* (Princeton, NJ: Princeton University Press, 1971), 44–5, 114–15 (originally published 1925). See also Avigdor W.G. Posèq, "Michelangelo's Self Portrait on the Flayed Skin of St. Bartholomew," *Gazette des Beaux-Arts* 124 (1994): 1–14.
28 Paul Barolski, *Michelangelo's Nose: A Myth and Its Maker* (Hoboken, NJ: John Wiley & Sons, 2007), 31.
29 The drawing is reproduced by Desmas, "Why Legros Rather than Foggini," 796.

30 Baldeschi and Crescimbeni, *Stato della SS. Chiesa papale Lateranense*, 11: "La quinta contiene la Statua di San Bartolomeo, scolpito egregiamente da Monsieur Legros Franzese colla propria pelle in mano, che fa riflettere al dolorosissìmo martirio sofferto dal Santo, quando fu per la Fede scorticato vivo."

31 Jacobus de Voragine, *The Golden Legend*, trans. William Granger Ryan, vol. 2 (Princeton, NJ: Princeton University Press, 1993), 124.

32 Sigmund Freud, *The Uncanny*, in *The Standard Edition of the Complete Psychological Works of Sigmund Freud*, vol. 17, *1917–1919*, ed. and trans. James Strachey (London: Hogarth Press, 1955), 235. Here, without citation, Freud quotes Rank.

33 The Greek word *martus* means to witness something, to swear testimony or testify to a known fact.

34 Vladimir Nabokov, *Transparent Things* (New York: McGraw-Hill, 1972), 1.

35 Bill Brown, "Thing Theory," *Critical Inquiry* 28 (Autumn 2001): 1–23.

8 Fear and Trembling in Sant'Ivo alla Sapienza

1 A much shorter version of this chapter appeared as "Sant'Ivo alla Sapienza, Rom," in *Rom – Meisterwerke der Baukunst, Festgabe für Elisabeth Kieven*, ed. Christina Strunck (Petersburg: Michael Imhof, 2007), 373–6. For Sant'Ivo, see Anthony Blunt, *Borromini* (Cambridge, MA: Harvard University Press, 1979); John Beldon Scott, "S. Ivo alla Sapienza and Borromini's Symbolic Language," *Journal of the Society of Architectural Historians* 41, no. 4 (December 1982): 294–317; Joseph Connors, "Comment interpréter un édifice? Le cas de Saint-Yves-de-la Sapience," *Cahiers de la recherce architecturale et urbaine* 9–10 (2002): 97–108; Joseph Connors, "Borromini's Sant'Ivo alla Sapienza: The Spiral," *Burlington Magazine* 138 (1996): 668–82; Joseph Connors, "Sant'Ivo alla Sapienza: The First Three Minutes," *Journal of the Society of Architectural Historians* 55 (1996): 38–57; Elisabetta Cirielli and Alessandra Marino, "Complesso della Sapienza: Le fasi del cantiere, gli interventi succesivi al Borromini, le manutenzioni," *Ricerche di Storia dell'Arte* 20 (1983): 39–64; Hans Ost, "Borrominis römische Universitätskirche S. Ivo alla Sapienza," *Zeitschrift für Kunstegeschichte* 30 (1967): 101–42.

2 St Augustine, Bishop of Hippo, *Expositions on the Psalms*, vols. 1–3, ed. John Rotelle, Maria Boulding, and Michael Fierowicz (Hyde Park, NY: New City Press, 2000–4).

3 Ost, "Borrominis römische Universitätskirche S. Ivo alla Sapienza," and Pierre de la Ruffinière du Prey, "Solomonic Symbolism in Borromini's Church of S. Ivo alla Sapienza," *Zeitschrift für Kunstgeschichte* 31, no. 3 (1968): 216–32.

4 Du Prey, "Solomonic Symbolism," 225.
5 *New Catholic Encyclopedia*, vol. 14, 2nd ed. (Detroit: Gale, 2003), 784.
6 Ernst Cassirer, *The Philosophy of Symbolic Forms*, 3 vols., trans. Ralph Mannheim (New Haven, CT: Yale University Press, 1953–7).
7 Noam Chomsky, *Language and the Mind* (New York: Harcourt, Brace, and World, 1986).
8 Craig Dworkin, "Against Metaphor," in *Architectures of Poetry*, ed. María Eugenia Díaz Sánchez and Craig Douglas Dworkin (Amsterdam: Editions Rodopi, 2004), 11.
9 As illustrated in Connors, "The First Three Minutes."
10 Ibid., 38.
11 "As to imperfect contrition, which is called attrition, since it commonly arises either from the consideration of the heinousness of sin or from the fear of hell and of punishment, the council declares that if it renounces the desire to sin and hopes for pardon, it not only does not make one a hypocrite and a greater sinner, but is even a gift of God and an impulse of the Holy Ghost, not indeed as already dwelling in the penitent, but only moving him with which assistance the penitent prepares a way for himself unto justice. And though without the sacrament of penance it cannot *per se* lead the sinner to justification, it does, however, dispose him to obtain the grace of God in the sacrament of penance. For, struck salutarily by this fear, the Ninivites, moved by the dreadful preaching of Jonas, did penance and obtained mercy from the Lord. Falsely therefore do some accuse Catholic writers, as if they maintain that the sacrament of penance confers grace without any pious exertion on the part of those receiving it, something that the Church of God has never taught or ever accepted. Falsely also do they assert that contrition is extorted and forced, and not free and voluntary." *The Canons and Decrees of the Council of Trent*, trans. Rev. H.J. Schroeder, O.P. (Rockford, IL: Tan Books and Publishers, 1978), 92.
12 Northrop Frye, *Fearful Symmetry: A Study of William Blake* (Princeton, NJ: Princeton University Press, 1969), 420: "If we follow [Blake's] own method, and interpret this in imaginative instead of historical terms, we have the doctrine that all symbolism in all art and all religion is mutually intelligible among all men, and that there is such a thing as an iconography of the imagination."
13 Connors, "The Spiral," 672.
14 Giorgio Vasari, *Lives of the Most Eminent Painters, Sculptors, and Architects*, trans. G. du C. DeVere (London: Medici Society, 1912), 9:105.
15 Martin Heidegger, *Basic Writings: From Being and Time (1927) to The Task of Thinking (1964)*, ed. David Farrell Krell (New York: Harper & Row,

1977), 59, quoted by A.S. Bessa, "Vers Une Architecture," in *Architectures of Poetry*, ed. María Eugenia Díaz Sánchez and Craig Douglas Dworkin (Amsterdam: Editions Rodopi, 2004).

16 Bessa, "Vers Une Architecture," 43.

17 Adolf Loos, *Ornament and Crime: Selected Essays*, trans. Michael Mitchell, Studies in Austrian Literature, Culture, and Thought Translation Series (Riverside, CA: Ariadne Press, 1998).

18 Robert Harbison, *Reflections on Baroque* (London: Reaktion Books, 2000), 3, where, under the chapter title of "The Case for Disruption," Harbison writes of the optical joke in Borromini's passageway at the Palazzo Spada, Rome. "For the rest of his career Borromini went on repeating this joke in subtler forms, creating false recessions in his façades and interiors, which multiply, and you could say theorize, the space we are looking at."

19 Rudolf Wittkower, *Art and Architecture in Italy 1600–1750*, 3rd ed. (Baltimore: Penguin Books, 1973), 132–4.

20 Ibid., 134.

21 Although musical pulse and poetic metre are not precisely the same thing. As my friend and colleague Ralph Lieberman informs me, "It is not entirely clear where the image of architecture as frozen music first appears. It is generally attributed to Goethe; in a letter of 1829 he wrote 'I call architecture frozen music.' From there the idea appears to have gone to Schilling, who declared in his Philosophy of Art that 'architecture in general is frozen music.' But in Madame de Stael's *Corinne* (Bk IV, ch. 3), which dates from 1807, we find 'The sight of such a monument is like a continuous and stationary music.'"

22 Cesare Ripa, *Iconologia, ouero, Descrittione di diuerse imagini cauate dall'antichità, & di propria inuentione* (Rome: Appresso Lepido Facij, 1603).

23 Deleuze, *The Fold*, 3.

24 Ibid., 5.

25 Ibid.

26 Ibid., 28.

27 Gregg Lambert, *The Non-Philosophy of Gilles Deleuze* (New York: Continuum, 2002), xii.

28 Ibid.

29 Giulio Carlo Argan, *Borromini* (Milan: Sansoni, 1996), 65: "La curvature dei piani é indicative della concezione borrominiana dello spazio architettonico."

30 Blunt, *Borromini*, 193–4: "In the middle window features from ... types used in the outer bays are combined, but with the basic difference that the whole window is set against the concave wall of the central niche. On each side of the window are two columns separated by a broken pilaster.

The outer column and the outer half of the broken pilaster are set against the curve, but the break in the pilaster initiates a convex curve which runs through the whole middle section and encloses an oval space, the covering of which is decorated with the dove of the Holy Ghost in stucco.

The relation between the two columns is complex, because they are each set orthogonally to the curve against which they stand, but this makes them just not at right angles to each other. Further, the sections of the entablature over the columns follow the curve of the niche and so add yet another complication to the whole effect.

At first sight the door seems simpler than the windows, but this is an illusion. The hood follows the familiar pattern of the Palazzo Barberini window, but in the three-dimensional version which the architect used at almost the same time in the door to the cloister of S. Carlino. The lower part is more complicated. The door is flanked by two piers which are neither columns nor pilasters. In plan they consist of two sides and two half-sides of a hexagon, each side being slightly concave, an effect that is even more reminiscent of late Gothic than the octagonal capitals in the cloisters of S. Carlino. Further Borromini has taken up Michelangelo's innovation in the Ricetto of the Laurentian Library and has made his piers narrower at the bottom than at the top, and to this he has added his own trick of making the flutings of unequal size. Drawings for the door and the central window show that Borromini intended to make them considerably richer."

31 Michael Baxandall, "The Language of Art History," *New Literary History* 10 (Spring 1979): 454.

32 Kant, *Critique of Judgment*, 107.

9 Baroque Conceits

1 Each of our eyes has 130,000,000 receptors, while the optic nerve has a "mere" 1,000,000 ganglion cells for collecting and processing that information. It is not unlike reducing a 1,300-word essay to 10 words. However, on the other side of that narrow passage, there are billions of neurons in the brain to process the visual information brought in by the optic nerve; still, what they have to work with is determined by that initial reduction of 130:1 that occurs inside the eyeball as receptors converge onto ganglion cells. Those billions of neurons, just the same, prompt us in our art-historical ekphrases, the metaphorical processing of visual information.

2 See chapter 8, "Fear and Trembling in Francesco Borromini's *Sant'Ivo alla Sapienza*."

3 Giovanni Pietro Bellori, *The Lives of the Modern Painters, Sculptors, and*

Architects, trans. Alice Sedgwick Wohl (Cambridge and New York: Cambridge University Press, 2005), 255. See also Richard E. Spear, *Domenichino* (New Haven, CT, and London: Yale University Press, 1982), 1:250, in which Spear identifies a head of Alexander in the Museo Barracco, Rome, as the source for Domenichino's preparatory sketches of John's head.

4 David Bordwell, *Narration in the Fiction Film* (Madison: University of Wisconsin Press, 1985), 16; as quoted in Remegius Bunia, "Diegesis and Representation: Beyond the Fictional World, on the Margins of Story and Narrative," *Poetics Today* 31, no. 4 (Winter 2010): 691.

5 Spear, *Domenichino*, relates this image to "the light which lighteth every man, coming into the world" (John 1:5 and 1:9).

6 Thomas Aquinas, *Summa Theologica*, trans. Fathers of the English Dominican Province, vol. 1 (Westminster, MD: Christian Classics, 1981), "Of the Angels in Comparison with Bodies, Question 51," 264–73, treats the angelic body as one merely assumed and one that does not engage in sex (which tends to remove issues of gender).

7 Ruthven, *The Conceit*, 46.

8 Relating to John's evangel "of love." Spear, *Domenichino*, 250.

9 Jacques Derrida, *Of Grammatology*, trans. Gayatri Chakravorty Spivak (Baltimore and London: Johns Hopkins University Press, 1982), 145.

10 The other pendentives carry the "The Four Doctors of the Latin Church," "Prophets of Israel," and "Lawgivers and Leaders of Israel."

11 Although I use various synonyms – such as "realm," "universe," and "world" – for an artist's fictional narrative, I tend toward "world," for it is part of a larger universe, as are paintings and their fictional representations. And "world" comes closest to where we all live.

12 Maurice Merleau-Ponty, *The Primacy of Perception*, in *The Merleau-Ponty Aesthetics Reader*, ed. Galen A. Johnson (Evanston, IL: Northwestern University Press, 1993), 4.

13 Theodore Kisiel, *The Genesis of Heidegger's Being & Time* (Berkeley: University of California Press, 1995).

14 Aquinas, *Summa Theologica*. See "Question 50: On the Substance of the Angels"; "Question 51: Of the Angels in Comparison with Bodies"; "Question 52: Of the Angels in Relation to Place"; and "Question 53: On the Local Movement of the Angels."

15 Tesauro, "Dell'argutezza e de' suo parti in generali," in *Il Cannocchiale Aristotelico*, 13.

16 Aquinas, *Summa Theologica*, "Question 51," 255.

17 R. Chris Hassel Jr., "Donne's *Ignatius, His Conclave*, and the New Astronomy," *Modern Philology* 68, no. 4 (May 1971): 329–37. For an easily

accessible text of the entire poem see http://www.bartleby.com/357/169.html.

18 Robert Enggass, *The Painting of Baciccio: Giovanni Battista Gaulli, 1639–1709* (University Park: Pennsylvania State University Press, 1964), 31–74. See also, for comments on the *apparati* installed for the 40 hours' vigil before Easter and their relation to Baciccio's paintings, Mark S. Weil, "The Devotion of the Forty Hours and Roman Baroque Illusions," *Journal of the Warburg and Courtauld Institutes* 37 (1974): 218–48.

19 Enggass, *Painting of Baciccio*, 178; P. Tacchi Venturi, "Le convenzioni tra Giov. Battista Gaulli e il generale dei Gesuiti Gian Paolo Oliva per le pitture della cupola e della volta del Tempio Farnesiano," *Roma* 13 (1935): 153; Jacopo Curzietti, *Giovan Battista Gaulli: La decorazione della chiesa del SS. Nome di Gesù* (Rome: Gangemi Editore SPA, 2011), 81–8 (who tackles the difficult task of identifying some of those – beyond Retti and Raggi – who contributed to the sculptural program).

20 For a discussion of the adoration of the Holy Name of Jesus in a painting by El Greco, see Anthony Blunt, "El Greco's *Dream of Philip II*: An Allegory of the Holy League," *Journal of the Warburg and Courtauld Institutes* 3, nos. 1/2 (October 1939–January 1940): 58–69.

21 Duane F. Watson, "A Rhetorical Analysis of Philippians and Its Implications for the Unity Question," *Novum Testamentum* 30, no. 1 (January 1988): 57–88.

22 Ibid., 62.

23 Aquinas, *Summa Theologica*, "Question 51," 268.

24 Ibid., 529.

25 John O'Malley, *The First Jesuits* (Cambridge, MA: Harvard University Press, 1995), 48.

26 *The Stanford Encyclopedia of Philosophy*, s.v. "Pseudo-Dionysius the Areopagite," last modified 31 December 2014, http://plato.stanford.edu/entries/pseudo-dionysius-areopagite/.

27 O'Malley, *First Jesuits*, 49.

28 Jacob Bronowski, *Origins of Knowledge and Imagination* (New Haven, CT: Yale University Press, 1978), 70.

29 Pseudo-Dionysius, *Pseudo-Dionysius: The Complete Works*, trans. Colm Luibheid, ed. Paul Rorem (New York: Paulist Press, 1987), 145.

30 Ibid., 154.

31 Ibid., 161–6.

32 Ibid., 173.

33 Ibid., 150.

34 Enggass, *Painting of Baciccio*, 44.

35 Ibid., 45.
36 Ibid.
37 "Storyworld" is used by David Herman in *Story Logic*. Throughout this discussion I adopt many of Herman's points.
38 I am adapting a quotation made by Sheldon Sacks, *On Metaphor* (Chicago and London: University of Chicago Press, 1978), v, in which he quotes from Ernst Cassirer's *Language and Myth*, trans. Suzanne Langer (New York: Harper & Brothers, 1946), the following: "But if this is indeed the case – if metaphor, taken in this general sense, is not just a certain development of speech, but must be regarded as one of the essential conditions – then any effort to understand its function leads us back, once more, to the fundamental form of verbal conceiving."
39 Pseudo-Dionysius, *Pseudo-Dionysius*, 146.

10 Bernini and the Metaphor of the Fiery Angel

1 This discussion of Bernini's angels is adapted from my article "Shapes of the Invisible: Bernini's Fiery Angels in Saint Peter's," *Artibus et Historiae* 19 (1989): 149–56.
2 For this chapter I use an earlier edition in English than I did in the last: Pseudo-Dionysius, *The Works of Dionysius the Areopagite*, trans. Rev. J. Parker (Merrick, NY: Richwood Publishing, 1976).
3 Ibid., 57.
4 Ibid.
5 Ibid., 61.
6 Ibid., 60.
7 Drapery pattern as *disegno* is treated in M.G. Poirer, "Studies on the Concepts of 'Disegno,' 'Invenzione,' and 'Colore' in Sixteenth- and Seventeenth-Century Italian Art Theory" (diss., New York University, 1976), 43ff. The references to Vasari, Dolce, and Pino are as follows: G. Vasari, *Le vite de' più eccelenti Pittori, Scultori, et Architettori*, 179; M.W. Roskill, *Dolce's "Aretino" and Venetian Art Theory of the Cinquecento* (New York, 1968), 150; P. Pino, *Dialogo di Pittura*, in P. Barocchi, *Trattati d'Arte del Cinquecento*, vol. 1 (Bari: Laterza, 1960), 114.
8 M. Black, "Metaphor," in *Philosophy Looks at the Arts*, ed. J. Margolis (New York: Charles Scribner's Sons, 1962), 218–35. Originally published as "Metaphor," *Proceedings of the Aristotelian Society* 55 (1954–5): 273–94.
9 Ibid., 234; emphasis in original.
10 Dio Chrysostom, "The Twelfth, or Olympic Discourse: On Man's First Conception of God," in *Dio Chrysostom*, trans. J.W. Cohoon, Loeb Classical Library, vol. 2 (Cambridge, MA: Harvard University Press, 1932–52), 83.

11 Erwin Panofsky, *Galileo as a Critic of the Arts* (The Hague: M. Nijhoff, 1954), 37.
12 Ibid., 9.
13 Domenico Bernini, *Vita del Cavalier Gio. Lorenzo Bernino*, 47.

11 Pascal, Jansenists, Jesuits, and the *Lettres Provinciales*

1 Hanns Gross, *Rome in the Age of Enlightenment: The Post-Tridentine Syndrome and the Ancien Regime* (New York: Cambridge University Press, 1990), 270.
2 Minor, *Death of the Baroque and the Rhetoric of Good Taste*, 6.
3 Translated and quoted in Joseph Wilhelm, "Pope Clement XIV," in *The Catholic Encyclopedia* (New York: Robert Appleton Company, 1908), accessed 16 September 2014, http://www.newadvent.org/cathen/04034a.htm.
4 The bibliography on the Jansenists is of a scale that defies a manageable summary. But see L. Mozzi, *Storia delle rivoluzioni della Chiesa di Utrecht*, 3 vols. (Venice, 1788); E. Picot, *Mémoires pour servir à l'histoire ecclésiastique pendant le XVIIIe siècle*, 7 vols. (Paris, 1853–7); R. Rapin, *Mémoires sur l'Eglise et la société, la Cour, la ville et le jansénisme*, 3 vols. (Paris, 1863); G. Ingold, *L'oratoire et le jansénism* (Paris, 1880); G. Ingold, *Rome et la France: La seconde phase du jansénisme* (Paris, 1901); M. Paquier, *Le jansénisme: étude doctrinale* (Paris, 1909); Nigel Abercrombie, *The Origins of Jansenism* (Oxford: Clarendon Press, 1936); L. Laporte, *La Doctrine de Port-Royale* (Paris, 1952); J.-R. Armogathe and M. Dupuy, "Jansénisme," in *Dictionnaire de spiritualité: ascétique et mystique, doctrine and histoire*, vol. 8 (Paris: Beauchesne, 1974), 102–48; and William Doyle, *Jansenism: Catholic Resistance to Authority from the Reformation to the French Revolution* (New York: Palgrave Macmillan, 2000).
5 Luther had begun with Augustine and moved to St Paul's emphasis upon justification by faith alone, thereby leading, if not inevitably at least somewhat logically, to a break from the church; the Jansenists had no such desire.
6 The reassertion of St Augustine's theology brought up again questions of Pelagianism, a set of heretical ideas on original sin and grace ascribed to the fifth-century Roman Pelagius.
7 An older but still useful assessment of the church's battle with the Jansenists, and the enmity between Jansenist and Jesuit, is Wallace K. Ferguson, "The Place of Jansenism in French History," *Journal of Religion* 7, no. 1 (January 1927): 16–42.
8 The condemnation was reaffirmed twice more by Clement XI, first with his bull *Vineam Domini* of 1705, which denounced the "respectful silence" adopted by Jansenists as passive resistance to the original bull, and then again with *Unigenitus*, in 1713, which certainly covered Jansenism but was specifically

directed at Pasquier Quesnel's *Réflexions morales*. Clement's latter bull was very thorough, prompting W.K. Ferguson to comment that it "caused many to feel that he had condemned not only Quesnel but Augustine and even Christ as well." Ferguson, "The Place of Jansenism in French History," 37.

9 Here is how Blaise Pascal described a subsequent event at the Sorbonne, this one in 1656, after Innocent's bull of condemnation: "The question of fact is whether M. Arnauld is guilty of temerity for asserting in his *Second Letter*: 'that he has carefully read Jansenius's book, that he has not found in it the propositions condemned by the late Pope, but despite this, since he condemns these propositions wherever they may be found, he also condemns them in Jansenius if they are there.'" *Pascal: The Provincial Letters*, trans. A.J. Krailsheimer (Harmondsworth, Middlesex: Penguin Books, 1967), 31. See the definitive edition: Blaise Pascal, *Oeuvres Complètes (Grand Ecrivans de la France)*, ed. L. Brunschwicg, P. Boutroux, and F. Gazier, vol. 4 (Paris: Librairie Hachette et Cie, 1914).

10 Richard Parish, *Pascal's "Lettres Provinciales": A Study in Polemic* (Oxford: Oxford University Press, 1989), 7: "it cannot be denied that the question of orthodoxy and the role of ecclesiastical authority is, in the contemporary context of an absolute monarchy, intimately bound up with the role of obedience to political authority." Parish then goes on to cite several sociopolitical studies and to refer the reader to his ample bibliography. He is no more inclined than am I to enter into a field in which we are both amateurs; suffice it to say, the political ramifications of the Jansenist-Jesuit controversy are legion.

11 The phrase "mystic hydra" is not Pascal's and is not especially well known outside of Italy; it comes from Vincenzo Gravina, *Hydra Mystica: con la ristampa della traduzione italiana del 1761*, ed. Fabrizio Lomonaco (Soveria Mannelli, Catanzara, Italy: Rubbettino, 2002); originally published in Latin in 1691. Something of Gravina's power for reformers, even into the nineteenth century (long after the events described here), can be detected in the following passage in Edith Wharton's *The Valley of Decision* (the early part of chapter 14): "Andreoni, famous throughout Italy for his editions of the classics, was a man of liberal views and considerable learning, and in his private room were to be found many prohibited volumes, such as Beccaria's *Crime and Punishment*, Gravina's *Hydra Mystica*, Concini's *History of Probabilism* and the Amsterdam editions of the French philosophical works."

12 Marc Fumaroli, "The Fertility and the Shortcomings of Renaissance Rhetoric: The Jesuit Case," in *The Jesuits: Cultures, Sciences, and the Arts*, ed. John W. O'Malley, S.J.; Gauvin Alexander Bailey; Steven J. Harris; and T. Frank Kennedy, S.J. (Toronto: University of Toronto Press, 1999), 90.

13 Jonathan I. Israel, in *Radical Enlightenment: Philosophy and the Making of Modernity 1650–1750* (Oxford: Oxford University Press, 2002), writes that "a prominent late seventeenth-century German court official, the Freiherr Veit Ludwig von Seckendorff (1626–92), observed in 1685 that what the radicals ultimately intended was to make 'life in this world' the basis of politics" (5). That of course would be a departure from the usual understanding of politics.

14 In an informative article on Jesuits and their meditations on images of early Christian martyrs, Kirstin Noreen, "Ecclesiae militantis triumphi: Jesuit Iconography and the Counter-Reformation," *Sixteenth-Century Journal* 29, no. 3 (Autumn 1998): 689–715 (and especially 703–6) writes effectively about the Counter-Reformation debate on justification, grace, and sin.

15 Antoine Arnauld, *De la fréquente communion: Ou les sentiments des pères, des papes, et des conciles* (Paris, 1683), in which he discourages frequent communion.

16 Pascal described his *Nuit de Feu* in a Latin inscription sewn into his leather cloak: Monday, 23 November [1654], feast of St Clement, pope and martyr, and others in the martyrology. Vigil of St Chrysogonus, martyr, and others. From about half past ten at night until about half past midnight,

> FIRE.
> GOD of Abraham, GOD of Isaac, GOD of Jacob
> not of the philosophers and of the learned.
> Certitude. Certitude. Feeling. Joy. Peace.
> GOD of Jesus Christ.
> My God and your God.
> Your GOD will be my God.
> Forgetfulness of the world and of everything, except GOD.
> He is only found by the ways taught in the Gospel.
> Grandeur of the human soul.
> Righteous Father, the world has not known you, but I have known you.
> Joy, joy, joy, tears of joy.
> I have departed from him:
> They have forsaken me, the fount of living water.
> My God, will you leave me?
> Let me not be separated from him forever.
> This is eternal life, that they know you, the one true God, and the one that you sent, Jesus Christ.
> Jesus Christ.
> Jesus Christ.

I left him; I fled him, renounced, crucified.
Let me never be separated from him.
He is only kept securely by the ways taught in the Gospel:
Renunciation, total and sweet.
Complete submission to Jesus Christ and to my director.
Eternally in joy for a day's exercise on the earth.
May I not forget your words. Amen.

17 Victor Cousin, *Jacqueline Pascal*, trans. H.N. (New York, 1854). Pascal's niece Marguerite Perier suffered from a *fistula lacrymalis*, an infected lachrymal gland. In 1656 a holy thorn, from Christ's crown of thorns, was given to La Mère Angélique, who in turn saw to it that during a ceremony Marguerite's eye was touched by the thorn. Her near-immediate recovery became known widely and became sanctioned by church authorities as a genuine miracle. Naturally, the Jesuits were up in arms over this but could say little. For a while at least, the pressures on the convent were relaxed.
18 Ibid., 41.
19 Ibid., 41–2. Although Pascal gives every indication of being both bemused and confused by the notion of "efficacious grace," in several of the later letters he seems to accept it without question.
20 See W. Bocxe, "Introduction to the Teaching of the Italian Augustinians of the 18th Century on the Nature of Actual Grace," *Augustiniana* 8, no. 3 (August 1958): 356–96, discusses at considerable length various teachings among Italian Augustinians on, among other issues, efficacious and sufficient grace; the author also distinguishes between Jansenist and Augustinian views of grace. "The Augustinian teaching … is that the free will is never reduced to nothing by a relatively stronger grace" (394).
21 Pascal, *Provincial Letters*, Letter IV, 61.
22 Ibid., Letter V, 75.
23 Ibid., Letter V, 85.
24 Fumaroli, "The Fertility and the Shortcomings of Renaissance Rhetoric," 97.
25 St Augustine himself was averse to having his words reduced to a single meaning: "were I to indite any thing that whatever truth any could apprehend on those matters, might be conveyed in my words, rather than set down my own meaning so clearly as to exclude the rest, which not being false, could not offend me." St Augustine, Bishop of Hippo, *The Confessions of St. Augustine*, trans. E.B. Pusey (London: J.M. Dent & Sons, 1907), 306 (12.31.42).
26 *Ecclesiastica Historia: integram ecclesiae Christi ideam complectens, congesta per aliquot studiosos et pios viros in urbe Magdeburgica*, 13 vols. (Basle, 1559–74).

27 "Il. V. Cardl. Passionei mi propose, essendone stato da me interrogato, di fare un Istoria Ecclesiastica come in compendia quasi come quella del Fleury, rilevare in vari discorsi tutti quei puntichye sono secondo il nostro sistema, siccome egli ne' suoi discorsi ha rilevati quelli che fanno a pro suo." Biblioteca Corsiniana, Rome, archives, 44 D 46, 139v. Heather Hyde Minor in her text from Pennsylvania University Press, *The Culture of Architecture in Enlightenment Rome*, provided me with this quotation (from a letter written by Giovanni Gaetano Bottari, another Jansenist adherent). She treats ecclesiastical history in the context of Roman eighteenth-century architectural programs.

28 On 24 August 1690, Alexander condemned the doctrine of "philosophical sin" (casuistry) – *il peccato filosofico*.

29 Aristotle, *The Art of Rhetoric*, trans. J.H. Freese (London: Heinemann, 1947), 13.

30 Patricia Topliss, *The Rhetoric of Pascal: A Study of His Art of Persuasion in the "Provinciales" and the "Pensées"* (Amsterdam: Leicester University Press, 1966), is the most focused *rhetorical* study of Pascal's rhetoric in any language.

31 Ferguson, "The Place of Jansenism in French History," 17: "Jansenism was essentially the revival, in a particularly acute form, of the perennial struggle of the few austere and deeply religious souls whose standards of theology, as of morals, are absolute, and to whom compromise with mediocrity is impossible, against the great mass of the people, whose standard is mediocrity and whose weight of inertia constantly tends to lower the spiritual level of the church."

32 Pascal, *Provincial Letters*, Letter XI, 164.

33 Ibid.

34 Nigel Abercrombie, *Saint Augustine and French Classical Thought* (New York: Russell & Russell, 1972), 116.

35 Pascal, *Provincial Letters*, Letter XI, 170–1.

36 Topliss, *Rhetoric of Pascal*, 1–41, upon whom I rely for Pascal as pamphleteer; see her text for sources and complete bibliography.

37 Increasing the chatter, he teased his public by appending a series of initials to the third letter: E.A.A.B.P.A.F.D.E.P (perhaps signifying Et Ancient Ami Blaise Pascal, Auvergna, Fils d'Etienne Pascal); just the same, his anonymity remained intact.

38 He undoubtedly felt some resentment towards them because they questioned the miraculous nature of his niece's cure.

39 Topliss, *Rhetoric of Pascal*, 92–125, summarizes Pascal's logic and escape from logic in the later *Provinciales*.

40 Fumaroli, "The Fertility and the Shortcomings of Renaissance Rhetoric," 90.

41 By "style" I do not mean something akin to a literary or artistic style; rather I see it in terms of a practice that is related to Jansenist ideals and attitudes in a fairly general sense.

42 Tad M. Schmaltz, "What Has Cartesianism to Do with Jansenism?" *Journal of the History of Ideas* 60, no. 1 (January 1999): 37.
43 See also Elmar J. Kremer, "Arnauld's Interpretation of Descartes as a Christian Philosopher," in *Interpreting Arnauld*, ed. Elmar J. Kremer (Toronto: University of Toronto Press, 1996), 76–90; and Steven M. Nadler, *Arnauld and the Cartesian Philosophy of Ideas* (Princeton, NJ: Princeton University Press, 1989), especially his section on Jansenism and Cartesianism, 18–34.
44 Nadler, *Arnauld and the Cartesian Philosophy of Ideas*, 18.
45 Marjorie Grene, *Descartes* (Minneapolis: University of Minnesota Press, 1985), 183, quoted by Nadler, *Arnauld and the Cartesian Philosophy of Ideas*.
46 Nadler, *Arnauld and the Cartesian Philosophy of Ideas*, 78, originally in René Descartes, *Oeuvres de Descartes*, 12 vols., ed. Charles Adam and Paul Tannery (Paris, 1897–1913), 7:251; hereafter AT.
47 AT 1:366, in which Descartes states that he isn't concerned with grace; Schmaltz, "What Has Cartesianism to Do with Jansenism?" 39.
48 Nadler, *Arnauld and the Cartesian Philosophy of Ideas*, 21.
49 Ibid., 19; Nadler writes about the objections of Louis-Paul Du Vaucel that Cartesianism "undermined the doctrine of Eucharistic transubstantiation by making extension the essence of body. Since it was traditionally held that the *substance* of Christ's body, but not its extension, replaces the substance of the bread of the sacrament, Cartesianism, which identifies a body with its local extension, cannot account for the 'real presence' of Christ's body in the Eucharist."
50 Schmaltz, "What Has Cartesianism to Do with Jansenism?" 39 (with translation); AT 4:157.
51 Bal and Bryson, "Semiotics and Art History," especially 176–80.
52 Michel Foucault, "What Is an Author?" in *Language, Counter-Memory, Practice: Selected Essays and Interviews*, ed. D.F. Bouchard (Ithaca, NY: Cornell University Press, 1977), 113–38.
53 See, especially for matters of taste, Minor, *Death of the Baroque and the Rhetoric of Good Taste*.
54 Richard Parish, "Port-Royal and Jansenism," in *The Cambridge History of Literary Criticism*, vol. 3, *The Renaissance*, ed. Glyn P. Norton (New York: Cambridge University Press, 2006), 475.
55 For Philippe de Champaigne see Bernard Dorival, *Philippe de Champaigne, 1602–1674; La Vie, l'oeuvre et le catalogue raisonné de l'oeuvre*, 2 vols. (Paris: Chez l'auteur, 1976) and Bernard Dorival, *Supplément au catalogue raisonné de l'oeuvre de Philippe de Champaigne* (Paris: L. Laget, 1992); also Lorenzo Pericolo, *Philippe de Champaigne* (Tournai: La Renaissance du Livre, 2002). For the Jansenist connections see H. Stein, *Philippe de Champaigne et ses*

relations avec Port-Royal (Paris, 1891), and *Philippe de Champaigne et Port-Royal*, Musée National des Granges de Port-Royal, 29 April–28 August 1995.

56 Louis Marin, *Philippe de Champaigne, ou La Présence Cachée* (Farigliano, Italy: Hazan, 1995), 11.

57 This is my admittedly loose reading of the following passage: "ce sont ces cadres de vision, ces schèmes de l'imagination, ces dispositifs de la sensibilité, un goût pour une certaine stridence des coloris, pour la mise en valeur sensuelle et comme tactile des textures, pour des scénographies amples et calmes, une attention à la densité de l'être dans les visages, les postures, les gestes" (Marin, *Philippe de Champaigne*, 11).

58 Dorival, *Philippe de Champaigne, 1602–1674*, tends to argue that Champaigne's basic style changed little after 1630 (giving him a good decade after his arrival in Paris to bring his early manner to full maturity), although Champaigne was known to adjust his style depending upon commission and patron.

59 "[D]ans [ses] divers tableaux destinés à l'autel, ou à la salle du chapitre, ou au réfectoire du monastère, sa peinture calme, sobre, serrée, sérieuse, tour à tour fouillée ou contrite dans l'expression des visages, s'accorde, d'un pinceau sincère, avec le sentiment qui le doit diriger; toute la couleur de Port-Royal est là." Charles A. de Sainte-Beuve, *Port-Royal*, ed. M. Leroy, vol. 1, *Discours préliminaire* (Paris: Libraire de L. Hachette, 1953), 107.

60 Quoted in Pericolo, *Philippe de Champaigne*, 229; a letter from Isaac Le Maître de Sacy to La Mère Angélique, dated 17 August 1660, Bibliothèque Municipale de Troyes, Manuscrit 2216, originally published in Bernard Dorival, "Récherches sur le portrait d'Antoine Le Maître par Philippe de Champaigne," *Gazette des Beaux-Arts* 70 (1967): 280. Pericolo also refers to Sainte-Beuve's association of Philippe de Champaigne with Port-Royal as the foundation myth of Champaigne as the good painter and good Christian, one who transposed onto the canvas the sensibility of the Jansenists.

61 Cicero, *De Amicitia*, vii, 23.

62 I follow Pericolo, *Philippe de Champaigne*, 228–62, and his discussion of Champaigne as "Le Prédicateur de la foi."

63 "I, (Name), submitting to the Apostolic constitutions of the sovereign pontiffs, Innocent X and Alexander VII, published 31 May, 1653 and 16 October, 1656, sincerely repudiate the five propositions extracted from the book of Jansenius entitled 'Augustinus,' and I condemn them upon oath in the very sense expressed by that author, as the Apostolic See has condemned them by the two above mentioned Constitutions (Enchiridion, 1099)." Jacques Forget, "Jansenius and Jansenism," in *The Catholic Encyclopedia*, vol. 8 (New York: Robert Appleton Company, 1910), accessed 22 March 2007, http://www.newadvent.org/cathen/08285a.htm.

64 Pericolo, *Philippe de Champaigne*, 230: "[C]e même jour ... mourut à Paris Philippe de Champaigne ... peintre très habile en son art, mais que sa piété rendait encore plus recommandable; il a toujours été fort affectionné a cette maison dont il a soutenu les intérêts en toutes rencontres, même devant les grands du monde."

65 Dorival, *Philippe de Champaigne, 1602–1674*, vol. 2, cat. nos. 128, 131.

66 Thomas N. Tentler, *Sin and Confession on the Eve of the Reformation* (Princeton, NJ: Princeton University Press, 1977), 80.

67 Rev. H.J. Schroder, O.P., trans., *Canons and Decrees of the Council of Trent* (Rockford, IL: Tan Books and Publishers, 1978), 89.

68 The image painted for Port-Royal derives from an earlier version (Houston Museum of Fine Arts), c. 1648, made for the Dames du Saint-Sacrament in the Marais, Paris.

69 Jacques-Paul Migne, *Patrologia Latina*, vol. 145, 308, as translated and quoted by Katherine L. Jansen, "Mary Magdalen and the Mendicants: The Preaching of Penance in the Late Middle Ages," *Journal of Medieval History* 21 (1995): 6. Jansen goes on to say: "Mary Magdalene had the gift of tears. According to the Evangelists she was preternaturally disposed toward them. She wept at the house of the Pharisee, bathing Christ's feet with her tears, she wept at the tomb of her dead brother Lazarus, and she most famously wept outside Jesus' tomb" (ibid.).

70 In fact, Antoine Arnauld makes this very point about the sublime in his *Art of Speaking*: "That which is called Great and *Sublime*, has given us an example of a sublime expression taken out of the First Chapter of *Genesis*, where *Moses* speaking of the Creation, uses these words; *And God said let there be light, and there was light*." Antoine Arnauld, *The Art of Speaking: Written in French by Messieurs du Port Royal: In pursuance of a former Treatise, Entitled, "The Art of Thinking"* (London: T. Bennet, 1696), 246.

71 Eric Méchoulan, in his "Immediacy and Forgetting," *SubStance* 34, no. 1 (2005): 154, makes the following observation on the tears in Champaigne's *John the Baptist*: "In the Christian religion, tears are repeatedly valorized: 'Blessed are those who mourn, for they shall be comforted' (Matt. 5:4); 'Blessed are you who weep now, for you shall laugh' (Luke 6:21); 'For godly sorrow produces repentance leading to salvation, not to be regretted; but the sorrow of the world produces death' (Corinthians II, 7:10). Man's awareness of sin inevitably brings fatal despair, but if this sorrow means a lack of faith in God, the sin is doubled. Now, tears function as an abandonment to God, the ambivalent sign of a renunciation and a waiting, the proof of the weight of the world and the joy of penitence. Evagrius Pontius (346–99) affirmed in his *Ad Virginem* 'Heavy is sorrow, unbearable

is bitterness, but tears before God are stronger than either of these.' This is the propitious reversal of tears – signs of sorrow become signs of joy. More than a catharsis, than a purging of the passions, crying is a way of entering into the very essence of passion: a submission where the soul and the body surprise one another and abandon themselves to one another."

72 The words "behold the lamb" (*Ecce Agnus*) and "Sin" (*Pecatum*) are visible, with the rest of the inscription hidden as the scroll furls about the cross and around the staff.

73 Svetlana Alpers, "Interpretations without Representation, or, the Viewing of Las Meninas," *Representations* 1 (February 1983): 39.

74 Méchoulan, "Immediacy and Forgetting," 152.

75 Christopher A. Dustin and Joanna E. Ziegler, *Practicing Mortality: Art, Philosophy, and Contemplative Seeing* (New York: Palgrave Macmillan, 2005), 9.

76 John Florio, *A Worlde of Wordes, or Most Copious and Exact Dictionarie in Italian and English* (1598), as cited in the *Oxford English Dictionary* under "theory."

77 "Events" as instances of hermeneutic seeing are discussed by Vattimo in his discussion of Sant'Ivo alla Sapienza (*Beyond Interpretation*, 58–74).

78 Heidegger, "The Origin of the Work of Art," in *Poetry, Language, Thought*, 25.

79 George Steiner, *Martin Heidegger* (New York: Viking Press, 1978), 79.

80 Vattimo, *Beyond Interpretation*, 66.

81 Heidegger, "The Origin of the Work of Art," 39.

82 Young, *Heidegger's Philosophy of Art*, 20, quoting from Martin Heidegger, *Denkerfahrungen 1910–76* (Frankfurt am Main: Klostermann, 1983), 70–1: "In the 1960s, Heidegger observes of Raphael's altarpiece known as the 'Sixtina' that it belongs to its church at Piacenza 'not merely in an historical-antiquarian sense, but according to its pictorial essence.' The painting 'is the appearing … the place within which the sacrifice of the mass is to be celebrated' so that were it to be uprooted and relocated in a museum, and so deprived of its world, it would lose its 'authentic truth' and become instead a mere 'aesthetic object.'"

83 The documentation for Catherine's cure can be found in the archival records published by J. Bruggeman and A.J. van deVen, *Inventaire des pièces d'archives françaises se rapportant à l'abbaye de Port-Royal des Champs et son cercle et à la résistance contre la Bulle Unigentus et à l'appel (ancien fonds d'Amersfoort)* (The Hague: M. Nijhoff, 1972); see also the fundamental article by Olan A. Rand Jr., "Philippe de Champaigne and the *Ex-Voto* of 1662: A Historical Perspective," *Art Bulletin* 65, no. 1 (March 1983): 78–93.

84 See Wendy Steiner, *The Colors of Rhetoric* (Chicago: University of Chicago Press, 1980), especially section 1, "The Painting-Literature Analogy."

85 Arnauld, *The Art of Speaking*, 247.

86 Ibid., 246.

87 Ibid., 248–9.

88 Ibid., 249.

89 A. Félibien, ed., *Seven Conferences Held in the King of France's Cabinet of Paintings* (London, 1740); all quotations take from 21–32.

90 Aristotle's language on tragedy was common currency among literati from the mid-sixteenth century on. The Christian story, with a risen and triumphant Christ, is not in the final analysis tragedy; yet, in the events of Christ's Passion, the elements of tragedy prevail.

91 Félibien defines peripety when recording Le Brun's analysis of *The Fall of Manna*; Félibien writes, "The groups of figures, which make different actions, are like so many episodes, that serve instead of what they call *Peripeties*, and by this means set forth the change which happened to the Israelites, when they were delivered from extreme misery and entered upon a more happy state" (Félibien, *Conferences*, 123).

92 Aristotle, *Poetics*, p. 38, sec. 53a1.

93 The emergence of drama in Europe comes from the church, not from the plays of antiquity; yet, given the humanists' fascination with ancient rhetoric, philosophy, and poetics, viewing these images through the "Aristotelian spyglass" is consistent with early-modern literary criticism.

94 Letter to Marquis Francesco Albergati Capacelli, 23 December 1760, in Voltaire, *The Complete Works*, ed. T. Besterman, 135 vols. (Banbury: Voltaire Foundation, 1972), 106:404. "J'ai entendu ce propos dans mon enfance, non pas une fois mais trente," as quoted in John Campbell, "Racine and the Augustinian Inheritance: The Case of Andromaque," *French Studies* 53, no. 3 (1999): 279–91.

95 *Jean Racine: 1699–1999*, ed. Gilles Declercq and Miche' le Rosellini (Paris: PUF, 2003) gathers 800 pages of Racinian criticism marking the tercentenary of his death. Port-Royal is given its due.

96 Campbell, "Racine and the Augustinian Inheritance."

97 Ibid., 284.

98 Ibid., 287–8.

99 Pericolo, *Philippe de Champaigne*; see especially 228–62 ("'Le Prédicateur de la foi': Champaigne et Port-Royal, 1643–67").

100 Ibid., 233: "En considérant ces différents témoignages, il paraît évident qu'il n'a jamais existé une esthétique de Port-Royal si l'on entend par

là un système cohérent de préceptes et d'interdictions concernant la pratique de la peinture."

101 Louis Marin, "Signe et répresentation: Philippe de Champaigne et Port-Royal," *Annales: Economies, Sociétés, Civilisations* 25, nos. 1–3 (1970): 1–28; and Louis Marin and Marie Maclean, "The Figurability of the Visual: The Veronica or the Question of the Portrait at Port-Royal," *New Literary History* 22, no. 2 (Spring 1991): 281–96.

102 Especially useful in this regard is Young, *Heidegger's Philosophy of Art.*

103 Ibid., 17.

104 For the transfer of the painting and a detailed discussion of its original placement, see Michael Rohlmann, "Raffaels Sixtinische Madonna," *Römisches Jahrbuch der Bibliotheca Hertziana* 30 (1995): 221–48.

105 Heidegger, *Denkerfahrungen 1910–76*, 70–1, as quoted and translated by Young, *Heidegger's Philosophy of Art*, 20.

106 Ibid.

12 The Corsini Chapel

1 Florence: Archivio di Stato, Carte Galilei, filza 14, fasc. 1, fols. 49–50: "Che ogniuno de d. Professori, tanto quelli, che fanno Ie Statue nelle Nicchie, e Siccome ancora i Bassirlievi, non devano con panni, Braccia, o altra cosa occupare, ne postare fuori dei vini o Spigoli dei contorni alle Nicchie, e di quelli alle Luci dei Bassirilievi, ma devono stare dentro di quelli, con obbligo, che facendolo debbano, e siano tenuti a mutarli, e ridurli a sodisfazione dell'Architetto." (That every one of these *professori* [sculptors], especially those who provide statues in the niches, as well as sculptural reliefs, may not allow clothes, arms, or anything else to project beyond the edges or contours of these niches or the frames of the sculptural reliefs, but must stay within these limits, with the requirement, that if they [the sculptors] do so, they are required to change them, and reduce them to the satisfaction of the Architect.)

2 One has no idea, of course, what precisely Galilei had in mind; he may in fact have been worried that too much detail – there is, after all, a great deal of sculpture in the chapel – would simply have been messy. Just the same, he made an aesthetic choice that suppressed the prevailing styles of the previous generation and therefore placed himself squarely in the camp of *"buon gusto"* (see Minor, *Death of the Baroque and the Rhetoric of Good Taste*). Elisabeth Kieven writes that the year 1732 (when Galilei received the commission for the Lateran façade) "was indeed a signal for the transition from Roman late Baroque to Neoclassicism." Elisabeth Kieven, "Rome in

1732," in *Light on the Eternal City*, ed. H. Hager and S. Scott Munshower (University Park: Pennsylvania State University Press, 1987), 255.

3 Francesco Valesio, *Diario di Roma*, ed. G. Scano and G. Graglia, vol. 5 (Milan: Longanesi, 1979), 758: "Celebrandosi oggi la festa di S. Andrea Corsini, si fece solenne musica nella nuova cappella fabricata da S. Beatitudine in S. Giovanni in Laterano ed ora terminata: vi assisté tutto il capitolo ed, essendo l'aria serena e temperate, vi furono a visitarla molti de' cardinali ed all'arrivo di ciascheduno di questi si sparavano Quattro mortaletti, il che fece fare lo scarpellino di detta cappella, ricca di marmi e metalli, ma non ha incontrata la soddisfazione di tutti, venendo riputata minuta e secca."

4 "In the Corsini chapel, Galilei left contemporary Roman architecture behind him and moved further toward neoclassical forms than would be possible again in Rome for many decades. Contemporary comments are more enthusiastic about the richness of the decoration than about the design. Valesio found the chapel '*dry* and boring.' The general reaction was more puzzlement than approval" (Kieven, "Rome in 1732," 258).

5 The French architect Antoine Dérizet believed that Alessandro Galilei's proposal for the Lateran façade was far from the "good" Roman tradition, which was about the "wild and unreasonable compilation of pilasters and columns and unnecessary projections." Kieven, "Rome in 1732," 23: "idea assai facile e semplice, un contorno troppo quadro, e senza interrompimento o risalto."

6 Jacques Derrida and Craig Owens, "The Parergon," *October* 9 (Summer 1979): 3–41.

7 Robert Enggass, "Two Contrasting Concepts of Color in the Architecture of the Roman Baroque," in *An Architectural Progress in the Renaissance and Baroque: Sojourns In and Out of Italy*, vol. 1, ed. Henry Millon and Susan S. Munshower (University Park: Pennsylvania State University Press, 1992), 407–9.

8 Jacques Derrida, *The Truth in Painting*, trans. Geoff Bennington and Ian McLeod (Chicago: University of Chicago Press, 1987), 9 (italics in original). I can imagine Derrida taking hesitant steps into the Corsini Chapel, pacing to and fro, squinting at details, and then bursting out through the gate, a manic expression on his face, pronouncing finally "But of course!" Sometimes seeing a physical instantiation of one's philosophical meditations can lead to a stunning post-eureka moment.

9 Jacques Derrida, *Writing and Difference*, trans. Alan Bass (London: Routledge, 2001), 281.

10 Derrida, *Truth in Painting*, 60–1.

11 See Bal and Bryson, "Semiotics and Art History," 180.

12 Edward S. Casey, *The Fate of Place: A Philosophical History* (Berkeley: University of California Press, 1997), 138. Casey's argument about early-modern space is that it is infinite, allowing little room for consideration of "place." *Where* something is does not affect *what* something is.
13 Ibid.
14 Louis Marin and Anna Lehman, "Classical, Baroque: Versailles, or the Architecture of the Prince," *Yale French Studies* 80, Baroque Topographies: Literature/History/Philosophy (1991): 176.
15 This is a substantially altered version of my chapter "La Capella Corsini: Un Museo Neoclassico?" in *Dopo il Museo*, ed. Federico Luisetti and Giorgio Maragliano (Turin: Trauben, 2006), 93–110.
16 Ludwig, Freiherr von Pastor, *The History of the Popes*, trans. Dom Ernest Graf, vol. 34 (London: Kegan Paul, Trench, Trubner & Co., 1941), 509–10. One presumes that the "voice" here is Pastor's, although the final text was prepared after his death in 1928. Most scholars agree that the text, prepared by a team of collaborators chosen by Pastor, follows very closely his detailed notes.
17 For instance see Pastor, *History of the Popes*, 506, specifically the comments on Alessandro Galilei's façade of San Giovanni: "Here also there are two storeys, but the upper storey above the open portico of 9 m. in depth and 56 m. in breadth forms with it an imposing unity, and the loggia of the upper storey ... harmonizes most happily with the main portal, yet stands out from it." Among Pastor's sources for this sort of formalist language may be A.E. Brinckmann's *Die Baukunst des 17. und 18. Jahrhunderts* (1915), which he frequently sites.
18 Elisabeth Kieven, "Überlegungen zu Architektur und Ausstattung der Capella Corsini," in *Studi sul Settecento: L'architettura da Clemente XI a Benedetto XIV – Pluralità di tendenze*, ed. Elisa Debenedetti (Rome, 1989), 69–91.
19 Ibid., 71: Zwischen "Architektur und Skulptur herrscht ein latentes Spannungsverhältnis, und die Zwiespalt zu tun haben."
20 Minor, *Death of the Baroque and the Rhetoric of Good Taste.*
21 Pastor, *History of the Popes*, 509.
22 Bachelard, *Poetics of Space.*
23 Michel Foucault, *The Archaeology of Knowledge* (New York: Harper & Row, 1972), 191.
24 See, for instance, Kieven, "Rome in 1732" and "Überlegungen zu Architektur und Ausstattung der Capella Corsini"; Gross, *Rome in the Age of Enlightenment;* Christopher M.S. Johns, *Papal Art and Cultural Politics: Rome in the Age of Clement XI* (Cambridge and New York: Cambridge University Press, 1993); Christopher M.S. Johns, *The Visual Culture of Catholic Enlightenment: Papal Art*

in Eighteenth-Century Rome (University Park: Pennsylvania State University Press, 2014); Minor, *Death of the Baroque and the Rhetoric of Good Taste*; Heather Hyde Minor, *The Culture of Architecture in Enlightenment Rome* (University Park: Pennsylvania State University Press, 2011). Here I list only books in English; the pertinent and vast bibliography in Italian can readily be culled from these texts.

25 For Ripa see *Iconologia*, ed. Piero Buscaroli, preface by Mario Praz (Milan: Editori Associati, S.P.A, 1992).

26 Minor, "Recollection and Undermining of Allegory."

27 See my discussion of this figure especially in "Art History and Intertextuality," *Storia dell'Arte* 92 (1998): 132–42.

28 Wolfgang Iser, *The Fictive and the Imaginary: Charting Literary Anthropology* (Baltimore and London: Johns Hopkins University Press, 1993).

Bibliography

Abercrombie, Nigel. *Saint Augustine and French Classical Thought*. New York: Russell & Russell, 1972.

Adorno, Theodor. *Aesthetic Theory*. Translated by Robert Hullot-Kentor. Minneapolis: University of Minnesota Press, 1997.

Alighieri, Dante. *Dantis Alagherii Epistolae: The Letters of Dante*. Edited by Paget Toynbee. Oxford: Clarendon Press, 1920.

Alpers, Svetlana. "Interpretations without Representation, or, the Viewing of Las Meninas." *Representations* 1 (February 1983): 30–42.

Alpers, Svetlana, and Michael Baxandall. *Tiepolo and the Pictorial Intelligence*. New Haven, CT, and London: Yale University Press, 1994.

Aquinas, Thomas. *Summa Theologica*. Translated by Fathers of the English Dominican Province. Vol. 1. Westminster, MD: Christian Classics, 1981.

Argan, Giulio Carlo. *Borromini*. Milan: Sansoni, 1996.

Ariès, Philippe. *Western Attitudes toward Death from the Middle Ages to the Present*. Translated by Patricia M. Ranum. Baltimore: Johns Hopkins University Press, 1975.

Aristotle. *The Art of Rhetoric*. Translated by J.H. Freese. London: Heinemann, 1947.

– *The Complete Works of Aristotle*. Edited by Jonathan Barnes. Vol. 2, Bollingen Series LXXI–2. Princeton, NJ: Princeton University Press, 1984.

– *Poetics*. Translated by Gerald F. Else. Ann Arbor: University of Michigan Press, 1970.

Arnauld, Antoine. *The Art of Speaking: Written in French by Messieurs du Port Royal: In pursuance of a former Treatise, Entitled, "The Art of Thinking."* London: T. Bennet, 1696.

– *De la fréquente communion: Ou les sentiments des pères, des papes, et des conciles*. Paris, 1683.

Auerbach, Erich. *Scenes from the Drama of European Literature*. Minneapolis: University of Minnesota Press, 1984.

Augustine, St, Bishop of Hippo. *The Confessions of St. Augustine*. Translated by E.B. Pusey. London: J.M. Dent & Sons, 1907.

– *Expositions on the Psalms*. Vols. 1–3, edited by John Rotelle, Maria Boulding, and Michael Fierowicz. Hyde Park, NY: New City Press, 2000–4.

Bachelard, Gaston. *The Poetics of Space*. Translated by Maria Jolas. Boston: Beacon Press, 1969.

Bacon, Francis. *Essays*. Edited by R. Whately. Boston: Life and Shepard, 1868.

Bal, Mieke. *Quoting Caravaggio: Contemporary Art, Preposterous History*. Chicago: University of Chicago Press, 1999.

Bal, Mieke, and Norman Bryson. "Semiotics and Art History." *Art Bulletin* 73, no. 2 (June 1991): 174–208.

Baldeschi, Alessandro, and G.M. Crescimbeni. *Stato della SS. Chiesa papale Lateranense nell'anno MDCCXXIII*. Rome, 1723.

Baldinucci, Filippo. *The Life of Bernini*. Translated by Catherine Enggass. University Park and London: Pennsylvania State University Press, 1966.

– *Vita di Bernini scritta da Filippo Baldinucci*. Edited by Sergio Samek Ludovici. Milan: Edizione del Milione, 1949.

Barkan, Leonard. *The Gods Made Flesh: Metamorphosis and the Pursuit of Paganism*. New Haven, CT: Yale University Press, 1986.

Barolski, Paul. *Michelangelo's Nose: A Myth and Its Maker*. Hoboken, NJ: John Wiley & Sons, 2007.

Baxandall, Michael. "The Language of Art History." *New Literary History* 10 (Spring 1979): 453–65.

Beaven, Lisa. *An Ardent Patron: Cardinal Camillo Massimo and His Antiquarian and Artistic Circle: Giovanni Pietro Bellori, Claude Lorrain, Nicolas Poussin, Diego Velázquez*. London: Paul Holberton Publishing in association with Centro de Estudios Europa Hispanica, 2010.

Bellori, Giovanni Pietro. *Lives of the Modern Painters, Sculptors, and Architects*. Translated and edited by Alice Sedgwick Wohl. Cambridge and New York: Cambridge University Press, 2005.

Bellow, A.A. "The Great Chain of Being and Italian Phenomenology." In *Analecta Husserliana: The Yearbook of Phenomenological Research*, vol. 11. Boston: D. Reidel Publishing, 2012.

Bemrose, Stephan. "'Una favilla sol della tua gloria': Dante Expresses the Inexpressible." *Forum for Modern Language Studies* 27, no. 2 (April 1991): 126–37.

Benjamin, Walter. *On Hashish*. Edited by H. Eiland and introduction by Marcus Boon. Cambridge, MA: Belknap Press, 2006.

– *The Origin of German Tragic Drama*. New York: Verso, 1998.
Bernini, Domenico. *Vita del Cavalier Gio. Lorenzo Bernino, descritta da Domenico Bernino, suo figlio*. Rome: Rocco Bernabò, 1713.
Bessa, A.S. "Vers Une Architecture." In *Architectures of Poetry*, ed. María Eugenia Díaz Sánchez and Craig Douglas Dworkin, 41–51. Amsterdam: Editions Rodopi, 2004.
Black, Max. "Metaphor." In *Philosophy Looks at the Arts*, edited by J. Margolis, 218–35. New York: Charles Scribner's Sons, 1962.
Bloom, Harold. *The Anxiety of Influence: A Theory of Poetry*. 2nd ed. New York: Oxford University Press, 1997.
– *The Western Canon*. New York: Harcourt Brace & Company, 1994.
Blunt, Anthony. *Borromini*. Cambridge, MA: Harvard University Press, 1979.
– "El Greco's *Dream of Philip II*: An Allegory of the Holy League." *Journal of the Warburg and Courtauld Institutes* 3, nos. 1/2 (October 1939–January 1940): 58–69.
Bocxe, Winfried. "Introduction to the Teaching of the Italian Augustinians of the 18th Century on the Nature of Actual Grace." *Augustiniana* 8, no. 3 (August 1958): 356–96.
Booth, Wayne C. "Criticism." In *Encyclopedia of Rhetoric*, edited by Thomas O. Sloane, 181–90. New York: Oxford University Press, 2001.
Boucher, Bruce. *Italian Baroque Sculpture*. New York: Thames and Hudson, 1998.
Bowron, Edgar Peters, and Joseph J. Rishel, eds. *Art in Rome in the Eighteenth Century*. Philadelphia: Philadelphia Museum of Art, 2000.
Bravo, Carlo del. "Sul significato della luce nel Caravaggio e in Gianlorenzo Bernini." *Artibus et Historiae* 4, no. 7 (1983): 69–77.
Bronowski, Jacob. *Origins of Knowledge and Imagination*. New Haven, CT: Yale University Press, 1978.
Brown, Bill. "Thing Theory." *Critical Inquiry* 28 (Autumn 2001): 1–23.
Bruggeman, J., and A.J. van deVen. *Inventaire des pièces d'archives françaises se rapportant à l'abbaye de Port-Royal des Champs et son cercle et à la résistance contre la Bulle Unigentus et à l'appel (ancien fonds d'Amersfoort)*. The Hague: M. Nijhoff, 1972.
Bullarium Romanum: Clementis XIV epistolæ et brevia. Edited by Theiner. Paris, 1852.
Bunia, Remegius. "Diegesis and Representation: Beyond the Fictional World, on the Margins of Story and Narrative." *Poetics Today* 31, no. 4 (Winter 2010): 679–720.
Campbell, John. "Racine and the Augustinian Inheritance: The Case of Andromaque." *French Studies* 53, no. 3 (1999): 279–91.
Casey, Edward S. *The Fate of Place: A Philosophical History*. Berkeley: University of California Press, 1997.

Cassirer, Ernst. *Language and Myth.* Translated by Suzanne Langer. New York: Harper & Brothers, 1946.

– *The Philosophy of Symbolic Forms.* 3 vols. Translated by Ralph Mannheim. New Haven, CT: Yale University Press, 1953–7.

Chomsky, Noam. *Language and the Mind.* New York: Harcourt, Brace, and World, 1986.

Conforti, Michael. "The Lateran Apostles." PhD diss., Harvard University, 1977.

– "Planning the Lateran Apostles." In *Memoirs of the American Academy in Rome*, vol. 35, *Studies in Italian Art History 1: Studies in Italian Art and Architecture 15th through 18th Centuries*, edited by James H. Ackerman and Henry A. Millon, 243–55, 257–60. Cambridge, MA: MIT Press, 1980.

Connors, Joseph. "Borromini's Sant'Ivo alla Sapienza: The Spiral." *Burlington Magazine* 138 (1996): 668–82.

– "Sant'Ivo alla Sapienza: The First Three Minutes." *Journal of the Society of Architectural Historians* 55 (1996): 38–57.

Cousin, Victor. *Jacqueline Pascal.* Translated by H.N. New York, 1854.

Crescimbeni, Giovanni Mario. *Storia dell'Accademia degli Arcadi Istituita in Roma l'Anno 1690.* 1712; repr., London, 1804.

Cropper, Elizabeth, and Charles Dempsey. *Nicolas Poussin: Friendship and the Love of Painting.* Princeton, NJ: Princeton University Press, 1996.

Curtius, Ernst Robert. *European Literature and the Latin Middle Ages.* Translated by Willard R. Trask. Princeton, NJ: Princeton University Press, 1990.

Curzietti, Jacopo. *Giovan Battista Gaulli: La decorazione della chiesa del SS. Nome di Gesù.* Rome: Gangemi Editore SPA, 2011.

Cusset, François. *French Theory: How Foucault, Derrida, Deleuze, & Co. Transformed the Intellectual Life of the United States.* Translated by Jeff Fort. Minneapolis: University of Minnesota Press, 2008.

Deleuze, Gilles. *Essays: Critical and Clinical.* Translated by D.W. Smith and M.A. Greco. Minneapolis: University of Minnesota Press, 1996.

– *The Fold: Leibniz and the Baroque.* Translated by Tom Conley. Minneapolis: University of Minnesota Press, 1993.

De Man, Paul. *Blindness and Insight: Essays in the Rhetoric of Contemporary Criticism.* Introduction by Wlad Godzich. Minneapolis: University of Minnesota Press, 1983.

– *The Resistance to Theory.* Minneapolis: University of Minnesota Press, 1986.

Dempsey, Charles. *Inventing the Renaissance Putto.* Chapel Hill: University of North Carolina Press, 2001.

Den Broeder, Frederick. "The Lateran Apostles." *Apollo* 85 (1967): 360–5.

Derrida, Jacques. *Of Grammatology.* Translated by Gayatri Chakravorty Spivak. Baltimore and London: Johns Hopkins University Press, 1982.

– *The Truth in Painting*. Translated by Geoff Bennington and Ian McLeod. Chicago: University of Chicago Press, 1987.

– *Writing and Difference*. Translated by Alan Bass. London: Routledge, 2001.

Derrida, Jacques, and Craig Owens. "The Parergon." *October* 9 (Summer 1979): 3–41.

Descartes, René. *Oeuvres de Descartes*. 12 vols. Edited by Charles Adam and Paul Tannery. Paris, 1897–1913.

Desmas, Anne Lise. "Why Legros Rather than Foggini Carved the 'St. Bartholomew' for the Lateran: New Documents for the Statue in the Nave." *Burlington Magazine* 146, no. 1221, Sculpture (December 2004): 805.

Didi-Huberman, Georges. "Artistic Survival: Panofsky vs. Warburg and the Exorcism of Impure Time." *Common Knowledge* 9, no. 2 (Spring 2003): 273–85.

Dio Chrysostom. "The Twelfth, or Olympic Discourse: On Man's First Conception of God." In *Dio Chrysostom*. Translated by J.W. Cohoon, Loeb Classical Library, vol. 2. Cambridge, MA: Harvard University Press, 1932.

Dorival, Bernard. *Philippe de Champaigne, 1602–1674; La Vie, l'oeuvre et le catalogue raisonné de l'oeuvre*. 2 vols. Paris: Chez l'auteur, 1976.

du Prey, Pierre de la Ruffinière. "Solomonic Symbolism in Borromini's Church of S. Ivo alla Sapienza." *Zeitschrift für Kunstgeschichte* 31, no. 3 (1968): 216–32.

Dustin, Christopher A., and Joanna E. Ziegler. *Practicing Mortality: Art, Philosophy, and Contemplative Seeing*. New York: Palgrave Macmillan, 2005.

Dworkin, Craig. "Against Metaphor." In *Architectures of Poetry*, edited by María Eugenia Díaz Sánchez and Craig Douglas Dworkin, 7–11. Amsterdam: Editions Rodopi, 2004.

Ecclesiastica Historia: integram ecclesiae Christi ideam complectens, congesta per aliquot studiosos et pios viros in urbe Magdeburgica. 13 vols. Basle, 1559–74.

Eck, Caroline van. *Classical Rhetoric and the Visual Arts in Early Modern Europe*. Cambridge: Cambridge University Press, 2007.

Enggass, Robert. *Early Eighteenth-Century Sculpture in Rome*. 2 vols. University Park and London: Pennsylvania State University Press, 1976.

– *The Painting of Baciccio: Giovanni Battista Gaulli, 1639–1709*. University Park: Pennsylvania State University Press, 1964.

– "Two Contrasting Concepts of Color in the Architecture of the Roman Baroque." In *An Architectural Progress in the Renaissance and Baroque: Sojourns In and Out of Italy*, vol. 1, edited by Henry Millon and Susan S. Munshower, 407–9. University Park: Pennsylvania State University Press, 1992.

Félibien, A., ed. *Seven Conferences Held in the King of France's Cabinet of Paintings*. London, 1740.

Ferguson, Wallace K. "The Place of Jansenism in French History." *Journal of Religion* 7, no. 1 (January 1927): 16–42.

Ferris, David. *Silent Urns: Romanticism, Hellenism, Modernity*. Stanford, CA: Stanford University Press, 2000.

Fletcher, Angus S. "The Perpetual Error." *Diacritics* 2, no. 4 (Winter 1972): 14–20.

Foucault, Michel. *The Archaeology of Knowledge*. New York: Harper & Row, 1972.

– "What Is an Author?" In *Language, Counter-Memory, Practice: Selected Essays and Interviews*, edited by D.F. Bouchard, 113–38. Ithaca, NY: Cornell University Press, 1977.

Freud, Sigmund. *The Uncanny*. In *The Standard Edition of the Complete Psychological Works of Sigmund Freud*, vol. 17, *1917–1919*, ed. and trans. James Strachey. London: Hogarth Press, 1955.

Frye, Northrop. *Fearful Symmetry: A Study of William Blake*. Princeton, NJ: Princeton University Press, 1969.

Fumaroli, Mark. "The Fertility and the Shortcomings of Renaissance Rhetoric: The Jesuit Case." In *The Jesuits: Cultures, Sciences, and the Arts*, edited by John W. O'Malley, S.J.; Gauvin Alexander Bailey; Steven J. Harris; and T. Frank Kennedy, S.J., 90–106. Toronto: University of Toronto Press, 1999.

Gombrich, E.H. "On Physiognomic Perception." In *Meditations on a Hobby Horse and Other Essays on the Theory of Art*, 45–55. London: Phaidon; distributed by New York Graphic Society Publishers, Greenwich, CT, 1963.

Grafton, Anthony. *Commerce with the Classics: Ancient Books and Renaissance Readers*. Ann Arbor: University of Michigan Press, 1997.

Gravina, Vincenzo. *Hydra Mystica: con la ristampa della traduzione italiana del 1761*. Edited by Fabrizio Lomonaco. Soveria Mannelli, Catanzara, Italy: Rubbettino, 2002.

Gray, Floyd. "The Essay as Criticism." In *The Cambridge History of Literary Criticism*, vol. 3, *The Renaissance*, edited by Glyn P. Norton, 271–7. Cambridge and New York: Cambridge University Press, 2006.

Greenberg, Clement. "Avant-Garde and Kitsch." In *Art and Culture*, 34–9. Boston: Beacon Press, 1961.

Grene, Marjorie. *Descartes*. Minneapolis: University of Minnesota Press, 1985.

Gross, Hanns. *Rome in the Age of Enlightenment: The Post-Tridentine Syndrome and the Ancien Regime*. New York: Cambridge University Press, 1990.

Gudiccioni, Lelio. *Latin Poems, Rome 1633 and 1639*. Translated and edited by John Kevin Newman and Frances Stickney Newman. Hildesheim: Weidmannsche Verlagsbuchhandlung, 1992.

Hallyn, Fernand. "Cosmography and Poetics." In *The Cambridge History of Literary Criticism*, vol. 3, *The Renaissance*, edited by Glyn P. Norton, 442–8. Cambridge and New York: Cambridge University Press, 1999.

Harbison, Robert. *Reflections on Baroque*. London: Reaktion Books, 2000.

Harris, Ann Sutherland. *Andrea Sacchi*. Princeton, NJ: Princeton University Press, 1977.

Hassel, R. Chris Jr. "Donne's *Ignatius His Conclave*, and the New Astronomy." *Modern Philology* 68, no. 4 (May 1971): 329–37.

Heidegger, Martin. *Denkerfahrungen 1910–76*. Frankfurt am Main: Klostermann, 1983.

– *Poetry, Language, Thought*. Translated by Albert Hofstadter. New York: Harper & Row, 1975.

– *What Is Called Thinking?* Introduction by J. Glenn Gray. New York: Harper & Row, 1968.

Herman, David. *Story Logic: Problems and Possibilities of Narrative*. Lincoln: University of Nebraska Press, 2002.

Holly, Michael Ann. "Interventions: The Melancholy Art." *Art Bulletin* 89, no. 1 (March 2007): 7–17.

– *Past Looking: Historical Imagination and the Rhetoric of the Image*. Ithaca, NY, and London: Cornell University Press, 1996.

Huxley, Aldous. *The Doors of Perception*. New York: Harper and Brothers, 1954.

Iser, Wolfgang. *The Fictive and the Imaginary: Charting Literary Anthropology*. Baltimore and London: Johns Hopkins University Press, 1993.

Israel, Jonathan I. *Radical Enlightenment: Philosophy and the Making of Modernity 1650–1750*. Oxford: Oxford University Press, 2002.

Jansen, Katherine L. "Mary Magdalen and the Mendicants: The Preaching of Penance in the Late Middle Ages." *Journal of Medieval History* 21 (1995): 1–25.

Johns, Christopher M.S. *Papal Art and Cultural Politics: Rome in the Age of Clement XI*. Cambridge and New York: Cambridge University Press, 1993.

Johnson, Samuel. "Life of Cowley (1779–81)." In *Lives of the English Poets*, edited by L. Archer Hind, vol. 1, 1–65. London: Everyman's Library, 1925.

Kant, Immanuel. *Critique of Judgment*. Translated by Werner S. Pluhar. Indianapolis, IN: Hackett Publishing Company, 1987.

Kieven, Elisabeth. "Rome in 1732." In *Light on the Eternal City*, edited by H. Hager and S. Scott Munshower, 255–76. University Park: Pennsylvania State University Press, 1987.

– "Überlegungen zu Architektur und Ausstattung der Capella Corsini." In *Studi sul Settecento: L'architettura da Clemente XI a Benedetto XIV – Pluralità di tendenze*, edited by Elisa Debenedetti, 69–91. Rome: Bonsignori Editore, 1989.

Kirwin, W. Chandler. *Powers Matchless: The Pontificate of Urban VIII, the Baldachin, and Gian Lorenzo Bernini*. New York: Peter Lang, 1997.

Kisiel, Theodore. *The Genesis of Heidegger's Being & Time*. Berkeley: University of California Press, 1995.

Koortbojian, Michael. "*Disegni* for the Tomb of Alexander VII." *Journal of the Warburg and Courtauld Institutes* 54 (1991): 268–73.

Krauss, Rosalind E. *The Originality of the Avant-Garde and Other Modernist Myths.* Cambridge, MA: Harvard University Press, 1985.

Kremer, Elmar J. "Arnauld's Interpretation of Descartes as a Christian Philosopher." In *Interpreting Arnauld,* edited by Elmar J. Kremer, 76–90. Toronto: University of Toronto Press, 1996.

Lambert, Gregg. *The Non-Philosophy of Gilles Deleuze.* New York: Continuum, 2002.

Lavin, Irving. "Bernini's Bumbling Barberini Bees." In *Barock Inszenierung: Akten des Internationalen Forschungscolloquiums an der Technischen Universität Berlin, 20–22 Juni 1996,* edited by Joseph Imorde, Fritz Neumeyer, and Tristan Weddigen. Zurich: Edition Imorde, 1999.

Lessing, Gotthold Ephraim. *Laocoön or the Limits of Poetry and Painting.* Translated by William Ross. London: Ridgeway, 1836.

Lingo, Estelle. *François Duquesnoy and the Greek Ideal.* New Haven, CT: Yale University Press, 2007.

Loos, Adolf. *Ornament and Crime: Selected Essays.* Translated by Michael Mitchell. Studies in Austrian Literature, Culture, and Thought Translation Series. Riverside, CA: Ariadne Press, 1998.

Löwy, Michael. *Fire Alarm: Reading Walter Benjamin's "On the Concept of History."* Translated by Chris Turner. London: Verso, 2005.

Mâle, Émile. *Religious Art.* New York: Noonday Press, 1970.

Mann, Thomas. *Death in Venice, and Seven Other Stories.* Translated by H.T. Lowe-Porter. New York: Vintage Books, 1936.

Marin, Louis. *Philippe de Champaigne, ou La Présence Cachée.* Farigliano, Italy: Hazan, 1995.

– "Signe et répresentation: Philippe de Champaigne et Port-Royal." *Annales: Economies, Sociétés, Civilisations* 25, nos. 1–3 (1970): 1–28.

Marin, Louis, and Anna Lehman. "Classical, Baroque: Versailles, or the Architecture of the Prince." *Yale French Studies* 80, Baroque Topographies: Literature/History/Philosophy (1991): 168–82.

Marin, Louis, and Marie Maclean. "The Figurability of the Visual: The Veronica or the Question of the Portrait at Port-Royal." *New Literary History* 22, no. 2 (Spring 1991): 281–96.

Martin, Frank. "Camillo Rusconi in English Collections." In *The Lustrous Trade: Material Culture and the History of Sculpture in England and Italy c. 1700–c. 1860,* edited by Cinzia Sicca and Alison Yarrington, 49–66. London: Leicester University Press, 2000.

McGinness, Frederick J. *Right Thinking and Sacred Oratory in Counter-Reformation Rome.* Princeton, NJ: Princeton University Press, 1995.

Méchoulan, Eric. "Immediacy and Forgetting." *SubStance* 34, no. 1 (2005): 145–58.

Menand, Louis. *The Marketplace of Ideas: Reform and Resistance in the American University*. New York: W.W. Norton & Company, 2010.

Merleau-Ponty, Maurice. *The Primacy of Perception*. In *The Merleau-Ponty Aesthetics Reader*, edited by Galen A. Johnson. Evanston, IL: Northwestern University Press, 1993.

Minor, Vernon Hyde. *The Death of the Baroque and the Rhetoric of Good Taste*. New York: Cambridge University Press, 2006.

– "Filippo della Valle's Tomb of Innocent XII: Death and Dislocation." *Gazette des beaux-arts* 112 (1988): 133–140.

– *Passive Tranquillity: The Sculpture of Filippo della Valle*. Philadelphia: American Philosophical Society, Transactions Series, 1997.

– "The Recollection and Undermining of Allegory in Eighteenth-Century Roman Sculpture." *Storia dell'Arte* 57 (1986): 183–91.

Missirini, Melchiorre. *Memorie per Servire alla Storia della Romana Accademia di S. Luca*. Rome: Nella Stamperia de Romanis, 1823.

Montagu, Jennifer. *Alessandro Algardi*. 2 vols. New Haven, CT, and London: Yale University Press, 1985.

Mormando, Franco. *The Life of Gian Lorenzo Bernini by Domenico Bernini: A Translation and Critical Edition*. University Park: Pennsylvania State University Press, 2011.

Morley, Edith, and Henry Frowde, eds. *Hurd's Letters on Chivalry and Romance with the Third Elizabethan Dialogue*. London: Henry Frowde, 1911.

Nabokov, Vladimir. *Transparent Things*. New York: McGraw-Hill, 1972.

Nadler, Steven M. *Arnauld and the Cartesian Philosophy of Ideas*. Princeton, NJ: Princeton University Press, 1989.

Noreen, Kirstin. "Ecclesiae militantis triumphi: Jesuit Iconography and the Counter-Reformation." *Sixteenth Century Journal* 29, no. 3 (Autumn 1998): 689–715.

O'Malley, John. *The First Jesuits*. Cambridge, MA: Harvard University Press, 1995.

Ost, Hans. "Borrominis römische Universitätskirche S. Ivo alla Sapienza." *Zeitschrift für Kunstegeschichte* 30 (1967): 101–42.

Palmer, Richard. *Hermeneutics: Interpretation Theory in Schleiermacher, Dilthey, Heidegger, and Gadamer*. Evanston, IL: Northwestern University Press, 1969.

Panofsky, Erwin. *Galileo as a Critic of the Arts*. The Hague: M. Nijhoff, 1954.

– "Iconography and Iconology: An Introduction to the Study of Renaissance Art." In *Meaning in the Visual Arts*, 26–54. Garden City, NY: Doubleday, 1955.

– *Tomb Sculpture: Four Lectures on Its Changing Aspects from Ancient Egypt to Bernini.* New York: Harry N. Abrams, 1964.

Parish, Richard. *Pascal's "Lettres Provinciales": A Study in Polemic.* Oxford: Oxford University Press, 1989.

– "Port-Royal and Jansenism." In *The Cambridge History of Literary Criticism,* vol. 3, *The Renaissance,* edited by Glyn P. Norton, 475–84. New York: Cambridge University Press, 2006.

Pascal, Blaise. *Oeuvres Complètes (Grand Ecrivans de la France).* Edited by L. Brunschwicg, P. Boutroux, and F. Gazier. 2nd ser., vol. 4. Paris: Librairie Hachette et Cie, 1914.

– *Pascal: The Provincial Letters.* Translated by A.J. Krailsheimer. Harmondsworth, Middlesex: Penguin Books, 1967.

Pastor, Ludwig, Freiherr von. *The History of the Popes.* Translated by Dom Ernest Graf. Vol. 34. London: Kegan Paul, Trench, Trubner & Co., 1941.

Pericolo, Lorenzo. *Philippe de Champaigne.* Tournai: La Renaissance du Livre, 2002.

Pestilli, Livio. "On Bernini's Reputed Unpopularity in Late Baroque Rome." *Artibus et Historiae* 63, no. 32 (2011): 119–42.

Pino, P. *Dialogo di Pittura.* In P. Barocchi, *Trattati d'Arte del Cinquecento,* vol. 1. Bari: Laterza, 1960.

Poirer, M.G. "Studies on the Concepts of 'Disegno,' 'Invenzione,' and 'Colore' in Sixteenth- and Seventeenth-Century Italian Art Theory." Diss., New York University, 1976.

Preimesberger, Rudolf. "Il San Longino del Bernini in San Pietro in Vaticano: Dal Bozzetto alla Statue." In *Bernini a Montecitorio: Ciclo di conferenze nel quarto centenario della nascita di Gan Lorenzo Bernini,* edited by M.G. Bernardini, 95–112. Rome: Camera dei Deputatiti, 2001.

Prince, Gerald. *Dictionary of Narratology.* Lincoln: University of Nebraska Press, 2003.

Pseudo-Dionysius. *Pseudo-Dionysius: The Complete Works.* Translated by Colm Luibheid. Edited by Paul Rorem. New York: Paulist Press, 1987.

– *The Works of Dionysius the Areopagite.* Translated by Rev. J. Parker. Merrick, NY: Richwood Publishing, 1976.

Radetsky, Paula Kadose. "To Will or Not to Will: The Evolution of Willy-Nilly." *Proceedings of the Twenty-Second Annual Meeting of the Berkeley Linguistics Society* 22 (1996): 302–15.

Rand, Olan A. Jr. "Philippe de Champaigne and the *Ex-Voto* of 1662: A Historical Perspective." *Art Bulletin* 65, no. 1 (March 1983): 78–93.

Riegl, Alois. *The Origins of Baroque Art in Rome.* Edited and translated by Andrew Hopkins and Arnold Witte. Los Angeles: Getty Research Institute, 2010.

Ripa, Cesare. *Iconologia, ouero, Descrittione di diuerse imagini cauate dall'antichità, & di propria inuentione.* Rome: Appresso Lepido Facij, 1603.

Rohlmann, Michael. "Raffaels Sixtinische Madonna." *Römisches Jahrbuch der Bibliotheca Hertziana* 30 (1995): 221–48.

Roskill, M.W. *Dolce's "Aretino" and Venetian Art Theory of the Cinquecento.* New York: RSART (Renaissance Society of America Reprint Text Series), 2000.

Ruthven, K.K. *The Conceit.* London: Methuen & Co., 1969.

Sacks, Sheldon. *On Metaphor.* Chicago and London: University of Chicago Press, 1978.

Sainte-Beuve, Charles A. de. *Port-Royal.* Edited by M. Leroy. Vol. 1, *Discours préliminaire.* Paris: Libraire de L. Hachette, 1953.

Schmaltz, Tad M. "What Has Cartesianism to Do with Jansenism?" *Journal of the History of Ideas* 60, no. 1 (January 1999): 37–56.

Schroder, H.J., trans. *Canons and Decrees of the Council of Trent.* Rockford, IL: Tan Books and Publishers, 1978.

Simmel, Georg. *The Philosophy of Money.* 2nd ed. Translated by Tom Bottomore, David Frisby, and Kaethe Mengelberg. 1907; New York: Routledge, 1990.

Spear, Richard E. *Domenichino.* 2 vols. New Haven, CT, and London: Yale University Press, 1982.

Spencer, John R. "UT RHETORICA PICTURA: A Study in Quattrocento Theory of Painting." *Journal of the Warburg and Courtauld Institutes* 20, no. 1/2 (January–June 1957): 26–44.

Stein, H. *Philippe de Champaigne et ses relations avec Port-Royal.* Paris, 1891.

Steiner, George. *Martin Heidegger.* New York: Viking Press, 1978.

Steiner, Wendy. *The Colors of Rhetoric.* Chicago: University of Chicago Press, 1980.

Stone, Shelley. "The Toga: From National to Ceremonial Costume." In *The World of Roman Costume,* edited by Judith Lynn Sebesta and Larissa Bonfante, 13–45. Madison: University of Wisconsin Press, 1994.

Summers, David. "'Form,' Nineteenth-Century Metaphysics, and the Problem of Art Historical Description." *Critical Inquiry* 15 (Winter 1989): 372–93.

– *Michelangelo and the Language of Art.* Princeton, NJ: Princeton University Press, 1981.

Summerson, John. *The Classical Language of Architecture.* London: Methuen, 1963.

Tacchi Venturi, P. "Le convenzioni tra Giov. Battista Gaulli e il generale dei Gesuiti Gian Paolo Oliva per le pitture della cupola e della volta del Tempio Farnesiano." *Roma* 13 (1935): 147–56.

Tatarkiewicz, W. "Mimesis." In *Dictionary of the History of Ideas: Studies of Selected Pivotal Ideas*, edited by Philip P. Wiener, vol. 3, 225–30. New York: Charles Scribner's Sons, 1973.

Tentler, Thomas N. *Sin and Confession on the Eve of the Reformation*. Princeton, NJ: Princeton University Press, 1977.

Tesauro, Emanuele. *Il Cannocchiale Aristotelico: Scelta*. Edited by Ezio Raimondi. Milan: Giulio Einaudi Editore, 1978.

Teskey, Gordon. *Allegory and Violence*. Ithaca, NY: Cornell University Press, 1996.

Topliss, Patricia. *The Rhetoric of Pascal: A Study of His Art of Persuasion in the "Provinciales" and the "Pensées."* Amsterdam: Leicester University Press, 1966.

Valesio, Francesco. *Diario di Roma*. Edited by G. Scano and G. Graglia. Vol. 5. Milan: Longanesi, 1979.

Vasari, Giorgio. *Lives of the Most Eminent Painters, Sculptors, and Architects*. Translated by G. du C. DeVere. 10 vols. London: Medici Society, 1912–15.

– *Vasari on Technique*. Translated by Louisa S. Maclehose. Edited by G. Baldwin Brown. New York: Dover Publications, 1960.

Vattimo, Gianni. *Beyond Interpretation: The Meaning of Hermeneutics for Philosophy*. Translated by David Webb. Stanford, CA: Stanford University Press, 1997.

Voltaire. *The Complete Works*. Edited by T. Besterman. 135 vols. Banbury: Voltaire Foundation, 1972.

Voruz, Véronique, and Bogdan Wolfe, eds. "Preface." In *The Later Lacan: An Introduction*, vii–xvii. Albany: SUNY Press, 2007.

Warnke, Frank J. *Studies in the Renaissance*. Vol. 2. New York: Renaissance Society of America, 1955.

Watson, Duane F. "A Rhetorical Analysis of Philippians and Its Implications for the Unity Question." *Novum Testamentum* 30, no. 1 (January 1988): 57–88.

Weil, Mark S. "The Devotion of the Forty Hours and Roman Baroque Illusions." *Journal of the Warburg and Courtauld Institutes* 37 (1974): 218–48.

Wilhelm, Joseph. "Pope Clement XIV." In *The Catholic Encyclopedia*. New York: Robert Appleton Company, 1908. http://www.newadvent.org/cathen/04034a.htm, accessed 16 September 2014.

Wimsatt, W.K., and Monroe Beardsley. "The Intentional Fallacy." In *The Verbal Icon: Studies in the Meaning of Poetry* by W.K. Wimsatt, 3–20. Lexington: University of Kentucky Press, 1954.

Winckelmann, Johann Joachim. *History of Ancient Art*. 4 vols. Translated by G. Henry Lodge. 1849–72. New York: Frederick Ungar, 1968.

– *Reflections on the Imitation of Greek Works in Painting and Sculpture.* Translated by Elfriede Heyer and Roger C. Norton. La Salle, IL: Open Court, 1987.

Wittkower, Rudolf. *Art and Architecture in Italy 1600–1750.* 3rd ed. Baltimore: Penguin Books, 1973.

Wölfflin, Heinrich. *Classic Art: An Introduction to the Italian Renaissance.* Translated by Peter and Linda Murray. London: Phaidon Press, 1952.

– *Principles of Art History: The Problem of the Development of Style in Later Art.* Translated by M.D. Hottinger. New York: Dover Publications, 1950.

Young, Julian. *Heidegger's Philosophy of Art.* New York: Cambridge University Press, 2001.

Index

Page numbers in *italics* refer to illustrations.